Interagency Coordination in Child Protection

CHRISTINE HALLETT

Studies in Child Protection

LONDON: HMSO

Acknowledgements

I am grateful to the Department of Health for sponsoring and financing the research project on coordination policies and practices in child protection on which this book is based and to the professionals in many agencies who participated in the study. I am also grateful to Pat Young who has typed and retyped the book with care, great patience and good humour and to Barbara Dobson, who coded and entered the questionnaires for SPSS-X and entered the data from the case record data collection instrument on a computerised database.

Finally, I am grateful to Dr Elizabeth Birchall and Professor Adrian Webb for their constructive comments.

Contents

List of figures

List of tables

Chapter 1 Introduction to the research topic

This book is based upon a study of interagency coordination in child protection services in England.

The empirical work for the book was undertaken as part of a larger study of coordination policies and practices in child protection funded by the Department of Health. The research project was in three phases. The first was an extensive literature review, published by HMSO under the title *Coordination and child protection: a review of the literature* (Hallett and Birchall, 1992). It covered the nature of coordination as a policy objective in health and welfare services generally and its particular application in collaborative working in child protection services.

The second phase comprised a postal survey of 339 practitioners (general practitioners, health visitors, paediatricians, specialist police, teachers and social workers) drawn from three diverse locations in the north of England. The questionnaire covered four main topics:

personal and professional data relevant to respondents' experience of work in child protection;

a child abuse severity rating exercise with a selection of brief case vignettes replicating, on a smaller scale, an earlier North American study (Giovannoni and Becerra, 1979);

an exploration of perceptions and proposed actions in an unfolding three-stage vignette of children in potentially abusive situations;

an exploration of respondents' experience and evaluations of the child protection procedures and interprofessional network in the locality.

This study was conducted by Elizabeth Birchall, under my direction, and was originally reported as *Working Together in Child Protection: Report of Phase Two: a survey of the experience and perceptions of six key professions* (Birchall, 1992 and published by HMSO in 1995).

The third phase of the study, on which this book is based, is a case study of interagency coordination drawing on data derived from a sample of 48 registered child abuse cases, in-depth interviews with 90 professionals and a brief questionnaire completed by a sample of 81 professionals in two research sites in the north of England. The research design and research instruments are described in the next chapter. Here, in Chapter One, the background to the research topic is outlined, some key themes from the literature are reviewed and their relevance to the study indicated.

Background to the study

A multidisciplinary approach to child abuse has been widely advocated since the 'rediscovery' of the problem associated with the work of Kempe in the early 1960s in the United States of America (Kempe et al, 1962). In the United Kingdom, central government emphasised the need for a coordinated interagency response in a stream of circulars of guidance issued from the late 1960s onwards, increasing in length and detail and culminating in *Working Together Under the Children Act* (Home Office at al, 1991). Interagency coordination thus lies at the heart of the system established in Britain for the management of cases of child abuse. It is reflected in mechanisms such as local interagency committees for policy-making and review, now known as Area Child Protection Committees (ACPCs), multidisciplinary child protection conferences and local child protection registers listing children who are considered to be suffering from, or likely to suffer from, significant harm and who are the subject of an interagency child protection plan. The government guidance constituted a mandate to coordinate, placed upon local agencies and professionals in health, social welfare, education, police and other services. The mandate, however, reflected accepted practice wisdom and professional advice about an appropriate response to the problem.

In 1974 an important DHSS circular (DHSS 1974(a)) specified management arrangements for dealing with non-accidental injury to children, as it was then called. These included a strong recommendation for the urgent formation of area review committees (renamed ACPCs in 1988) as policy-making bodies for the management of cases where such committees did not already exist. Area review committees (or similar bodies) were in existence in some areas prior to 1974. Forerunners of the area review committees had been recommended in 1950 in a Home Office circular entitled 'Children neglected or ill-treated in their own homes' which called for the establishment of local interagency coordinating committees (Home Office, 1950). Similar guidance appeared in the circular on 'battered babies' in 1970 which asked Children's Officers and Medical Officers of Health to hold local consultations with interested agencies to review the situation and decide what further arrangements might be necessary (DHSS and Home Office, 1970). The latter called for a report on the consultations and, in 1972, in another circular letter (DHSS, 1972), the DHSS reported that most areas had in existence a review committee to plan local policy and management and to cooperate with adjacent areas.

The 1974 circular, however, outlined much more fully the role and functions of the area review committees. The circular began:

> *Although we realise how busy you are with reorganisation, recent events have left us in no doubt of the need to repeat the professional guidance*

> *about the diagnosis, care, prevention and local organisation necessary for the management of cases involving non-accidental injury to children.*

In particular, the circular states:

> *Recent cases have underlined the need for regular joint review of all aspects of the management of cases and the main thing we are asking you to do is to set up area review committees for this purpose* (DHSS, 1974(a), p1).

Uppermost in the Department's mind was undoubtedly the case of Maria Colwell. The committee of inquiry's report was published in 1974 and concluded:

> *What has clearly emerged, at least to us, is a failure of the system compounded by several factors of which the greatest and most obvious must be that of the lack of, or ineffectiveness of, communication and liaison* (DHSS, 1974(b), p86).

The circular recommended that the area review committees were to:

a   advise on the formulation of local practice and procedures to be followed in the detailed management of cases

b   approve written instructions defining the duties of all personnel concerned with any aspect of these cases

c   review the work of case conferences in the area

d   provide education and training programmes to heighten awareness of the problem

e   collect information about the work being done in the area

f   collaborate with adjacent area review committees

g   advise on the need for inquiries into cases which appear to have gone wrong and from which lessons could be learned

h   provide a forum for consultation between all involved in the management of the problem

i   draw up procedures for ensuring continuity of care when the family moves to another area

j   consider ways of making it known to the general public that eg health visitors, teachers, social workers, the NSPCC and police may be informed about children thought to be ill-treated

k   prepare a report for 1974.

The recommended membership was to include representatives at senior level of key local authority departments (chief executive, education, housing and social services), health services, the police, the probation service and the NSPCC. The circular also recommended other coordinative activities, notably the establishment of local registers of abused children and the holding of multidisciplinary case conferences.

While some voluntary networks existed at local level before 1974, the DHSS circular constituted an administrative mandate to cooperate. It acknowledged that the informal and local arrangements, where these existed, had failed adequately to coordinate services, as the Maria Colwell case had demonstrated. Since then, the mandate has been extended and elaborated in a succession of government circulars of guidance, increasing in scope, length and specificity. These circulars built incrementally upon the foundations laid in the 1974 circular. In 1976, a circular (DHSS 1976) recommended the inclusion of children at risk of abuse on child abuse registers (as they were then called). In 1980 another circular (DHSS 1980) widened the registration criteria, as occurred again in 1986 with the addition of child sexual abuse.

A major extension of central guidance was issued in 1988 under the title *Working Together* (DHSS and Welsh Office, 1988). A draft had been completed in 1986 but publication was delayed until 1988, following the publication of the report of the committee of inquiry into events in Cleveland (Cm 412, 1988). The guidance contained in *Working Together* (DHSS and Welsh Office, 1988) was in force while the fieldwork for this study was undertaken and its content and implementation are examined in detail in the book. Here, in Chapter One, it is important to note that while it contained significant changes, for example, clearly designating social services departments as the lead agency in child protection and the recommendation that parents should normally be invited to attend initial child protection conferences, it contained to place a central emphasis upon the importance of interagency coordination.

Coordination as a policy objective

That interagency coordination was emphasised so strongly in the government's response to child abuse in the late 1960s and early 1970s is not surprising since there was a widespread preoccupation with the issue at that time in social welfare delivery systems, in the UK and elsewhere, for example in Australia (Duckett, 1977) and Western Europe (Westrin, 1987). It was particularly marked in the USA with its highly fragmented health and welfare system, in which responsibility for funding and service provision is shared between federal, state and local levels, with a wide array of specialised agencies in the private, voluntary and statutory sectors (Clark Turner and Ten Hoor, 1978, Fandetti, 1985). In Britain, as Wistow (1982) has demonstrated, an interest in coordination preoccupied earlier generations of policy analysts and social reformers. The rationalisation of the distribution of charitable relief for the poor in the mid 1860s with the establishment of the Charity Organisation Society is one example, as is the Royal Commission on the Poor Law in 1909. Later, in the plans for the reconstruction of social welfare in the post-war period, Beveridge explicitly acknowledged the interdependence of, for example, health and employment policies with social security.

In the 1960s and 1970s the search for coordination was at the forefront of the policy agenda in Britain, reflected in a number of policy developments. At central government level the creation of mega-government departments such as the Department of the Enviroment and the Department of Health and Social Security by amalgamating their smaller component ministries was designed, in part, to secure a greater degree of coordinated planning across related policy areas. So were the several administrative reorganisations in health and welfare services and in the structure of local government. An explicit aim of the Seebohm Report (Cmnd 3703, 1968) in recommending the unification of the personal social services in one new local government department was to remedy the gaps and duplications in service provision arising from the fragmented and administratively separate children's, mental health and welfare departments. The large scale reorganisation of the national health service in 1974 with the creation of administrative units spanning hospital and community services (with the exception of family practitioner services) was also intended to increase the capacity for rational planning and coordinated service provision. The contemporaneous reorganisation of local government into bigger units with stronger corporate decision-making structures is properly seen within the same policy tradition.

An important feature, however, of the administrative reforms of the NHS and of local government in 1974 was the continued structural separation between health and the personal services. The issue was addressed in the government's policy proposals issued in the early 1970s (DHSS, 1970 and Cmnd 5055 (1972) and in the report of a special working party on collaboration between the services (DHSS, 1973). The decision to retain structural separation was based on the view that services should be organised according to the main skills required to provide them, rather than by any categorisation of primary user. It should be noted, however, that it would have been politically difficult so soon after the unification of the personal social services and the separation of the former local authority welfare and mental health services from the aegis, and sometimes the control, of local medical officers of health to suggest bringing health and personal social services together. The newly emerged occupation of generic social worker was flexing its organisational muscle and celebrating its autonomy in the new local authority social service departments.

An important consequence of the decision to retain the structural separation of health and welfare services was that arrangements for collaboration between them were required. The NHS Reorganisation Act 1973 included a statutory requirement for health and local authorities to cooperate with each other and to establish machinery – the Joint Consultative Committee (JCC) – comprising members of local authorities and area health authorities for the purpose. JCCs were to be supported by working groups of officers. This process was facilitated (outside London) by the coterminous boundaries established upon reorganisation between health authorities and local authorities. The Act required collaboration in the supply of goods and services, the planning and operation of services and joint action to secure and advance the health and welfare of the population served. Of these, the DHSS gave greatest attention to joint planning. However, progress was slow and in 1976 joint finance was introduced to encourage collaborative planning. Booth (1981) suggests that the introduction of joint finance was necessary because the assumptions underpinning the 1974 reorganisation (that rationality and an altruistic concern with collaboration in the general interest of clients and patients would, by themselves, lead to collaboration) had proved to be false. Booth concludes: 'above all, joint finance taught that some sort of tangible inducement, in the form of reward or sanction which can be measured in terms of their own organisational interests, was an essential ingredient of any partnership between the health and social services' (1981, p27). The purpose is not to review these policy developments in detail here but rather to draw attention to the fact that the arrangements for collaboration between the health service and local authority social services were laid down in legislation and then supplemented in 1976 by a financial inducement in the form of joint finance. This was not the case in child protection, since the requirement for interagency collaboration was not embodied in primary legislation (at least until Section 27 of the Children Act, 1989 which was implemented in 1991) nor were earmarked funds provided to support it. This posed particular challenges in implementation.

Defining Coordination

One starting point for this study was that while interagency coordination was widely advocated in child protection, as in other health and welfare services, its meaning and content remains unclear. Aiken et al describe it as a word which is 'overworked, underachieved and seldom defined' (1975, p6) and Challis et al observe that coordination is 'a largely rhetorical invocation of a vague ideal' (1988, px). Thus Weiss asserts:

> the definitional ambiguity which makes coordination a handy political
> device has led to a chasm between rhetoric and operationalisation:
> coordination is discussed in the political arena as though everyone knows

precisely what it means, when in fact it means many inconsistent things and occasionally means nothing at all (1981, p41).

In a similar vein, Challis et al (1988) note that the conceptual elusiveness of coordination initially posed problems of method in their study. Mulford and Rogers summarise the definitional difficulties as follows:

> *Because coordination means different things to different people, because the process must be accomplished through several strategies, and because a number of different elements can be coordinated, the term has been used synonymously with or confused with a variety of related concepts . . .. Because of this lack of agreement about meaning, propositions about coordination are, at best, tenuous . . .* (1982, p9).

This study aimed to specify more closely the meaning and content of coordination in child protection services as it appeared to have been practised in a sample of registered cases of child abuse and as it was experienced by a sample of professionals.

The lack of clarity in the definition of the term coordination, and its close allies collaboration and cooperation, poses problems for such a study. Turning to the dictionary for clarification proves to be of limited use. The verb coordinate is defined in the Concise Oxford Dictionary as to 'make coordinate; bring parts, movements, etc into proper relation; so coordination', This, ofcourse, begs the question as to what is the 'proper relation' of the 'parts' – a matter on which there may be disagreement in child protection as in other spheres. The related terms collaboration and cooperation are defined in similar ways – the former as 'work jointly' and the latter as 'working together to the same end', but, as is noted below, the idea of shared goals is problematic.

There are two principal approaches to the definitional issue. One is simply to proceed on the basis of unstated 'common-sense' assumptions about what terms such as coordination, collaboration and cooperation might mean and thus to avoid offering specific definitions. An alternative approach, also adopted in the literature on coordination, is for authors to propose their own definitions, often, but not always, without specifying the basis for selection. Examples include:

> coordination is *the extent to which organisations attempt to ensure that their activities take into account those of other organisations* (Hall et al, 1977, p459);
>
> coordination is *the process whereby two or more organisations create and/or use existing decision rules that have been established to deal collectively with their shared task environment* (Mulford and Rogers, 1982, p12);

coordination is *the articulation of elements in a social service delivery system so that comprehensiveness of, compatibility among and cooperation among elements are maximised* (Aiken et al, 1971, p9);

coordination is *a structure or process of concerted decision-making wherein the decisions or action of two or more organisations are made simultaneously in part or in whole with some deliberate degree of adjustment to each other* (Warren et al, 1974, p16);

coordination is *a pursuit of competence, consistency, comprehensiveness and harmoniousness or compatible outcomes* (Challis et al, 1988, p25).

Other authors appear to use the term collaboration synonymously with coordination. Examples include Williams who suggests that collaboration is 'joint working in the interests of a common aim, that aim being to achieve more effective and efficient services to patients (1986, p39) and Armitage who defines collaboration as 'the exchange of information between individuals . . . which has the potential for action in the interests of a common purpose' (1983, p75).

While some appear to use the terms coordination and collaboration synonymously, others differentiate. The report on collaboration between the NHS and local government (DHSS, 1973) defined coordination as 'working independently but in harmony' and collaboration as 'working together' (Booth, 1981, p25).

An additional complication is that yet others use the term cooperation synonymously with the way in which some use the terms coordination and collaboration. Westrin (1987), for example, in a cross-national study of interprofessional cooperation in primary health care in eleven counties defines cooperation as 'all conscious efforts of agencies or individuals to direct their work towards common goals' (1987, p7).

Some definitions suggest a simply dichotomy between the presence or absence of coordination (or collaboration). It either exists, as defined, or it does not. Others, however, have elaborated the idea of a continuum whereby activities are distinguished in terms of the extent or degree of coordination which they do or do not imply. One such by Westrin (1987) categorises cooperation (in parimary health care) in terms of a hierarchy from the lowest level to the highest, as follows:

1   the existence of at least some concern about the need for cooperation;

2   the implementation of experimental or model projects in the field;

3   explicit policy statements from responsible community authorities, especially governments;

4   implementation of such policies;

5   systems of follow-up and evaluation.

In terms of child protection in the UK it would seem that level four at least has been achieved but, while there has been some activity at local and central levels in monitoring the interagency management of child abuse (for example through the work of Area Child Protection Committees and the collection and publishing by the Department of Health of data about registration) there has been relatively little systematic evaluation.

Another classification by Bond et al (1985), used in a large-scale study of interprofessional collaboration in primary health care organisations in the UK, is based upon the work of Armitage (1983), and outlined in Table 1.1.

Table 1.1   **A taxonomy of collaboration (after Armitage, 1983)**

Stages of Collaboration	Definitions
1 Isolation	Members who never meet, talk or write to one another.
2 Encounter	Members who encounter or correspond with others but do not interact meaningfully.
3 Communication	Members whose encounters or correspondence include the transference of information.
4 Collaboration between two agents	Members who act on that information sympathetically; participate in patterns of joint working; subscribe to the same general objectives as others as a one-to-one basis in the same organisation.
5 Collaboration throughout an organisation	Organisations in which the work of all members is fully integrated.

Source: Bond et al, 1985, Vol 2, p89

A similar approach is adopted by Gough et al in their longitudinal study of 147 families (202 children) on the child protection register in one Regional Council in Scotland. They suggest 'interdisciplinary cooperation exists on a continuum, that can be described by the following four levels:

working separately;

keeping each other informed;

coordinating work;

and being part of a true team' (1987, Vol 1, p101).

The operational indicators which distinguish one level from the next are not, however, defined. It is nonetheless possible to identify some indicators or intermediate outputs of coordination as is discussed below. First, however, it should be noted that given the ambiguities associated with the terms, this study sought to avoid the imposition of tight a priori definitions of the term and, instead, to explore the key mechanisms commonly accepted as contributing to coordination in child protection services and respondents 'assumptive worlds' regarding the processes. It was an exploratory rather than a hypothesis-testing study.

Routinised and radical coordination

One distinction drawn in the literature – that between routinised and radical coordination – proved to be particularly important in this study. Routinised coordination is that which is 'so well established it can be taken for granted' (Webb, 1991). As Webb notes, 'This is most obviously so when it is embedded in and becomes a function of a well-accepted technological process, division of labour or operational rules' (1991, p231). The latter two, a relatively clear division of labour and operational rules (contained in central government guidance and in local interagency procedural manuals) were much in evidence in this study of coordination in child protection. Webb notes that such routinisation has dangers and limits, for example in inhibiting innovative responses demanded by novel problems, a concern noted also by Benson (1982) and Warren (1973). Warren criticises coordination strategies for their potential to reinforce existing policies and practices and to screen out those with unorthodox or different views. He identifies the latent function served by coordination strategies in strengthening and preserving existing organisations and their mandates and suggests that the strategy is particularly important when social agencies are under attack for their ineffectiveness in remedying social problems, using the example of social problems associated with poverty in the USA. In such situations, change is widely heralded as necessary but 'change must take place in and through existing agencies . . ..
In the process, agencies have a dominant voice in what is to be done, work is with problems as they define them and in terms of the technology they have developed for dealing with them' (1973, p360). Warren emphasises that the key point is 'that the problem gets defined by local agencies in a way which makes their services appear the key to the solution and which expands their services while leaving untouched much more important aspects of the macro-system which can and do continue to produce poverty and dependency' (1973, p361). This analysis of coordination, developed in relation to anti-poverty strategies which defined poverty as an individual problem and underplayed its structural origins, has parallels with the account of the British response to child abuse elaborated by Parton (1985).

By contrast, a more radical form of coordination may exist which 'implies change and the disturbance of the existing order' or 'the crossing of boundaries between mutually exclusive, competitive or previously unrelated interests and domains' (Webb, 1991, p231). This, as Dartington (1986) suggests, is more creative and risky, involving an additive component, something beyond existing agency mandates which neither agency could achieve alone. It is likely that in such radical coordination, interpersonal issues of trust, openness, status, power and respect for the competence of other professionals will prove to be more salient and necessary than in more routinised forms. Identifying the existence and relative importance of each of these forms of coordination in child protective services was a part of this study.

The outcomes and outputs of coordination

Several authors point to the limited data on the outcomes of coordination. Mulford and Rogers, for example, noted that 'little is known about the impact of coordination with any high degree of certainty' (1982, p93) and Weiss observed that 'a host of researchers have noted that, because of data problems, they were unable to test the hypothesis that coordinated systems are better than uncoordinated ones' (1981, p35). Among the problems in evaluating outcomes are the multiple and sometimes conflicting objectives in coordination, the difficulties of establishing causal links between coordination as an input and varied outcomes, and the lack of outcome measures noted by many authors (for example, by Webb and Hobdell, 1978, Clark Turner and Ten Hoor, 1978, Westrin, 1987, Rogers and Whetten, 1982, and Mulford and Rogers, 1982). A study by Clark Turner and Ten Hoor (1978) of county support programmes in mental health in the USA noted the researchers' wish to develop outcome criteria but also the complexity of establishing outcomes for users, their families, communities and agency staff. Widner (1973) reported similar difficulties in evaluating the Appalachian development programme in the USA (which involved setting up coordinating councils). The underdeveloped state of the art of evaluation and associated methodological problems led to 'a normative and descriptive approach which measured performance against expectations . . . data were used not to discover and prove scientifically, but to illustrate' (Widner, 1973, p26). More recently a sophisticated study of coordination in several policy arenas in the UK (Challis et al) focused 'not on outcomes as such' but 'firmly on the policy and administrative purposes' (1988, p24). No doubt the difficulties of researching outcomes in this field led to this approach.

This study is no exception. It concentrates on process rather than outcome. In child protection services, the outcomes are principally the extent to which children are protected and their welfare promoted. This was not explored in this study. However, an attempt was made to identify whether there was evidence of 'intermediate outputs' (Knapp, 1984) of coordination, which can include:

a reduction in duplication and overlap evidenced, for example, in the minimisation of repeated interviews with children or of multiple medical examinations

clarity concerning professional roles

systems for the referral of cases between agencies

mechanisms for information sharing and joint decision-making

the existence of agreed interagency child protection plans

joint collaborative working in investigation, assessment or intervention

unified interagency records

unified child protection agencies.

It was not possible in the study to explore systematically the relation between coordination policies and practices and intermediate outputs. This was partly because of the methodological difficulties of establishing causal relations between inputs and outputs but also because such a study would require data collection in a large number of sites which had different policies and practices in respect of coordination. This was beyond the scope of the study and the available resources. Such an approach is also rendered problematic in the context of coordination in child protection services because the central government mandate and associated procedural guidance have led to a relatively standardised and homogenous system which limits, but does not eliminate, local variation in coordination policies and practices (Birchall, 1992).

Coordination as problematic

A second point of origin for the study was that, despite the widespread invocation of coordination as a policy objective, there is widespread agreement in the literature that working together is difficult. Challis et al suggest that coordination is problematic 'because in practice, it turns out to be extremely difficult to achieve' (1988, p267). Others writing of coordination in the sphere of health and welfare generally make similar observations, for example, Kahn and Thompson, 1971, Wilson and Akana, 1987, and Norton and Rogers, 1981. In the field of child protection specifically, the difficulties of collaboration are also widely accepted. Blyth and Milner suggest that 'given the opportunity, professionals would probably work better alone' (1990, p195) and numerous other authors (Wallen et al, 1977, Gustaffson et al, 1979, Benjamin, 1981, Fox and Dingwall, 1985, Molin and Herskowitz, 1986) assert the difficulties of collaboration. Stevenson encapsulates these views in the question 'why has it been so difficult to achieve the cooperation necessary to protect children at risk?' (1988, p5).

Many problems involved in working together are identified and they are explored in this study. They include different professional perspectives and frames of reference about the nature of child abuse and of intervention, different agency mandates and operational priorities, organisational tendencies towards autonomy, the time and other resource costs of collaborative work and interpersonal difficulties of trust and openness, gender and status differentials.

A perception of interagency collaboration in child protection as problematic is powerfully shaped and reinforced in the UK by a succession of inquiries into child abuse, beginning with the inquiry into the case of Maria Colwell, established in 1973. Initially the inquiries investigated the cases of individual children who had died or been seriously injured as a result of physical abuse. Latterly some have focused upon wider failures in the system involving multiple victims of alleged sexual abuse as in Cleveland (Cm 412, 1988) and Orkney (Clyde, 1992). The inquiries, some of which attracted considerable publicity, have had a powerful impact upon popular and professional consciousness and on official policy. While the lessons to be learned from them may be more complex than is sometimes portrayed (Dingwall, 1986, Hallett, 1989 and Hill, 1990), one of their most persistent and powerful messages is of recurrent failures and shortcomings in interagency coordination.

However, perceptions of collaboration as problematic are also evident in countries such as the USA and Sweden which have not been rocked by a succession of inquiry reports, nor are they confined to the sphere of child protection. There is, therefore, a paradox, in that interagency coordination is mandated by central government, required by local agencies, widely advocated by professional writers in the field of child abuse and yet revealed in the literature and in the inquiry reports to be difficult to achieve. Nonetheless, an interagency approach is widely practised and evident in the thousands of cases on child protection registers (which numbered 38 600 in England in 1992 (Department of Health, 1993(a)), at least in the sense that the cases must be processed through multidisciplinary child protection conferences in accordance with local interagency guidelines issued by the ACPCs.

It, therefore, seemed important in this study to examine coordination with reference to a sample of the generality of cases (as opposed to those where, by definition, things had gone wrong) and to explore whether working together was indeed perceived by the professionals involved to be intrinsically difficult and problematic.

Perspectives on interagency coordination

Increasingly, societal problems in advanced industrial or post-industrial societies are framed in organisational and interorganisational terms. Case studies of the process by which child abuse was transformed in the USA (Nelson, 1984) and Britain (Parton, 1985) from a private sorrow to a public ill emphasise how responses to the newly constructed social problem were located within health and welfare agencies. In both countries, there was an emphasis on interorganisational cooperation.

The study of organisations in recent years has moved through three overlapping but discernable phases marked by shifts in the predominant focus of concern. In the first, the primary focus was upon single organisations and their intraorganisational processes. This approach was criticised for its parochial and decontextualised character which isolated organisations from the societal structures in which they are located. In the second phase, the concern was with organisations and their environments. As external constraints on organisational functioning were identified as increasingly important and organisations sought to control environmental exigencies, attention was focused on the interface between organisations and their environments. In the third phase, the focus moved to the study of interorganisational relationships per se. This reflected a growing awareness of organisational interdependency and the existence of networks through which public policy is made and implemented (Benson, 1975, Hanf and Scharpf, 1978 and Rhodes, 1990).

The third phase has spawned a literature on interorganisational relations or, as it is often called, reflecting one of its dominant biases, interorganisational coordination. The literature is multidisciplinary and draws on studies in marketing and economics, public and social policy and, perhaps most important, organisational sociology. Three of the key perspectives in the sociological tradition of the study of interorganisational relationships, namely exchange, resource dependency and political economy are reviewed below.

The exchange perspective

The concept of interorganisational exchange developed by Levine and White has been influential in the analysis of interorganisational relations. Levine and White suggest that human service organisations need three main elements – clients, personnel and non-human resources, such as equipment, knowledge and funds, in order to achieve their goals. Often these are in short supply and, under conditions of scarcity, organisations cooperate or engage in interorganisational exchanges of the resources essential to goal attainment. Levine and White define organisational exchange rather broadly as 'any voluntary activity between two organisations which has consequences, actual or anticipated, for the realisation of their respective goals or objectives' (1961, p583). One of the factors likely to affect the extent to which interorganisational exchange takes place is the degree of domain consensus, or interagency agreement, about matters such as goals, functions, populations served and ideologies of intervention.

According to the exchange perspective, interorganisational relations form when members of organisations perceive mutual benefits or gains from interacting. The motivation to participate is internal to each organisation and, in consequence, it is suggested that the relationships which ensue are characterised by a high degree of cooperation and problem solving. This perspective assumes both the goal-directed nature of interorganisational activity and organisational decisions calculated rationally on the basis of self-interest. As will be seen later, both assumptions are open to question. The exchanges need not involve material goods but can include items such as legitimacy and status. They may be for short-term as well as long-term purposes and there need not be a symmetry or equality in the exchange. This suggests that exchange relationships may be compatible with the existence of power and dependency in interorganisational relationships, concepts which are central to the second key perspective.

The power/resource dependency perspective

The power or resource dependency approach to interorganisational relations is associated especially with the work of Aldrich (1972, 1976 and 1979), and the early work of Benson (1975). This perspective emphasises the links between organisations and their uncertain environments and it assumes that interorganisational relations are instrumental in controlling organisational environments. It shares with the exchange perspective a focus on the resource acquisition activities of organisations, especially securing an adequate supply of money, and of authority, defined as the legitimation of activities or a mandate. The resource dependency approach assumes that organisations seek to manage their environments to reduce dependencies and uncertainties, including those stemming from other organisations. It also assumes that environmental resources are in short supply because of inter-organisational competition and that organisations survive in so far as they can acquire scarce resources at the expense of other organisations.

Aldrich summarises the resource dependency approach as follows:

> *Other organisations are the key elements in most organisations' environments, as they control the flow of resources in a society. The interorganisational division of labour, under the pressure of resource competition, ensures that most organisations must seek out others with the specialised resources they require. If an organisation seeking resources from another controls strategic resources, has access to alternative sources, can use coercive power, or can modify its goals and technologies to do without the resource, it can avoid becoming dependent on the supplier. If, however, these conditions are not met or if the supplying organisations make effective countermoves to blunt attempts at interdependence, an organisation in*

*need may find itself in a dependent relationship. An organisation in a
dependent position vis-a-vis a dominant organisation might be forced to
comply with requests inimical to its own interests. Dependence is thus the
most important interorganisational relation, and the resource dependence
perspective on administrators' behaviour gives a primary role to the
concepts of dependence and power* (1979, p290).

In this approach, the feelings and attitudes associated with domain consensus,
an important feature of the voluntary relationship of the exchange perspective, are much less prominent. Power is more important than sentiments and
the motivation to interact is asymmetrical, with relationships forming when
one or more organisations have the power to force or induce other parties to
interact. For those forced to interact, the motiviation is external and
involuntary and not the result of the free pursuit of organisational self-
interest. As a result bargaining and conflict characterise these relationships, in
contrast to the cooperative character of the exchange perspective, although in
both interorganisational dependence is central to the analysis.

Exchange and resource dependency perspectives are sometimes presented
as alternative or competing paradigms developing along parallel but separate
paths. Schmidt and Kochan (1977) suggest that this is unhelpful since
interorganisational life is not as simple as the perspectives might indicate.
Rather than engaging exclusively in one or other type, organisations are in
reality likely to engage in some exchange and some power dependency
interorganisational relationships. Furthermore, they suggest that real-life
relationships are, as might be exected, unlikely to fit exactly the ideal-types
identified in the models but rather to reflect mixed motives. Schmidt and
Kochan, therefore, call for an integrated view of interorganisational relations
which can incorporate the basic propositions from both models, as does
Cook (1977) in her article on 'Exchange and power in networks of
interorganisational relations'. This highlights the extent to which both
perspectives adopt a similar conceptual framework, despite some marked
differences of emphasis.

Because of this degree of commonality, some of the criticisms which may
be made of one perspective apply also to the other. For example, both assume
that interorganisational relationships result from the attempts by individual
organisations to secure resources required for goal achievement. The utility of
the concept of organisational goals has, however, been questioned by
organisational sociologists, including Hall (1977) and Perrow (1979). They
highlight the difficulty of identifying clear and unequivocal goals for reasons
which include the distinctions drawn between what organisations say they do
and actually do (official and operative goals), the existence of multiple and
often competing goals and the different perception of goals by different
members of the organisation.

Similarly, both the exchange and resource dependency perspective emphasise the capacity of organisations to engage in rational decision-making in pursuit of the goals. The ability of organisational actors to make such rational decisions has also been questioned by Lindblom (1959), amongst others. Whetten and Leung suggest that the rational decision-making model assumes that key staff in organisations have considerable freedom to choose between alternatives and can do so on the 'basis' of 'rational' considerations, but, they argue:

> *Within the context in which linkages between public agencies are established, frequently these assumptions cannot be met. There are environmental conditions that restrict the autonomy of the administrators to choose freely between alternatives, and there are organisational conditions that restrict their use of rational criteria* (1979, p238).

The resource dependency model acknowledges this in respect of organisations forced into linkages they would not have chosen, but the focal organisations are nonetheless assumed to act on the basis of rational self-interest. In fact, however, all the organisations in a horizontal interorganisational network may be constrained by a legal or administrative directive from a higher level, as is the case in child protection in the UK.

Mandated coordination

The exchange and resource dependency perspectives both accord a central importance to the circumstances in which individual organisations choose or are forced to engage in coordination with other agencies in their environment. The emphasis is principally, although not exclusively, upon lateral relationships between agencies at the same government level, albeit sometimes of unequal power. The exchange perspective in particular may be criticised for its assumptions concerning rationality in the decisions to establish interorganisational linkages, portrayed as the outcome of deliberate and thoughtful process involving as degree of choice. In practice, a multitude of factors can interfere with this rational decision-making process, particularly in the public sector. In particular, some linkages are essentially forced upon participating agencies by third parties which mandate coordination. Hanf notes that

> *for a significant range of policy problems the kind and amount of coordination produced through the voluntary and spontaneous actions of individual organisations is neither appropriate nor sufficient. Effective problem-solving for these problems requires corrective interventions into the self-organisation of the system. The conventional response in such circumstances has been to provide central government with the capacity to*

> *formulate comprehensive and integrated policies to ensure that lower level agencies will be more effectively guided by the policy objectives of more inclusive higher levels of government* (1978, p2).

This 'mandated' coordination characterises current coordination policies in child protection in the UK, in which agencies are directed or required to coordinate their activities by those in superordinate positions in the hierarchy in central government.

Some authors, for example, Hall et al (1977) argue that the exchange model does not apply when interorganisational relationships are mandated by law or regulatory agencies. Does the existence of mandated coordination then mean that the exchange and, to an extent, also the resource dependency perspectives can be ignored in situations such as child protection in the UK? The answer is no, for two principal reasons. The first is that the mandates themselves may emerge from situations in which linkages based on exchange (or it may be argued resource dependence) already exist. It is rare for mandates to coordinate to be established in situations where no prior coordinating activity took place. As Hall et al (1977) note mandates will be developed to regularise exchange and exchanges will occur to modify mandates. Cook (1977) argues that an analysis of the exchange process may lead to an understanding of the emergence of mandates. This occurred in the UK since advice from central government in the field of child protection was founded upon the dominant understanding about the importance of an interagency response, essentially developed from voluntary exchanges between professionals and agencies in the USA and here. Secondly, the problem of securing agreement to mandates suggests that several of the concepts of relevance in understanding the emergence and particularly the sustaining of voluntary coordination activities, such as domain consensus, power and status, are also of relevance in studying the implementation of coordination policies when these are mandated. Nonetheless, mandated coordination poses particular problems in securing adherence to the mandate and achieving effective implementation, as is discussed below.

The policy sector or political economy approach

While the concepts and insights associated with the exchange and resource dependency perspectives cannot be ignored in studying mandated coordination, their limitations should be noted. The interorganisational literature based upon these perspectives usually reflects a limiting and practical reformist concern, with an interest – sometimes explicit, at times implicit – to improve service delivery through the reduction of duplication and overlap. This has had important consequences. First, as both Hall and Clark (1974) and Neghandi 91975) note, the reformist orientation has led to little attention being paid to more radical changes in service delivery or alternative means of meeting need, leading to an inherent conservatism in the literature. Secondly, the concern with rationality and coordination has led to an emphasis on cooperative forms of interrelationship at the expense of the analysis of conflict and to a framing of the issue from the perspectives of service providers rather than users. Thirdly, within this paradigm, interorganisational relationships are abstracted from their broader societal context and theorised in a self-contained and decontextualised way. Aiken et al reviewed the literature on interorganisational relations for their study of the coordination of services for people with a severe learning difficulty and concluded that it was:

> only partly applicable since it ignored matters of community power, state and national politics and the like, which were as important in explaining the outcomes of these projects as organisational or interorganisational factors (1975, pxi).

A concern to articulate the relationship between interorganisational linkages and the wider social structure is a characteristic of the third perspective reviewed here, the political economy or policy sector appraoch.

This perspective, associated particularly with the work of Benson (1975 and 1982), acknowledges the contribution of earlier theories, especially resource dependency theory, to the analysis of interorganisational relations but sees them as embedded in a limiting problematic, characterised by its decontextualised nature. Benson suggests:

> the problematic does not include a concern with or theory about the larger societal context and its institutional arrangements. Interorganisational phenomena – dyads, sets, networks, are theorised as if context-free. Resource dependencies and other interorganisational relations are then analysed without regard to the larger political and economic structures in which they are embedded particularly those of the capitalist mode of production and capitalist state apparatus (1982, p145).

Benson also suggests that:

> the ideological incorporation of the problematic suggests the advanced societies face no fundamental structural problems or contradictions, that their problems are merely organisational and interorganisational in character, and that an organisational and interorganisational technology can be created to deal with the problems. By this route the interorganisational problematic is incorporated into a technocratic ideology. The use of this ideology dissolves class conflict, relations of state and economy, bureaucracy and other critical macro-structural problems into the more palatable and seemingly more manageable difficulties of resource blockage,

domain conflict and duplication of services. This ideology is also linked to strategies of piecemeal problem-solving (1982, p146).

In a similar vein, Weiss suggests that coordination acts as a vehicle for the expression of social commitment to rationality, comprehensiveness, simplicity and efficiency and that 'coordination simplifies the problems in human services by implying that the worst problems are merely administrative and that improvements in service quality will follow automatically once the organisational questions are resolved' (1981, p39). In practice, however, she argues 'coordination cannot generate new resources, cannot devise new treatment methods, cannot solve problems of alienation or mistrust, cannot transmute ineffective service systems into effective ones' (1981, p43).

These are powerful critiques of the traditional, dominant approaches in the analysis of interorganisational relations. Benson suggests that interorganisational relationships need to be analysed in the context of a policy sector viewed as an interorganisational political economy. Briefly, a policy sector as defined by Benson, is an arena in which public policies are made and implemented (such as health care, or welfare) composed of complexes of organisations connected to each other by resource dependencies. A policy sector is a social structure, a patterned set of practices, operating at several levels (as follows) with each level limited by succeeding or higher levels.

Level 1:

1   Administrative arrangements (division of labour)
2   Policy paradigms
3   Interorganisational dependencies

Level 2:

1   Interest-power structures
2   Rules of structure formation

The components in level 1 relate closely to the concepts and issues identified as important in the typologies and perspectives outlined above. The administrative arrangements are those made for the division of labour and control over activities within the policy sector. Policy paradigms are the substantive content or policy orientations as revealed in the practices actually taking place, rather than declared policy intentions. The third component, the structure of interorganisational resource dependencies is developed in the context of the particular policy paradigm and administrative structure. For example, changes in administrative arrangements, (such as reorganisation) or in policy paradigms would alter the patterns of resource dependency. Similarly, the pattern of interorganisational dependency in existing power structures may constrain the development of alternative policy paradigms and administrative arrangements. An example of this is the position of general practitioners in Britain where their continued position as independently contracted practitioners constrains certain developments in integrated health care services.

Benson suggests that the resource dependency perspective is useful for analysing interactions in level 1 but that to understand them it is necessary to move to a deeper level of analysis in what he terms 'historically specific macro-structural' contexts. The components of Level 2 identified by Benson for undertaking this task are interest-power structures and rules of structure formation. Benson suggests that the administrative arrangements, policy paradigms and interorganisational relationships must be understood in relation to underlying power structures, in which groups which Alford (1975) describes as 'structured interests' are embedded. The structured interests are groups whose interests are built into the sector in that it serves or conflicts with them. Benson identifies five as important: demand groups (the users or recipients); support groups (those providing financial and political resources); administrative groups (those in administrative control within organisations); provider groups (those engaged in service delivery) and coordinating groups (those engaged in rationalising programmes and services between sectors). Within these groups there may, of course, be conflicts of view, as there are likely to be between them. Benson suggests that the operation of policy sectors reflects these structured interests, usually defending some at the expense of others, and changes within the policy sector which threaten these are likely to be resisted.

In addition to these interests, the structure underlying a policy sector includes rules (or practices) which limit its operation – the rules of structure formation. These are generated in part, in advanced capitalist societies, from the changing demands of capital accumulation and legitimation and their impact would vary between policy sectors depending upon how closely the sector impinged upon the core functions of the state. Benson distinguishes two types of structure formation rules – negative selection rules which define limits or boundaries (in public policy in general, or in particular policy sectors) such that actions which directly threaten the character of the capitalist state are not permitted or will be counteracted. The second type, positive selection rules require a policy sector to contribute to structure formation. In child abuse both these processes can be seen at work. In terms of negative selection rules, the operational definitions of child abuse adopted in law and welfare in countries such as the USA and the UK are not such as directly to threaten the nature of the state. Definitions such as those offered by Gil 'abuse of children is human-originated acts of commission or omission and human-created or tolerated conditions that inhibit or preclude unfolding and development of the inherent potential of children' (1981, p295) with their implicit agenda of wide-scale social change, for example, to reduce inequalities in childhood, do not gain acceptance in the public policy arena. In respect of positive selection rules to contribute to structure formation, however, child protection activities may be viewed both as a demonstration of the state's caring function (thus contributing to its legitimacy) and state control of deviant behaviour which, if unchecked, may undermine 'the family'. Benson stresses a degree of autonomy from these 'rules' which allows for some negotiation and variation. The rules are not deterministic or rigid but rather place limits upon the mobilisation of interests within the policy sector. In this sense, there is some similarity with the idea of a 'bounded pluralism' in public policy as outlined by Hall et al (1975), although that view is propounded within a more liberal pluralistic system then is suggested by Benson's neo-Marxist perspective.

This study of coordination policies and practices in child protection does not investigate specifically the macro-political and economic context in which child protection policies have developed in the UK in the last twenty-five years. Such a task is beyond the scope of this more limited study and has been attempted by others, notably Parton (1985 and 1991) and Frost and Stein (1989). The macro-level changes of significance include the disaggregation of the family as a unit with greater attention paid to the rights and needs of children (and women) as individuals rather than as the property of authority figures in the household and changing relations between the family and the state. However, changes in the political economy of welfare, notably the extension of markets and quasi-markets in social policy, proved in the course of this study to be significantly affecting interagency coordination in child protection, founded on traditions of collaboration rather than competition. More broadly, the study explores whether there is support for Benson's observations about the nature of coordination as a force for conservatism in response to newly emerged (or re-emerged) social problems.

The interpersonal base to interagency coordination

The literature on interorganisational relations has a predominant focus on the form, structure and mechanisms of interagency coordination. They are relatively straightforward to identify and operationalise in research terms. Some such organisational arrangements for promoting coordination are reviewed in this study. They include Area Child Protection Committees, child protection case conferences and child protection registers. However, Challis et al (1988) note the limitations in studying coordination which result simply from the outputs (for example, records of meetings, service agreements, joint planning documents, etc). They assert also the importance of the many informal relationships and coordinating activities which may exist alongside the formal machinery. The child protection system in the UK is characterised by an elaborate set of organisational arrangements designed, inter alia, to secure coordination among the many agencies involved. It is, however, supplemented by a variety of less formal interactions at the case level.

Several authors have commented on the emphasis in the interorganisationa relations literature on structures and mechanisms. Whetten (1981), for example, suggested that considerably more is known about the form of interorganisational relationships than about their content and highlighted the need for a shift from study of structural characteristics and dimensions to an emphasis on context and content in the study of interagency relations. Gough et al (1987) has also argued for better description and analysis of the realities of practice and Tibbitt noted the need to put people back into organisation theory since 'interorganisational relationships occur through the interactions of individuals' (1973, p166).

In respect of interagency work, issues such as trust, respect for the competence and contribution of other professionals, status and power are important. This study, therefore, tried to meet the criticisms of the focus of much earlier work in the field, by studying these issues as they were experienced by practitioners in the course of collaborative work in child protection in the research sites.

Implementation

In circumstances in which coordination is required rather than voluntarily sought by agencies in pursuit of their own interests, a key problem concerns securing adherence to the mandate. Since a central tenet of the literature on coordination is a basic organisational tendency towards the preservation of autonomy and independence and since changes in interorganisational systems are costly in time, effort and morale, Weiss suggest that 'organisations are unlikely to take up cooperation with one another simply because someone says it would be a good idea for them to do so' (1981, p29). As Scharpf notes, in the absence of coercion, unless governments can offer positive incentives to participants

> *the would-be creators and managers of policy networks cutting across the boundaries of formal organisations . . . will either have to persuade participants that it is in their own interest to join a proposed policy network . . . or that it is their duty to do so* (1978, p366).

When coordination is mandated by central government, its implementation needs to be considered within the framework of relationships between central and local government (Rhodes, 1981, 1986 and 1988). There is an increasing awareness of the problematic nature of central government control in complex societies and awareness of the power of local agencies to resist and subvert policy initiatives or engage in delaying tactics. Policy analysts have, therefore, been particularly concerned in recent years with the issue of implementation of public policy.

Two contrasting approaches, widely known as the 'top down' and the 'bottom up', characterise the literature. In the former associated, for example, with the work of Derthick (1971), Pressman and Wildavsky (1973), Van Meter and Van Horn (1975) and Sabatier and Mazmanian (1980), the emphasis is on the identification of a clear 'policy' and how its objectives were or, often, were not achieved in the course of implementation. The bottom up approach, associated with the work of Barrett and Fudge (1981), Barrett and Hill (1984), Hjern (1982) and Hanf and Scharpf (1978), emphasises the study of implementation from the perspective of other actors in the policy process besides the central decision-makers. It explores the extent to which policies are shaped, and in effect created, in the course of implementation as street level bureaucrats (Lipsky, 1980) subvert or divert them to their own ends. They thus question both the existence of unambiguous policies whose implementation can be studied and the distinction conventionally drawn between policy formulation and implementation, noting that many of the same structured interests and policy networks are involved both in formulation and implementation.

As Marsh and Rhodes (1992) suggest, the dichotomy between the two approaches, while useful, runs the risk of simplifying to the point of inaccuracy. They advocate the selection of an approach best suited to the problem at hand. Sabatier (1986a) has attempted to produce a synthesis which combines top down and bottom up approaches in the analysis of policy change. This acknowledges the importance of studying a policy problem over time rather than the implementation of a single policy decision, but also emphasises the extent to which interventions by central government, as well as broader socio-economic factors, influence and change the implementation network.

Such a synthesis seems particularly helpful in studying interagency coordination in child protection. As the literature discussed above makes clear, the motivations, reactions and experience of those in local implementation networks are likely to be critical in securing adherence to the mandate. However, with respect to interagency coordination in child protection, in contrast to some other policy arenas, central government guidance in the UK has been detailed and relatively specific. There has been a clearly articulated central government policy on the issue, changing over time but still relatively stable, whose nature and implementation is capable of being studied. Two important topics in the analysis of public policy, namely mandated coordination and policy implementation, are, therefore, brought together in this study.

As a result of the review of the literature, certain themes were identified as particularly important for reflection in the research design. The first was that, given the definitional problems associated with the terms coordination, collaboration and cooperation, the topic was studied through an exploration of what appeared to constitute coordination in policy and practice, rather than through the prior imposition of a tight, and possibly restrictive, definition.

Important aspects of the topic identified in the literature included whether the coordination was routinised or radical, whether it was perceived as inherently problematic and the identification of its intermediate outputs. There is limited evidence about the outcomes of coordination, reflecting both a rather uncritical acceptance of its benefits in much of the literature and the methodological difficulties of establishing links between coordination and outcomes. The outcomes of coordination policies and practices in child protection services for the children and families concerned were not explored in this study. However, there was a focus upon the existence and nature of intermediate outputs.

Secondly, the literature revealed that two intellectual traditions, those of exchange and resource dependency, were dominant in accounting for the development and maintenance of interorganisational relations. They highlight certain features as likely to affect interagency coordination, for example the degree of consensus about domain, motivations to work together and the resource levels required. However, the purchase of these two perspectives on the topic was limited by the existence of a central government mandate to collaborate in British child protection services. This led to an exploration in the study of the extent to which there was adherence to the mandate and to its implementation.

Thirdly, despite the dominance in the literature of the structures and mechanisms for coordination, the interpersonal base to interorganisational relations nonetheless emerged as important. The research design was, therefore, sensitive to issues such as trust, status, power and respect for the competence of the professionals involved.

Finally, the literature pointed to the potential for coordination strategies to tend towards conservatism, reinforcing an existing division of labour and accepted ways of working. This issue was, therefore, explored in the study. The research design and methods adopted to explore these themes in the context of child protection services in two areas in northern England are presented in the next chapter.

Chapter 2

The research design

The aim of the study was to explore coordination policies and practices in child protection by reviewing coordination as it appeared to have taken place in a retrospective, purposive sample of cases of child abuse and by exploring the topic through depth interviews and a brief questionnaire with a sample of professionals. The study is an exploratory, descriptive account of interagency coordination rather than a hypothesis-testing study or an evaluation of the final outcomes of coordination. In research design, data collection and analysis the study sought to relate the empirical findings to selected key themes and concepts identified in the literature review, which were outlined in the previous chapter. This chapter outlines the research design adopted for the study and describes the characteristics of the research sites, the cases in the case sample, the professionals who were interviewed and those who completed a questionnaire.

The research design: a case study

The research design adopted was a case study of interagency coordination in two areas. Yin defines a case study as 'an empirical inquiry that investigates a contemporary phenomenon within its real life context . . . in which multiple sources of evidence are used' (1989, p 23). The methods typically include analysis of records and documents, depth interviews, structured surveys and participant or non-participant observation. This study concentrated on the first three, although some limited non-participant observation of meetings of the ACPC was undertaken in one research site. The triangulated research design chosen to illuminate the topic of coordination in child protection comprised multiple data sources. The three primary ones were

the social services department case files of a sample of children on the child protection register

a semi-structured interview with a sample of professionals

a questionnaire completed by a sample of professionals

In addition, a variety of documentary sources was consulted, including central government guidance, the local interagency guidelines in the authorities concerned, internal agency procedures and working papers. Finally, three meetings of the ACPC were attended in borough as a non-participant observer 'orientation' exercise.

The research design was intended to complement the empirical work conducted by Birchall (1992). Birchall used a postal questionnaire survey with a sample of 339 respondents. Such an instrument cannot explore in depth the motivations, experiences and perceptions of respondents. Since the literature indicated that the interpersonal base to interorganisational coordination is significant, the present study selected a smaller sample of professional respondents to allow for exploration of the topic through depth interviews. Secondly, Birchall explored the views and intended actions of professionals in response to hypothetical situations, through the use of case vignettes. Since there may be a difference between the reported intentions of respondents in such situations and their concrete actions in practice, the present study incorporated a retrospective study of interagency coordination as recorded in agency case files.

Reflections on the case study method

The case study method reportedly has certain strengths. Yin suggests that case studies 'contribute uniquely to our knowledge of individual, organisational, social and political phenomena' principally through allowing 'an investigation to retain the holistic and meaningful characteristics of real-life events' (1989, p 14). In a similar vein, Hakim suggests that 'using a variety of data collection techniques and methods allows a more rounded, holistic study than with any other design' (1987, p 61). Case study methods can be particularly appropriate when the content and context of a phenomenon are unclear – as coordination was argued to be in the previous chapter.

Nonetheless, the case study method poses problems of central relevance to social scientific inquiry, namely those of validity and reliability. One charge against case studies, with their traditional reliance on qualitative methods, has been that of lack of rigour. As Hakim notes, the allegation of lack of rigour can be addressed in research design. She suggests 'the case study is the social research equivalent of the spotlight or the microscope; its value depends critically on how well the study is focused'.

More problematic is the issue of whether, given their local and specific focus, case studies can provide a basis for generalisation. In some respects this is based on a misunderstanding of the nature and aims of case studies. As Platt notes 'it is curious how often criticisms of case studies, as a basis for generalisation, use ideas of representative sampling, appropriate only for estimating the prevalence of a characteristic in a population, to dismiss their adequacy for making contributions to a theoretical explanation (Platt 1988, p 17). Case studies can be designed to be generalisable to conceptual issues described by Yin (1989) as analytic generalisation rather than to enumerate frequencies (statistical generalisation).

Some strategies can be adopted in research design to minimise (although not to eliminate) these difficulties. One is to conduct the study in more than one site. As Sudman suggests the significance and robustness of research findings increase with the number of sites noting that 'the largest gain occurs when the number of sites is increases from one to two' (1976, p 26, in Hakim 1987). Two research sites were used in this research.

Secondly, the characteristics of the research sample can be related to national data and to the findings of other studies. This is done later in this chapter in respect of the selection of the research sites, the purposive sample of registered cases and the characteristics of the professionals interviewed.

Thirdly, multiple data sources can be used. In this study, data were principally collected from case files, depth interviews, a questionnaire and from documentary analysis. In particular, some quantitative data derived from the sample of case files were compared with data from depth interviews, as outlined by Bryman (1988). Furthermore, the numbers involved, although small by comparison with large quantitative surveys, were not restricted to one. As Bryman notes, there is a 'tendency to approach a case study as if it were a sample of one drawn from a higher universe of such cases'. However, he suggests that 'within a case study a wide range of different people and activities are invariably examined so that the contrast with survey samples is not as acute as it appears at first glance, especially when the widespread tendency for survey researchers to draw samples from localities rather than on a national basis is borne in mind (1988, p 90).

Fourthly, as Bryman (1988) and Silverman (1993), (among others), note, attention can be paid in presenting qualitative data to the selection, representativeness and typicality of the views expressed and, in particular, the avoidance of the temptation to report solely the exotic or only 'a good quote'. As outlined below, attention was paid to this in this study.

Finally, it is possible to use the respondent validation technique, as recommended by McKeganey and Bloor (1981) and Yin (1989). This is designed to explore the extent to which research respondents accept the representation of themselves and of the topic as valid. The limitations of this technique have been noted, for example by Bryman (1988) and Silverman (1993). They include the possibility of the censoring of research findings by respondents and the fact that it is unlikely that respondent validation will greatly facilitate the researcher's interpretation of the data. Nonetheless, the technique was used in this study. A draft of the research report was sent to key informants for comment. While not all recipients of the draft responded, those who did so accepted the general picture portrayed in the report as valid.

However, while the strategies outlined above can strengthen claims to validity, reliability and the capacity to generalise from case studies, they cannot entirely meet the criticisms. The issue of reliability remains at the heart of qualitative methods, particularly when a single researcher has collected and analysed the data. A degree of subjectivity is inherent. No doubt in the study reported here, other researchers would have asked different questions, utilised different concepts and, perhaps, reached different conclusions. Ultimately, a case study must be judged by the appropriateness and rigour of the methods selected, by what Hammersley (1990) terms its credibility and plausibility and whether the conclusions are supported by the data. The research methods adopted in this study are described below, together with the characteristics of the samples which are compared with those used in other studies.

The research sites

It is not easy to present the contextual data about the research sites selected whilst protecting their anonymity which was a condition of research access. The strategy adopted is to present the information in deliberately rather vague terms, while, it is hoped, giving sufficient information for the context of the research to be appraised.

The research took place in two local authority areas (referred to as city and borough) in the north of England. This region was selected partly because of its relative proximity to Scotland, where the research was based at the University of Stirling, but also because much previous research in child care and child protection had been based in southern England. Two research sites were selected since this was the maximum considered feasible within the resources available for the research and since this was thought likely to increase the robustness and significance of the findings (Sudman, 1976). The research sites were selected using several criteria. One was that there should be coterminous boundaries with the health authority. While coterminous boundaries do not necessarily guarantee collaboration, (Challis et al, 1988, Wistow and Fuller, 1986, Pugh-Thomas 1987) their absence is recognised to render it more difficult to achieve and so areas with non-coterminous boundaries were avoided.

A region of the north of England was selected, from which the county councils were excluded since they did not have boundaries which were coterminous with the health authorities. One metropolitan authority was also excluded since it was one of the three principal research sites included in Birchall's (1992) study. Using data from the remaining eight metropolitan districts in the region a 'regional sample average' score was calculated on a number of different indicators which could be compared both with the average for England as a whole and for all metroplitan districts.

Deprivation

The research sites selected were ranked sixth from bottom (city) and seventh from bottom (borough) of the metropolitan districts in the regional sample in terms of the Department of the Environment Z scores which rank deprivation on various factors, using census data. These provide scores which at zero indicate 'average' deprivation, at plus five 'severe' deprivation and at minus five 'little' deprivation. The regional sample ranged from minus 1.03 to 2.68 and the two authorities selected had Z scores of between 1 and 2.

Ethnicity

The regional sample average for the percentage of the residences where the head of the household originates from the New Commonwealth or Pakistan (based on the 1981 Census data) was 3.2% (compared with a metropolitan district average of 5.0% and an average for the whole of England of 4.7%). The range in the regional sample was from 0.4% to 11.2%. The two research sites chosen were close to the regional sample average, at between 3% and 4%.

Social services department resources

The aim in selection was to avoid those authorities with the lowest expenditure levels on social services provision since the literature indicated, unsurprisingly, that, in general, severe resource shortages have a deleterious impact upon interagency collaboration (Broskowski et al, 1982, Challis et al, 1988). The authorities selected ranked first (city) and joint third (borough) of the eight in the regional sample of gross current expenditure on personal social services per capita. With specific reference to per capita expenditure in 1984/85 on the population under 18 years of age, they ranked joint second (city) and fourth (borough). In terms of social work staff per 1000 population, the regional sample average was 4.9. City was top and borough was fourth, both above the average for England as a whole and above the regional sample average. Borough was, however, below the average of 5.9 for all metropolitan districts.

Child protection registrations

The rate of child protection registrations per 1000 population under 18 in the regional sample in 1989 ranged from just under 9 to just below 3. The regional sample average was 4.5 compared with an average for England as whole of 3.7. The rate in city was slightly above the regional average at under 5 and in borough slightly below at under 4.

City and borough compared

City was much larger than borough, with over two and a half times the population of borough. In terms of interagency work in child protection, the key features were that, in both authorities, at the time of the study the child protection register was on the point of being transferred to the social services departments (from the health authority in city and the NSPCC in borough); that, in both, the police had established special units dealing, inter alia, with child abuse; and that, in both, the social services departments operated on a generic basis, although they were on the point of creating specialist child care teams/practitioners. Dickinson (1993) estimates that about 85% of police authorities have established specialist units but only about 38% of social services departments in England have done so (although there are varying degrees of informal specialisation). The authorities selected are, therefore, broadly representative of the national position in this respect.

The principal contrasts were that, in city, paediatric services were provided by teaching hospitals including a specialist children's hospital staffed with a full complement of junior paediatric staff in training posts; that in city there was a separate school nursing service and that, in borough, there was an NSPCC child protection team. The impact of these contextual issues is discussed more fully throughout the book.

From a researcher's point of view one of the most significant characteristics of each locality was the remarkable openness of members of the interagency network and their willingness to take part in the research, reflected in very high participation rates.

Research access

Research access was negotiated initially through the Director of Social Services in each of the two research sites. This was partly because the ACPC in each locality was chaired by the Director of Social Services but also because if the social services department, as the lead agency, had opposed the research it could not have taken place. Both social services departments were initially welcoming and a formal request for research access was then put to each ACPC. It was granted in both cases, on the understanding that the participation of individual professionals would be voluntary and with an assurance that the research sites would not be identified.

Data sources and data collection instruments

The three primary data sources were a sample of 48 registered cases of child abuse, interviews with a sample of 90 professionals and questionnaires completed by 81 professionals. Each is described in turn below.

The case sample

Drawing the case sample

The purposive sample of 48 cases was drawn by identifying cases from the child protection registers in borough and city which met the research criteria. These were selected principally to limit the scope of the study, reflecting Dixon et al's (1987) advice that global topics, such as interagency coordination, need to be translated into researchable issues, limited in scope and confined to a certain time, place and set of conditions. The first limitation placed was on type of abuse. Two types of abuse, physical and sexual, were selected from the available register categories which included, at that time, neglect, emotional abuse and grave concern, although the last was removed as a separate register category in 1991. The two categories were selected partly because physical abuse contributed the largest single registration category (23% of cases in 1990) and sexual abuse the second largest (14%) (Department of Health, 1991). They also offered opportunities to examine the contrasting roles of medical assessment and of the police and the criminal justice system in response to the two different types of abuse.

The second criterion was to restrict the children concerned to those of primary school age (defined in the study as those aged between four and a half and eleven years at the date of registration). This afforded an opportunity to explore the role of teachers in interagency coordination – a topic relatively little explored in the literature (Maher 1987, Hallett and Birchall, 1992, pp 147–148).

The third criterion was to select cases registered within the two years preceding data collection. This time period was chosen for two principal reasons – first so that the majority of the cases would have been registered for long enough for the initial peak of interagency activity in investigation and initial conference to have passed offering an opportunity also to examine collaborative work in intervention and case review. Secondly, so that there was not too long a time gap between registration and the field interviews with the professionals engaged with the sub-sample, so that the likelihood of people having moved jobs was not too great and their capacity to recall the cases not too impaired by the passage of time.

Since the child protection registers in the research sites were not at that stage computerised, selecting cases to meet these criteria required a manual search. In borough, it yielded 25 cases, but two were subsequently removed (one because the social worker did not wish to participate in the research and a second because the child was subjected to abuse in residential care and the case had already been the subject of an internal case review), so 92% of the eligible cases were included in the sample. In city, 66 cases met the sampling criteria. Since it was intended to produce a case sample size broadly comparable in each authority, the cases in city were stratified to reflect the spread across the different social services divisional offices and then sampled at random, to produce a list of just over 30 (to allow for some wastage). As requested, this list was presented to the divisional officers for information and feedback as to whether any case would be likely to cause particular difficulty. None did, although it was revealed that a few did not meet the criteria (having originally been registered for neglect, for example) so a final sample of 25 cases was achieved in city.

The case record data collection instrument

Data were collected in respect of the case sample principally by extracting information from the social services department case files. A data collection instrument, reproduced as Appendix 1, was developed and piloted on a sample of cases in a London borough. Following that stage, it was decided to omit a section which had tried to map all the interagency communications on the basis of the information recorded in the files concerning the initiators and receivers of interprofessional exchanges, the method of communication (ad hoc meeting, telephone conversation, letter etc) and a broad classification of the purpose of the exchange (seeking information, passing on information, requesting action etc). This was because it appeared that some interprofessional exchanges were not fully recorded, if at all, a finding confirmed by Birchall (1992).

The case record data collection instrument was, therefore, confined to the following five main areas:

i   data concerning the registered child and siblings eg household composition, age, ethnicity, gender;

ii   referral – eg the source and data of referral; the primary reason for referral; the number, sex and relationship to the registered child of the alleged abuser(s); the referral route to the social service department and previous contact between the family and the social services department;

iii   investigation – eg the agencies contacted during investigation, interviews with children, parents and abusers, medical examinations, police investigation, emergency protective action (eg immediate removal of the child from home, removal of the alleged abuser from the home);

iv   initial child protection case conferences – eg timing; location; chairs; patterns of attendance and non-attendance; conference recommendations; family involvement; professional dissent concerning recommendations; the child protection plan;

v   case review – eg subsequent child protection conferences; core groups; other interagency meetings.

In addition to the data extracted in standardised form for each of the 48 cases in the case sample, a brief 'pen picture' of the case was compiled to serve as an aide-memoire.

Data analysis of the case sample

The case sample data collection instrument comprised principally nominal data. It was analysed using a computerised database (Data Ease) which involved entering the data on a standard data entry sheet and retrieving the collated data in respect of particular categories or combinations, as required.

The characteristics of the case sample

The case sample comprised 48 cases in which at least one child of primary school age was entered on the child protection register in the category of physical or sexual abuse or, in a few cases, grave concern thereof. When one child in a family was the principal victim of abuse and the subject of the initial referral, he/she was designated the index child. When there was more than one primary school aged child registered and all children were equally abused or at risk of abuse, a child was selected at random and designated as the index child.

The cases selected for the case sample were all registered in 1989 or 1990 with the exception of one in borough, registered in November 1988; 13 cases (27%) in 1989 and 34 cases (71%) in 1990. The distribution between the years and between borough and city is shown in Figure 2.1. This yielded a sample in which, on average, 16 months (14 in borough and 17 in city) had elapsed between the date of registration and the date on which the file was studied to complete the data collection instrument. The patterns are as shown in Figure 2.2

As is shown in Figure 2.3, 27 of the 48 cases were registered as physical abuse, including two cases of grave concern, (15 in borough and 12 in city) and 21 as sexual abuse, including three cases of grave concern (8 in borough and 13 in city). The case mix in the sample in terms of types of abuse is not identical in the two authorities, there being proportionately fewer cases of sexual abuse in borough.

Characteristics of the index children

There were slightly more girls in the sample of index children than boys, 27 (56%) compared with 21 (44%), as is shown in Figure 2.4. This corresponds with the sex of the 9628 children reported in the NSPCC research on child protection registers where the proportions registered

Figure 2.1   **Year of registration of cases in the case sample: borough and city compared (N=48)**

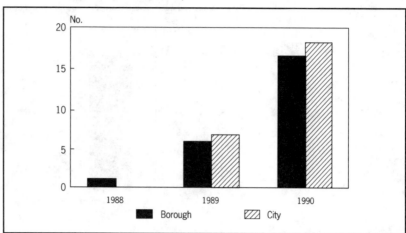

Figure 2.2   **Time elapsed between registration and completion of the case record data collection instrument: borough and city compared (N=48)**

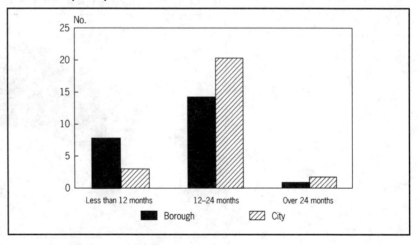

between 1988 and 1990 were 54% girls and 46% boys (Creighton, 1992). The ethnic origins of the index children are shown in Figure 2.5. It is predominantly a white sample. At the time of the research, the ethnic origin of the children on the child protection registers in the research sites was not separately recorded, so it is not known whether the case sample reflects the ethnic composition of the population of children registered as abused in the authorities concerned.

Figure 2.3   **Case sample by type of abuse: borough and city compared (N=48)**

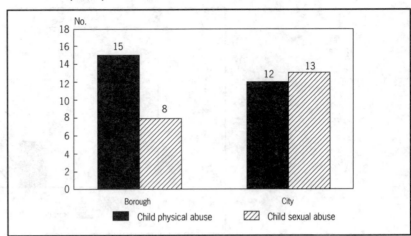

Figure 2.4:   **Sex of index children in the case sample (N=48)**

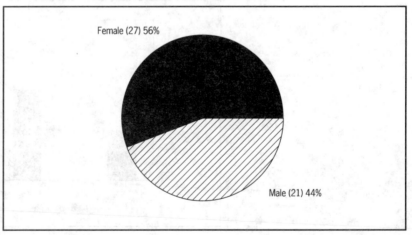

The index children were fairly even spread across the age range, with the exception of the two children aged 11 at the time of registration, as is shown in Figure 2.6. The modal age was five, but the mean age was 7.54 years, 8.19 in borough and 6.93 in city.

Figure 2.5: **Ethnic origin of the index children in the case sample (N=48)**

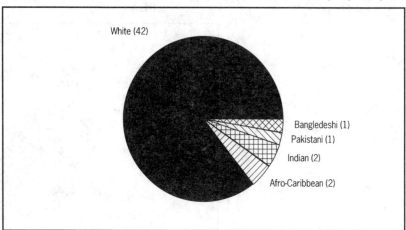

Figure 2.6   **Age of the index children in the case sample (N=48)**

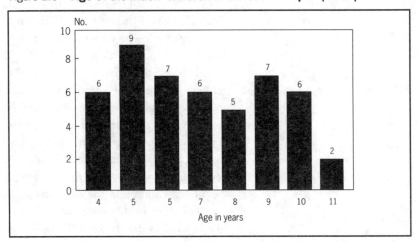

Family composition

The composition of the parental household of the index children at the time of referral is shown in Figure 2.7.

The largest category of children lived with their natural mother and a male cohabitee or step-father, followed by those who lived with their mother alone. Only a fifth lived with both birth parents. Data about the household composition of children on child protection registers are not available on a national basis. However, the NSPCC research on registers (Creighton, 1992),

Figure 2.7   **Household composition of the index children in the case sample (N=48)**

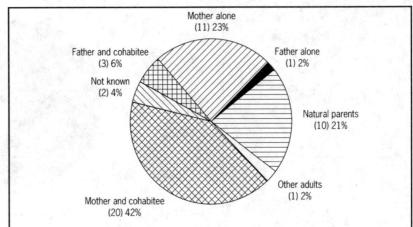

which covers approximately 10% of the child population in England and Wales, revealed that of the 972 children registered for physical injury from 1988–1990, 26% lived with their natural mother and father substitute, 23% with their mother alone and 35% with both birth parents. Of the 525 children registered for sexual abuse, 30% lived with their natural mother and father substitute, 24% with their mother alone and 30% with both birth parents. Creighton observes that these children were 'considerably less likely to be living with both their natural parents and considerably more likely to be living with their natural mother and a father substitute, than the national distribution of children from similar social class' (Creighton, 1992, p 25). This tendency was even more marked in the household composition of registered children in the case sample, although data about social class were not collected in this study, since it was not systematically recorded in the social services departments' files. The proportions in the case sample living with their mother alone, and the very small numbers living with their father alone or with others were comparable with the rates in the much larger NSPCC data set.

Most of the index children lived in households where there were siblings. Of the 104 siblings, 62 were female and 42 male. Eight registered children were the only children in the family but most were in families comprising three or four children. As is shown in Figure 2.8, 42% of the households in the case sample contained four or more children. Again, national data on the family size of registered children are unavailable but the NSPCC research on registers reported that 18% of registered physical injury cases in 1988–90 and 25% of sexual abuse cases were in households with four or more children.

Figure 2.8   **Family size of the index children (N=48)**

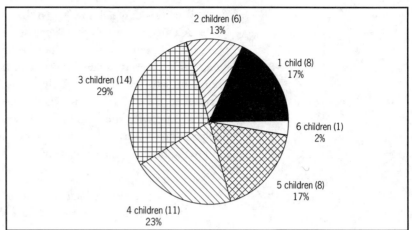

The national distribution of families of this size for social classes IV or V is 13% (Creighton 1992). In the case sample there were, therefore, over three times as many families with four or more children than would be expected, a factor which was likely to lead to increased poverty and stress.

As is shown in Figure 2.9, in 24 of the 48 cases (including the 8 where the index child was the only child), only the index child was registered. In a further 20 cases, the index child and all siblings were registered and in four cases some siblings only were registered along with the index child. Thus, 99 (65%) of all the children in the households were registered while 53 (35%) were not.

Figure 2.9   **Numbers of cases in which index children and/or siblings registered (N=48)**

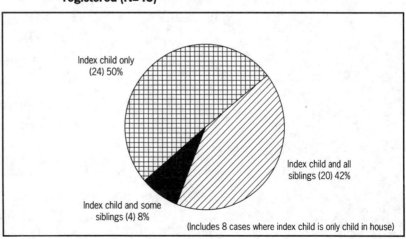

The nature of the cases

It is increasingly acknowledged that the term child abuse is wide. It is a label attached to certain forms of child maltreatment, notably physical and sexual abuse, emotional abuse, neglect and, latterly, organised and ritualistic abuse. The harm is usually inflected, or not prevented, by parental figures in domestic settings, or, particularly in cases of sexual abuse, by other people known to the children concerned. There has been increasing concern in recent years with the abuse of children in substitute care. In government policy, other forms of harm to children of the kind identified by Gil in the following definition are normally excluded from the term 'child abuse':

> *Abuse of children is human-originated acts of commission and human-created or tolerated conditions that inhibit or preclude unfolding and development of the inherent potential of children* (1981, p 295).

Even within the narrower definition operationalised in child protection practice in the UK, the term 'child abuse' covers a multiplicity of behaviours, with a variety of causes, differing degrees of severity and with varying short and long term consequences for the children concerned. The term is ripe for disaggregation. The cases in the case sample were registered as cases of physical or sexual abuse but there was considerable variety within these broad categories.

The nature of the sexual abuse cases

The nature of the sexual abuse in the case sample was classified using the schema outlined in Child Sexual Abuse in Northern Ireland. This ranks sexually abusive behaviour in five categories reflecting the degree of bodily violation inflicted as follows:

Degree of Physical Contact	Types of Abuse
Penetrative Sexual Contact	Digital Penetration.
	Oral Genital Contact.
	Attempted Anal Intercourse.
	Anal Intercourse.
	Attempted Sexual Intercourse.
	Sexual Intercourse.
	Rape – Sexual Intercourse with violence.
Non-Penetrative Sexual Contact	Physical Attack with Clear Sexual intent.
	Inappropriate Fondling or Caressing.
	Masturbation of Child by Adult or Adult by Child.

	Genital to Genital Contact.
No Physical Contact	Exhibitionism to Child.
	Exhibitionism to Child with Suggestions for Further Sexual Activity.
	Inspection of Child's Genitals.
	Viewing Adult Sexual Activities.
	Child Photographed in Sexual Pose.
	Viewing Blue Videos.
Miscellaneous	Other Types

(The Research Team, 1990, p 25–26)

It should be emphasised that this is a classification only of the sexually abusive behaviour and not of the severity of the abuse as experienced by the child. A variety of contextual variables including, but not restricted to, the age of the child, the degree of coercion involved, the nature of the relationship between the abuser and the abused, the duration and frequency of the abuse and the support offered to the child following identification all affect the nature of the abuse as experienced by the child.

Where multiple forms of sexually abusive behaviour occurred in this study, as in the Northern Ireland study, the highest contact level was recorded. Where the nature of the abuse was unclear from the social services department file 'not known' was recorded. The abusive behaviours are classified as they were stated at the point of referral or as identified during the course of investigation. The distributions shown in Figure 2.10 indicate that the largest group involved penetrative sexual contact with children who, in this study, were of primary school age.

The miscellaneous cases involved two where Schedule 1 offenders were associated with households and two where the child was displaying sexualized behaviour. The two cases classified as 'not known' involved either penetrative or non-penetrative sexual contact; the precise nature of the activities was unclear in both cases, one of which involved a child with learning difficulties.

When the case sample of 21 registered cases of sexual abuse is compared with the distribution of cases in the Northern Ireland study, the rank orderings are similar with the largest group experiencing penetrative sexual contact, followed by non-penetrative sexual contact and only a small minority experiencing abuse involving no physical contact. In the Northern Ireland study, however, with a sample of 408 established cases, the differential between penetrative sexual abuse, which comprised 65% of cases in the study, and non-penetrative abuse, which comprised 28% (The Research Team 1990), was greater than in the case sample reported here.

Figure 2.10 **Classification of the forms of sexual abuse identified in the case sample (N=21)**

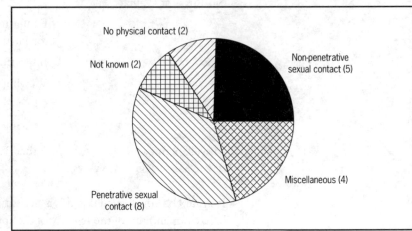

The severity of physical abuse

The physical abuse cases by definition involved some physical injury (or grave concern thereof). The cases in the sample were classified using the definitions used in the NSPCC research on registers (Creighton, 1992) which are as follows:

Fatal: All cases which resulted in death

Serious: All fractures, head injuries, internal injuries, severe burns and ingestion of toxic substances.

Moderate: All soft-tissue injuries of a superficial nature.

Classifying the physical injuries in the case sample according to this schema, the distribution is as shown in Figure 2.11. The fatal case involved the death of a baby, in respect of which the mother was charged and pleaded guilty. The one serious case involved the ingestion of cleaning fluid. There were two cases of burns (not severe) and the remainder were cases of bruising. Two cases were registered as grave concern of physical abuse. In one a Schedule 1 offender convicted of physical injury had returned to the family home. In another, a mother with a history of psychiatric illness and of the loss of several children in early infancy referred herself as she considered herself to be in danger of harming (killing) the older children, although there was no evidence of inflicted injury.

The majority (85%) of the cases were, therefore, subsumed in the 'moderate' category. This is broadly in line with the data in the NSPCC

Figure 2.11 **Classification of the severity of physical abuse in the case sample (N=27)**

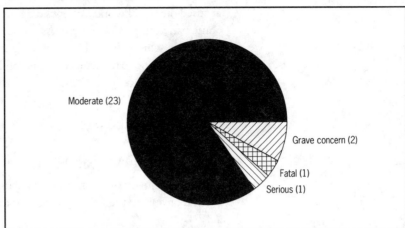

register research which reported that 88% of the cases registered as physical injury in 1988–90 were in the 'moderate' category, with 11% classified as serious and 0.5% as fatal (Creighton, 1992). The 'moderate' category is, perhaps, insufficiently differentiated since it included, in this study, cases in which implements (eg a belt or a shoe) were used to inflict the injuries, those in which there was bruising (albeit of a superficial nature) on multiple sites as well as cases in which one blow resulting in a single bruise was said to have been inflicted with a hand.

The physical punishment of children in British society is not uncommon. The Newsons (1978), for example, reported that 83% of the mothers in their sample smacked children under the age of four. Smith's (1993) study reveals that over 90% of children in a sample of 560, aged between one and eleven years, had been smacked at some time, with 16% subjected to hitting classed as severe. While it may be argued that no child should be subjected to inflicted physical injury, it is clear that the assaults in the sample of 27 cases were not, in the main, severe or life-threatening, especially given the age of the children concerned. With the exception of the child who had ingested cleaning fluid, none of the children had injuries which required medical treatment from hospital doctors. Had it not been for the requirement to seek a paediatric opinion about the nature of the injuries, it appeared that none would have needed to attend hospital. They thus comprised a group who may not be readily distinguished, in terms of their injuries, from others in the same age group with similar backgrounds. Since this study did not directly explore parental (or the children's) perceptions of the process of intervention, it is not known whether few or many would have thought that they had been unfairly picked out and identified as having abused their children. One mother of a child with a cigarette burn, noticed at school and said by the child to have been inflicted by a relative, is recorded in the case notes as having accused the social worker of 'picking on one little burn' when a lot of serious abuse was going on elsewhere. As is discussed more fully below, many of the families in which physical abuse was identified were previously known to the social services department and child abuse was only one of several family difficulties.

The alleged abusers

The number of abusers

In the majority of cases, only one abuser was identified at the time of the referral or during the course of the initial investigation, as is shown in Figure 2.12.

Figure 2.12   **Number of alleged abusers per case (N=48)**

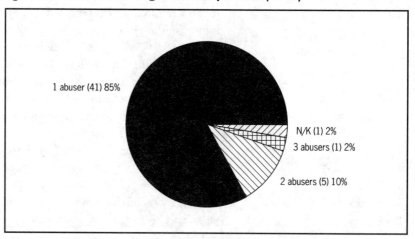

The patterns are shown in more detail in Table 2.1

In total, 54 alleged abusers were identified, of whom 74% were men. All cases of sexual abuse in this study involved alleged abusers who were male. Women were more involved in allegations of physical abuse (53% men and 47% women) but men were overrepresented given that 23% of the children in the sample were living with their mothers alone. This is consistent with the findings in Creighton's study (1992).

As is shown in Figure 2.13, most of the abuse was intrafamilial: 52% of the alleged abusers were one or other of the birth parents of the child concerned, and a further 20% were stepfathers or male cohabitees. Another 20% were

Table 2.1. **Alleged abusers by number per case, by gender and by type of abuse: borough and city compared**

Alleged Abuser	Borough No of cases		City No of cases		Total
Male	CPA	CSA	CPA	CSA	
1 abuser	9	7	5	10	31
2 abusers	–	–	–	2	2
3 abusers	–	1	–	–	1
Female					
1 abuser	6	–	4	–	10
2 abusers	–	–	1	–	1
Male and Female Abusers					
1 male & 1 female abuser	–	–	2	–	2
Not known	–	–	–	1	1
N=	15	8	12	13	48

Figure 2.13 **The relationship of the alleged abuser(s) to the index child (N=54)**

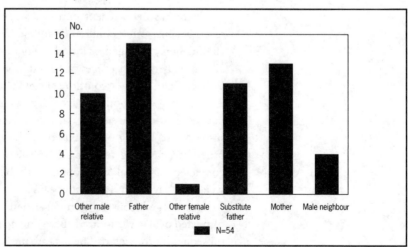

other relatives, all but one of them male. Only four of the alleged abusers were extrafamilial, all being neighbours or friends of the family.

The patterns are shown in more detail in respect of the type of abuse in Table 2.2, which reveals that extrafamilial abuse is confined in this study to sexual rather than physical abuse, and that 'other male relatives' are more likely to be engaged in sexual than physical abuse.

Table 2.2. **The relationship of the alleged abuser(s) to the registered child by type of abuse**

	Borough	City	Total N
Child Physical Abuse			
Father	2	6	8
Father substitute	6	0	6
Other male relative	1	1	2
Sub-total	9	7	16
Mother	6	7	13
Other female relative	0	1	1
Sub-total	6	8	14
Child Sexual Abuse			
Father	3	4	7
Stepfather	2	3	5
Other male relative	4	4	8
Male neighbour	1	3	4
Sub-total	10	14	24
Total	25	29	54

There has been recent concern with children and young people who sexually abuse other children (National Children's Home, 1992). In 1989, of all offenders cautioned or found guilty of sex offences in England and Wales, 32% were between the ages of 10 and 21 and 17% under the age of 16 (Home Office, 1990). Only two of the alleged abusers in this study were aged 16 or under. They were both involved in cases of sexual abuse; one, a nine year old boy alleged to have sexually abused a neighbour, was subsequently himself suspected of having been abused by the father of the child concerned; the other was a young man (aged 16), who admitted and was subsequently convicted of sexual intercourse with his sister (aged 7) while home on weekend leave from residential care.

The alleged abusers were classified in terms of whether they were suspected of abuse, admitted abuse during the course of investigation or were subsequently convicted. The data are presented in Table 2.3. Details concerning prosecution and conviction are discussed more fully in Chapter Five, The Role of the Police and Joint Investigation. Of the 54 alleged abusers, most (61%) remained 'suspected'. Only 22% admitted abuse. The majority of admissions were in respect of physical abuse and only one concerned sexual abuse. National data about the status of alleged abusers are unavailable but the NSPCC research on registers reported that 72% of alleged abusers in their study were categorised between 1988 and 1990 as 'certain (defined as the person having admitted the abuse or the case having been proven in a court of law) in respect of physical injury and 46% in respect of sexual abuse (Creighton, 1992). The proportions in the case sample are much lower, at 43% for physical abuse and 33% for sexual abuse.

There appears to be an interaction between the sex of the alleged abuser and the nature of the abuse, physical or sexual, in respect of a propensity to admit to the alleged abuse. As is discussed more fully in Chapter Five, the greater societal disapproval and the harsher responses of the police and the criminal justice system to sexual abuse are likely to lead to fewer admissions in this category of cases. Furthermore, the absence or equivocal nature of medical evidence in some of these cases may afford greater possibility of outright denial. By contrast, in cases of physical abuse, the medical evidence may be clearer and physical injury to children apppears to excite less opprobrium and different responses in the police and the criminal justice system. A greater number of admissions to having inflicted the injuries in such cases would, therefore, be expected, as was the case in the sample. There is, however, a gender differential in the rate of admissions of physical abuse, with women alleged abusers (who were all the mothers of the children concerned) more likely to admit than men.

The reasons for the gender difference were not explored empirically in this study but they are likely to include the responsibility for family life attributed to mothers, and a greater preparedness by women to discuss problems or, at

Table 2.3. **The 'status' of the alleged abuser**

	Suspicion	Admission	Conviction	N
Child Physical Abuse				
Father	6	1	1	8
Stepfather/male cohabitee	3	3	0	6
Other male relative	1	0	1	2
Sub-total	10	4	2	16
Mother	6	7	0	13
Other female relative	1	0	0	1
Sub-total	7	7	0	14
Child Sexual Abuse				
Father	5	0	2	7
Stepfather	3	1	1	5
Other male relative	5	0	3	8
Male neighbour	3	0	1	4
Sub-total	16	1	7	24
Total	33	12	9	54

least, their greater frequency of contact with health and welfare agencies (Balbo, 1987). There were instances in the case sample of mothers having approached their general practitioner to seek help, having injured their children, and other similar examples were cited in interviews. There was only one example of an alleged male abuser having voluntarily sought help and admitted abuse. Since acknowledging that abuse has occurred and accepting responsibility for it is recognised by some as a prerequisite for effective work with abusers, this gender difference may have implications for the possibility of engaging in constructive work to protect children, particularly since men were responsible for most of the abuse in the case sample.

Previous contact of the families with the social services department

Four sets of data were collected about previous contact between the families concerned and the social services department. The first was whether there was an indication on the file that the child or family had been previously referred for whatever reason, before the current referral which resulted in registration. 73% of the families had been previously referred or had referred themselves; the patterns were broadly similar in borough and city as is shown in Figure 2.14. The proportions were similar in respect of sexual and physical abuse, with slightly more, 74%, of the physical abuse cases previously known than the cases of sexual abuse, 71%. Again, the patterns were similar in both city and borough. Packman and Randall (1989) report that of 62 children in their study who were on child protection registers in the early 1980s, only five per cent were new referrals with no history of contact with the social services departments. In Corby's (1987) study of 25 registered cases, only three of the families had no previous contact with social services departments. Gibbons et al's (1993) study of 1888 referrals of child protection concerns revealed that two thirds of the families were already known to the eight social services departments involved.

The second was whether there had been previous ongoing contact of the family or children with the social services department, defined as the case having been open for three months or longer. Thirty three per cent had previously been open for three months or more, as is shown in Figure 2.15. The patterns were broadly similar in borough and city, as is shown in Figure 2.16.

The third was whether the case was open at the time of the referral in connection with the current registration. As is shown in Figure 2.17, only 9 cases were open cases when the child protection concerns which resulted in this registration were raised. Again, the patterns are broadly similar in city and borough (Figure 2.18). Finally, the files were scrutinised to ascertain whether there had been previous referrals about child protection concerns prior to the

Figure 2.14   **Previous family conctact with the social services department:
                borough and city compared (N=48)**

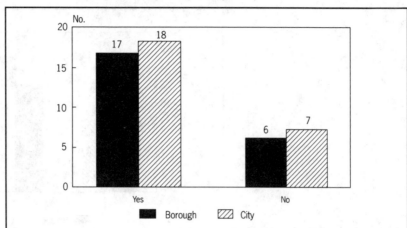

Figure 2.15   **Previous on-going contact of the family with the social services
                department (N=48)**

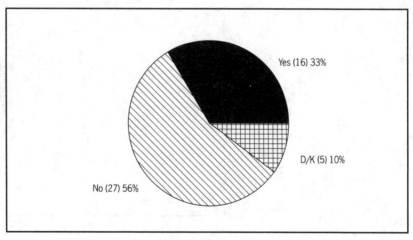

referral which resulted in the current registration. This is obviously to some
extent a subjective judgement since referrals are not necessarily clearly
distinguished between child protection and non-child protection concerns.
Nonetheless it was estimated that in 54% of the cases there had been previous
referrals to city or borough social services department raising child protection
concerns. When previous referrals to other social services departments are
included the number rises to 63%. There was a stronger likelihood of

Figure 2.16   **Previous on-going contact of the family with the social services
department: borough and city compared (N=48)**

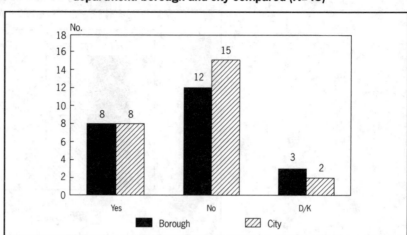

Figure 2.17   **Number of open cases at the time of referral in connection with
current registration (N=48)**

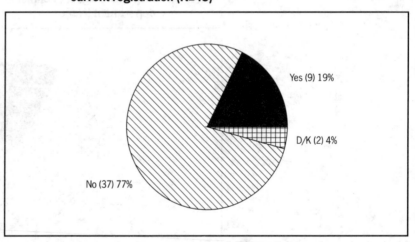

previous child protection referrals in borough as is shown in Figure 2.19. In
Gibbons et al's (1993) much larger data set, 47% of the families had previously
been investigated for suspected maltreatment of their children. Since the
outcome of the previous referrals was not explored in this study, it is not clear
whether the rate of previous child protection referrals indicates that the social
services departments failed to deal effectively with these concerns at an earlier
stage or whether they had been resolved effectively at the time, only to re-
emerge later.

Figure 2.18 **Number of open cases at the time of referral and in connection with the current registration: borough and city compared (N=48)**

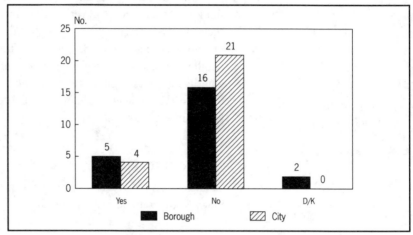

Figure 2.19 **Previous child protection referrals to the social services department: borough and city compared (N=48)**

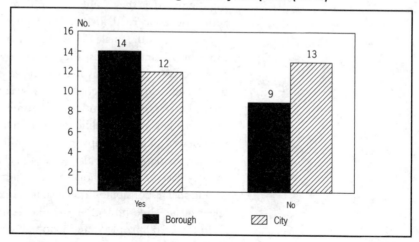

The proportion of the local population with children known to the social services departments in borough and city is not known. Goldberg and Warburton's (1979) work demonstrated the residual nature of the personal social services in the 1970s revealing that between three and five per cent of the population (or between nine and fifteen per cent of households) were in contact with the social servies department. The 1980s witnessed a rise in the proportion of children and families in poverty and increased the numbers in contact with social services departments (Becker and MacPherson, 1986, Social Trends, 1993). The fact that 73% of the families in the study had previous contact with the social services department may indicate the significance of family poverty and stress in the causation of child abuse (Pelton, 1981, Irvine, 1988, Creighton, 1992). It may also reflect labelling phenomena (Parton, 1985), notably the greater surveillance of certain families by health and welfare agencies and the propensity of professionals to identify and refer child protection concerns in particular families rather than in others (O'Toole et al, 1983, Parton, 1985, Herzberger and Tennen, 1988, Dingwall et al, 1983).

The interviews

The second key data source in the study comprised the in-depth interviews with a sample of 90 professionals.

Drawing the professional sample

The sample of professionals to be interviewed was drawn by selecting a sub-sample of eight cases, five in borough and three in city. The cases were stratified so that they came from different area or divisional offices in the authorities concerned, included both physical abuse (5 cases) and sexual abuse (3 cases) and both female (5 cases) and male (3 cases) index children. Within those broad stratifications, they were however selected at random. Those professionals who were involved in the cases, in terms of having attended the initial child protection conferences, were invited to be interviewed and formed the core of the professional sample. It was supplemented by inviting others in key roles in child protection in the localities concerned to be interviewed. These comprised: the administrators of the child protection register, the register custodian (city), the chairs of the ACPCs (the director of social services in each authority), two assistant directors of social services with operational responsibility, inter alia, for child protection services, and minute-takers at the child protection conferences.

In total, 100 people were identified for interview. Six were subsequently removed from the list because they had left the district (two consultant paediatricians, one health visitor) or were on long-term sick leave, (one teacher, one clinical nurse manager, one social worker). A seventh, a social worker in the court section in city, participated in a group discussion with colleagues in the section. This left an effective sample of 93. Of these, 90 (97%) agreed to be interviewed. Those identified for interview were contacted by letter inviting them to take part, followed up with a telephone call to make the arrangements. Only three people refused to participate (one general practitioner and two teachers) – a remarkably high participation rate.

The interview schedule

The interviews with the 90 professionals were semi-structured and usually tape recorded. Six of those interviewed chose not to be tape recorded and notes were written up immediately following the interviews. In a further two cases there was mechanical (or, more likely, operator!) failure with the tape recorder. In the remainder of the cases the taped interviews were transcribed onto hard and soft copy.

The semi-structured interviews lasted between one and two hours, usually nearer two than one, and covered the following topics:

1 the respondent's job title and role in child protection

2 the interagency referral network

3 the child protection register

4 initial investigation

5 initial child protection conferences

6 intervention, monitoring and review

7 local interagency child protection procedures

8 the ACPC

9 general issues concerning working together in child protection

10 concluding section including other topics identified by respondents.

A copy of the interview schedule is at Appendix 2.

The topics were selected to follow the 'natural history' of cases from identification and referral through to deregistration, to cover the key components of the machinery of interagency coordination (the child protection register, the initial conference, interagency review, the local interagency procedures and the ACPC) and, in the final phase of the interview, to explore respondents' views about and experiences of working together.

Data analysis of the interview schedule

The data from the interviews were analysed using qualitative methods (Miles and Huberman, 1984). Initially, the transcripts were read and re-read in hard copy to gain a familiarity with the data and to develop a preliminary set of analytic codes. Some of these were derived from the topic headings used in the interview schedule, which themselves represented key topics and concepts. These included, for example, the different phases of a case from referral to closure, links between particular professions, aspects of the collaborative machinery in child protection, issues of trust, status, power and many others. Some analytic codes emerged from the data itself, for example, the emphasis placed by many in interview on the stress and anxiety engendered by work in child protection, or the emerging impact of internal markets and delegated budgets on interagency collaboration. The list of codes was then inserted into the copies of the interview texts on a micro-computer to enable the relevant passages to be retrieved using the search facility in a word processing package. The relevant passages of the interviews were then read and scrutinised for the information and light which they shed on specific topics. During the course of the research a variety of dedicated computer packages for the storage, retrieval and analysis of qualitative data became increasingly available and used within the social scientific research community (Fielding and Lee, 1992). With hindsight, the use of such a package could have streamlined and aided the analysis of the qualitative data in this study. The less sophisticated method used nonetheless served its purpose.

A key issue in the analysis of and reporting of qualitative data is the use of direct quotation, especially the criteria for selection. In preparing this account, a working draft was produced in late 1992 which incorporated much more extensive quotation than is reported here. From this draft, the qotations cited here were selected to represent typical or, in some cases, atypical views, as appropriate, and to try to avoid too idiosyncratic an approach or the reporting of only the pithiest views (Hammersley, 1990). This was an attempt to structure the selection process, but it does not, of course, avoid the necessity for subjective judgement which is an inescapable part of qualitative research.

The characteristics of the interview sample

The broad composition of the interview sample is shown in Table 2.4.

A fuller breakdown is presented in Table 2.5.

Sex of the interview sample

The interview sample comprised 57 women (63%) and 33 men (37%). The patterns were broadly comparable in borough (67% women, 33% men) and city (59% women and 41% men). All the community nurses were women but other professions were more evenly divided. A full breakdown by job title and gender is given in Table 2.6.

The questionnaire

The third key data source was a brief questionnaire, devised and issued to those who were interviewed and, in borough only, to the remaining members of the ACPC. The questionnaire was in two forms – one for professionals

Table 2.4. **Interview sample by agency/profession**

	Borough	City	Total (%)
Social Services	21	18	39 (43)
Education	9	7	16 (18)
Community Nursing	6	8	14 (16)
Police	3	6	9 (10)
Doctors	2	4	6 (7)
NSPCC	4	0	4 (4)
Legal	1	0	1 (1)
Probation	0	1	1 (1)
Total	46	44	90 (100)

who were also members of the ACPC incorporating some questions about its functioning (reproduced at Appendix 3) and one for those who were not members (reproduced at Appendix 4).

The questionnaire was in five sections:

the first covered data about the respondents' age, sex, ethnicity, job title and job mobility

the second covered the extent of their involvement in child protection

the third, their experience of basic, post-qualifying/in service and multi-disciplinary training in child protection

the fourth, their access to, use of and views about the local interagency procedures

the fifth – a series of eight scaled questions about interagency work in child protection covering respondents perceptions of the ease of collaboration with other professionals, the role clarity of other professions, the importance of the role of other professions, the role performance of the other professions, the degree of role overlap, the extent of interprofessional consensus about the handling of cases, the urgency with which the different professions approached child protection and, finally, preference as to collaborative partners.

The version of the questionnaire for ACPC members excluded the fourth section on the interagency procedures and excluded two of the series of eight scaled questions (on role overlap and preference as to collaborative partners). In their place, it included a series of questions on the working of the ACPC.

Table 2.5. **Interview sample by job title (N=90)**

	Borough N=46	City N=44
Social Services N=39		
social worker	10	5
family aide	1	0
team leader/principal	2	4
area/divisional officer	2	3
administrative/clerical staff	3	2
directorate	2	2
child protection coordinator	1	2
Education N=16		
head/deputy	2	4
class teacher	3	3
education officer	1	0
education welfare officer	2	0
senior education welfare officer	1	0
Community Nursing N=14		
health visitor/school nurse	3	4
senior health visitor	2	0
clinical nurse manager/cp specialist	1	4
Police N=9		
special unit	2	3
crime/community division	0	3
other	1	0
Doctors N=6		
paediatrician	1	1
general practitioner	1	1
PCMO	0	1
child psychiatrist	0	1
NSPCC N=4	4	0
Probation Officer N=1	0	1
Local Authority Solicitor N=1	1	0

Data analysis of the questionnaire

The questionnaire responses were coded (by a research assistant) and analyzed using SPSS-X. Since the sample comprised 81 respondents, when sub-divided by profession and/or locality many of the cell sizes were too small for tests of significance, with large numbers having expected frequencies of less than five. The data were, therefore, analyzed principally by frequency counts of the variables and simple cross-tabulations.

The questionnaire respondents

The majority of those interviewed also completed the questionnaire but

Table 2.6. **Interview sample by job title and gender**

	Borough N=46		City N=44	
	Women N=31	Men N=15	Women N=26	Men N=18
Social Services				
social worker	5	5	3	2
family aide	1	–	–	–
team leader/principal	1	1	1	3
area/divisional officer	–	2	1	2
administrative/clerical staff	3	–	2	–
directorate	1	1	1	1
child protection coordinator	1	–	1	1
Education				
head/deputy	1	1	2	2
class teacher	3	–	2	1
education officer	1	–	–	–
education welfare officer	2	–	–	–
senior education welfare officer	–	1	–	–
Community Nursing				
health visitor/school nurse	3	–	4	–
senior health visitor	2	–	–	–
clinical nurse manager/cp specialist	1	–	4	–
Police				
special unit	2	–	2	1
crime/community division	–	–	–	3
other	–	1	–	–
Doctors				
paediatrician	–	1	1	–
general practitioner	1	–	1	–
PCMO	–	–	1	–
child psychiatrist	–	–	–	1
NSPCC	3	1	–	–
Probation Officer	–	–	–	1
Local Authority Solicitor	–	1	–	–

seven respondents were not asked to do so (the five administrative and clerical staff and the two directors of social services) since the questionnaire was principally designed for those engaged in direct work in child protection, those with first line or middle management responsibilities or those in specialist child protection advisory posts. The questionnaire was left with the respondents at the end of the interview, with a request to complete and return it by post.

Of the 42 interviewed in borough who also received a questionnaire 39 were returned, a response rate of 93%. In city, of the 41 interviewed who also received a questionnaire, 35 were returned, a response rate of 85%. The overall response rate of questionnaire completion among those who were interviewed was 90%. In addition, one questionnaire was completed by a respondent who did not agree to be interviewed. A further nine questionnaires were issued in borough by post to those members of the ACPC who were not in the inteview sample; of these, six were returned. In total, therefore, 93 questionnaires were issued of which 81 were returned, an overall response rate of 87% – again a remarkably high rate. This pattern of responses is summarised in Table 2.7.

Table 2.7. **Questionnaire response rate**

	No. issued	No. completed	Response Rate
Borough			
Interview and questionnaire	42	39	93%
Questionnaire only	10	7	70%
City			
Interview and questionnaire	41	35	85%
Total	93	81	87%

The characteristics of the questionnaire respondents

The broad professions/agencies comprising the questionnaire respondents are shown in Table 2.8.

Table 2.8. **Questionnaire respondents by profession/agency in borough and city**

	Borough	City	N (%)
Social work	19	12	31 (38)
Education	11	7	18 (22)
Community nursing	7	7	14 (17)
Police	4	5	9 (11)
Doctors	3	3	6 (7)
Other	2	1	3 (4)
Total	46	35	81

In borough the 19 classified as 'social work' include four staff from the NSPCC and the 11 classified as education include three staff from the education welfare service. The 'other' category comprises one local authority lawyer and two members of the Probation Service.

Sex of the questionnaire respondents

Forty seven (58%) of the questionnaire respondents were women and 34 (42%) men. This was a slightly lower proportion of women than in the interview sample (63%). The patterns were similar in borough and city as is shown in Table 2.9.

Table 2.9. **Sex of the questionnaire respondents**

	Borough N=46	City N=35
Women	26 (57%)	21 (60%)
Men	20 (43%)	14 (40%)

Ethnicity

Seventy seven (95%) of the questionnaire respondents were born in the UK and 76 (94%) classified themselves as white.

Age

The age distribution of the sample is shown in Figure 2.20.

Figure 2.20   **Age of the questionnaire respondents (N=81)**

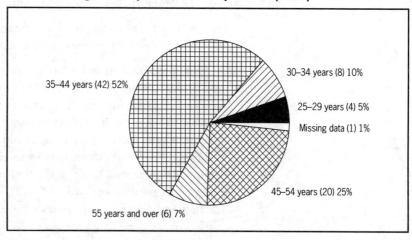

35–44 years (42) 52%

30–34 years (8) 10%

25–29 years (4) 5%

Missing data (1) 1%

45–54 years (20) 25%

55 years and over (6) 7%

Time spent on child abuse

Respondents were asked to estimate the amount of time spent working on child abuse matters in the four working weeks prior to completing the questionnaire including any aspect of child abuse investigation, treatment, administration or management. The responses in Figure 2.21 reveal that a third of respondents spent three days a week or more. A further 17% of respondents spent less than half a day per month and a similar proportion one to two days per week.

Figure 2.21 **Estimated amount of time spent on child abuse matters in last four working weeks (N=81)**

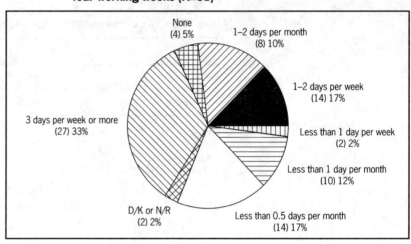

Sixty nine per cent of respondents reported that the preceding four weeks had been typical in terms of the amount of time they spent on child abuse matters, with equal numbers of respondents, 10%, reporting it either lower or higher than normal as is shown in Figure 2.22.

The allocation of time to child abuse was, not surprisingly, differentially distributed across the professions, as is shown in Table 2.10.

Half of the teachers and half of the doctors (two general practitioners and one clinical medical officer) spent less than half a day per month, while the majority of social workers, the police and community nurses were skewed towards the high end. This demonstrates that the interagency network comprises both those whose primary and sometimes exclusive tasks involve child protection and others, notably teachers and general practitioners, for whom it represents a small proportion of their total workload. A similar pattern was revealed by Birchall (1992), although in that study half of the teachers and general practitioners reported no involvement in child abuse matters in the preceding four weeks.

Figure 2.22 **Whether the estimated time spent on child abuse in the preceding four weeks was typical (N=81)**

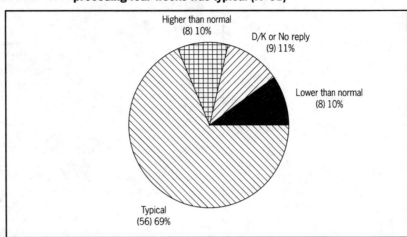

Table 2.10. **Estimated amount of time spent on child abuse matters in last four working weeks by agency/ profession**

	None	Less than 0.5 days per month	Less than 1 day per month	1–2 days per month	Less than 1 day per week	1–2 days per week	3 days per week or more	D/K	N/R
Social work (N=31)	1	2	1	4	4	7	15	0	0
Education (N=18)	1	9	0	2	2	2	0	1	1
Comm. Nursing (N=14)	1	0	0	3	3	3	4	0	0
Police (N=9)	0	0	1	2	0	0	6	0	0
Doctors (N=6)	0	3	0	0	0	2	1	0	0
Other (N=3)	1	0	0	0	1	0	1	0	0
Total	4	14	2	8	10	14	27	1	1

Another indication of the salience of child protection in individual workloads is the number of cases which people have handled. Respondents were asked how many cases they had been involved with in the last two working months, including new referrals and on-going cases, suspected or confirmed. The results are shown in Figure 2.23.

The modal response (22%) was between one and four cases, followed by five to nine cases and 20 to 39 cases, each at 16%. Again there were interprofessional differences in the responses with those in specialist child protection roles in community nursing and social work and a local authority lawyer reporting over 40 cases in the preceding two months as shown in Table 2.11.

Figure 2.23 **Number of child abuse cases in which respondents had been involved in the preceding two months (N=81)**

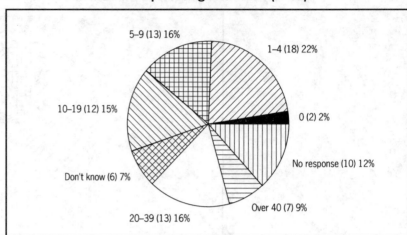

Table 2.11. **Respondents' involvement in child abuse cases in the preceding two months by profession**

	0	1–4 cases	5–9 cases	10–19 cases	20–39 cases	Over 40 cases	D/K	Total
Social work (N=31)	0	5	5	7	4	2	5	31
Education (N=18)	–	2	1	1	–	1	3	18
Comm. Nursing (N=14)	1	3	1	2	2	1	–	14
Police (N=9)	–	1	4	2	–	2	–	9
Doctors (N=6)	–	1	1	1	–	–	1	6
Other (N=3)	–	1	–	–	1	–	1	3
Total	2	13	12	13	7	6	10	81

Training in child abuse

Respondents were asked about the extent of the training they had received in child abuse and/or child protection at basic qualifying and post qualifying/in service levels and how much of this had taken place in multidisciplinary groups. The diversity in terms of the importance of child abuse as a component of the workloads of the various professions discussed above was also reflected in the differing levels of training they had received, confirming the heterogeneity of the interagency network.

Basic training

Forty three respondents (53%) had received no input in child abuse in their basic qualifying training, while 35 (43%) reported that there was some coverage of the topic. Those most likely to have received no training in child abuse at the basic qualifying stage were the teachers, 14 of whom had received none, and the police 8. Social workers and community nurses were most likely to have covered the topic in basic training as shown in Table 2.12.

Table 2.12. **Input on child abuse in basic qualifying training**

	No	Yes	N/R
Social work (N=31)	12	19	–
Education (N=18)	14	3	1
Comm. Nursing (N=14)	4	9	1
Police (N=9)	8	1	–
Doctors (N=6)	3	3	–
Other (N=3)	2	–	1
Total	43 (53%)	35 (43%)	3 (4%)

However, as is shown in figure 2.24 this training was not extensive, with 20 respondents (57%) reporting less than a week's training on the topic.

The pattern of responses by profession is shown in Table 2.13., confirming, as expected, that the topic was accorded greater priority in basic qualifying training for social work than for other professions, although the total amount remains meagre.

Figure 2.24 **Length of child abuse input in basic qualifying training (N=35)**

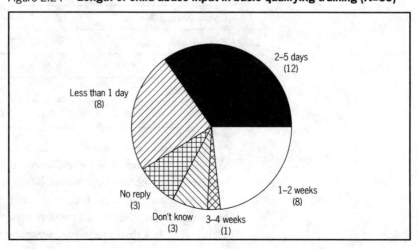

Table 2.13. **Time input on child abuse in basic qualifying training by profession**

	Less than 1 day	2–5 days	1–2 weeks	3–4 weeks	D/K	N/R
Social work (N=31)	2	7	6	1	2	1
Education (N=18)	1	1	–	–	–	1
Comm. Nursing (N=14)	4	2	1	–	1	1
Police (N=9)	–	–	1	–	–	–
Doctors (N=6)	1	2	–	–	–	–
Total	8	12	8	1	3	3

Post-qualifying and in-service training

Eighty per cent of the respondents reported having received some formal training (apart from supervised experience) in relation to child abuse or child protection since their basic qualification. As is shown in Table 2.14, those most likely to have done so were social workers, and teachers the least likely. Similar patterns were reported by Birchall (1992) although, in that study, the proportion reporting no experience of post-qualifying or in-service training in child protection was higher at 41%.

Table 2.14. **Post-qualifying and in-service training in child protection**

	Yes	No	N/R	Total
Social work (N=31)	30	1	–	31
Education (N=18)	9	7	2	18
Comm. Nursing (N=14)	12	1	1	14
Police (N=9)	7	2	–	9
Doctors (N=6)	5	1	–	6
Other (N=3)	2	1	–	3
Total	65 (80%)	13 (16%)	3 (4%)	81

The most frequent length of such training (either in a single block or more usually in total) was 3–4 weeks, reported by 25% of those who had training, followed by 1–2 weeks reported by 23%. Only 8 people reported having attended more than 3 months of training, as is shown in Figure 2.25. Again, these figures are higher than those reported by Birchall (1992) where no such training, or less than one week, were the most frequent responses.

The breakdown of length of post-qualifying training in child abuse or child protection by profession, shown in Table 2.15 reveals that a higher proportion of the police and social workers had received over one month's training compared with the other professions.

Figure 2.25 **Estimated amount of time spend on post-qualifying, in-service training, short courses or conferences on the topic of child abuse/child protection (N=65)**

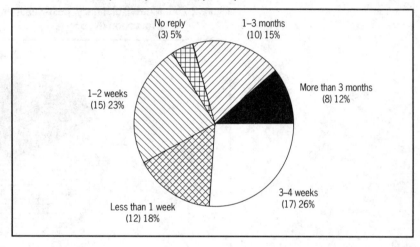

Table 2.15. **Estimated amount of time spent on post-qualifying, in-service training, short courses or conferences on the topic of child abuse/child protection by profession**

	Less than 1 week	1–2 weeks	3–4 weeks	1–3 months	D/K	N/R	Total
Social work	3	5	10	5	5	2	30
Education	5	1	2	1	–	–	9
Comm. Nursing	1	6	2	1	1	1	12
Police	1	–	2	3	1	–	7
Doctors	1	3	–	–	1	–	5
Other	1	–	1	–	–	–	2
Total	12	15	17	10	8	3	65

Multidisciplinary training

Of the 65 respondents who had attended post-qualifying or in-service training in child protection, 48% had undertaken some of it in a multi-disciplinary forum, lasting in total less than a week. 43% had undertaken more than one week's multidisciplinary training as is shown in Figure 2.26.

As is shown in Table 2.16 social workers and the police were more likely to have undertaken longer multidisciplinary training than the other professions.

Figure 2.26   **Multidisciplinary post-qualifying or in-service training in child protection (N=65)**

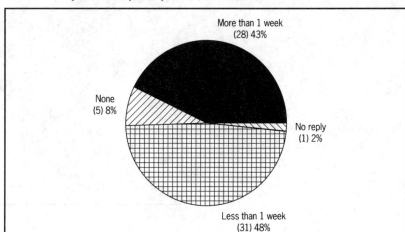

Table 2.16.   **Multidisciplinary training in child protection, by profession**

	None	Less than 1 week	More than 1 week	N/R
Social work (N=30)	3	12	15	–
Education (N=9)	–	6	3	–
Comm. Nursing (N=12)	1	8	3	–
Police (N=7)	–	3	4	–
Doctors (N=5)	1	2	2	–
Other (N=2)	–	–	1	1
Total (N=65)	5	31	28	1

Given the importance attached in policy and practice to interagency work in child protection, the fact that more than half of the respondents had received less than a week's multidisciplinary training is a cause for concern.

When the responses to questions concerning the amount of involvement in child protection matters and of child protection training are compared between this study and Birchall's larger sample, this study revealed more involvement with cases and greater amounts of training. This may be explained by the different sampling strategies adopted in the two studies. Since respondents in this study were drawn from a sample of existing cases, they may reflect a greater propensity to involvement than in the stratified random sample drawn from staff lists by Birchall. Nonetheless the general pattern of professional responses on these dimensions is similar with the social workers and the police most heavily involved in child protection work and most extensively trained at post-qualifying level.

This chapter has reviewed the research design, the research methods adopted and the choice of the research sites. It has presented an overview of the 48 cases in the case sample, of the sample of 90 professionals interviewed in the study and of the 811 professionals who completed the questionnaire and compared these to data derived from other studies. The succeeding chapters prevent the principal findings of the study.

Chapter 3

Referral

Since children cannot be protected in the absence of effective arrangements for case-finding, the identification of cases of child abuse and their referral to the investigating agencies is a key element in any system of child protection and an important dimension of interagency work. Among the issues identified in the literature on interorganisational relations as affecting the referral process are those of the protection of domain (Muldoon, 1981), the need for trust and respect for the competence of those to whom cases are referred (Brill, 1976, Gustaffson et al, 1979, Mouzakitis and Goldstein, 1985), the preservation of organisational autonomy (Reid, 1975) and fear of loss of control over the subsequent responses and handling of cases reported, for example, in respect of teachers and doctors (Maher, 1987, Dingwall et al, 1983). In child protection there are concerns also about the extent to which there is interprofessional agreement about the nature of cases which should be referred, given the complex and subjective processes involved in the attribution of the label 'child abuse' to a variety of harms to children (Gelles, 1975).

The policy framework within which interagency referral takes place in child protection is detailed and specific. While the exercise of discretion which causes individual professionals to perceive an event or a child's situation as evidence of potential or actual abuse is hard to prescribe in rules or guidance, once that threshold of suspicion is passed central government guidance (for example *Working Together* (1988) and (1991)) and local interagency procedures are clear as to the required response: cases must be referred to the investigative agencies, principally the social services department or the police, for appraisal or action. Referral was studied in this research with reference to the notification pathways of the case sample and was discussed in more general terms in the interviews with professionals.

Referral pathways in the case sample

The case comprised 48 children of primary school age, registered as 27 cases of physical abuse (including two cases of grave concern) and 21 cases of sexual abuse (including three cases of grave concern). The person or agency making the initial referral of abuse is shown in rank order in Table 3.1. This shows mothers as the persons most likely to do so, referring 18 of the 48 cases. When all family members are added together, including the two children who referred themselves, 27 cases (56%) were initially brought to the attention of agencies by the families themselves. The propensity of family

Table 3.1. **Person or agency making initial referral by type of case (N = 48)**

	Physical Abuse	Sexual Abuse	Total
Mother	7	11	18
School	9	0	9
Father	4	0	4
Other relative	1	2	3
SSD Staff	1	2	3
Child	1	1	2
Photoprocessing	0	2	2
Other	2	2	4
Not Known	2	1	3
	27	21	48

members to seek help may be some corrective to a view of child protection services as exclusively engaged in the intrusive surveillance or policing of certain sections of the population. As is made clear below, the cases which were identified first by official agencies, without having been alerted to the problem by a family member, are in a minority.

The agencies to which initial referrals were made are shown, by type of abuse, in rank order in Table 3.2.

Table 3.2. **Initial referral by type of abuse and agency to whom initial referral made (N = 48)**

	CPA	CSA	Total
Social services department	19	9	28
Police	2	7	9
General practitioner	3	1	4
Accident & Emergency	2	1	3
School	0	2	2
Education Welfare Officer	1	0	1
Health Visitor	0	1	1
	27	21	48

This table includes cases in which family members referred cases and those identified first by other agencies and subsequently referred to the social services department.

Referral

Since the case sample comprised registered cases, all cases were referred ultimately to the social services department. However, as is shown in Table 3.2, 20 of the cases were referred initially to other agencies rather than direct to the social services department. The principal agencies involved are shown in Figure 3.1 and the referral sources and nature of abuse in Table 3.3. Seventeen of these 20 cases were referred by families or members of the community. The principal sources to which the families, including children, who referred themselves were, first, direct to the social services department (10 cases) and then, in order, to the police (five cases), to general practitioners (four cases) and to schools (two cases).

There was a tendency in both authorities for child physical abuse cases to be referred directly to the social services department more frequently than cases of child sexual abuse, as illustrated in Figure 3.2, while sexual abuse was more likely to be referred to the police. In total, about three fifths of cases of physical abuse were referred direct compared with only about half of the cases of child sexual abuse.

Figure 3.1 **Agencies to which referrals were made when not initially to the social services department (N=20)**

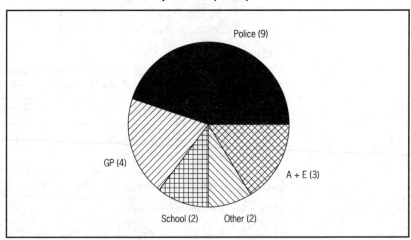

The 13 referrals made by family members to other agencies were compared with the ten made direct to the social services departments, with reference to previous family involvement with social services departments counted on four dimensions: whether there were previous referrals to the

Table 3.3. **Person referring and agency to which referral was made when the initial referral was not made direct to the social services department, by type of abuse**

Person referring	(N = 20)	Agency to which referral was made	Physical abuse (N = 10)	Sexual abuse (N = 10)
Mother	3	GP	2	1
Child	1	GP	1	–
Mother	1	HV	0	1
Father	1	hospital	1	0
Mother	4	police	2	2
Father	1	police	0	1
Photoprocessing	2	police	0	2
Train driver	1	police	0	1
Neighbour	1	police	0	1
Child	1	school	1	0
Aunt and grandmother	1	school	0	1
Class teacher	1	school nurse	1	0
Head teacher	1	EWO	1	0
Head teacher	1	Probation	1	0

Figure 3.2 **Direct and indirect referrals: physical and sexual abuse compared**

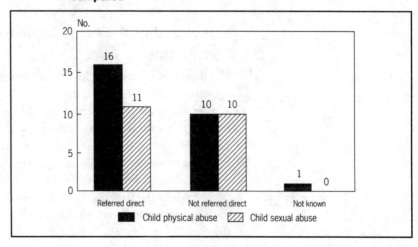

department recorded on the files; whether the case had previously been open for a period of three months or longer; whether the case was open at the time of the referral in connection with the current registration and whether previous referrals concerning child abuse were recorded on file. The data are presented in Table 3.4.

Table 3.4. **Prior family involvement with social services department: a comparison of cases in which families referred themselves directly to social services departments with those who referred themselves elsewhere**

	Direct Referral to SSD (N = 10)	Referral to other agency (N = 13)
Number previously referred to the SSD	10	9
Number which had previously been open cases	3	6
Number which were currently open cases	4	1
Number in which there had been prior child abuse referrals	7	6

Although the cell sizes are too small for tests of significance, it is notable that all families who referred themselves direct had had prior contact with the social services department. The families who referred themselves direct were also much more likely to be current open cases of the department and somewhat more likely to have been the subject of previous notifications to the departments concerning child abuse.

Referral of the case sample to the social services department

Ultimately all cases reached the social services department, referred by the sources identified in Figure 3.3.

The age range of the sample probably accounts for the low rate of referral from health visitors and day nursery staff. The five cases recorded as referred from within the social services department for child abuse investigation included four identified by staff (a family aide, a social work assistant, a residential social worker and a field social worker) in the course of their work with children and families. The fifth concerned the death of a child where the identity of the person who had notified the department was not recorded on the file.

Figure 3.3   **Referral source to the social services department (N=48)**

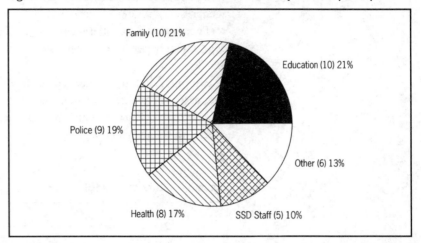

Figure 3.4   **Persons (or units) referring cases to the social services department (N=37)**

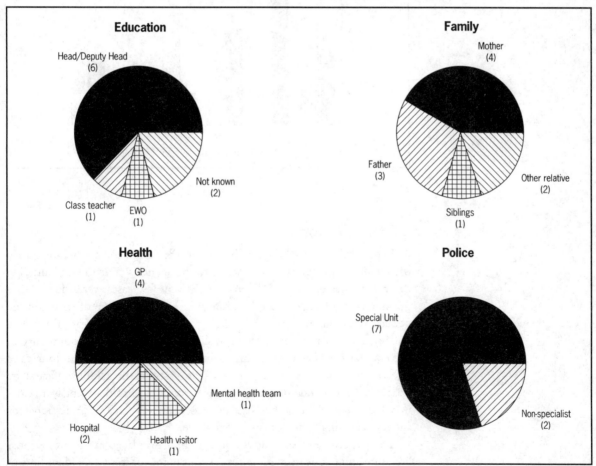

The persons (or units) making the referrals within the principal referring agencies are shown in Figure 3.4.

There were some differences in the referral pathways to the social services department between cases of physical and sexual abuse, as illustrated in Figure 3.5.

Although the numbers are small, schools were four times more likely to refer cases of physical abuse than sexual abuse and the police over three times as likely to refer cases of sexual abuse, reflecting the different patterns of initial referral to these agencies.

Figure 3.5   **Referral (N=48)**

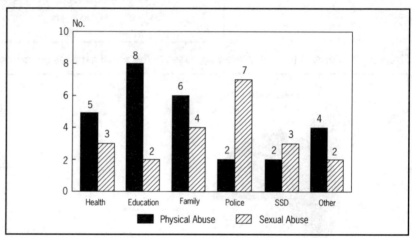

Identification

In over half of the 48 cases in the sample, the family, and much more rarely the children, had referred themselves to the agencies concerned identifying the problem as one of child abuse. Relatively few cases were identified as possible cases of child abuse by professionals in the course of their routine contact with children. For example, all nine cases referred from the police were specifically referred to them by family members or the community in the context of alleged sexual or, more rarely, physical abuse. All four cases referred by general practitioners and the cases in the sample referred by hospital accident and emergency departments and a health visitor were cases in which a family member had presented directly to the professional or agency reporting actual or suspected abuse.

This pattern casts some doubt on the emphasis placed in the professional literature and in government guidance on the role of front-line identifiers of abuse in health care settings, notably in general practice and in accident and emergency departments. *Working Together* (1991) says, for example,

> *General practitioners have a vital role to play in child protection. As family doctors . . . they are well placed . . . to notice in the child indications of significant harm or likelihood of significant harm.*
>
> (Home Office et al, 1991, p20)

The data in this study suggest that such identification is extemely rare, unless the case is presented to them as child abuse by a family member. This appears to be confirmed by the low rate of enquiries from general practitioners to the child protection register in city (comprising one per cent of the total in 1990), an issue discussed more fully in Chapter Four.

In this study, it was the teachers and, to a lesser extent, social services department staff in contact with children and families for reasons other than abuse who identified cases of abuse on the basis solely of the presenting signs without a report or disclosure. It is to be expected that health visitors and day nursery staff would also have figured prominently in case identification had the sample included pre-school children. Given the importance of school teachers as primary identifiers of children at risk, their relative paucity of training in child protection discussed in the previous chapter is a cause for concern.

Referrals: the interview data

All the cases in the case sample had come to the notice of the social services department and subsequently resulted in registration. Registered cases, however, constitute only a small proportion of child protection referrals. As Gibbons et al (1993) have demonstrated with a sample of almost 2,000 referrals, a significant proportion (29%) were filtered out of the system at an early stage. A further 50% were filtered out following further investigation and only 15% finally resulted in registration following a child protection conference. The in-depth interviews with the professionals concerned, therefore, explored the issue of referral more generally, covering topics such as the appropriateness of referrals in content and timing; the referral process; the social services department's response to referrals and the perceptions held by the other agencies of the social services' response.

The appropriateness of referrals

Key problems in reporting abuse are the overenthusiastic identification of cases, resulting in significant numbers of unsubstantiated cases and associated intrusions into family life (Besharov, 1987), and the under-identification of cases which can arise from ignorance about the presenting signs or from denial of the existence of child abuse, a reluctance to breach the parents' trust or confidentiality and/or fear that control of the case will pass to the investigative agencies (O'Toole at al, 1983, Mrazek et al, 1981, Finkelhor, 1984). In contrast with countries with mandatory reporting systems, the child protection system in England relies on the voluntary reporting of concerns to the investigative agencies by lay people and by professionals, although the responsibilities of the latter are set out in local procedural guidelines.

Two issues in particular were explored in interviews concerning the appropriateness of child abuse referrals reaching the social services department – first, whether they were appropriate in terms of the thresholds of concern, especially whether there was evidence of perceived over or under reaction on the part of the various professionals involved, and, secondly, in terms of their timing.

In general, social workers and their immediate and more senior managers were satisfied about the pattern and timing of referrals from the other agencies, of which the two most important, in terms of volume, were said to be the schools and the health visiting service. Views such as the following were typical.

> *I think it's increasingly appropriate, it's better and better in many ways*
> *. . . the majority of referrals that we get are appropriate and it's improving*
> *as other agencies become more aware . . . It's not a major problem for us.*

Many of those interviewed described relatively close working relationships established in the various localities which facilitated referral:

> *We're very close to health, we're very close to housing, we're very close to*
> *education welfare; the latter two even being in the same building. Our*
> *relationships with those agencies are so close that I suspect that we have*
> *perhaps sorted out some misunderstandings and we appreciate each other's*
> *systems better than in most places.*

This led to a degree of discrimination in appraising the information received, as illustrated in the following quotations:

> *It depends on who we're dealing with. You get to know from the ground*
> *the people who you can take their word that if they're worried then there*
> *really is something to be worried about. . . . We have had some excellent*
> *relationships on the ground with head teachers and health visitors whom*
> *we've worked with for a long time.*

and:

In terms of health visitors, we have a corps of health visitors who have been round for quite some time now, and in the schools once you get to the headship. The headships are stable and it's generally those people whom we've met already who actually would ring in.

There was an almost universal denial that referral thresholds were an overreaction and inappropriate in the sense of unwarranted intrusion into family life for minor infractions of societal norms of childrearing. As one head teacher commented:

I think it's about right. I don't think we're going over the top at all in this and I've read, I've followed all that's gone on in Rochdale and Cleveland and elsewhere and I've never felt that it's an over the top situation here.

and a school nurse remarked:

I think honestly if you've got professional people they're used to dealing with children and if they have worries usually they're founded. I don't think you're meddling in people's lives at all because we're there supposedly to be looking after the kids and the families, trying to help them as well. I mean that's what it's all about. You're not pointing the finger – if you can alleviate a crisis well that's better than ending up in the children's hospital with injuries isn't it really?

Among many social services staff there was a stance of encouraging the referral of concern at an early stage, as the following quotations illustrate:

We're not always saying to people 'oh no don't trouble us with that one'. We tend to have the philosophy 'tell us, you know, we're glad to hear', we'll make a judgement about whether it's something we need to go out on or investigate or whatever, or we'll log it or whatever but we certainly don't give out the message (I hope anyway) to people that we're not interested and that we would overreact to a situation or whatever.

When we're talking about child protection, I don't feel that any referral that comes along or any child is inappropriate.

No, no they don't inappropriately refer and no they don't panic, and even if I thought there was an element of panic, I don't necessarily think that's a problem because I don't think it's other people's province to define abuse. I think it's ours.

Certainly they're referring in things that they're worried about and maybe they're right to share their worries even if, at that time, we're not going to do anything more than just help them to cope with them.

The social worker who responded in the following terms was rare:

> *Generally, the problems tend to be that they're unspecific so we get a teacher phoning up and saying 'you know there's something here I'm not quite happy about', rather than saying 'look there's a bruise on the child. I've asked for an explanation and I'm not happy with the explanation.' They're a lot vaguer than that so it's difficult to determine from the first whether they're actually complaining about an unexplained injury or what.*

Most social workers, it appeared, were not exclusively interested in or solely attuned to child protection.

> *I feel that most of the referrals are appropriate, on the basis that somebody else is concerned about the child and so, for me, that's an appropriate referral. Because we've had that kind of policy I think we've made it much easier for the different agencies, and particularly schools, who are our largest referrals really, to feel able to ring us up about things . . . We would rather people told us than they didn't tell us anything at all.*

In the context of generally high levels of satisfaction about the nature of the referrals from other professionals received by the social services departments, there were concerns of three kinds. First that there was a degree of *under reporting*, in that information which should properly have been passed on had not been, as in the following examples:

> *I think under reporting is more of a problem. . . . I've lost count of the times when something serious has happened and then they'll say 'ah but he had a little bruise last week'. I've lost count of the occasions where that's happened.*

> *My biggest worry is really the other agencies, their own training and ability to recognise and detect child abuse at first step because they're the ones that are seeing the kids every day. If they're not trained, then we are not going to know.*

> *My own view is that there was under reporting of child abuse and there's been under reporting of child sexual abuse. The cases that we see are serious. They are incredibly damaging to the kids and we ought to know about it.*

Secondly, that information had been shared too late:

> *I think that the difficulty is that usually their timing of their referral is not usually good. I'm always happy that we get the referrals and then we decide rather than they don't refer or they refer late. . . . . Either they phone*

up at four o'clock or they phone up a day and a half later. I would rather have the referral and then make a judgement because one could always decide not to react. I really like to know.

Sometimes it's worried me that we received referrals about a child and then I suddenly find like from a nursery that there's been other injuries that haven't been followed through, maybe very minor ones that people haven't referred to us properly and I find myself quite worried about that. It's hard to say. I mean I prefer to have referrals as early as possible.

Thirdly, but very rarely, it was said people had overreacted, either from lack of experience or because they were the 'panicky sort'. These were, however, said to be a small minority of the referrals received.

Lay referrals

In responding to questions about the appropriateness of the referrals received, many social services department staff differentiated between those received from fellow professionals in other agencies and those from the community at large. The latter were seen as much more problematic because of their lack of specificity but, principally and commonly, because of concerns that they may have been motivated by malice, as illustrated in the following examples:

I have a bit more difficulty with the anonymous telephone call or the vague type telephone call which doesn't identify the child, you know, the child who lives on the third landing, the second door in. Those kind of referrals worry me. Our area has got a lot of single parents, it has poor housing so we get a lot of split families in that area and there's quite a lot of vindictive kind of malicious referrals. What always worries me about that is that amongst all of that malicious rubbish, kind of general rubbish, there's probably true referrals and I worry about the response to that but, in general terms, I don't really think we should complain about any referral we receive. I think we should receive it and encourage people to give you that information. I think we get a few mischievous allegations or they may seem so to me when I've investigated them. It's always difficult to separate out whether they're mischievous though or whether they're just overzealousness.

I would say that from the public we get quite a lot of variety from serious allegations to quite petty malicious allegations. I think the malicious ones particularly come about 'so and so has left their children on their own; they are a bad mother; this has been happening for a long time' and you get cited a lot of examples of their bad parenting, their lifestyle but you find out, after investigation, that it's the partner basically stirring up the dirt.

> *. . . There might be some truth in the allegations but basically they are stirring and there's probably a custody thing or some bitterness between them, or . . . you get neighbours who fall out with each other and who can report somebody and you go round and there's no foundation for the allegation; it's just malicious and fabricated.*

Referrals of this kind posed particular challenges to the social services departments. The child abuse inquiries of the last two decades reveal some stark examples of warnings and referrals from neighbours which appear not to have been taken sufficiently seriously, with tragic consequences. The evidence of the inquiries (eg Maria Colwell (DHSS, 1974(b)), Lucie Gates (London Borough of Bexley, 1982)) demonstrate that for many lay members of the community, referral to the investigative agencies is not an easy option or a first resort, but action taken after considerable agonizing and often considerable delay since suspicions were first aroused. However, with the exception of Gibbons et al's (1993) study, there appears too be little systematic national information about the frequency with which lay referrals prove to be unsubstantiated on investigation and, even if there were, such probabilities could not obviate the need for careful consideration of each individual case since, although motivated by malice, the allegation may nonetheless be true.

The social services response to such referrals was said to be one of careful appraisal, with a good deal of preliminary checking with the interagency network, resulting in the routinised exchange of information, before investigation, as in the following examples:

> *What we would tend to do in those cases is certainly to take the referrals seriously and then to do some checking out with our colleagues on the ground to see whether they can find anything else that substantiates the anxiety of what we're being told. We would always respond but the response would be generated by what else we can find out quickly from colleagues on the ground who know the family, know the situation. If we can't find anything then we have to go and look fairly quickly but, generally, we'll say to ourselves 'who's the GP, who's the health visitor, what schools are likely to be involved?' and try and pick up other people's feelings to go with.*

One social worker with experience of working in child protection abroad compared the two systems in this respect, as follows:

> *I think we do a lot of what I call homework, before we go out. Just comparing it to where I've been, there I think it was a case of jumping up and going out. Our brief was to go out to anything that came in and we did very little checking out because that was seen as an infringement on human rights. So you went out very often cold and blind on abortive trips.*

. . . My experience is that we don't do that here. We spend time checking out referrals to know whether or not there is any substance to them and invariably there is some substance. It might not be full blown abuse but there are concerns.

The referral process: health visiting and schools

Because of the importance of referrals from schools and health visitors the referral processes within these agencies were explored in interviews in some detail. (Referrals between police and the social services departments are discussed in Chapter Five, The Role of the Police and Joint Investigation).

Health visiting

The process for health visitors appeared somewhat more direct and straightforward than in some, but not all, schools. Essentially health visitors and school nurses identifying child protection concerns reported that they would inform their nurse manager and the social services department. Unusually amongst those referring child abuse cases to social services departments, the health visitors stated that they would usually record the referral in writing. This was confirmed in the study of social services department case records where examples of such written referrals were found. It also confirms Birchall's finding that health visitors appear to be the most punctilious in recording and were perceived by other professionals in the network to be so (Birchall, 1992, pp 53–56). In city there was an elaborate system within the health visiting service for recording and monitoring child protection issues, which is discussed in more detail in Chapter Seven with reference to child protection conferences and in Chapter Nine with reference to monitoring and review. In borough there appeared to be more local variation, but nonetheless referrals followed broadly the same route and were usually be confirmed in writing, as the following quotation illustrates:

> *If I went to see the family and I felt that something untoward was going on, I would write a report to the senior nurse manager, I would telephone her first and I would put a written report in to the effect of what I'd found and why I'd felt it was not right for that child. I would contact the social services department by phone and then I'd follow it up with an inter-service referral form, a written form.*

A nurse manager in city described the process as follows:

> *In the initial stages of concern, if they've got somebody they are concerned about they will come in here and discuss it with me. I'll ask them to write it down on a form and to write it in their notes.*

Subsequently,

> *If the concerns become more and more heightened, then we involve social*
> *services and then it's a referral by telephone, followed by a written referral*
> *and then depending on the response we get from that depends on whether*
> *it's followed up by a telephone call from me or whether we actually involve*
> *the nurse specialist in child protection, because if we're getting really het up*
> *then we involve her and ask where we stand and what we can do.*

In urgent cases:

> *If a health visitor goes round and there's been what I would call an*
> *incident, she would either come in or ring in, it depends on the gravity*
> *again. And I would get to know anyway and we would discuss it, then*
> *social services would be informed immediately and I would expect*
> *immediate action from the social services.*

Schools

The referral process from schools was more varied and uneven. In borough, a change in policy had been instituted which barred education welfare officers from investigating child protection allegations as they had done in the past. Schools were therefore required by the child protection procedures to relay their concerns direct to the social services department, as was also the case in city. Some of those interviewed were clear about the procedures and the need to refer and reported this to be their practice, as in the following example:

> *If it's a form of physical abuse the teaching staff have got better. I think*
> *they now know the procedure. What happens now in most of the schools,*
> *if there's a child who has got an injury which the teacher suspects is non-*
> *accidental, then most of the schools will contact the child protection liaison*
> *teacher who will then take on board the need to get social services involved*
> *and they know the procedure.*

Some head teachers reported that they gave child protection matters top priority, for example:

> *(Child protection) . . . is one of the most important things that I do and I*
> *do feel that I've always got to keep my finger particularly on what's*
> *happening to those children;*

and:

The job of a head teacher now is a very busy one, as you've seen this morning, but if a member of staff came to me and said 'I am really concerned about what the child has said to me' or evidence of marks or anything like that, that is one thing that I would close on the routine of the day for. It is, if you like, the top of the list.

This was not always easy, given that the primary task of schools is not child protection and that there are many demands placed upon teachers by the introduction of the national curriculum, responsibility for devolved budgets and other changes in education policy. One teacher, working in a deprived inner city area, described the dangers of overload and the difficulties of identifying child abuse among a myriad of other problems, as follows:

Because of the area we're in our teachers become very quickly well qualified to spot children with a real need. The thing that does concern me, and I'm talking about personal experience here when I was in the classroom myself, each teacher is faced with say twenty five children. Out of those you may be already aware of five or six children who are on the at risk register or whatever because that's been passed to you through internal notes and that's a lot of children to be hyper aware of, and hyper concerned about. I'm thinking of one particular child I had in my class, who I really had no suspicions, you know, the child was just coming and going as he pleased; again the other facet to this is the fact that we do have a lot of discipline problems because of the nature of the area, all sorts of things. The children are very hyperactive, they're very challenging and very boisterous, etc, etc, so whereas the behaviour that was shown by this child in another side of the city would have been perhaps picked up within a day or two, it took me about a fortnight to think 'hang on, there is something wrong with this child' and then I said to (the head), 'look I'm concerned about this child', I began to get a bit more specific and then we picked up the phone and contacted social services and the child was in fact being physically abused. But that really shocked me and really concerned me and really upset me to be quite honest because I hadn't noticed this child because I was so wrapped up with the bad behaviour and boisterousness of the class in general.

Despite such difficulties, however, some schools were clear about their role and the appropriate action to take, as was illustrated in the case sample when teachers had identified and reported cases of suspected child abuse on the basis of presenting signs observed in the school.

Respondents in some schools, however, displayed anxiety about initiating referrals and described their practice of calling upon others in the education system for advice or action before contacting the social services department.

A school nurse described this as follows:

> *That varies from school to school, it depends on the head and who is the named child protection teacher. In my opinion, it seems pretty good they seem to know their role. If I'm in school and they're worried about someone and they say, you know, 'what do you think', then I'll advise. But ultimately if they're identifying the problem then obviously they have to follow the procedure which is quite clear in (city). Sometimes they feel as though they do need a bit of back up if it's something that's very difficult, sometimes if they've got a lot of worries about children and yet there is nothing really definite like an injury and sometimes feel they need support as far as referring. So I mean I help depending on what they call me for whether I'm in school or not.*

A deputy head teacher, to whom family members had relayed a disclosure made by a child the previous evening about her sexual abuse, reported her actions thus:

> *Yes, I phoned actually for advice from the education department first. I needn't have done. I felt I knew what I needed to do but I just wanted a bit of back up, a bit of reassurance.*

Another head teacher who had reported several cases to the social services department and was familiar with the procedures referred to 'pressing the panic button'; indicating a level of anxiety:

> *I'm thinking across to another instance when, if you like, I pressed the panic button over a family and all the support agencies were involved very quickly, I was very impressed by that. I mean we follow the procedures laid down in the local guidelines obviously, but I thought long and hard about this particular issue and then decided that, yes, I'd press the panic button and social services visited the house. At the end of it all my fears were quite unfounded and the mother was extremely cross and rightly so and I can understand why she was, and came into this room and gave me quite a blasting, but you know I hope that she went away quite calmed and realised that I did what I did, and why I did it were obviously in her child's best interest. Presented with the same circumstances again I would . . .*

The social services department also picked up the anxiety from some schools:

> *The schools, in particular, are an interesting source because – talking about junior schools – there's a large number of them and, no matter what statistics say about child abuse, every time one happens in school – oh my God, it's the first time we've ever faced this and people are naturally somewhat taken aback, or so it comes through.*

In the examples cited above, although making the referrals had provoked a degree of anxiety among school staff, the procedures were followed. In others, particularly in city there were examples of an alternative system or sub-network in operation based upon schools in which direct referral was not always to the social services department. This confirms the findings in Birchall's (1992) study. The following is an example:

> *I've just thought of another case we did have and that was [x] with the black eye, in [y's] class. What we do is acually get in touch with the EWO first but we don't need to do that, we can go directly to, you know, we can phone up the register and ask but we like to go through the EWO and then they start contacting . . .*

This teacher described the close relations with the school nurse and the education welfare officers:

> *and, of course, they know the social, you know, the people who, social workers and so on, again it's easier for them to phone, they know immediately who to get in touch with and so on. . . . We go to the sound professional person who's used to dealing with these things . . . but we work from the premise that we're teachers. We're nothing else really although people think that we're everything and we go to people who have expertise in the field.*

One school discussed several cases which on the face of it might have been of concern to the social services department. One concerned a primary school aged child who, although presenting no difficulties in school, was 'wandering the street at eleven or twelve o'clock at night because his mum's not in'. This was recorded in a book held in the school in which concerns were noted when 'we don't feel the need to take further action but it's so that if we get incidents cropping up again and again at least there are dated entries there'. In another school, the practice was described as follows:

> *Well it depends really on the nature of the problem, if it's something such as bruising we would do probably an internal investigation. Such as the head or myself would take the child away somewhere safe, you know, they knew who they were with but away from other children and try and do just a bit of gentle investigation. Well you know the kind of thing 'how did you get your bruises, etc, etc'. . . . If the child is forthcoming which, I'm thinking of one case in particular last year that I was involved with, the child had no qualms about telling us that it was dad, stepdad, who'd done the abusing. Then it's straight down to the phone and pick up the phone and contact social services. If the child gives no indication really as to why the bruises have occurred then its always noted down but the procedure is usually to send the child back to the class and the class teacher and the*

child protection liaison teacher and the head are very much on the alert to watch out for anything, you know, in the future.

There was, then, variation in the schools between those highly attuned to child protection, according it a high priority and familiar with the procedural requirements regarding referral and others less so, either routing their concerns to or via others, notably school nurses and education welfare officers, and, in some instances, confining the problems in the school-based arena.

Perceptions of the social services departments' response to referrals

In general, those referring cases to the social services departments were reasonably satisfied with the response, at least in cases where there were serious and specific concerns regarding physical injury or sexual abuse.

A general practitioner commented:

I've been very impressed with the amount of support that they've been giving the family.

A school nurse said:

Quite good, quite good. They listen and sometimes we are instrumental in getting a case discussion in the school. I would at the same time discuss this, all the arrangements, with my senior nurse and the health visitor as well but, yes, considering the fact that they are very pushed, they do listen.

A teacher commented as follows when asked if referrals from the school had been taken seriously:

Well every case I've been involved with, yes they have. The social services usually initially come out to school and they'll have a chat with the child and usually take the child home and confront the parents with the child there. All the social workers that I've had contact with, really without exception, have, in my opinion, operated superbly with children. They really have.

There was, however, an important caveat to these responses. While it was generally agreed that the social workers would listen, the nature of the response varied with the type of case referred. There was a clear view that physical injuries and allegations of sexual abuse would receive a prompt response. This is unsurprising given the history of the social construction of child abuse as a social problem in recent years and the prominence accorded to physical and sexual abuse. Together they comprise 39% of cases on child protection registers in England (Department of Health, 1993) and they have been the subject not only of much professional and public concern but also, and perhaps not coincidentally, of child abuse inquiries. The response to other types of child abuse, particularly emotional abuse and neglect where the presenting signs were less clear-cut and evidence was more difficult to gather, was reported to be much less satisfactory. So was the response to more general child welfare problems. Health visitors, in particular, expressed these concerns, since they were often in the position of trying to support the families without the aid of social workers.

One nurse manager summarised the position as follows:

> *It it is very serious they'll respond immediately, if it's less serious they hum and hah.*

Others, in varied professions, supported this view:

> *[They respond] in a case that is pretty urgent, either there has been an injury or we're really worried about the child. Otherwise, if we can see problems arising or think that something is about to occur, I'm afraid there is little response but they are unable to take that sort of work on, any preventative work is very difficult for them to take on.*

> *Sometimes if the health visitor is the only worker going in and the concerns are mounting but there is no incident or sexual abuse, they're the difficult ones and they're the ones I think the health visitors feel uncomfortable with because they're the only one going in.*

> *It depends what sorts of things you're talking about, I mean if you go in and there is a bruise, then yes it's very speedy. If it's something a bit more intangible like a child failing to thrive it may be more protracted because in terms of priority it may not be top of their list and that may take quite a bit of chivvying along to make it quite clear that we're taking this very seriously. You know we would have to sort of use centile charts . . . .*

> *Because social services are busy etc, they're perhaps not as quick off the mark to listen and to act. If it's not something that we can say look we've actually seen a great big yellow bruise on Jonathon's leg or whatever. It is, I suppose, again because of staffing it's far harder for them to put input into every area. We must appreciate in an area such as this we have nine classes and I know this is a generalisation but we could have five families that we are quite desperately worried about in each class. It could be for all sorts of reasons, for different reasons, I can appreciate their side, you know, they've got such a large area to cover.*

I have on several occasions contacted social services and said 'do you have involvement with this family, it looks as though things are building up, the children are suffering' and I've been told on more than one instance that 'we would love to do preventative work, we don't have the resources', and that's the message clear and strong.

As is evident from the quotations above, the situation did not appear to generate great interagency tensions or anger. The professionals involved appered to acknowledge and accept, although with some sadness, that the ruthless prioritising of work in social services departments led to many families and children in difficulty remaining unsupported unless and until a crisis resulting in clear harm to the child led to their involvement. The social workers, too, shared these concerns, acknowledging their very limited capacity to work preventatively with families in difficulty.

The consequences of this situation were that in some circumstances referrals were not made, with schools and health visitors noting their concerns, doing what they could to help but waiting until the position became more serious or more concrete, if it did, before alerting social services. A teacher gave a case example:

I am concerned about a child. But, from my experience with the family, I don't feel that it's a case where we would intervene, I wouldn't have the grounds for it. You know they wouldn't be strong enough. I don't feel I could go to social services and say 'I'm concerned about this girl because she doesn't make friends in school, she can't accept any criticism, she won't communicate with her teacher'. When I think of the grounds that we do go to them with, they're not going to listen to those because they're, it's the effects of the way of the system in a way isn't it, that I know that social services are so pressed that if I went to them with that kind of conversation about a child they wouldn't take me seriously . . . I mean obviously if that child came to school with a bruised back one day then those things might emerge but I don't think she ever will.

In other situations, professionals reported that they would nonetheless pass on their concerns so that the extent of unmet need was logged in the social services department. One teacher said:

All I can suggest is that you keep a written record of the thing that worries you and that you pass it on, it has to be passed on.

A school nurse spoke of the problem in an inner city school with high levels of deprivation and children in need:

They do worry a lot and a lot of it is justified. I mean the head has said to me sometimes 'oh well what's the point', then maybe think a child's being sexually abused, she's fidgety, she's not paying attention and falling behind with the work and maybe the family situation is not too wonderful and, 'well there's no point in phoning social services' they've actually said to me. But I've said 'but you must because you're actually logging a worry and that is the first start'. . . . If everybody decided there's no point in referring then nobody would actually ever get together.

The position, then, was one in which referrals indicating physical injury or allegations of sexual abuse met with a speedy response from social services departments, in which the investigation of such referrals was a top priority, as is discussed in the next chapter. However, referrals about other forms of child abuse and more general concerns about the welfare and well-being of children did not receive a level or speed of response which others in the itneragency network, and the social workers themselves, wished to see. It may be appropriate that thresholds of concern for entry in the child protection system are high, given the procedural requirements and the often unwelcome consequences for the children and families concerned of a full-blown child protection investigation. However, if this is the case, accessible and acceptable child care services are also required, triggered at lower levels of need for the kinds of cases revealed as causing concern in this research study.

At the time of the field research, the Children Act 1989 was being implemented, with its requirements both that services should be made available to children in need as well as to those needing protection and that interagency collaboration in child welfare should not be restricted to child abuse. It is too soon to assess whether this legislation has increased services to the large group of children and families revealed in this study as in need of help but whose problems were not yet serious enough or presented in such a way as to claim a service under the rubric of child protection. This study provides further evidence of the tendency of child protection to overwhelm other child care services, upon which others, notably Packman and Randall (1987) and Parton (1991), have commented.

Feedback

Although there were generally reasonable levels of satisfaction with the social services departments' response to referrals in serious cases, a few respondents complained of inadequate feedback following referral. A teacher, for example, having reported a child in the case sample with bruising to the social services department spoke of having later received a telephone message that no explanation for the bruising has been found. In fact, the social worker had visited the family and had been told that the child had been injured when his brother had thrown a toy at him in temper. The social worker had checked the story with a pre-school liaison teacher who had been visiting the home just before the alleged incident. She confirmed that the parents' account was a likely explanation in view of the younger brother's behaviour when she had left the house. The social worker had, therefore, investigated the allegation and concluded that the injury was accidental – but this did not appear to have been communicated clearly enough to the teacher. It is not known how frequently such instances occurred. One nurse manager said:

> *One of the problems we have is that the information sometimes only flows one way and we don't ever seem to get enough information coming back, particularly from social services. Health visitors are ringing them, passing information on and they don't get the same courtesy back. Sometimes I think the social services ought to be a little bit more forthcoming.*

Some social workers spoke of the importance of feedback to referrers if their continued involvement in the referral process was to be sustained. One social services manager, for example, said:

> *Or what we've also done is actually established that maybe there are concerns about certain children but that we can't necessarily take it on and we tend to tell other agencies that we're not taking it on but please refer it again and please let us know and keep us informed. I think as well at the point of referral, when they're referring things to us, to actually involve them in that referral process because one thing I'm very keen on is that people don't dump referrals on us; it isn't just my referral, it's their referral and so I think that you have to do right at the point of referral. It's not just about taking the information it's about taking it and saying what we are going to do about it and involving them in decisions all the way along not just at the formal stage but at the informal.*

Summary

It appears, both from the case sample and from the interviews, that the interagency referral process for child protection cases was generally experienced as working reasonably well. Once the threshold of suspicion was passed, there was a clear procedure for interagency referral with which many in the study proved to be familiar and which many appeared to implement in practice. In this, as in other topics studies in the course of the research, there was a degree of variation and differential compliance as field staff implemented the policy guidance. However, information, of an appropriate kind, was generally passed routinely between the agencies without undue preoccupation with the preservation of agency domain and organisational autonomy. The thresholds of concern for initiating interagency referral were not considered to be too high. On the contrary, it appeared that there were high levels of unmet need among children and families which the understandable preoccupation with physical injury and sexual abuse had pushed aside.

Chapter 4

Social work investigation

The investigation of allegations or suspicions of child abuse has been accompanied by the development of a significant degree of interagency collaboration in the UK in the last twenty years. Three principal agencies are involved: social services departments, the police and the health service, through the involvement of doctors in the medical assessment of children. In addition, the investigative phase routinely involves the collection and appraisal of information about the children and families concerned from others in the interagency network, notably teachers and health visitors.

One of the most significant changes in the role and function of social services departments in recent years has been the volume of work associated with the statutory duty to investigate child protection referrals and the priority awarded to the task. The role of social workers in initial investigation is discussed in this chapter.

As is shown in Figure 4.1 almost half of the cases in the sample in each authority were investigated jointly by police and the social services department with approximately one third investigated principally by social workers. About one fifth were initially investigated by the police alone. Joint investigation and police investigation and the process of notification of referrals between these two agencies are discussed in the next chapter.

Figure 4.1   **Agency responsible for initial investigation (N=48)**

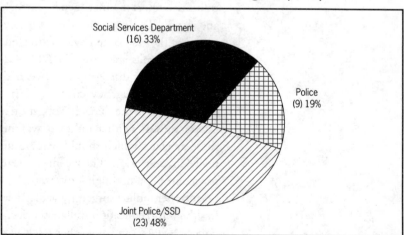

The cases where social workers were the principal investigators were mainly those involving physical abuse, as is shown in Table 4.1. Only two were cases of sexual abuse, in both of which the problem presented at referral was the association of a Schedule 1 offender with the household.

Table 4.1: **The investigating agency by type of abuse: borough and city compared**

	Social Services department alone	Police alone	Joint Investigation	N
Physical abuse				
borough	7	1	7	15
city	7	1	4	12
Sexual abuse				
borough	–	4	4	8
city	2	3	8	13
Sub-total	16	9	23	48

Interagency checks

As indicated in Chapter Three, concerns about child protection reached the social services departments in a variety of forms and by diverse routes, sometimes clearly identified as child protection but at other times much more nebulous. In both cases, unless the referral indicated the need for emergency protective action, the first response of social workers was a considered but routinised resort to other agencies to seek further information about the child and family. The patterns of interagency consultation during initial investigation of the case sample were extracted from the social services department files. The results are shown in Table 4.2.

There was a discrepancy between the case records and the interviews concerning interagency checks and it is clear that not all such checks or conversations at the initial investigation stage were recorded separately in the case records. In neither authority was there a standard proforma in use listing those agencies which should be consulted (although one was in use informally in one area). The agencies were, however, identified in the local procedures. In borough, for example, the following were listed: general practitioner, police surgeon, paediatrician or other relevant hospital doctor, health visitor, education welfare service, school or nursery, probation service, police, NSPCC and any other relevant statutory or voluntary agency.

The interviews with social workers and others in the interagency network indicated that such consultations were more frequent and extensive than was

Table 4.2: **Agencies recorded as having been contacted by the social workers during the initial investigation of the 48 cases**

Paediatricians	20
Police	20
School	16
Health Visitor	11
Police Surgeon	6
NSPCC	4
GP	1
Other	28
Total	106

revealed by the case records. Relationships between health visitors and social workers were said, on both sides, to be generally good and social workers identified health visitors as particularly helpful and cooperative in the exchange of information in the investigative stage. As one health visitor said:

We're quite happy to give the information, we're quite happy to share. We've no problems with that, the staff now are all perfectly clear as to their role and that's in the child's best interest, that's not problematic.

Schools were also said to be contacted frequently and to respond to requests for information, but general practitioners were perceived as much less forthcoming. One social worker described the process of interagency checks in respect of a nebulous referral:

I'd check with the local school. I'd let them know that what I've got is something very limited, is there anything that might lead them to think that I should go out on it, without giving away too many details because I think there is an element of intrusion, you know, of human rights. So I'd check with the school, and probably with the local general practitioner, although at that stage they are incredibly uncooperative because of their brief of confidentiality so usually that's not a particularly good source. I'd check perhaps with health visitors, who are excellent, if it was an under-5, I'd check and say 'look we've had something come in and you know these kids are at this address and do you think there is anything that might make you think I should go out'. So I do a lot of checking out and then at that stage I'd feed back. I'd say 'right, have we got anything here that is concerning enough for us to act? Does it need acting today? Could it wait

> *until tomorrow, could it be done in a more planned way, in a less sort of*
> *crisis-ridden way.' You can get all sorts of panic buttons pressed in people.*
> *It's about having worked in an area for a certain number of years. I think*
> *you do build up relationships with other professions who know, when you*
> *ring they know exactly what you are looking for and I don't think it's*
> *compromising children. I don't think it's putting children at risk. I think*
> *there is a really sound argument for saying sit back, hold fire, do a bit of*
> *checking out and then act if we need to, whereas if you were to read the*
> *tabloid press, you'd think we were just sitting here waiting but for the word*
> *abuse to come through on the telephone and we're out there like the charge*
> *of the light brigade. It isn't that at all, it's sad.*

Contact with others in the interagency network was central to this task and, depending on the outcome of such inquiries, some cases might be diverted at an early stage from the child protection procedures. A social work manager in one area where workloads were said to be manageable and interagency links were described as close, said:

> *I can say with a fair degree of comfort – but there's still the hot breath of*
> *Louis Blom-Cooper on my neck – that we haven't used conferences just to*
> *exchange information, there has been a culture of planned meetings,*
> *discussion meetings between agencies outside of the child protection*
> *procedures. We wouldn't leap . . . you know, say 'Oh well that might be*
> *child protection, bang that into a conference' – we'll talk about it first and*
> *try to get involved at the early stage, . . . seriously look at it together,*
> *sharing information that we already have between us, looking at what we*
> *can do about it, bringing it to the family's attention. Most of the time there*
> *is that contact early enough that we don't have to wait for somebody to*
> *come and panic.*

This was an area of the authority where the rate of case conferences was said to be low, reflecting a conscious policy decision made at local level that if the work was being done, there might be nothing to be gained by invoking the child protection procedures. There was a danger, however, that other factors might lead to differential responses within departments. For example,

> *It's often down to individual responses and what would concern me is there*
> *is often some disparity between different divisions; they would respond*
> *differently to similar circumstances and we hear of cases where we feel that*
> *intervention should have taken place and people didn't respond appropri-*
> *ately. That is sometimes about resources but I am also concerned that*
> *resources are sometimes used as an excuse for not responding because*
> *people feel debilitated by child protection. They don't want to get into*
> *what is increasingly an area of aggravation for them I think, you know,*

worry, concern, anxiety and so on. The expectations are so high in terms of procedural issues and all the new guidance that's come out 'Working Together', 'Assessment Processes', 'The Children Act' and so on. It's fairly overwhelming for workers and I think that sometimes they are very prone to take the line of least resistance and not respond according to our very fundamental statutory duty to investigate when we receive a referral. And I guess it's one of our roles to actually pick up on that, assuming that we do get to hear about it in the first place. We actually try to ensure that there is some consistency of response across the department but there is this feel for a disparity that takes place, perhaps even within divisions between different team leaders and so on.

This is one of several points in the data where there was evidence of unevenness in implementing the procedural guidance, a point discussed more fully in Chapter Ten.

Checking the child protection register

The local procedures in each authority required social workers undertaking child protection investigations to check the child protection register. At the time of the fieldwork, the register was held in city by the health authority but transfer to the social services department was imminent. In borough, the register was transferred from the NSPCC to the social services department in the course of the research. At the time, both registers were held manually but they were being computerised on transfer. In addition to information concerning children registered following child protection conferences, a record was kept of details of unregistered children (name, address, age and identity of enquirer) about whom inquiries had been made in the preceding period. Calls were received by the register clerks/administrators in each authority and information passed on using a call back system. The frequency and pattern of use of the rgister in borough is shown for the months January to June 1991 in Table 4.3 and in city for the whole of 1990 in Table 4.4, using the categories recorded in each authority. The estimated annual number for borough in 1991 (if the patterns for the first six months had continued throughout the year) is 754. Inquiries to both the registers were increasing annually, for example from 425 in city in 1989 to 672 in 1990, an increase of 63%. In both authorities the social services department (including hospital-based social workers) was the largest source of enquiries to the register.

When child protection registers (or at risk registers as they were then called) were developed in the late 1960s and early 1970s, their value in alerting front-line agencies to existing concerns about particular children and families was emphasised, particularly in relation to accident and emergency departments and the alleged propensity of some parents to take their injured

Table 4.3:   **Register enquiries borough, January to June 1991**

Social Services Department	172 (46%)
Emergency Duty Team	29 (8%)
Probation	64 (17%)
NSPCC	44 (12%)
Health	28 (7%)
Police	20 (5%)
Other[1]	20 (5%)
Total	377

[1] includes calls from outside the local authority (9) Education Welfare service (2) Day Nursery (2)

Table 4.4:   **Register enquiries City 1990**

Social Services department	189 (28%)
NSPCC	143 (21%)
Health Visitors/Snr nurses	82 (12%)
School nurses/Snr nurses	61 (9%)
Education Welfare officers	53 (8%)
Probation service	30 (4%)
Court Officer	18 (3%)
Clinical medical officers	11 (2%)
Head Teachers	10 (1%)
GP's	9 (1%)
Other registers	45 (7%)
Others[1]	21 (3%)
Total	672

[1] comprises A & E (7) Police (5) Hospital consultants (3) Psychological service (6)

children to multiple hospital sites to avoid detection. This study reveals accident and emergency departments in district general hospitals to be infrequent users of the registers. They were rarely involved in the initial identification of abused children, a finding reported also by the British Paediatric Association and British Association of Paediatric Surgeons (1973), Dingwall et al (1983) and by the Children's Research Fund (c. 1987). Front-line agencies in contact with universal or near universal child populations such as schools and general practitioners are also revealed as infrequent users of the register. In city, usage rates for health visitors and school nurses are somewhat higher, reflecting the procedural requirement to indicate in a box on the inter-service referral form that a register check had been undertaken. The rank order of register users, therefore, suggests that the child protection register is principally consulted by social services department staff as a procedural check in the course of investigating child protection referrals, rather than by other front-line identifiers of abuse. By the time of this study, the principal function of the register appeared to have shifted to the more managerial one outlined in *Working Together* (1991) as follows,

> *The purpose of the register is to provide a record of all children in the area for whom there are unresolved child protection issues and who are currently the subject of an interagency protection plan and to ensure that plans are formally reviewed every six months. The register will provide a central point of speedy inquiry for professional staff who are worried about a child and want to know whether the child is the subject of an interagency protection plan. The register will also provide useful information for the individual child protection agencies and for the ACPC in its policy development work and strategic planning (Home Office at al, 1991, p 48).*

As is shown in Figure 4.2, register checks were recorded on the social services department file as having been carried out in only 10 cases in the case sample.

Figure 4.2 **Record of register check on social services department file (N=48)**

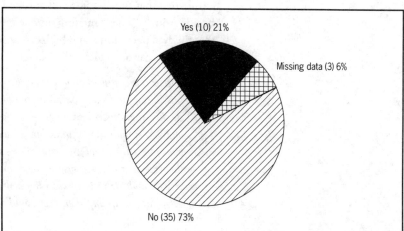

There was no record of a check in the remaining 35 cases. The rate of recording register checks on the files was higher in borough than in city as is shown in Figure 4.3.

Of the ten recorded register checks, six were carried out by social workers, one by a community mental health team and, in three cases, the person checking the register was not recorded. Since these figures represent apparently low levels of compliance with procedural guidelines (or at least the recording of them), the use and usefulness of the register was discussed in interviews with the respondents.

Figure 4.3 **Record of register check on social services department file: borough and city compared (N=48)**

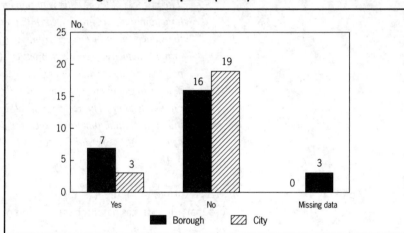

The health visitors and school nurses asked about the use of the register confirmed that they had used it and said they would do so. In city, the initial health visiting/school nursing service referral form included a space to record that this had been done, and high rates of usage are recorded in the register. As one health visitor explained:

> *If there is an incident or we've had something reported to us, then we've got this initial form that you fill in and on that it says, you know, have you checked the register and are they on the register and all that sort of thing, and you ring the appropriate bit. So we do that as a matter of course and one of the values that we see in it as well as it tells you whether they are on the register or not, but also it acts as an alerting system. So if we ring the register and the register was rung perhaps a week or so ago, it's probably been flagged up and then they could say so.*

Many social workers and their managers, in both authorities, also said that register checks would always be done, although apparently not always recorded. Typical replies were 'we check the register for every child', and 'if a duty social worker talked to me about a brand new child protection referral and they haven't checked the register before they came to see me, I'd be quite surprised'. However some suggested that it was not always done. The following were among the replies given:

> *I think that probably varies from staff member to staff member in terms of to what extent they automatically go into a child protection mode. I suspect we don't use it for routine allegations.*

> *We were talking about this. I don't know whether it was your presence that stimulated this discussion but it might well have been – it has cropped up in the last few weeks – about whether people do automatically check the register, and it's newer staff who do because they get their booklet out and they follow it. If social work training achieves nothing else, it's achieved sufficient fear that people read their book, follow the procedures and older staff, more established staff, are saying 'well actually, now you come to mention it, it was three weeks before I realised we'd taken the register back from the NSPCC'. So the honest answer is that no, it's not always checked but because it's being discussed, we could perhaps get back into the idea of automatically checking.*

Staff are likely to undertake register checks either because they are required to do so by the procedures and/or because they perceive it to be useful; the two are not necessarily mutually exclusive. Some stressed the former:

> *If it's a referral concerning child abuse, we have to by our procedure. It's a matter of course now . . . it's not really useful, no. Well it is actually, I mean I suppose it is. I think it's good from a point of view that it's always good to have some form of registry in case you miss out but, generally speaking, I suppose it's more often than not when you ring you find that they're not registered so it's a bit unfair of me I suppose to say that. In terms of child abuse the registry is just another port of call as it were to check up.*

> *I didn't get any information, no. I mean it's part of the routine procedure but I've always known beforehand whether a child was on or off the register.*

> *I always check it, not because I think it is useful but because it's something that you get picked up on. It sounds so stupid but I've been through sort of reviews of cases where things have gone wrong and the questions are asked 'did you check with the health visitor? Did you check with the register? If not, why not?'. Now one particular case where the child wasn't on the register I was criticised for that even though it wouldn't have made the slightest difference to the outcome of it. So I make it a matter of routine*

now. It's not a bad thing anyway to have a kind of checklist of things to do. It doesn't take two minutes to phone the register up and get them to ring you back so it's not a major hassle, but in terms of its value, marginal. Well I suppose it's less than marginal; it doesn't have a purpose. In terms of the early stages of an investigation, we know the children that are on the register anyway by virtue of the files.

Already knowing that families were on the register in the area was given most frequently as the reason for not checking the register or not finding it useful to do so; a finding confirmed by Corby (1987) and by Birchall (1992). Others, however, spoke of the value of checking the register for three additional reasons: first, that it was useful if families had recently moved into the area; secondly, that it could help in respect of families moving within the authority. This was particularly important in city where, in contrast to borough, there was no centralised, computerised client index in operation in the social services department so that to ascertain whether a child or family was known necessitated separate checks with each divisional office. Thirdly, the register check would reveal whether others had made previous inquiries about the same child in the preceding months. Knowledge of the existence of this facility seemed patchy which may suggest that the number of cases in which there were prior recorded concerns was low. Some workers reported it to be helpful:

When we do register checks it doesn't matter whether a child is registered or not, the previous register checks go in the register. The information will be there so, in that respect, it is useful to have it around.

Where a register check reveals that there have been previous referrals, sometimes it's useful from the point of view that the referrals indicate a signal you know there may be a number of referrals from different people which obviously would give cause for more concern. Sometimes a register check reveals that the same person had made numerous referrals so, yes, I mean it is a useful tool for gaining some fairly quick background on which to decide how to progress.

Others, however, seemed unaware of or had not experienced this facility.

You know I've never used that facility. . . . I can honestly say I must have phoned the register a hundred times myself. I've never, even when there is nothing there, nobody has ever said 'well they're not on the register but somebody phoned about this'. That might just be that it's not the kind of cases I phoned up on, but no I couldn't say its a useful facility because its never occurred to me.

It seems from the responses in interview that register checks were carried out more frequently than the social services case records suggested, but that some workers relied on knowing the register status of families in their area and were less concerned perhaps than they should have been about mobile families or about using the register to pick up earlier indications of concern. The latter seemed more a consequence of lack of awareness than principled objections to the practice of recording concern about families without their knowledge. Indeed in discussing the use of the register, there was little evidence of the civil libertarian concerns of earlier years (Geach, 1983, and Family Rights Group, 1986). Very few of those interviewed mentioned anxieties on this score. One, who did, said:

> *I can remember when I first came to [borough] and I hadn't actually seen the register. I'd checked it as a social worker and I hadn't actually seen it and I was horrified when I came here that the register was actually not only children on the register but where there had been register checks on families. Then when I actually sat down and thought about it, I could see the sense from a professional point of view of keeping a check on the register checks. So I can live with that now, it feels uncomfortable because families don't actually know that there has been a register check done on their little one, but I can just about live with that. One issue that certainly crossed my mind is the whole sort of ethos of working together isn't it, of well the Children Act is letting the parents know at each stage and I wonder now if we're actually, because of the way we've always done it, is that we get, and it's in our procedures, the new ones that have come out, is that we get the referral and we automatically check other agencies, the register all sorts of people, all the different professional agencies without . . . before we contact the parent. Now this is an issue that I wonder is something that if we're talking about contacting the parent at each stage along the way are we, should we be saying should we go to the parents straight away, first off and say to them 'look we've had this referral, this complaint, allegation, whatever. Our procedures say we've to contact other agencies and the register and we're just letting you know that this is what we're doing'. Do you know what I mean how far do we go along the line? I haven't got the answer.*

Whatever the answer should be, in practice there was frequent routinised interagency contact in the early stages of investigation, often carried out before parents or children were notified of the existence of concerns about them.

The allocation of social work investigations

In all areas, initial investigations were treated seriously and urgently and other work was reorganised as necessary to accommodate them within the requisite timescales. Unsurprisingly, the investigation of child protection referrals was recognised as a high priority within both social services departments and it often received relatively close supervision from managers. As one social worker said:

> *Well yes, our sort of line management thing is if there is a child abuse case come up you have to drop everything else and go for it and the backup is there from our own line manager.*

An inability to process initial investigations was seen as particularly worrying since responsibility for taking emergency protective action rested with the social services department, as the following quotation indicates:

> *Ultimately, the most dangerous thing is not going out and having a look at it . . . My own view is that the responsibility for the child's safety lies with the investigating agency and not with the case conference. . . . I don't think we, as a department, can avoid that responsibility.*

Although at the time of the research, there were not formally designated specialist child protection workers in post in either authority, there was a degree of informal specialization in the work. In most, but not all, parts of the areas studied there was a possibility of using more experienced staff for initial investigations rather than allocating them to newly qualified or very inexperienced social workers.

In some offices in the authorities it was the departmental practice for social workers to undertake child protection investigations in pairs with, for example, one worker accompanying the child and parents to a medical examination while another undertook checks and discussions with members of the interagency network and both workers interviewing the child and parents. In the case sample, this had occurred in approximately one third of the cases investigated by the social services departments. Where staffing levels permitted, some managers were able to pair less experienced with more experienced workers in an apprenticeship model but, in some offices, staffing did not allow for people routinely to conduct initial interviews in pairs.

It was departmental policy in borough for two people to go together if they 'needed' to, but need was defined principally in terms of risk of violence, as in the following examples:

> *It depends, it's a matter of what the referral is and whether there might be any violence towards social services . . . I've mostly been on my own but I have been on quite a few where I've been with other people as well, and*

> *we've got a sort of policy that where there's any chance of any danger to*
> *social workers that you're accompanied, not that that would do any good if*
> *they had a gun!*

and

> *The only time that two people can go out on an investigation is if you*
> *know there's a man at the other end with a gun or a knife or sixteen*
> *neighbours who will join in the fight.*

The arguments in favour of using two workers rather than one included the safety of workers in situations of potential violence, an opportunity to share perceptions and pick up on missed information, helping workers with the anxiety of sole investigation, developing the skills of newer workers and acknowledging the import of the decisions to be made. One social worker argued as follows:

> *My own perception is that all child protection should be done jointly . . .*
> *principally because it reduces the anxiety level of the person interviewing*
> *and, therefore, leads to a more reasoned and more considered interview*
> *and secondly, it gives the person being interviewed the benefit of a second*
> *opinion which, given the seriousness of what we're going to talk to them*
> *about, I think they deserve. Certainly in some of the joint interviews I've*
> *done it has been useful and there has been a measure of disagreement*
> *about interpretation of signals that were sent out and there were signals*
> *sent out which were missed. People who are doing initial interviews on*
> *their own are anxious and that reduces their ability to make a reasoned*
> *judgement, to actually see what's going on because they are more conscious*
> *of their own anxiety and their own agenda. It's ludicrous and from a wider*
> *point of view, it just shows a total disregard by management for the safety*
> *of staff, I mean essentially what you're doing is you're going in to people*
> *and saying 'well we suspect that you may have committed a crime'. I*
> *mean at it's most basic you wouldn't get a copper to go out and do that on*
> *their own, they go out in twos and they all have radios. I'm not suggesting*
> *that we should have all that paraphernalia but I do think that we should*
> *have a regard for the safety of people and their stress levels. I also think*
> *from a social work practice point of view it is just good practice.*

Only one social worker spoke of the potential drawbacks emphasising the need to work consistently with a partner to feel comfortable with each other's style, which was difficult to organise given the resource constraints. She also said:

> *Sometimes if two of you go, it causes more aggravation because they think*
> *you're coming with a heavy, like if I ever go with anybody here, they say*
> *'look she's got her bodyguard'.*

While it was possible, in many work locations anyway, to allocate child protection investigations to experienced workers and to increase the level of supervision, this was not so easy when the concerns arose or should have been identified in open cases allocated to workers initially for reasons other than child protection. The difficulties of switching roles from a supportive to a more investigative mode were acknowledged, as in the following example:

> *It's especially difficult on experienced workers who've had relationships with clients for a long time, which have developed into a comfortable cosy relationship. Suddenly they're presented with a situation where they are having to change role completely and having to do an investigation, that's very difficult. Somebody who would be very much on the ball about a fresh new case doesn't always give you the same sort of information on a case that they've had for some time because they worry about whether they should have picked up on something more, something before for instance, it's a different level of information.*

The nature of social work investigations

In addition to the interagency consultations described above, the other principal component of the social workers' initial investigation was interviews with the parents and children concerned.

Interviews with children

Sixteen cases in the sample were investigated by the social services department without police involvement. The number of interviews with the children is shown in Figure 4.4. In four cases, there was no record in the social services department file that the children were interviewed. In two of these, Schedule 1 offenders were present in (or associated with) the household and there was no current allegation that the children had been subjected to abuse. A third was a case where a child had ingested cleaning fluid and the fourth a child, noticed at school with bruising who was reported to have told the teacher that his father had inflicted the injury.

In the majority, eight cases, only one interview was carried out, in two cases two interviews and in the remaining two cases, three and four. The total number of interviews with the children in these 12 cases was 19, 13 of which were conducted by one social worker. Five were conducted by two social workers and only one (with a health visitor) by another member of the interagency network.

The definition of 'interviewing children' that was adopted in gathering the data was a loose one, requiring only that there was an indication in the case file that the social worker(s) had spoken to the child concerned. This may

Figure 4.4 **No. of interviews with children per case in cases which the
social services departments investigated alone (N = 16)**

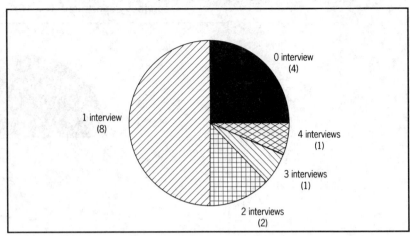

not necessarily have involved an extensive conversation nor seeing the child away from his/her parents when, as was usually the case, they were also the alleged abuser(s). This may account for the fact that the case records, at the initial stage, generally revealed rather scant evidence of assessment of the child, of his or her feelings, responses to the abuse or general well-being as opposed to the child's account of the 'incident' under investigation – a point explored further below. There was certainly little evidence from the case files of repeated intrusive or oppressive interviews with the children concerned, as has been reported in some child abuse inquiry reports, for example Cleveland (Cm 412, 1988) and Orkney (Clyde, 1992). Those cases jointly investigated by the police and social workers discussed in Chapter Five were more likely to have had a more extended investigative interview, but there were cases of sexual abuse or more serious physical assault.

Interviews with parents

In the 16 cases investigated by the social services department alone, a total of 38 interviews was carried out with the parents or parent substitutes. The frequency of the interviews is shown in Figure 4.5. Just one parent or parent substitute was the alleged abuser in all but two of these cases. Of a total of 28 interviews, 18 (64%) were carried out by a single social worker, and ten by social workers acting in pairs.

The nature and quality of initial investigations

There was widespread agreement within the interagency network and in the social services departments that the nature and quality of initial social

Figure 4.5 **No. of interviews per case with parents or parent substitutes in cases where the initial investigation was carried out by the social services department (N = 16)**

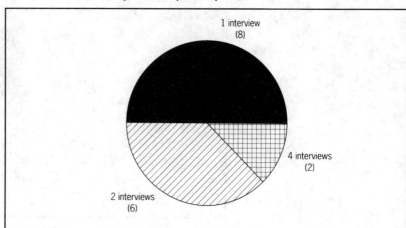

work investigation varied considerably. Soem social workers and their managers in both authorities expressed confidence. For example:

> *Generally the staff here do a good job in their investigations. Yes my team members are very good. I feel very positive about the work they do on that; We consider in a quiet kind of way we are competent on this, that doesn't mean that we can't be caught out by something at any time but we think that we're actually more competent than some of the divisions . . . I would say I am usually happy with the quality of the social work investigation.*

> *I have a lot of confidence in the workers here. I think we're in the position to do good investigations usually and I think what we manage to do, because we've not got high bombardment and we can take a little bit of time to think about it and there's no substitute for thought . . . We know what we need to find out and we can give ourselves the space to do that.*

This generally positive view was sometimes shared by other professionals who received social workers' reports of their investigations at child protection conferences. More common, however, was an acknowledgement of unevenness based partly on the different skills and experience of individual workers and partly on the uneven workload on different work sites. The following were typical comments. One NSPCC worker said:

> *I think again they tend to vary. I think there's a lot of good workers here and there's a lot of people who can do good work. I think that sometimes*

their work, like our work here, may not always be as good as it is able to be because of the resources and other things, limitations that are put on them because basically they are worn down . . . If you use people who perhaps aren't as experienced as other people and expect the same output from them, you don't always get that, so we don't always get a lot of consistency.

A nurse manager reported similarly:

I think it varies enormously, having gone to a lot of case conferences recently throughout the city, I think it varies enormously. I think some of them are very good and they produce very good reports and it's very clear and concise. Others, I suppose, didn't go in for very much preparation and they have very entrenched ideas and it varies, that's all I can say.

A social work manager said:

Yes well I think I'd say it would apply also to the police and the doctors that, clearly, there are good and bad social workers as there are doctors and this sort of thing, trying to take that into account as well. Obviously it's not good. I hope I'm not being over critical of social workers, that's down to the fact that really they don't have the experience. There are some workers out there who I trust implicitly, whose judgement is very very sound, who are thorough, who are sensitive, assertive, know their stuff and I would trust them. There are others who I wouldn't. I would have grave doubts about some of the information they provide. I would take that into account if I were chairing a case conference. There are, from this divison, probably 40 social workers who, potentially, could be involved in investigations. Maybe ten of them are experienced, in that they are level three social workers who have been doing it a long time and have sufficient training or whatever, know the ropes, been to a lot of case conferences but the others maybe only do two or three a year perhaps and don't have the knowledge really about the situation and don't have enough knowledge about the procedures really to know what they're doing.

The major problems were said to be the pressure of time and insufficient appropriately trained and experienced staff to cope with the workload. Sometimes the initial child protection conference was called too soon (a point discussed further in Chapter Six) which resulted in inadequate investigation. As one social worker said:

Because of the pressure of work we're in, we are actually, as social workers, going to case conferences with inadequate assessments. We know they're inadequate, I mean we've no reports and things like that. Case conferences are being done on duty with the most cursory of investigations which doesn't do justice to the families, it doesn't help the case conference because, invariably, no in most cases the majority of the information is coming from the social services and we don't . . . we're just badly prepared. I think the job, with the present level of resources, is unmanageable – that's the top and bottom of it – and it wouldn't matter how long you held it up for. If there is nobody able to devote the time to investigating it and to sort of digging around it, then the quality of information going in is not terribly good.

In some circumstances there was insufficient information at the early stage and then child protection conferences would be reconvened, as the following quotation illustrates:

If I'm chairing there's no point in me having a go at the social worker. I don't feel that's appropriate because I can sort of sympathise, empathise with her right, but I will try to point out that we are actually wasting time or we could use time more productively, and I have actually adjourned case conferences, two so far, that I've chaired. I think the difficulty is that we have got a workforce generally that feels, particularly within the [main town area], stretched the way that they're dealing with investigations and it, at times, feels like make do. It's first aid; there's no in-depth investigation, that's a resource problem, and I don't think there's any other way of describing it.

However, more fundamentally, some staff in the social services departments and the NSPCC questioned whether the focus and nature of the inital investigations was appropriate and adequate. The concern was that the social work element of the assessment had been lost in a concern with detailed forensic investigation, as illustrated in the following quotations:

Some of it's very good and some of it's poor . . . I think that depends on the social worker involved and all the bits that go with the pressure of the caseload and, again, what they see. When I walk into a house and I see like a myriad of layers of interaction going on but I know that not all workers operate like I do, so the kind of information that they're going to get to put into a case conference is going to be very different.

Yes, we'll get a report that goes through the incident, right. Little one had a bruise, I took him to the doctor's. The doctor said this and I notified them and that's it, we then don't have any social work bit and that's what I was like. I can actually remember my first report for a case conference and that was what my report was like when I first qualified, right. My reports are nothing like that now and I would expect, to some extent, newly-qualified staff to have that maybe a little bit more if they've got the management support. But there are qualified, experienced staff who are not doing that social work element of an investigation. From a social work point of view, the gaps are that they don't actually do a social work assessment as part of that investigation into the family dynamics and the strengths and weaknesses, and what we're getting more recently and more frequently is an allegation of abuse, all the checks are done, the medical is done and a case conference is called and, if you are lucky, a social worker will visit the family and let them know that and that's it.

A routinised response with a focus on the abusive incident was confirmed in many cases by the written records of the social work investigation available in the case files, which often concentrated more upon the incident and the explanations offered rather than on an assessment of family functioning, or indeed of the child's responses and reactions. It was not easy to gain from the social service records an impression of the child, his/her functioning and well-being or reactions to the alleged abuse. Some suggested that this was principally because of the constraints of time and resources rather than the skills and approach of the social workers, as in the following example:

It's not down to the quality of the worker, I'm quite convinced of that because, given the space to begin to think about the issues, the workers, who I've given a hard time in case conferences and told to go away and come back when they've done some work, have come up with some superb stuff.

Clearly, finding the space and time posed enormous problems, at least in some areas of the authorities concerned, but it also appeared that the nature of the initial investigations reflected an orientation to the task which was primarily forensic.

This is a difficult issue. Social workers were severely criticised in some of the earlier inquiry reports for their naivety in accepting dubious explanations of injuries to children and for failing to probe in sufficient depth and detail what had actually happened; when, where, how, to whom and by whom. In consequence, greater attention was paid to this aspect of the investigative task by social workers but this study suggests that, in the process, the social work element of investigation in the sense of a broader assessment of child and family functioning may have been lost.

Some of those interviewed were relatively unconcerned about this, emphasising the importance in the early stages of a case of a clear, factual account of what had occurred. For example, one said:

At initial conferences, I'm not too worried about that because I think that you need clear factual stuff because we always have this debate really about timing of conferences. I'm pleased the new draft guidance seems to ease up on the notion of timescales because my own view is, as somebody who chairs a lot of conferences, there's very little point in having a conference where you don't know what you're dealing with. You might as well accept that if a place of safety order needs to be taken, somebody is going to have to make a speedy assessment of that and do it but the multiagency thing is about planning services for families and looking at assessment of risk that has to be based on good information and I think, in an initial conference, I'm quite happy to have people tell the sort of bare bones because what I would like to see is them coming back together for another conference after a full assessment.

The sting may be in the tail for, as is discussed in Chapter Eight, the majority of the cases in the sample were not characterised by subsequent full assessment of the kind envisaged in the Department of Health guidance *Protecting Children* (1988).

Summary

Almost one third of the cases in the sample were investigated by the social services department, without police involvement in joint investigation. The investigative activities of the social workers proved to be routinised. They were undertaken within a clear framework of procedural guidance which shaped their actions, although variations in compliance were apparent, for example in implementing the requirement to check the child protection register. In the course of investigation the social workers had frequently to resort to others in the interagency network for the exchange of information about the children and families concerned and agreement as to a division of labour. With the exception of general practitioners, most professionals in the network were willing to participate in this collaborative process. In this activity, there was little 'hands-on' collaborative work requiring two or more professions to work closely together simultaneously. This contrasts with the kind of coordination envisaged in joint investigation involving police and social workers which is discussed in the next chapter.

Chapter 5

The role of the police and joint investigation

The British child protection system is distinguished from some others, for example the Dutch, in the importance attached to police involvement in the investigation of abuse and, potentially, to the prosecution of criminal offenders. As Parton (1991) notes this represents a significant change since the elaboration of central government guidance for child protection management in the early 1970s, dominated then by a socio–medical rather than a socio-legal discourse. The shift is evident in comparing current practice concerning the role of the police with that set out in the 1974 circular of guidance issued following the Maria Colwell inquiry. It listed professions and agencies which 'a case conference should normally include' as follows:

a   persons having statutory responsibilities for the continuing care of the child, eg the appropriate senior member of the social services department, the consultant in charge of the patient's medical care;

b   persons concerned with the provision of services likely to be relevant to the case, eg area social worker, voluntary agency representatives, family doctor and health visitor, psychiatrist treating child or parents, day nursery matron;

c   persons with information regarding the child and his family, eg family doctor and health visitor (if not included under (b), social workers including probation officers in previous and present contact, paediatrician and members of medical and nursing staff. (DHSS 1974(a), p4).

The dominance of health and social service staff is evident. The police were then included in the category of 'others who may also be invited when appropriate'. By contrast, a senior manager in social services summarised the current position as follows:

> I think, in many ways, our closest colleagues are the coppers. They are in it up to their necks as we are. They are exposed to the allegations, all the really heavy material although they have a different starting point and I don't want to romanticise it; their position is very blunt and crude but that's what they're there for and they are certainly sharing the grit of the business with us in a very direct way.

The collaboration envisaged between the police and social workers in joint investigation constitutes a more radical form of interagency coordination. As was noted in Chapter One, it implies a fundamental challenge to the existing division of labour in which the interpersonal base to interorganisational relations, particularly issues of trust, mutual confidence and respect for the skill and competence of collaborative partners, appears to be particularly salient.

Notification between the social services department and the police

Collaboration between social services and the police in the investigation of child abuse requires that the agencies notify each other of relevant cases coming to their attention and reach decisions as to future action. There were reported variations in practice on these matters within and between area or divisional offices within the social services departments and between various police units.

In nine of the 48 cases in the case sample, the referral was initially made to the police. In 34 of the remaining 39 cases there was a record in the social services case file that the police were notified by the social workers of the referral. They were also notified in the remaining five at the point of issuing invitations to the initial child protection conference. In some cases, however, the notification to the police appeared to have occurred some time after the initial referral and after social workers had undertaken some initial investigation, and the notification to the police took the form of a request for any information about the criminal records of the alleged abusers and for police attendance at the initial child protection conference.

The practice of cross-referral between the police and social services was explored in interview. In general, staff in social services departments said they would notify the police (almost always the Special Unit in city and borough) of allegations of child sexual abuse, and the Special Units would notify the social services departments. Such cases would be likely to be investigated jointly – a process discussed more fully below. There were said to be few exceptions to this practice in the field of child sexual abuse. Two were mentioned. One concerned occasions where there was no clear allegation of sexual abuse and no report of a suspected crime but where a child's behaviour was giving rise to concern that she or he may have been sexually abused. In such situations, the police would leave the investigation, at least in the early stages, to the social services department. The other exception involved cases in which there appeared to be inappropriate sexual play/exploration involving young children (below or near the age of criminal responsibility). Again, the police were said to be likely to agree to the social services department making some initial enquiries.

The patterns of cross-referral were much more varied in respect of physical injury to children. The official position in both city and borough was that suspected criminal offences or assaults should be reported to the police. As one police officer explained:

> *What happens is that we would expect to start off with the social services ringing us with any allegation and we would discuss it and make a decision at that stage whether we would go in together, or whether they would go and look at it and then come back to us because it does happen from time to time, social services will go and come back and say 'look, this is more serious than we first thought' but we would always expect that, having been discussed at the original referral, that we would consult with each other after that.*

In practice, social workers and their managers often made judgements about the circumstances in which they would notify the police of cases of physical injury. Some said they would routinely inform the police of the vast majority of cases although they might expect to handle the investigation alone. For example:

> *Well I always involve the police partly because that is the procedure, so I would always involve them. However, I may be saying 'this, this and this, I don't wish you to be involved at this point, do you agree to that?' But I would always involve them in every step of the way. I tend anyway to discuss most of them now with them and just say what we're handling and we're thinking or we're going to do it this way, if we can get hold of them. If it's definitely a child protection matter where there has been an injury, or a suspected abuse or whatever then the police would always be involved. If it was something where it was a bit iffy, we might ring them and say 'do you want to be involved right from the initial in this or do you want us to go and suss it out and then get back to you?'*

Others reported that their practice varied:

> *I think it varies, in all honesty. I think some of them are clear cut, the sexual abuse ones and the serious injuries are fairly straight forward. I think the sexual abuse is the most straight forward one for us and for the police. I think my response would vary really, sometimes it depends what the referral is and how much information . . . I mean we might go and have a look or we might tell them that's what we're going to do and they say 'yes let us know if you want us to be involved.' I couldn't say I had a rigid policy about it. I think experience has probably told you that for the ones that are very vague they're not going to come and have a look anyway so perhaps that's affected what I might tell them. We make it a policy of contacting them where there's very clearly been an injury and there's an offence been committed.*

The police were not unhappy with this:

> *I think its fair to say we do get incidents where social services call me and sort of say 'I've got concerns about this child, nothing concrete but I've just got concerns and we're going to monitor him' and then we, quite rightly in my opinion, agree that that's the best course of action.*

Yet other social workers were in contact with the police over physical injury much less frequently, making decisions on the seriousness of the case, or, more usually the seriousness of the injuries, referring fractures, severe bruising and burns but not routinely doing so in respect of minor injuries, as the following quotations illustrate:

> *In terms of physical abuse that's much less clear cut; if I think it's gross physical abuse there's no question about it but in terms of sort of more minor physical abuse maybe over a period, I'm not sure we necessarily would involve them. So that varies.*

> *If a referral comes to social services we would look at it before we make a decision whether or not to involve the police. I would think that there's only a minority of cases where the abuse is so serious that you would feel the necessity to involve the police.*

The interview data and the case sample both revealed that serious injuries are rare among child protection cases, a finding confirmed by the much larger data set in the NSPCC research on registers (Creighton, 1992). So, in some offices, many physical abuse cases would be investigated without police notification at least in the early stages. This was reflected in the case sample where over half of the cases of physical abuse were investigated by the social services department alone.

Calculating the necessity for police involvement on the basis of the seriousness of injuries could potentially be a dangerous practice. Clearly, there are times when the seriousness of injury, for example extensive and serious bruising or fractures, is an indication of serious and/or prolonged assault. But, in some cases, the outcome of an assault or blow to the child in terms of the resulting injuries is a matter of chance (for example whether a child, when pushed or hit, falls against a sofa rather than against a table or a fireplace) and a relatively minor injury should not necessarily be taken as indicative of the degree of risk to the child in the home.

However, in general, police staff in the Special Units and those in the social services departments considered that each notified the other of most of the relevant referrals. Those that went astray or awry were thought to be a 'small minority.' This was one of several points in the data where significant improvements in interagency liaison were reported to have occurred in recent years:

> *We expect if there is a suspicion that this child may have been physically or sexually assaulted that they notify us and, conversely, that is how I expect it to work*

and broadly it did:

> *. . . things have changed a lot in the last four years. We've both re-examined our position. All the agencies have. I'm broadly happy that we are getting referrals straight away.*

There were, nonetheless, some complaints on both sides that referrals had not been passed on quickly enough, for example:

> *I guess if we're honest all agencies stray from the procedures and, from time to time, I would certainly occasionally criticise social workers for not informing us of an incident which we should at least have been informed of and given the chance to decide whether to investigate or not rather than wait for the case conference which can be sort of the following week and we've lost time.*

In these cases, the problem was not simply that there was delay in the specialist police beginning their investigation but that the child might need to be re-interviewed, which was regarded as unacceptable practice and indicative of a lack of coordination, as the following quotation illustrates:

> *Sometimes . . . they go too far with the disclosure before they call us in. I think we are asking a very, very, very great thing for children to disclose if they have been abused, physically or sexually . . . and I feel they should only have to disclose it once. And so . . . I am critical of people . . . from the police side and also from the social services . . . where they've gone too far and we've then got to go over old ground. I think that's wrong.*

From the social services point of view, delay in notification to them was more likely to occur when cases had been first identified by the divisional police rather than the Special Units. These were often cases when the police were called out of hours to deal with domestic disputes involving, inter alia, physical assault to children. The police would visit the home and take the requisite action without alerting the social services. Non-specialist police were said to be very unlikely to deal with sexual abuse and would refer such cases to the Special Units. The police acknowledged this to be a problem noting the relative lack of experience and training in child protection of non-specialist police officers. One police officer said:

> *To us, it's an unusual event. I could take you downstairs and take half a dozen policemen picked at random and you could ask them questions on*

care of children and they wouldn't be able to answer any of them. I would doubt if they would be able to unless they'd had a case where they've educated them. That's why I like to take police officers involved in the cases to the case conference because not only do they give valuable information to that case conference but it also broadens their education and they see what actually happens after they've dealt with it. They see the process and the progress of that case and they then have a much broader knowledge for next time, and hopefully they'll pass it on to their colleagues as well. That is informal training which is very positive 'hands-on' training but we don't push it as a topic of police training. There is a little input but not a lot. Similarly we don't train every officer in fraud because fraud is a very complicated specialised subject and so you get the group of officers who have certain talents and abilities in that area, and you train them how to do it so when a fraud job comes in, you give it to them and the same thing happens with a child abuse case, it goes to the Unit but assault is assault whether it's on a child or a person or on an old person. We know how to deal with assaults.

Police investigation

As the quotation above illustrates, when cases of physical injury were referred, usually by members of the public, to uniformed officers or when they came across such situations in the course of their duties they were likely to deal with them themselves, although they may refer to the Special Units for advice. There were two such cases in the study. A further seven cases, all of sexual abuse, were investigated initially by the police alone. In these cases, the person suspected could be arrested or bailed to return to the police station or reported on summons awaiting a decision as to future action and such action might be taken before involving the social services department and long before the child protection case conference.

Joint Investigation

In the case sample just under half the cases (23) were investigated jointly by social workers and the police. Pressure of resources on both sides was said to militate against a greater use of joint investigation. As is shown in Table 4.1 in the previous chapter, joint investigation occurred in a higher proportion of sexual abuse cases. The procedures in city specified that joint investigations should take place in all cases of alleged sexual abuse or serious physical abuse, but the guidelines in borough were less specific on this point.

Joint investigation was loosely defined in this study. It did not necessarily imply that children would be interviewed jointly by the police and social workers. Rather, it implied that the police and social workers were both concurrently engaged in some investigative activity/interviews with children, parents or other alleged abusers, although they may not necessarily undertake these tasks together. This is in accordance with the findings of Moran-Ellis et al (1991) who note that a simple dichotomy between sole or joint investigation does not represent the realities of practice where there are degrees of 'jointness' in investigations.

Interviews with children

An important objective of joint investigation and an indication of a coordinated approach is the minimisation of the number of times children are interviewed and required to repeat their story to different people. This appears to have been largely achieved in the case sample. In the 23 cases investigated jointly, a total of 31 interviews with children were carried out. Their frequency is shown in Figure 5.1. In 11 cases only one interview was undertaken and, in a further five cases, there were two.

Figure 5.1   **No. of interviews with children per case in cases involving joint investigation (N = 23)**

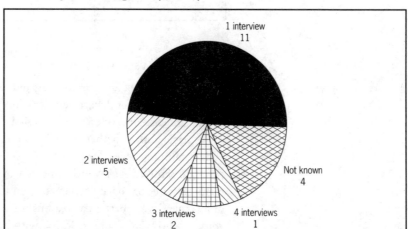

As is shown in Figure 5.2, 13 of these interviews were carried out by social workers alone and 11 jointly by social workers and the police. The three which involved other professionals were two interviews where a social worker interviewed with a YTS worker to whom a young woman had disclosed her own sexual abuse and expressed her anxieties about her younger siblings (who were subsequently registered), and a third involving a social worker and a school nurse. It is clear that, even in joint investigation, the frequency of the police and social workers working together to interview children is not high in this case sample, at a third of the total of 31 interviews.

It should, however, be noted that the interviews in the case sample preceded the publication of the Memorandum of Good Practice (Home Office and Department of Health, 1992) which would be expected to lead to more joint investigative interviews being undertaken by police and social workers.

Figure 5.2   **Persons interviewing children in cases investigated jointly by the police and social services department (N = 31)**

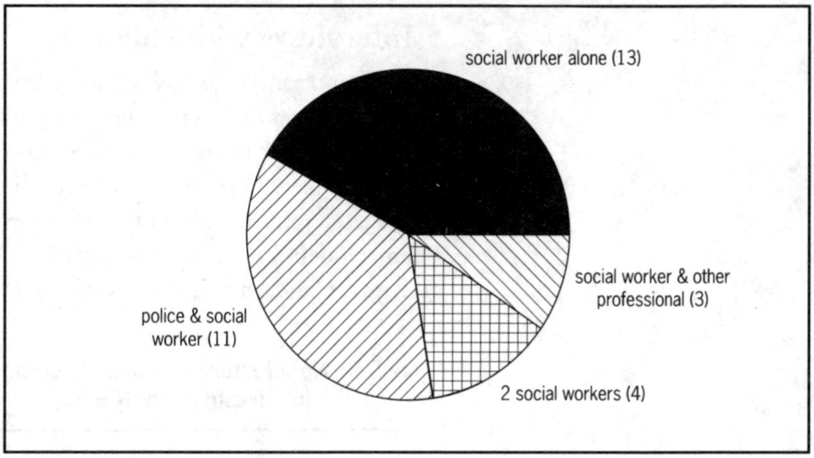

Pie chart segments:
- social worker alone (13)
- social worker & other professional (3)
- 2 social workers (4)
- police & social worker (11)

Interviews with parents

In the sample of 23 cases investigated jointly, 32 interviews were recorded in the social services departments case file as having involved a social worker acting alone, six interviews were carried out by two social workers and three took place jointly with the police. It is likely that the police undertook additional interviews alone with the parents when, as was often the case in this case sample, they were suspected of the abuse. It was reported to be relatively rare for social workers to join the police in interviewing suspects, unless there were particular reasons for doing so, for example with alleged abusers who were young or those with learning difficulties.

The experience of joint investigation

Respondents were asked about their experience of joint interviewing and it was clear that there were several problems. Perhaps the most crucial was the absence in the social services departments in both city and borough at the time of the field research of an identified corps of specialist social work staff trained with the police to undertake joint investigation. This was emphasised by the police in the Special Units, by other professionals and by the social workers themselves. The revised 'Working Together' (1991) emphasises the importance of this stating:

> *Difficulties will be encountered in joint interagency investigations but these can be minimised by the selection of specialist staff who undergo appropriate interagency training* (Home Office et al, 1991, p17).

The government advice is that staff should not be selected for this work unless they are of acknowledged competence and have undergone appropriate (although unspecified) staff development and training. However the guidance in operation at the time of the interviews was less specific, stating only that agencies 'should try to ensure as far as is practicable' that cases of sexual abuse 'are handled only by staff who have had preparation and training for the tasks involved . . .' (Department of Health and Welsh Office, 1988, p36).

In both city and borough, the appointment of such specialist staff was imminent as part of wider departmental reorganisation, and was widely welcomed as necessary and desirable both within the social services department, by the police and by other professionals in the locality. The absence of specialist social workers at the time of the research was said to result in difficulties. These were of two main kinds: first, a lack of knowledge and confidence among some social workers involved in joint investigation and secondly, the lack of familiarity, predictability and trust which joint training and repeated working together could engender. The former is illustrated by the following quotations:

> *I think the other worrying thing in terms of social workers, however, and for children in [city] is that social workers, if they continue to work this way, are giving a very bad service to the children because the police, even if one wishes to criticise the way they interviewed, are doing it every day so they're getting their practice whether it's good, bad or indifferent; it's certainly being confirmed every day and validated to them and by them every day whereas if social workers maybe only going out maybe possibly once, twice a year, they never have the actual experience and I think that is very frustrating because I think the only way you learn is through practical experience. No amount of head knowledge is going to change and inform your practice.*

> *The police officers take over and run the interview as they would want it to be run, or they think it should be run, and the social workers either haven't got the confidence or the skill to challenge that. There doesn't seem to be much space for that at the moment which is regrettable and I think the losers are, well, the young people themselves because we don't tend to get the result sometimes which we should be getting and things go so wrong, so it troubles me that.*

While clear that the lack of specialist social workers made the task much more difficult, the police officers interviewed seemed to be surprisingly understanding of the position. One, in city, where plans for specialist social workers had been around for some time but had not been implemented (it appeared because of union opposition and an insufficient determination on the part of senior management to see them through) spoke as follows; the views are indicative of harmonious working relationships between social services and the police in both city and borough at senior and generally at operational levels, and also reflect the improving relationships over time, on which many in the interagency network commented.

> *I'm not resentful of it, because I've worked with [city] social services very closely now for four years and I started off as the traditional police stereotype looking at social workers as a typical social work stereotype should be but I have changed my views dramatically over the last four years of social workers. I mean, I'm just not giving them a hard time over this. I'm convinced that the important role that they play in society, I think they've got an absolutely awful job to do, with awful working conditions and very little thanks and I've met some very very skilled professional people and I have a very good relationship with the manager of the [city] social services, in particular, the Child Protection Coordinators, who are doing everything in their power to develop the social services in [city] and to take on a specialist role in child abuse and the politics of the area overrides, at the moment, what they are trying to do. So I don't feel it's right for me to be in a position to feel resentful because the politics are what they are. They've got to sort that out, meanwhile we'll carry on working in the best possible way. We learnt a lot, you know, from the social workers in [city] and from the NSPCC social workers when we first started our investigations and I don't think we should forget that and when all else fails you see, it's all left with them. When we've moved on the next day, the next inquiry, there's this awful mess within the family is left with the poor old social worker and any subsequent repercussions or problems within that family are left with them to help them. I've not had time for social services being castigated in that way. I think before you can start criticising them, you've got to understand what their problems are. I can't imagine why anyone would want to be a social worker.*

Training was reported to help, as illustrated in the following quotation:

> *In many ways we've got a lot to learn because I don't think personally we have enough training certainly for interviewing children. If we had specialists we could maybe start ironing those things out at this sort of level. Certainly I feel, having done a joint investigation course with some of them, that that gives me more ways to handle it. I could say 'don't you remember when we did that course, we said we'd never do a, b, c, or something' and it would be a much easier way than them trying to address*

it rather than formally saying 'I think you are being quite abusive or destructive of this child'. I mean we don't bring that up and I'm sure they must feel immense frustration.

A consequence of the lack of a specialist role and associated training was that the police were said to have a tendency to take control and dominate the interviews, as noted also by Thomas (1988). The police were seen by some social workers as more confident and, sometimes, more skilled in the task:

The social workers feel very unhappy and uneasy about getting into joint working arrangemnts but I think, we too, have certainly contributed to that process by failing to identify specific workers who have sufficient competence and skill to work in this area, to genuinely work alongside the police, to go in there and say 'hey, I don't agree with the way you conducted that interview, don't you think we ought to . . .', you know, to sort of influence the police practice and what tends to happen is that the police, because they are operating specifically in this area and have been for some time, know what they are about and know what they are seeking to achieve from an investigatory process and they go in there and do it, and our social workers are somewhere in there tagging behind and uncertain about their role and what they are seeking to achieve where if they have an idea about what they would like to be doing, they are not in an equal partnership/relationship at all. That's this agency's failing, I'm not necessarily blaming the police for that, it's our failure to influence their practice in any real sense.

As in other parts of the data (for example concerning the quality of social work initial investigations or of initial medical examinations), there was reported to be considerable variation in the way in which individual police officers and social workers handled the interviews. This is unsurprising in the work of 'street level bureaucrats' (Lipsky, 1980) operating with varied training, experience and a good deal of delegated discretion, and in advance of the degree of formalisation and standardisation of the task outlined in the Memorandum of Good Practice (1992) and the Open University Training Pack (1993). The variations were ascribed to the aptitudes of individual staff, as the following quotations illustrate:

I have sat in on some very good ones and joined in some very good ones. I've watched one police officer interview a child and I was sat this side of the screen and she'd got another social worker in with her and this kid was very clearly saying that this man had put the penis on the back of it's throat and it had been sick. As clear as that and she just left it at that and I said to her afterwards 'why didn't you get any more detail?' She said 'I couldn't have got it' but she'd already got that amount of detail and she just didn't go for any more and I can't remember what actually happened with that but I thought, well she'd been in there five to ten minutes which is no time to build a rapport, establish whether kids know the difference between right and wrong, colours, left and right, private parts, public parts and all the rest of it. It was 'in, ask the question and out again' and I was appalled because she didn't give the child the opportunity to say what it needed to say but I know other police officers who actually work a lot harder and will do things over two or three sessions, take their time, take it at the kids pace, etc, etc, so I think it depends on the officer;

Again, it depends on which officer is involved. I mean, some of the officers are more receptive, more willing to listen to advice from social workers in a working partnership. Others tend to have a more high handed approach where they know best and, again, I think there's a bit of professional arrogance comes in as well. They haven't much time for social workers attitudes so I think there are more problems there;

I think I've got mixed impressions, there's one or two workers I've seen who I've been quite impressed and pleased with, happy to work with. Whether that's a coincidence, that one I'm thinking of is a woman, I don't know;

The police also reported variations in the capacities of social workers, as illustrated in the following:

Joint investigation varies. It varies from very good to poor. Some social workers are very experienced in dealing with child abuse and those – it tends to be a real joint investigation with both parties contributing equally but because you haven't got specialised workers, our officers are faced with the situation sometimes where they may be going on a case with somebody who's never been on a child abuse investigation and, in those circumstances, the officer takes the lead and does everything that is required in the investigation and the social worker tends to go along and do their social work bit but not as a child abuse investigator.

Logistics

While most, if not all, of the social workers and police interviewed accepted the principle of joint investigation, there were severe logistical and practical problems. Besides a lack of specialist trained social workers, there was pressure of work on the Special Units which were both small in staff complement and thus severely affected by staff absence on training or leave and by their own operational priorities. Both units, for example, dealt with cases of rape which were said to absorb staff resources, inevitably unpredictably and for a considerable length of time and, in some circumstances, therefore, social workers investigated alone.

> *One of the problems they have is coordinating – everybody says that a joint investigation is a good thing, if anything's well done it is, but the actual mechanics of organising it are becoming increasingly problematic. It feels from our side that we have to fit in with their shift system and their other commitments and, for an alleged emergency service, it's been quite an eye-opener to see how long they're willing to leave things to wait and we will now give them a reasonable time to . . . but we will say 'if you can't do it by then, we'll have to go through it without you, we'll try not to muck it up too much but we have a responsibility to this family' and, by and large, that is understood. I think they're unhappy about their own workload and the spread of their commitments.*

> *They are a very small unit and, therefore, one person missing is actually quite crucial and they seem to suffer staff being pulled in and out with monotonous regularity so that they are very easily depleted and that has a very dramatic impact. That combined with our own resource problems means that, and the intake model that we had, means that if you ring up the domestic violence unit and you get the answerphone, the odds are that you bat on without them and that's thoroughly irretrievable in terms of its impact on the case.*

Another practical problem was arranging ongoing work when those involved worked different hours and different shift systems, a finding which confirms Moran-Ellis et al's study (1991). It was generally agreed that social workers would work into the evenings to see through a case begun during the day and police officers were said to have changed their shifts to continue with a specific case. Nonetheless:

> *Sort of typical thing that everybody knows is that you get a referral and then you manage to get a joint interview which is the first time at 4 o'clock on a Friday, then we find that we're well into an interview and that particular officer is working over the weekend and doesn't see why, understandably, doesn't see why everybody else shouldn't and we get our two systems just sliding down the sink.*

> *Another difficulty is the ordinary difficulty of the police working different hours to us, to their shift system needs – it might not be working the same hours during the day, and whether they are or not, it's almost certain that their rota system will mean that they go missing for two or three days during the investigation weeks which means that we have to wait three or four days to get hold of a particular officer whose been involved with the family, or where you might have to wait for ages because he's gone on leave for two or three weeks so there are practical difficulties there.*

While there was considerable goodwill on both sides to work round these problems, they were a recurrent source of frustration and difficulty.

The pressure of work and high turnover of cases in the Special Units was alleged, by some social workers, to have led the police to 'revert to type', a finding also noted by Moran-Ellis et al (1991). The service was said to have deteriorated as the police came under pressure. One social worker gave the following example:

> *[A young girl] started telling the teacher at school, they started telling the youth worker, only dribs and drabs, it's deeply damaging and painful to that girl to disclose. The police were, we actually set up a meeting where we took her down to the Special Unit to be interviewed by one of the women officers there and it went disastrously wrong because I think they were under such a pressure, or that particular officer was under such a pressure, it was about getting the statement, getting it all down and, you know, 'why are you wasting our time?' sort of thing whereas what we had intended, what we really made clear that we wanted to happen, was that this girl was sort of introduced into a non-threatening environment where she was allowed to take her time and develop some trust with the people down there. I'm afraid that didn't happen. She was frightened off . . . she was basically put under pressure to disclose and it all went. I think that shows you how the insensitivity that was resulting from the pressure can easily tip the scale in this sort of case and I think that's where the resource and support has got to come in. The resource has got to be adequate to allow people not to feel under pressure and to take their time, to go at the pace the kids want to go at because, particularly the older girls, or boys for that matter, a disclosure for them is not like a child of four saying 'Daddy did something to me'. They are aware of the consequences.*

Another explained the position as follows:

> *You are just aware that they might not, for instance, be able to devote the time to an investigation that we would wish them to. They have had a tendency to revert to type, I think. When they were set up initially and it was written into the code of practice that there was a need to focus on the needs of the child and all the rest of it and there was a distinct feel that that was being accepted but the sheer weight and volume of cases that they are being hit with means that they have to get some throughput which means that they tend to interview children, take statements and if the information isn't forthcoming then forget that one, move on to the next and that's not really . . . The whole assumption in this kind of joint working arrangement is that you can devote some time and energy to a particular case to enable that child to disclose any information that they may want to*

give and there is a distinct feeling these days that they may have lost sight of that, the police have lost sight of that.

One casualty of the pressure upon resources was sometimes the 'strategy discussion', recommended in Working Together (DHSS and Welsh Office, 1988). A meeting was required by the local procedures in city which read:

> *a strategy meeting involving face to face discussions must take place in every case. The police officer, social worker and, where appropriate, supervisory officers will hold a strategy meeting to reach agreement on a preliminary action plan. Crisis 'doorstep' planning is not acceptable. The strategy meeting may be deferred and replaced by telephone consultation only in exceptional circumstances where it is considered that immediate action is necessary to secure the protection of the child, to secure vital evidence or to prevent the escape of an offender or suspect.*

The tasks of the strategy meeting were to consider the need for action to ensure the safety of the child victim and others at risk; the results of the check of the child protection register and the records of the investigative agencies; the need to consult with others in the interagency network and the arrangements for interviewing informants, victim and the family, for a medical examination, place of safety order, etc. and for the investigation of crime. The procedural guidance in borough was less prescriptive on this issue suggesting that close cooperation especially among the investigating agencies was essential but that strategy meetings should be held in the event of more complex or contentious circumstances.

In practice, strategy meetings were not always held in either authority. This was partly because of pressure of time and resources but there were other reasons, including a lack of confidence and fear on the part of some social workers of losing control and ceding power to the police in such situations. There was also some questioning by the police of the necessity for such a meeting in every case. If cases were particularly complex or sensitive or if the workers did not know each other then a meeting was deemed appropriate but:

> *if they know the social worker and they've had a chat over the phone, then they should be able to meet at the appropriate point. I feel that the arguments for the strategy meeting were to stop the police officer and the social worker turning up separately at the house. You know if you walk in, I've walked in and I've said, you know, 'Are you?' . . . and she's said 'Well, no, I'm the social worker' and it's not good practice, it's not professional. I think you've got to go and be seen as a team rather than two independent people, and I think that should be the philosophy behind it*

> *rather than to sit around for hours on end talking about what you're going to do.*

Nonetheless,

> *I think being experienced in dealing with this type of work doesn't necessarily mean that in every circumstance, set of circumstances, you know what to do and we have great difficulty sometimes making decisions as to how we are going to proceed. The majority of investigations tend to have their own parameters but there are some very difficult decisions to make and I would expect there that we all sit round and talk about it.*

The revised <u>Working Together</u> (1991) appears to reflect this more pragmatic approach advising that 'it is essential that there is an early strategy discussion which may not require a meeting' (Hone Office at al, 1991, p28).

A difference in approach

Behind the very real practical problems some workers saw a more fundamental difference in approach. This was a difference not so much about outcomes but about process, which caused difficulties in collaborative working. Some social workers, while acknowledging the importance of the police role in securing evidence, considered that they, rather than the police, had greater skill in interviewing children and that their more discursive methods were more sensitive and appropriate than those employed by some police officers. As was argued in respect of strategy meetings, the social workers' anxieties were about losing control and the work being undertaken on police terms, and at their pace, as the following quotations illustrate:

> *There is still some uncertainty about who has which role to play and how we play it and whether we go along with them because they're technically the experts in terms of evidence, but when you look at it we're obviously the experts in terms of our expertise in talking to kids but not necessarily maybe in talking to kids in a way that they find appropriate so I think there's a balance that hasn't been struck, we haven't worked together enough to actually work out that balance. I think they're not very good at saying 'let's wait, you know let's hold fire here' and I don't know why that is. I don't know whether that's about police training or whatever but I don't think they are very good at saying 'let's hold on, let's think about what the implications of our presence in this child's home, in this child's school might mean to this child.' I think it's very much I think they hear abuse and they think evidence and they think procedures and they think court and it's quite sequential and I think sometimes we don't have to charge at it. I can think of incidents that have happened where myself and*

another colleague have been up in arms saying, you know, 'we can hold fire, we can do this in a planned way, there is no need to be charging down, you know' and we've frantic calls saying 'we're at the school, be there', you know, we haven't discussed roles we haven't done the plan, we haven't done anything that the procedures say we should do. Even if their procedures were strictly right, but I think it's all new. It's a relatively new unit and we're relatively new at joint working so there's a lot of headway to be made. I think a great sadness is that, as a field worker, you have to have had several experiences with the unit and hopefully several positive experiences before you do feel confident to pick up that phone and know that you are not going to lose control. I think that's a great sadness because that's the reality. I don't think it's just here, it's in other authorities as well.

An NSPCC worker, in a specialist setting in borough, explained the difficulty:

It's actually trying to understand the way that we operate and the way that they operate and we come from two different stances and it doesn't work out so easily in trying to bring those two different disciplines together although we'd agree the common objective is the protection of children but after that then it gets very unclear and I think that I would say that if we were talking about skills that this team holds, we develop significant skills interviewing children, very young children and there are issues in terms of how that can best be maximised. I don't want to present the scenario that there's no good work that goes on, that's not true. There are some good interviews that take place involving social worker and police officer but it always seems to be on police terms.

Joint interviews were perceived as being particularly problematic in cases in which interviews were conducted with young women in the context of allegations of sexual abuse. Part of the police rationale for adopting a 'tough' approach was said to be the need to test the evidence and to reach a view about how the young woman would present and stand up to cross-examination in court. Nonetheless, as social workers explained:

I think there are different ways of dealing particularly with young women who've been abused which are more time-consuming, less clear cut but eventually will arrive at where they want. What's often happened is that their approach has been so abrasive almost that the young person has said 'I don't want anything more to do with that, I don't want to give, I don't trust you, you don't believe what I'm trying to tell you, you think that I'm lying, you think I'm making it up', all this sort of stuff and they refuse and I know there have been young girls who've gone back to abusing situations because of the way the police have handled that.

I don't know whether it will actually improve when children are videoed. I think the actual interviews can be very frustrating because I think they're still very much caught in question and answer statement and I think social workers probably, in general, interview in a much more free-flowing way and let children talk and ramble and go all around the houses and then maybe at the very end you might go back and say 'now could you just tell me a little bit more about this' whereas in the situations I've been in with the police, they may have started 'well yes you were walking down this road' . . . and you can see the child desperately needs to sort of bring it all out in one big burst, and they say 'yes but where was this road' and 'where was that in relation to that' and it stops them in their tracks and I've found that, particularly with teenagers, and I think every joint investigation I've done with teenagers has just descended into utter chaos with the teenagers very quickly saying 'they don't believe me, do they?' because some of the questions have not been the most, they maybe needed to be asked, but they've not been tactful like 'have you had a boyfriend before? are you sure you were just petting and led him on a bit?' and that immediately puts up barriers 'you're blaming me'. And, again, that's frustrating when you're not working closely because by and large they are women police and they work in a very male-dominated hierarchy far more so than women social workers and sometimes I feel maybe they have pressures on them that they have to be almost more manly than male police officers who have nothing to lose.

Quite often their questioning is very rigorous and maybe asking questions of, particularly, teenage girls who may be raped or assaulted that I keep on thinking 'but you must realise how painful this is, you are a woman yourself, all women who have been subjected on one level or another to some sort of sexual abuse in it's widest context you must, surely you must, understand how awkward, painful, embarrassing . . . surely you must understand the dynamics that women immediately think 'it's my fault, I've done something to deserve this' and yet their questioning, as police officers, quite often doesn't reflect that and I found that a real problem and I know other social workers have, particulary with teenage girls, who are often assumed to be liars, fickle, promiscuous, giddy etc, etc, and, that more than younger children, can be very frustrating.

These views about the interviewing of young women in the context of sexual abuse offer some confirmation of the findings of Blagg and Stubbs (1988) and Horley (1988(a) and (b)) that, despite some improvements in recent years, work remains to be done in developing the attitudes and skills of police officers to undertake this task sensitively and effectively.

The outcomes of police involvement

As was discussed above, police involvement in the investigation of child abuse was extensive, both in the sense of their notification of allegations or suspicions in many, although not all cases, and in their routine attendance at child protection conferences (discussed in Chapter Seven). The outcomes of the police involvement in terms of the decisions and actions taken following investigation are discussed here.

The revised Working Together (1991) outlines the police role as follows:

> *Police involvement in cases of child abuse stems from their primary responsibilities to protect the community and to bring offenders to justice. Their overriding consideration is the welfare of the child. In the spirit of* Working Together, *the police focus will be to determine whether a criminal offence has been committed, to identify the person or persons responsible and to secure the best possible evidence in order that appropriate consideration can be given as to whether criminal proceedings should be instituted,* (Home Office at al, 1991, p16).

The Government guidance goes on to outline the factors to be taken into account in deciding whether to prosecute:

> *The decision whether or not criminal proceedings should be initiated will be based on three main factors: whether or not there is sufficient substantial evidence to prosecute; whether it is in the public interest that proceedings should be instigated against a particular offender, and whether or not it is in the interests of the child victim that proceedings should be instituted,* (Home Office at al, 1991, p16).

The ordering of these is interesting, given the primacy accorded to the welfare of the child earlier in the paragraph. A child welfare orientation is even more marked in the central government guidance issued to the police in 1988, in a Home Office Circular entitled The Investigation of Child Sexual Abuse. It concluded:

> *It is essential that all professional agencies concerned with the protection and welfare of children work together in harmony and towards a common goal. . . . the success of the police intervention . . . is not to be measured in terms of the prosecutions which are brought, but of the protection which their actions bring to children at risk* (Home Office, 1988, p10).

The case sample

As reported in Chapter Four, in 16 cases the social services department conducted the initial investigation alone, and the police were involved at a subsequent stage. In the reamining 32 cases (66%) there was either a joint investigation or the police undertook the initial investigation alone. The outcomes of their involvement in the 48 cases is shown in Table 5.1.

Table 5.1. **Outcomes of police involvement in the registered cases**

	Borough	City	N
No police investigation	7	9	16
Investigation and no further action	10	5	15
Police caution	2	–	2
Referral to Crown Prosecution service – no prosecution	1	2	3
Prosecution	3	9	12
	23	25	48

In appraising these figures it is important to emphasise that the case sample comprised registered cases which are, by definition, those considered most serious, requiring a multi-agency protection plan for the child, and/or those in which the evidence is clear-cut. Even so, there was a prosecution in only twelve cases. Nine of the prosecutions were in city and three in borough. Of these twelve prosecuted cases, seven were sexual abuse cases and five involved physical abuse. The outcomes are shown in Figure 5.3. The length of prison sentence was recorded on the social services file in five of the seven cases where custodial sentences were imposed; the average length of sentence was two years and two months. So, in seven of the 48 registered cases, police involvement led to the imprisonment of the abuser, in most cases for approximately two years.

Figure 5.3 **Outcome of prosecutions (N = 12)**

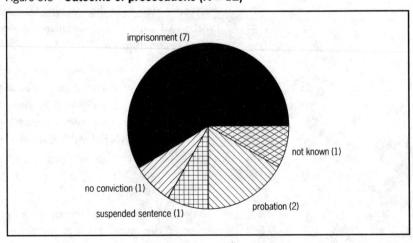

Although the numbers are very small, the prosecution rate in the case sample is higher in city (36%) than in borough (13%). It is unclear whether this is due to different operational philosophies in the two police services, to clearer medical findings in city than in borough, to the interviewing skills of the police officers concerned, to other reasons or whether the finding would change with a larger case sample. To clarify this, information was sought on this issue in both police authorities, but it was supplied only by the police authority in whose boundaries borough was situated. This revealed that the outcome of police involvement in all child abuse referrals in the police authority in 1989 and 1990 was as shown in Table 5.2.

Table 5.2.   **Outcome of police investigations of referrals of child abuse in one police authority**

	1989	1990
	No. of referrals	**No. of referrals**
No further action	2214 (72%)	2469 (62%)
Caution	181 (6%)	223 (6%)
Prosecution	436 (14%)	251 (6%)
Outstanding at the year end	234 (8%)	1008 (26%)
	3065 (100%)	3951 (100%)

The rate of no further action (72% in 1989 and 62%) is similar to the rate (63%) in the case sample in borough; as is the prosecution rate (at 15% in 1989 and 6% in 1990) and 13% in the case sample. These figures are broadly comparable with those reported by Moran-Ellis et al (1991) who in a study of outcomes of investigations of sexual abuse cases only in 1989 and 1990 found prosecution rates of 12% in one research site and 7% in another. Creighton's (1992) study reported that criminal proceedings occurred in 17% of registered sexual abuse cases in the sample of 1,732 and in 9% of the sample of 2,786 physical abuse cases in 1988–90, a combined rate of 12%. The contribution of law enforcement to the protection of children is discussed further below.

The exercise of police discretion

Police decision-making in respect of child abuse, the difficulties of balancing potentially or actually competing interests and the response of other professionals to police actions in cases of child abuse were explored in interviews.

First, in decisions about prosecutions, a distinction was made between sexual abuse and physical abuse. In general, sexual abuse was viewed more seriously by the police and, it was said, by the courts. This reflects both broader societal attitudes and the views of other professionals working in the system. The responses to brief vignettes concerning potentially abusive situations used in Birchall's study indicated that cases involving sexual activities with children were ranked as more serious by the professionals concerned (Birchall, 1992). Finkelhor (1992) has contrasted the particular characteristics of the sexual abuse of children and the societal reactions it provokes with the response to other forms of child maltreatment. Similar points were made in the UK (Campbell, 1988) during and after the events in Cleveland.

The consequence of this for decisions concerning prosecutions was that the quality of evidence appeared to be the overriding consideration. If the evidence were good enough in cases of sexual abuse, offenders would be prosecuted, at least if they were adults. It seemed to be taken for granted that this would also be in the public interest and in the interest of the child victim. The position was said to be as in the following quotations, from police officers:

> *Sexual abuse, it's more likely that, well, the seriousness of the offence is one thing that's worked in consideration and a sexual offence against a young girl or a young boy for that matter is a serious offence so we're starting at a different level then, very much so.*

> *In a small proportion you get very good evidence. You know, children perhaps seven and over, children that you can get to court . . . and if there is evidence then we'll put it to court;*

The position was rather different in respect of physical abuse. As noted above, some cases of physical injury were investigated by the social services department, some by the police alone and in others, usually cases of more serious injury, joint investigations occurred. The police appeared to exercise much more discretion over decisions to instigate proceedings or to recommend prosecution in such cases. In making such decisions, more emphasis was placed upon the impact of prosecution on the family, and on the child, than appeared routinely to be the case in respect of sexual abuse. Except in cases of serious physical assault, such cases were lower down the tariff and more discussion was likely to take place between social services and the police in respect of decisions concerning prosecution and the likely consequences. The nature of the offence, the motivation of the abuser, the willingness, or otherwise, to accept voluntary social services intervention, and the interests of the child were reported to be important considerations. So was the predicted value for the future protection of children of having abusers clearly identified in police records as Schedule 1 offenders. Police officers gave some examples:

> *I would look to what we know about the family, background of the family, the information coming from other parties involved as to whether it appeared to be a one off. What the reasons were for the incident and the reaction of the family to the incident and what sort of input was going to be made to the family whether there's a prosecution or not. They're the sort of areas that I'd be looking at. If we got a situation whereby a youngster had been assaulted by her father and all the background details were good, there had been no concerns in the past, the injury although it's bruising perhaps is not overly severe and it was because the youngster had been such a difficult child and this was coming from the school and the health worker and so on, then that's the sort of case where I'd be erring against a prosecution.*

> *But it can be difficult sometimes finding the right balance of it, make no bones of that. What do you look for? You look for a lot of things: the background of the family, how they have accepted social work input which must have taken place by that time. Again I'll just give you another example where I've just argued on the side of verbal caution where a young girl, she is fourteen years of age, started drinking, the father took a belt to her and caused bad bruising on her buttocks. I didn't see that a prosecution there would help them. The social workers had been involved with the family and when I spoke to them, before I actually made my recommendation, the social worker had said we've been talking about how to deal with the child and what have you, and that social worker was quite happy that some progress had been made and they realised the seriousness of the offence and were working with them to make sure it didn't happen again.*

> *It may be, in the long run, that to proceed would be contrary to the best interests of the child. It may be over-chastisement, that's the typical thing where you've got a kid with a bruised bum and obviously you've got an assault . . . It's an assault and that's it but now we think, under the circumstances, was she justified in slapping the kid? If the answer to that is yes, but did she just hit him a little too hard? Maybe she did but does that mean to say that we've got to take her to court. She's very probably a very caring parent but she's just overstepped – she's gone over that very thin line between justifiable chastisement and assault, you see. So yes, it's an assault but no, we don't think we ought to prosecute.*

> *There are times when, although the actual offence itself, in isolation, is not that great, looking to the future, might it be useful if we have a conviction for this person which makes them a Schedule 1 offender. That is sometimes a difficult area that. I can just recall one for instance where a lad*

who assaulted a young baby, whilst babysitting. The lad was a little retarded, the injuries were not that great but, having said that, any assault on I think it was something like a three or four month old baby is serious. There was no chance that he would reoffend against that youngster because the family had made sure of that following the incident. What people were saying was that really a verbal caution would be appropriate because that youngster had been safeguarded. My concern was that the young man obviously had difficulties in, you know, being able to parent a young person. It might be that in a couple of years time he got married and had a youngster himself. If things started to go wrong there, at a fairly early stage, we might need some intervention; a) a conviction stays on his record longer than the verbal caution and b) it gives us a little bit more ammunition should we need it. So, in that case, there I was arguing for a prosecution, not particularly to have that lad punished but simply as a marker for future information and action if needs be. The fact that someone is recorded as a Schedule 1 offender does give us a lever on certain occasions.

The exercise of police discretion in such cases was said by some social workers occasionally to cause problems since it was, by its nature, unpredictable as situational judgements had to be made in specific cases. As a police officer explained:

But it's not always an easy decision to make and I'm quite sure that there'll be some cases where I'll be recommending a prosecution and my counterpart on the other side of the city would be giving the other advice. I'm not saying very frequently but there would be times, I'm sure.

The police were keen to stress their dual role in child protection and in the detection and prosecution of crime. They placed the emphasis on competent investigation and securing the best evidence in order to establish what had occurred and to prosecute, if appropriate, but there was some tension and ambivalence in the role, as the following quotations illustrate:

In the main, you know, I'm satisfied because alright we've only got 13% of the referrals into court, investigations to court, but in one of the Home Office circulars, it says that the performance of the police isn't to be measured in terms of how many people we get convicted and that would be wrong. It's got to be measured in terms of how many children are protected and are we protecting children adequately? Because that's another thing that comes across to you, people's morale dips if we don't win that often so it's good for morale when we win. But the officers know, and this is an important point that I stress greatly on training courses that it's important to do a very thorough investigation but sometimes you just can't win. The cards are stacked up against us so much but the main thing is that the child must win, you know, and they accept that I think.

We're here to present the best evidence, to make a decision on that, ie whether we don't think it's abuse or we do think it's abuse and we've enough evidence to put it to court and that's up to us. That's what we're all about, and I see our role very clearly as that and if you can get those aspects right then I think you will be achieving some success for the department because I don't measure success on the number of convictions.

For this police officer, part of the success of conducting a good investigation was obtaining evidence:

In a way that is not harmful to the child and family . . . when you're dealing with this sort of work you soon realise that you are not just into the investigation of crime, you're into something else, another area, ie children and their welfare.

The difficulties in securing good enough evidence, particularly in cases of child sexual abuse, were profound and a source of frustration to both police and social workers. The formidable problems faced by children in speaking about sexual abuse were acknowledged as were the difficulties of securing medical evidence in such cases. In some, of course, no medical evidence would be expected from the nature of the reported abuse. In many cases the evidence was the uncorroborated evidence of a child ranged against the denial of the alleged abuser and:

usually, I'm sorry to say, if a person exercises his right to silence that usually there's no evidence.

There were cases in the case sample and many more examples from interviews where the police, social workers and, when appropriate, the doctors were convinced that abuse had occurred but it was not possible to prosecute.

You've got the word of the child against the adult and, it seems to me, not the police but the courts are needing more than that. They're wanting medical evidence or somebody actually has seen it, preferably an adult and videoed it while they've been doing it. It's that, and that is a frustration for me and my colleagues in the police unit, and we are able to share that. The police will say 'yes something has happened here but the chances of getting a successful prosecution are zilch', and that's a frustration for us both.

Some social workers complained that the police did not push hard enough for evidence or that police interviewing styles and the pressure of work in the Special Units militated against getting the best possible evidence:

I think, in some instances, if they actually allowed the children time then I think, they may – I'm not saying they would – but they are more likely to get evidence

I quite often come away thinking they haven't done enough, they haven't investigated enough and because, like the other day there was a case conference on a family where it was quite clear from what these little people were saying, that they'd been sexually abused by their uncle but their uncle had got learning difficulties and the policewoman was saying we had to explain to him what sex was and, even then, he couldn't answer the questions and so they just let it go. Almost, almost I was thinking, okay these kids no longer have access to this man but that doesn't stop him from going out there and doing it to anybody else . . . I didn't feel very happy about that because I felt that maybe they could have pushed this guy more and, on some levels, it never feels like enough, you know, with the amount of kids that you see and the amount of perpetrators who actually get done for it.

More common than complaints about the police not pursuing investigations with sufficient vigour, however, was a shared frustration between social workers and the police that the Crown Prosecution Service (CPS) would not pursue proceedings. This is confirmed by the findings in Moran-Ellis at al's (1991) study that 67% of the police reported disagreements with the CPS over decisions about prosecutions or the speed with which the case was processed. The evidential requirement in criminal cases is proof beyond reasonable doubt that the person accused has committed the offence (as opposed to the balance of probabilities required in civil courts). The CPS is required to appraise the evidence and only to pursue cases if there is a reasonable chance of securing a conviction. They are also required to consider whether prosecution is in the public interest. Police views concerning decisions taken by the CPS in child abuse cases varied. One said:

We are at variance. We are often at variance . . . in general, not only specifically in child abuse. It seems that we would prosecute when they wouldn't. We are dismayed on occasions, shall we say that.

A social worker agreed:

We normally find that it's not the police that we disagree with it's the CPS but I think that the officers at the Special Unit have actually broken new ground and have consciously, on some occasions, said 'right, this is the sort of case where we would expect CPS to be saying it's dodgy we don't want to take it, we're going to push it to them and see if we can change their minds on it' so they have done that on some occasions which has been good.

One police officer explained the position as follows:

> *You see I can understand the contraints placed upon the CPS and the guidelines that they have to take into account . . . when they are making a decision as to prosecution. Are we likely to secure a conviction? There is the fifty fifty rule, have we got a fifty fifty chance of getting it home. Also there's a bit of personal pride in it. . . . how many do they take to court and how many do they get home. We all like to have high returns I suppose. I have an argument about rape and child abuse to a certain extent, that it should be the right of the woman if she wants to go and give evidence and make that allegation, let the jury decide. You see they recommend off paper, do the Crown Prosecution Service. They just see a file and you can't get a feeling out of paper. When a woman stands up at court, or a child, and gives evidence it's not just what she says, it's how they say it. That's a very important part, I think, of people giving evidence. From an officers point of view, they know that woman or that child is telling the truth or they're pretty much convinced they are and, for it then not to go anywhere, they feel that they're letting the client down and the justice goes out of the window perhaps if an abuser or a rapist got away with it by not even having to stand trial, it's very, very frustrating. It's like cricket if you don't go and have a bat you won't score any runs.*

However, another reported that:

> *We don't have problems with CPS in the main. We have specialised work solicitors in CPS who we relate directly to and they are very good and very supportive obviously of the cases and if there is evidence then we'll put it to court and we get even uncorroborated accounts to court now.*

The potential for criminal proceedings to further traumatise the child is well recognised (King and Trowell 1992, Jones and McQuiston 1988, Flin and Tarrant 1989), and likely to remain problematic despite changes such as the acceptance of video recordings for the child's evidence-in-chief and the use of screens in court. The impact on the child of having to give evidence was reported to be considered both by the police and the CPS, as the following quotations illustrate:

> *I normally send them through with the evidence that is presented to let them make the decision but I do give guidance as to the witness. I believe that some of the witnesses who are truthful, I can't stress that enough that I do believe the witnesses, but I feel they won't stand up to court and I give that guidance, if I feel sure. You know some people feel so strongly about going to court and airing their story and they're not really bothered about how they're treated in court but it's a traumatic experience, it really is. I wouldn't want my children to go through it.*

> *They do take that into account, what's in the best interests of the child. In other words, having this child stand up and give evidence could be worse and I'm very conscious of that as well. The officers are, you know, it could well be worse for the job to go to court, it could have a worse effect on the child than to just let it ride and, you know, what concerns me there though is that there might be an abuser there who's still at large.*

The consequences of decisions not to prosecute (or, more rarely, cases in which prosecutions had been unsuccessful and convictions had not been secured) were said to be serious, both at individual and societal levels. Unsurprisingly, those individuals suspected of abuse were likely to construe decisions not to prosecute (or the failure to secure a conviction) as confirmation of their innocence.

> *I think that when files comes back from the CPS and it says 'no charges' that will temporarily make our job more difficult because they will be saying things like 'well see, we told you she hadn't done it.' Actually getting through to people the difference between the different burden of proof, of evidential proof, is quite difficult.*

> *Yes. If there has been a problem, it's been problems where there hasn't been a prosecution where, in my view, that's given a false message to the family and the family or the perpetrator has chosen to interpret it that way. They've been able to say either it was only a caution, as people do, and caution isn't quite guilty is it? Or it wasn't followed through in those situations where there's been enough proof to satisfy a juvenile court, a civil court, but in terms of CPS they've said it's not worth the effort and that's certainly difficult.*

On a societal level, some argued in favour of the effect of prosecution as a deterrent, and as a demonstration of the community's abhorrence of the abuse of children:

> *Human nature is such that people will, I'm not saying that all people will but a lot will, do things if they don't think there'll be any comeback on them and that's why I think it's important that we investigate. I don't think we can decriminalise this sort of behaviour, I mean what sort of society would allow this to happen anyway?*

The importance of securing convictions in some cases so that people could be identified in future as Schedule 1 offenders was acknowledged by both the police and social workers.

A social work manager commented as follows:

> *I think we see the value in offenders being removed from a situation if at all*

possible but also having people labelled as Schedule 1 offenders. It's a pretty blunt instrument as a way of dealing with child protection but at least it gives us some kind of marker on people who are worrying and we always case conference on Schedule 1 offenders, if we have some. So it's a check for us but, unless you've got somebody who's a Schedule 1 offender, you don't always have the grounds to have a case conference and also necessarily the grounds to remove the child if it seems right. So it's important wherever there is a serious injury, if at all possible, to get a conviction. We're not usually saying to the police 'don't take this one away and prosecute'. We're happy to let them make the judgement and sometimes we encourage them to do that.

The absence of a record of Schedule 1 offences was said to be a drawback when the police used cautions, which occurred usually in cases of physical rather than sexual abuse. They were used to demonstrate to abusers that assaulting children was a criminal offence and were said to have a role to play in helping people change their behaviour, putting up a marker that similar actions in future could have serious consequences.

Most social workers, in both authorities, said that they rarely disagreed with police views and actions in cases in which they had initiated proceedings or decided that they would seek prosecution. Comments such as 'we don't have too much difficulty' were typical, and were shared by others such as teachers and health visitors in the interagency network. A general practitioner commented:

Yes, I mean I do feel a bit uncomfortable when the police are there at case conferences and knowing that somebody could be arrested as a result of what you say. Then so they should be if they're guilty. Obviously people in a stressful situation, depressed, with family problems you can sort of understand it. But then plenty of people are in that situation and don't hit their kids, so.

In general, it appears that few decisions to prosecute were taken in the face of advice from social workers or others that such action would be harmful or counter-productive. On the contrary, some social workers argued that they wished to see more rather than less prosecutions:

I am reasonably happy with the outcomes. I'm reasonably happy. If anything, they're on the side of liberalness. The situations where there's been a debate about whether there's any point in prosecution, by and large, the debate hasn't been a polarised one where it's involved certain types of police saying a cop's a cop and a crime's a crime and social workers saying 'well, there were extenuating circumstances and will it help the family?' It's not been that sort of stereotype, it's been an open debate and, on occasions, we've asked them to prosecute. They've been quite happy to say caution and we've said no, prosecution would actually be beneficial in our view in terms of ongoing protection.

I can't really think of a case where we've said 'well we don't want to prosecute in this case' and they've gone off and arrested and prosecuted. Usually it's been more the case that we've wanted to prosecute and they haven't. They felt that there wasn't evidence. I think that, you know, there's a popular view that social workers are over-soft and gullible and wishy-washy, and it doesn't hold good really. Generally most social workers wish these matters to go to court.

No, no I don't think any of the cases that I've worked on jointly with the police have been prosecuted. I mean some quite rightly but some I've disagreed with. Shall I give you an example of what I find unsatisfactory? I had a case recently where the child was quite badly knocked about by his father, very extensive bruising and photographs, and the police got photographs, they interviewed him and got photographs. Quite clear bruising that he admitted to on the child's buttocks, very severe bruising on his buttocks, and he admitted to it and they didn't prosecute because they said they wouldn't get a conviction, because they felt the court would not convict, even though he admitted, it they would be likely to say 'oh well it was probably a one off'. Well, from my point of view, that was a serious decision they made because it was giving him the wrong message. It was giving him the message 'it's not serious'. Whilst at the same time we're going for care proceedings, got our care order upheld but the police hadn't prosecuted so the father was able to say 'even the police didn't think it was serious', so I was disgruntled about that. But on other occasions, within the context of police follow-up to joint working, there probably hasn't been enough to prosecute with and perhaps there wouldn't have been a good reason to. It wouldn't have done anybody any favours to do so.

This is awful, you can feel it's inevitable that's why I said about the child protection procedures not really being set up to protect children because you have the procedures on this side and you have a criminal justice system which actually does very little about men who do things that they shouldn't, and what we end up doing is punishing the woman and the children all the time and we end up picking up the ricochet of all that and the men go and move on, find another family and do it all over again. So it feels like an inevitability. It's, I'm best putting my energy into getting women to protect themselves and their kids rather than – I used to get very, very angry about it but six years has taught me.

There were several reasons for wanting an increased rate of prosecution. Some spoke of the importance of prosecution in demonstrating societal disapproval and the seriousness of certain behaviours, particularly in cases of physical abuse which, as noted above, were less likely to be prosecuted than sexual abuse.

> *I think sometimes when it's a minor thing, if the police took it more seriously, this might sound a bit topsy turvey to you but the people honestly believe that they can hit their children and mark them and nobody can do anything about it and that's quite common. They seem to think that if you bruise a child it's not actually assault and I think, in some families, sometimes the police, I don't mean they would be more heavy but just make people more aware that they have actually committed a criminal offence in doing that. I mean I don't know if that would act as a deterrent but I've had times when I've thought, well they won't listen to you the people, maybe they would just sort of take note of the police. You could end up in serious trouble but people don't seem to believe that. It's got to be a fairly serious offence, a serious assault on a child for any criminal proceedings to be taken but with a sexual offence it tends to go straight up and back, bang, locked away it's serious straight away.*

Others commented on the therapeutic value of prosecution in that it helped validate for the child that what had happened was wrong, is recognised by society as such and that they are not to blame, as suggested for example by Terr (1986) and Flin (1988). As social workers remarked:

> *Because, in terms of child protection, that is as valid as five years of case work sometimes, especially for young girls who have been sexually abused. What they go through is seen as punishment but the offender gets off scot free unless he's taken to court and that I know, in several situations, it's been really very important for them to see the offender, even if it's a relative, punished in some way, that's crucial.*

> *I think my criteria are very definite in respect of the crimes being committed and they should face the consequences of that. I still think there's a debate and dilemma where children say and they, you know, are obviously anxious about 'I don't want this person to go to court and I caused this', and it's about quite clearly explaining if I break a window the police are going to come and I'm probably going to get a fine for that because we know there's a tariff system and we know what's going to happen and I think once you explain that to children that people who commit these sort of offences they are adults, they know what the outcome is going to be and they're taking the risk of that outcome and that we have a law in our society to keep law and order so, as much as that's going to cause you some anxiety, it's not you who's doing that it's the law by which society's standards are upheld, that often helps.*

As suggested earlier in the chapter, some saw prosecution as being in the public interest in protecting potential future victims, if only temporarily, from abuse and some also valued the clear identification of abusers as Schedule 1 offenders in terms of an increased capacity to protect children in the future.

> *I feel, generally, that male abusers have to go to court. It's more difficult to get them to admit in the first place and I think the ones that do admit have to go to court. I'm quite clear about that. I think we have to have in most situations, we have to have a conviction which gives us the firm basis for saying 'I'm sorry, you know, you are convicted, you have done it'*

The general view, from social workers then, concerning prosecution was that they rarely disagreed with police decisions to prosecute. A more widespread concern was that, while acknowledging the evidential difficulties, they wished to see higher rates of prosecution. As was made clear above, this applied particularly in some cases of physical injury where evidence was often available but they perceived a reluctance to prosecute. This study, therefore, offered little support for the emphasis on prosecution which characterised police involvement in child abuse in the 1970s (Mounsey, 1975, Wedlake, 1978).

There were, however, important exceptions to this majority view and a few social workers articulated a case for less involvement by the police and criminal justice system, at least in its current form, in child protection. For some, this was based on the view that imprisonment, the usual outcome of conviction particularly in child sexual abuse, did little, if anything, to help abusers change their behaviour. While imprisonment provided some temporary protection to potential victims, the offenders would, sooner or later, be released, often to offend again. Furthermore some argued, since imprisonment was the very probable outcome of admitting abuse, abusers were deterred from seeking help and prevented from seeking access to services/therapy which might help them to control or change their behaviour. Three of those interviewed referred to systems elsewhere, for example in Holland and Belgium where a more therapeutic approach was in operation with a much more restricted role for the criminal justice system.

> *To my thinking, it shuts the door on any possibility of communication with the abuser. I've taken over a case from my colleague and I know full well that there is no way in which that stepfather could ever admit the slightest bit of inclination to sexual abuse because it puts himself in prison and that seems to be an enormous block to really helping the family, even helping an abuser. There are things which strike me as working very badly and there do appear to be other ways of handling investigation, evidence etc, in different parts, the United States, for example, which seems to be more effective in reaching the end of (a) stopping the person abusing*

*children, other people's children, anybody, and (b) helping the abused get
over the effect of the abuse.*

The tensions between clinical and legal approaches to interviewing children
have caused widespread concern in recent years, as evidenced in the
Cleveland and Orkney inquiries and in the practice literature (Glaser and
Frosh, 1988, Jones and McQuiston, 1988, Sgroi, 1982). In this reseach study,
a number referred to the harmful effects on children of evidential interviews
required by the criminal justice system. This was said to interfere with an
outright therapeutic approach from the very beginning and prevented work
to enable children to talk about their experiences (including leading them to
do so as appropriate) and direct work with them to help them cope with their
stress, while decisions as to prosecution or court cases were pending.

> *I'm concerned about the way in which clarity of taking evidence, of not
> interfering with the clarity of evidence holds up therapeutic work, holds up
> the process of our actually personally dealing with the kids. In this case, for
> example, apart from the initial interview or interviews by the police, there
> could be no further discussion with the children about any of those issues
> that came up, like their sexual abuse, at least until after it had been
> decided whether to go ahead with any prosecution. The Crown Prosecu-
> tion Service took five months to reach that decision. Now what concerns
> me is that, because there is this heavy overlay of getting the evidence,
> getting a prosecution, getting all of these things in the criminal justice
> system, it runs a danger of delaying the process of actually personally
> dealing with the sufferer, the abused person.*

A very few raised more profound questions about whether child abuse was
better conceptualised as a symptom of individual or family malfunctioning or
as a crime. One, a senior manager in a social services department, spoke of the
consequences of the criminalisation of abuse:

> *All I do know is that some kinds of social work intervention can be very
> damaging however carefully you do them and, in particular, the interven-
> tion where there has been intrafamilial abuse because we have criminalised
> it, we do have processes about justice and we do have external interven-
> tions that can't be controlled and, inevitably, in that situation parents,
> particularly, have to make choices either for a spouse or a child to
> understand and forgive and to help or to punish and reject and betray and
> those are impossible very basic emotions. The problem about the British
> system, and about criminalising this, is that once that process has started
> there is no alternative but to continue into the criminal arena where the
> assumptions are tested and where, all of a sudden, the needs of the child
> are of infinitely less significance than the interests of justice.*

Another social worker was grappling with the complexities.

I think that would depend on where you saw the origin of child abuse being. How much you saw people doing it purposely or unconsciously which, again, is going to depend on how you, yes, interpret, how you interpret why you think people do it.

Whether, like one of the fears we've sometimes chucked around here is about having the computer, having the register on a computer and whether that's actually going to be broken into by the paedophile rings, who, from the stereotypes that we're given of them are quite clearly purposely gathering information to purposely abuse the kids and the adults that get involved with them and, in that respect, that is criminal for want of a better word. Whereas I also work with people who are abusive because they don't know any other way to behave and I don't know whether criminalisation's the right thing. Unlless you actually get people to understand where their abilities are to be a perpetrator and to be a victim and that they have control over those. I'm not sure that criminalising them is the way to do that but what I wouldn't go for is the legitimisation of so called consensual sex between adults and kids, no I don't, I'm not sure about it at all; it doesn't feel right because kids just don't have the power to make those sorts of decisions.

Summary

It should be emphasised, however, that those speaking in these terms were in a minority. For the majority of those in the interprofessional network, the role of the police in the investigation of child abuse was accepted as important and interprofessional relationships, although at times strained, for logistical reasons, were not characterised by deep and entrenched conflict, as is discussed more fully in Chapter Eleven. It appeared that, in general, at least for cases of sexual abuse and for the minority of cases of physical abuse involving serious injuries, there was an effective routinised exchange of information in both directions between the two services. While there were expected and occasional lapses from the procedural requirements to inform each other, information was considered to pass in a timely and appropriate way in most cases.

In joint investigation involving the police and social workers a more radical form of coordination was involved. This required interagency cooperation in planning the investigation and agreeing a division of labour and, most difficult of all, close collaboration when children were interviewed jointly. The study revealed that joint interviewing of children occurred relatively infrequently in the case sample. It was affected by logistical considerations, including staff shortages, but also by the lack of formal specialisation in child protection work among the social workers. This had important consequences for their ability to develop skill, confidence and competence in the work and to undertake joint training with the police which contributed to a degree of familiarity and trust, revealed to be important in working together on this task. The experience, greater training opportunities and confidence engendered in the work of child protection by the deployment of police in specialist units contrasted with the position for many social workers. It was, however, clear that there were anxieties for some social workers that, for varied reasons, close collaboration with the police in initial investigation could lead to a dominance of a police view and police ways of working which some saw as inappropriate and, at times, as unhelpful to children. There was a fear of a loss of organisational autonomy and of control of the case on the part of social workers. Nonetheless, a dominant finding is of improved and improving working relationships between the two services in recent years.

The study also revealed the limited outcomes of police involvement in terms of the prosecution and conviction of alleged abusers. The problems of securing good enough evidence were acknowledged by the police and social workers and others in the interagency network, many of whom wished to see higher rates of prosecution than were achieved. Interagency decision-making on this matter was generally characterised by consensus rather than dissent and there was very little evidence for the stereotypical view of the police wishing to prosecute against the advice of others in the interagency network.

Chapter 6

Medical assessment

The role of physical medicine was central in the rediscovery of the problem of physical abuse of children, both the work of paediatric radiologists such as Caffey, and paediatricians, notably Kempe (Parton, 1985, Pfohl, 1977). The recognition of sexual abuse posed some challenge to the medical certainty and dominance of earlier years, with disputes about the interpretation of clinical findings in some cases and the absence of any physical signs of abuse in others. In this situation, the role of the police took on increasing prominence, as discussed in the previous chapter. Following Cleveland, the government advised in *Working Together* (DHSS and Welsh Office, 1988) that 'the investigation of child abuse or risk of child abuse always requires both social and medical assessment'. This phrase was incorporated in the procedures manuals in both borough and city. In this chapter the medical contribution to the investigation and assessment of child abuse is discussed, drawing on data from the case sample and from interviews with a few of the examining doctors and others in the interagency network with whom they worked.

The local facilities and arrangements for medical examinations varied between borough and city. In borough the work was mainly divided between the local paediatricians and a woman police surgeon, with the former seeing cases of physical injury and the latter sexual abuse. The paediatric service was provided by three consultant paediatricians, all male, based in the district general hospital located in the main town in the authority. Partly, but not exclusively, because of the distance of some areas from this hospital, there was a more extensive involvement of general practitioners in the examination of children in borough. In city, by contrast, the work (at least for pre-pubertal children, the focus of this study) was more closely concentrated in the hands of paediatricians who were located on two sites in the city, at a children's hospital with its own accident and emergency department and at a general hospital.

Medical examinations were recorded in the social services department file as having been carried out in 42 (88%) of the cases in the sample of registered cases of primary school age children, as is shown in Figure 6.1. The patterns were very similar in city and borough, as is shown in Figure 6.2. In four cases there was no medical examination. Three involved Schedule 1 offenders who had moved into or returned to homes in which there were children but there were no specific allegations of contemporary assaults necessitating examination; another case involved concern for the younger siblings of a young woman who disclosed sexual abuse having taken place a long while earlier. In the remaining two cases it was unclear from the file whether any medical

Figure 6.1 **Cases in which there was a medical examination of the child (N = 48)**

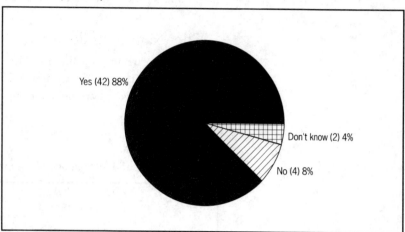

Figure 6.2 **Cases in which there was a medical examination of the child: borough and city compared (N = 48)**

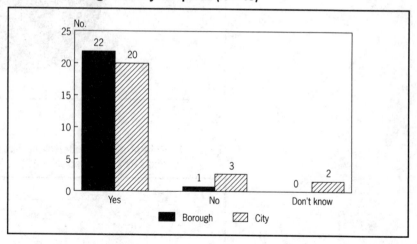

examination had been carried out in connection with the registration episode. One was an allegation of child sexual abuse by a neighbour said to have occurred six months previously. The second was a case of physical injury where the initial investigation was undertaken by police officers called to the house by a mother alleging that her cohabitee had kicked her son in the course of a domestic dispute. The cohabitee admitted assault, was arrested and reported on summons. Nine days elapsed before the referral reached the social services department and although it appeared that the mother had been advised by the police to visit her general practitioner the next day and may have done so, there was no record of a medical examination on the file.

The examining doctors

The persons carrying out the *initial* medical examinations are presented in Figure 6.3 for the sample as a whole and for each authority separately reflecting the different arrangements in Figure 6.4.

Figure 6.3 **Role of doctor undertaking *initial* medical examination (N = 42)**

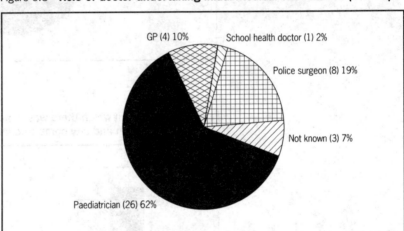

Figure 6.4 **Role of doctor undertaking *initial* medical examination: borough and city compared (N = 42)**

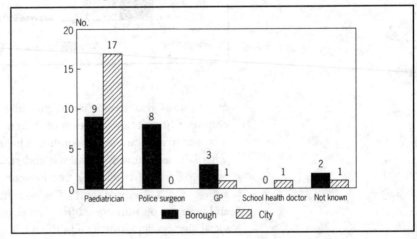

Only four children in the sample of registered cases were examined by their general practitioner in connection with the abusive incident, confirming Staltmeir and Mackenzie's (1987) finding in a study in Tower Hamlets, and only one child was examined by a clinical medical officer, a school health doctor. This reflected wider practice in both city and borough, where the involvement of clinical medical officers in the medical assessment of children suspected of child abuse was minimal, as it was also revealed to be in Birchall's (1992) study.

The number of examinations

In the interests of children, an important objective of interagency cooperation in recent years, emphasised particularly in cases of sexual abuse, has been to minimise the number of medical examinations performed in each case, and to ensure they are conducted with sensitivity and in appropriate locations. The number of medical examinations per case in the case sample is shown in Figure 6.5.

Figure 6.5 **Number of medical examinations per case (N = 42)**

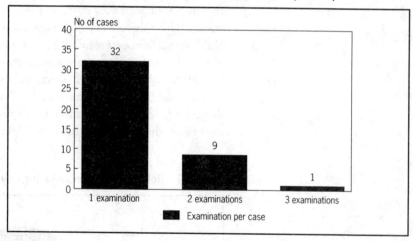

In about threequarters of the registered cases in the sample, where a medical examination was undertaken, only one was required, two were carried out in about a fifth of the cases and, in one case, three. The patterns were broadly similar in borough and city as is shown in Figure 6.6 with borough achieving a slightly higher proportion of single medicals.

Of the cases requiring two medical examinations, four were cases of physical abuse in which the general practitioner was initially contacted by the parent(s). In one case the general practitioner had arranged overnight admission to hospital of the child where he was seen by a paediatrician, and in the others subsequent paediatric assessment had been organised by the

Figure 6.6 **Number of medical examinations per case: borough and city compared (N = 42)**

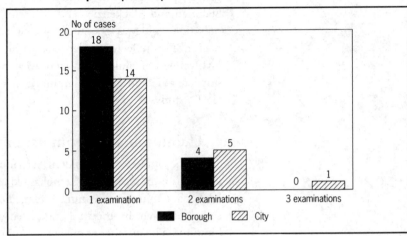

investigating agencies. In two other cases of sexual abuse, the child was seen first by junior paediatric staff and then re-examined by a consultant paediatrician. The only case in which a child was examined three times was a case of child sexual abuse presented by the mother to hospital in which three paediatric examinations were recorded as having been carried out on three successive days while the child was in hospital.

These additional examinations involved eleven more doctors and their distribution can be compared in Figures 6.7 and 6.8 with those who undertook the initial examinations (Figures 6.3 and 6.4).

Figure 6.7 **Role of doctor undertaking any examination (N = 53)**

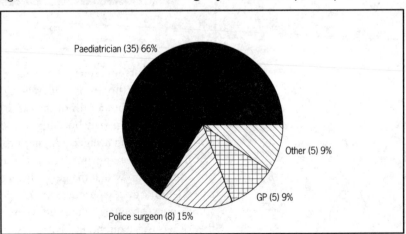

Figure 6.8   **Role of doctor undertaking any examination: borough and city compared (N = 53)**

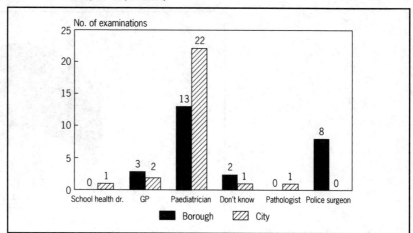

Joint medicals

In neither authority were joint medicals often carried out. In borough, this was reported to reflect some reluctance on the part of the police surgeon attributed to an incompatibility in styles of work between herself and the local paediatricians. The police, in both authorities, accepted the competence and professional expertise of either the police surgeons or the paediatricians working alone. One worker commented that assessments undertaken only by the police surgeon were reliant on the information presented by the child, parents and social worker and were not supplemented by medical evidence available in the hospital, but the absence of joint medicals was not generally viewed as problematic.

Timing

Another important aspect of interagency collaboration is that the investigating agencies should have timely access to medical assessment. While central government advice concerning the timing of medical investigation of cases of child sexual abuse notes that 'hurried intervention may cause more harm to the child and the family. There is rarely a need for immediate clinical examination', (DHSS, 1988, para 5.3) most investigations into cases of child physical and sexual abuse in the sample were undertaken promptly. As Figure 6.9 shows, in over half the cases the medical examination was carried out on the same day on which the social services department or the police received notification of the abuse. Over two thirds of children were examined within two days. The pattern was similar in both authorities. This confirmed the views expressed in interviews and discussed below that, in both authorities,

Figure 6.9   **Length of time between referral to social services department/
police and initial medical examination (N = 42)**

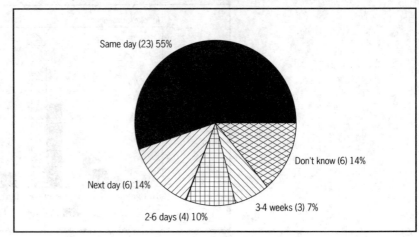

the relevant doctors were generally accessible and made themselves available
to examine children.

Location

In order to minimise the trauma to the children, recent years have seen an
emphasis on finding an acceptable environment for the medical examination,
particularly the avoidance of examination in a police station. The location of
medical examinations undertaken in the total case sample is shown in Figure
6.10 and is broken down between city and borough in Figure 6.11. None was
carried out in a police station. One took place in a police Special Unit which
was housed in a separate building.

The pattern in borough reflects the preference of the police surgeon to
conduct examinations in the general practice surgery whenever possible since
this was less threatening and more familiar to children, although the
examination suite in the police Special Unit would be used at night. The site
for the examinations conducted in hospital varied. Those in borough and in
the general hospital in city took place on the paediatric ward. Those, for
physical injury, at the children's hospital were conducted in the accident and
emergency department. For those social workers in city who could choose
between the two locations, this was important in leading some to go to the
general hospital to avoid the accident and emergency department, as is
discussed below.

Figure 6.10   **Location of initial medical examinations (N = 42)**

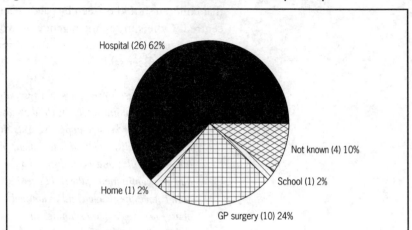

Figure 6.11   **Location of initial medical examinations: borough and city compared (N = 42)**

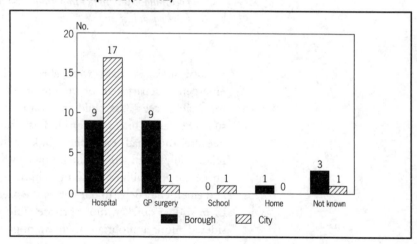

The choice of doctors

Different practices existed between the two research areas in the choice of doctors for medical assessment in child protection. In city, with the exception of post-pubertal young people who might be seen by gynaecologists and/or police surgeons, most children suspected of physical or sexual abuse were seen by paediatricians. A rota of senior staff, including a principal clinical medical officer, saw children suspected of sexual abuse. This represented a change in practice from a former position where sexually abused children were seen at a medical-legal centre by male police surgeons in an examination suite described as 'cold and clinical' The change was instituted by doctors who felt that children should be seen by paediatricians or by doctors who were child-centred. Others in the interagency network appreciated the involvement of paediatricians in examining children suspected of being sexually abused. As one police officer said:

> *When we first started, we always called on the services of the police surgeon to examine anybody, child or adult, but, as we started progressing in this area, it became apparent to us that a child who has been abused needs a specialist paediatric assessment, not just of the private parts but of the whole child, and I can think of a few in the early days where we only had an examination of the child's genitals and I've lived to regret it that we didn't have the whole child examined . . . We're not just investigating abuse, we're going into famiies and splitting up families and there are children involved and you take that on if you're going to have any success at all. And I think part of taking that on is the realisation that you wanted a qualified paediatric assessment and all the things that the hospital and the paediatricians can give you, and that the actual medical examination of genitalia was of minor importance. So that's why we call on the services of the paediatrician.*

In city, social workers were able to choose between the accident and emergency department of the children's hospital and, if they were within reasonable access, the children's wards at the general hospital. Some made such choices on pragmatic grounds (such as distance, ease of parking), others because they had established links and developed easier interpersonal relationships with staff in one hospital rather than another. Some specifically chose the general hospital so that children would be seen not in the accident and emergency department but on the paediatric wards which were reported to provide a quicker, more private and more straightforward service, considered more appropriate than waiting to take a turn in a busy accident department.

A social worker explained the position:

> *They do respond. You can phone up the senior registrar at casualty and they'll say 'yes, come down', they take the detail, take it seriously, not put you off but there is no sense in which you're any different from all the other broken feet and fingers and stuff that are down in casualty and you wait. You don't have a special sort of fast track. They just have you sat there in casualty for hours and hours waiting for the whole thing to take its course, you know, they're busy. I mean for us that day is a priority, for them it's one of many people that are in need of their services.*

The police and social workers were not unsympathetic to the doctor's position:

> *They are very busy and, while we are wanting kids looked at, they're saving babies' lives, so you've got to fall in with that.*

Nonetheless, waiting with the parents and child or children for a medical examination was a time-consuming and difficult task for social workers, usually taking place on the first day of the child protection investigation when parents were likely to be distressed, fraught or angry and the children anxious and unsettled.

In city there was a long-standing practice by which children suspected of abuse could be admitted fairly readily to paediatric beds. This was reflected in the local procedures which stated that any child suspected of abuse should be taken, with the parents if possible, to one of the two hospitals:

> *where he/she will usually be admitted. The extent or degree of abuse is not relevant to this requirement. The purpose of admission is to aid diagnosis and to protect the child until other examinations concerning the safety of the home are complete.*

This was generally valued by the social workers and, it was said by the parents, at least in preference to the alternatives. It was reported to have enabled social workers to avoid more coercive and stigmatising interventions in the early stages of investigation and to have contributed to the low rate of place of safety orders (as they were then called) in the city. The following comment illustrates that social workers positively valued the facility:

> *It did contribute significantly to our ability to keep our rates of place of safety orders extremely low. Parents found it more acceptable, less stigmatising, to agree an admission to hospital – lots of children get admitted to hospital. They were reasonably content as content as you could be under the circumstances, to allow that to happen and it didn't force us to make decisions whether it was safe for that child to go home there and then which might have promptd us to have a different route and place of safety and alternative care for perhaps a short period, but nevertheless that would be damaging, traumatising for the child and family and so on. So it has worked very well.*

However, the practice was changing at the time of the research, largely because of pressure on resources, as one doctor explained:

> *We haven't got as many children's beds as we had and, therefore, the facility of actually admitting children is more difficult. So far we've sort of hurtled along but . . . that's going to get more difficult.*

A social worker gave a case example illustrating the difficulties of establishing close working relationships, and giving an acceptable standard of care to the child in the context of straitened resources:

> *And there was another incident, more this was just the hospital about keeping a child in rather than having to drag it across the city to an emergency foster home. Recently I got into a dire row with this. It's just about the lack of understanding of child protection which we didn't have before with the hospital. I found myself there, you know, flaunting the procedures saying 'look it actually says in here that we could decide we'd use a hospital bed to accommodate a child'. It was ten o'clock, we'd had the child there since four and she was crying. She was tired and there was no way she was going home and her mum was saying 'I don't want her' type of thing. So it was that or traipse across the city to a new place at ten o'clock at night, and we got into a dire argument but what it was about was this doctor who said 'I can't use the bed – we've stretched resources' and that's what we are into now. And it really is a sign of the times, yes, we talked about it afterwards. It's not her. She's having to cut clinics, services are being stretched, so that's what it's about but it doesn't stop me saying that child protection is suffering.*

The difficulties were linked by doctors and social services staff with the National Health Service reforms consequent upon the National Health Service and Community Care Act 1990:

> *The whole attitude has changed because the medical staff have changed and the economic atmosphere in which the National Health Service is now operating has changed, the children's hospital are seeking trust status from April of next year. There has been mention at the ACPC on several occasions of social services being required to buy beds, contract for beds at the children's hospital and everything is moving in a very different direction. It's been mentioned by the paediatrician, certainly I feel very ambivalent about it. I don't feel at all happy with the basic principles, about the direction in which it's going. I'm anxious to save this kind of approach really because it has worked very well in the interests of children, families, professionals alike, and I think we'll lose it.*

This was one of several examples in the data discussed more fully in Chapter Ten where broader changes in social policy, particularly the creation of internal markets and a degree of decentralisation, cut across and undermined collaborative working practices which had been established in the past.

The arrangements for medical examinations were rather different in borough. Cases of child sexual abuse were seen normally by a female police surgeon who was said to be accommodating and, generally, readily available to do the work. The examination of children with physical injury was principally, but not exclusively, concentrated in the hands of three consultant paediatricians based at a hospital in the main town. There was a rota to cover the work but some social workers with a preference for a particular consultant circumvented the rota by seeking direct access. Few problems were, however, reported in terms of relatively speedy access to a medical consultation. Some social workers working some distance from the main town made more use of general practitioners, as is discussed below.

Figure 6.12 **Outcomes of medical examinations in cases of child physical abuse (N = 25)**

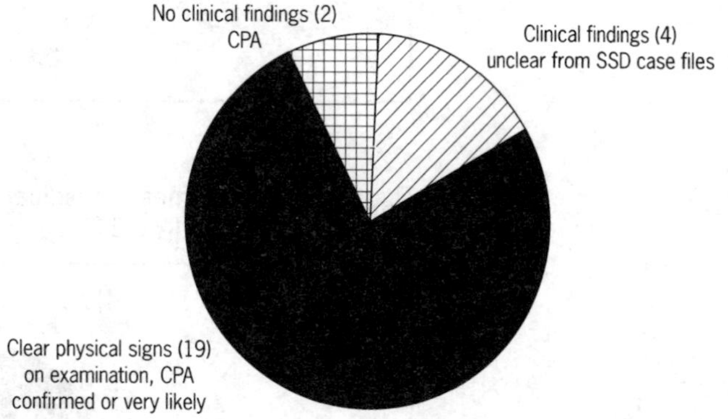

No clinical findings (2)
CPA

Clinical findings (4)
unclear from SSD case files

Clear physical signs (19)
on examination, CPA
confirmed or very likely

The outcome and nature of medical examinations

As expected from the nature of the presenting conditions and the relative difficulty of diagnosis, the outcome of medical examination differed between cases of physical and sexual abuse. Since these were examinations of children whose names were subsequently entered on the child protection register, it is likely at least in respect of physical abuse, that they represent a group where the clinical signs were clearer than might sometimes be the case. The outcomes of medical examinations as recorded in the social services department file, including case conference minutes, are presented in Figure 6.12 for the sample as a whole, and in Figure 6.13 for each authority separately. Although the numbers for each authority are small, they appear to reflect the concern expressed in borough but not in city about a reluctance on the part of some consultants to commit themselves in respect of physical injury. This is discussed more fully below.

The outcomes of the cases subsequently registered as sexual abuse in which medical examinations took place are shown in Figure 6.14. The

Figure 6.13 **Outcomes of medical examinations in cases of child physical abuse: borough and city compared (N = 25)**

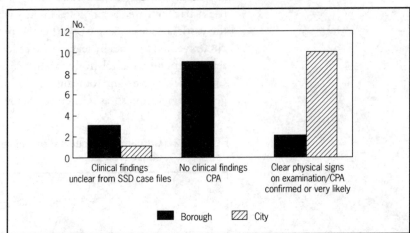

Figure 6.14 **Outcomes of medical examinations in cases of child sexual abuse (N = 17)**

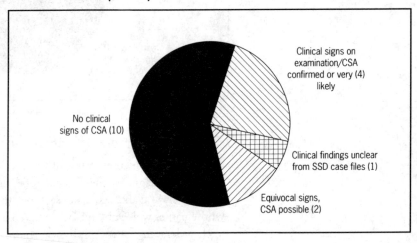

patterns were similar in both authorities. The low levels of positive identification of clinical signs of sexual abuse are unsurprising. As the government guidance states 'doctors should be aware that the probability of finding definite clinical evidence is low, but the absence of signs does not mean that child sexual abuse has not taken place.' (DHSS, 1988, para 5.4).

In general, as is discussed below, those in the interagency network reliant on the outcomes of medical assessment as part of the process of child protection appreciated the limitations. The following comments from social workers were typical:

I think they are as clear as they can be. I don't regard it as an exact science diagnosing which bruise came from what cause. I think they're fallible like the rest of us.

They will say there is no way I can tell you whether this is a non-accidental injury or not, there isn't sufficient evidence or it is too late or whatever and that's fine. I don't expect them to be able to give me clear answers on everything.

Nonetheless the difficulties faced by doctors in the clear identification of child sexual abuse in particular have contributed to a position in which, in some cases at least, a socio-legal discourse had risen to prominence at the expense of the socio-medical. A police officer summarised the position:

My view now, after dealing with child abuse for years, is that generally the medical examination of victims of abuse is a very inexact science. Locally we have a very good service with the [paediatricians here in [city]. We have people who work very hard to accommodate children who have been abused, or suspected of abuse, but the evidence that is produced varies. We're at a stage now in child abuse investigation that the defence are producing medical evidence by paediatricians to counteract the evidence that our paediatricians have got, and my experience now is that the medical evidence is not terribly compelling in a court unless the child has suffered gross injuries, but very rarely do we get gross injuries to the child and I see now arguments coming from all sides, for example about sexually transmitted diseases, and that all lessens the impact of that evidence in court. I don't feel, as a police officer, that I am qualified to comment really on what a doctor or a consultant paediatrician or police surgeon is saying because they are the experts but it's not got the same impact that it used to have.

A paediatrician commented, in respect of the medical assesment of child sexual abuse:

the more you see, the more you are asked to see and the more uncertain you become.

In the context of interagency collaboration in child protection, it is important that the outcomes of medical examination are reported clearly to the investigating agencies. This may be done orally or in writing, before or during the initial child protection conference. In only 16 cases (38%) was there a written report of the medical examination on the social services department file; no written report was on the file for the remaining 26 cases (62%). The rate was higher in borough than in city as is shown in Figure 6.15. This was principally because of the practice of the police surgeon routinely to

Figure 6.15 **No. of cases in which any written report of a medical examination on SSD file: borough and city compared (N = 42)**

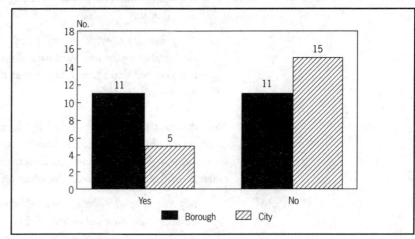

provide a copy of the written report to the social services department. Paediatricians were more likely to present their clinical findings orally at the child protection conference. These were usually fully minuted.

Nonetheless, as Figure 6.16 shows, in 15 cases (35%) in which medical examinations had been carried out, there was no written report nor was the examining doctor able to be present at the conference. Although the numbers are small, Figure 6.17 indicates that this was more problematic in city than in borough. This suggests that the problem of the irregular or low profile of essential health staff at case conferences noted by the Department of Health remains problematic (DHSS, 1982, DHSSI, 1990(a) and (b)).

While access to medical examinations was not reported as particularly problematic in either area, there were different levels of satisfaction reported concerning the outcomes of medical examinations. In city there was general satisfaction with the accessibility and quality of the medical contribution, despite some interpersonal difficulties. Comments such as 'on the whole, they are very helpful, very prepared to come to case conferences and are quite aware of what the issues are, what needs to be drawn out and what their examination has found'; 'I've no real beefs about the judgements they make'; 'the input to case conferences from the paediatricians is excellent'; 'by and large, no problem whatsoever' and 'they are as constructive as they possibly can be' were typical. Many social workers and others commented on the recent loss (at the time of the research) of two paediatricians with a particular interest in child abuse. This was said to have had a serious impact at the general hospital where the paediatrician who had left had clearly established close interagency links and was highly regarded by many. As one social worker said:

Figure 6.16 **Number of cases in which either a written report of medical examinations was on SSD file or the examining doctor(s) were present at initial case conference (N = 42)**

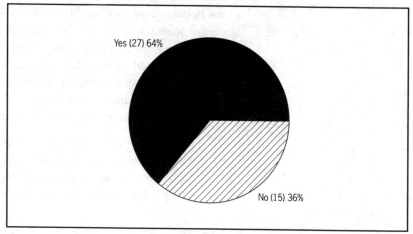

Figure 6.17 **Number of cases in which either a written report of medical examinations was on SSD file or the examining doctor(s) were present at initial case conference: borough and city compared (N = 42)**

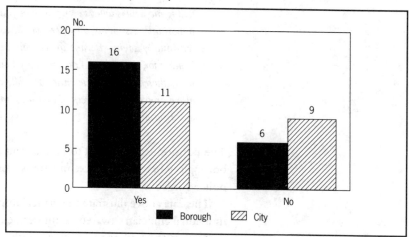

You just begin to worry that when you don't hear so much about child protection from the [general hospital] as you used to do when this particular consultant was there you know, what the hell is going on? you know, why is it that it's not being recognised, that it's not being picked up there and so on? So the atmosphere has changed.

In borough the problem was reported to be one of different levels of experience, interest, competence and confidence in the field of child protection among the local paediatricians. Some expressed their satisfaction with the service available, for example 'I'm quite satisfied with what we got from them', but others described what they saw as 'a huge deficit'. Partly this was because it was not possible to offer children an examination by a woman paediatrician but there was also said to be a reluctance, on the part of some consultants at least, to give a clear diagnosis. The observations above did not seem to be based on unrealistic expectations or fundamental misapprehensions about the genuine difficulties of diagnosis in some cases, since workers contrasted the position unfavourably with previous work experiences elsewhere. One case conference chair explained the position as follows:

> *It varies I think. In case conferences it's like drawing teeth trying to get an opinion sometimes . . . but if you pursue it doggedly, you get there in case conferences . . . but a social worker trying to get a diagnosis in a different setting – I can see that it's impossible . . .*

One social worker described her strategy in such situations:

> *We sometimes have to say to them 'I need to know from you categorically, in this consistent or is it not consistent? Does it fit or doesn't it fit? And you're going to need to tell me that now. You know we can't be saying 'oh it could be or it couldn't be' and I need you to stick with that – what you're telling me now is what's going to be in your report because that is also very important'. I suppose they perceive me as a really mouthy person who is continually saying I want to see you, it's important, this is what I'm looking for, and I don't know actually how they perceive that, not only as men, there's an age differential as well, a gender differential and there's also a professional differential that they are consultant paediatricians and I am a social worker.*

The position was reported to be different in respect of child sexual abuse in borough, where medical examinations were usually performed by a woman police surgeon.

The data above illustrate the critical importance in child protection of the individual clinician's awareness, interest, experience and competence in child protection and willingness to work with others. The relative scarcity of key personnel such as consultant paediatricians and their central role in the child protection network mean that the influence of an individual on the quality of child protection services in a local area could be profound.

The role of general practitioners in medical examinations

As was shown above, the role of general practitioners in the medical examination of the registered cases in the sample was limited and all general practitioners who were involved had been contacted by the families themselves. None had identified the abuse in the course of routine consultation with their patients. A limited use of general practitioners seemed to reflect the widespread practice of social workers in city who, as was discussed above, had access to a choice of hospitals and broadly expressed satisfaction with the paediatric services offered. This was reinforced by the procedures which stated that while, in some circumstances it may seem more appropriate to use a general practitioner, it is usually preferable to use a hospital paediatrician. Three reasons were offered. First that the hospital constituted a place of safety and so could achieve the primary aim of securing the child's immediate safety; secondly, to reduce the number of medical examinations and thirdly, because hospital paediatric departments could often carry out more comprehensive assessments. These were also among the reasons cited by social workers in city for rarely involving general practitioners in medical examinations. But they added others, for example that general practitioners were less familiar with what was required and would not be regarded as expert witnesses in court and that the service was more uneven, as the following quotation illustrates:

> *General practitioners, certainly in [city] – I don't know what other areas are like – their experience of dealing with NAI is very patchy, very inconsistent. You can't ever predict really what their knowledge is going to be like so unless the family adamantly won't to to anybody but the GP, and unless you know that a particular GP is experienced and will give you a proper judgment about an injury, then social workers always take the child to the hospital.*

Others commented that the general practitioners were less likely to confront parents with difficult questions, because of their continuing relationship with them as patients, a problem which was less acute for paediatricians.

In borough, the procedures were less prescriptive and the practice reported to be more varied in respect of the use of general practitioners, although they were still not often used for initial examinations. One social worker expressed surprise at the flexibility:

> *What I feel, having worked elsewhere before where the procedure was that all children where NAI was suspected had to be referred to the paediatrician or his colleagues at the hospital, I find it very strange coming to an authority where we can pick any GP under the sun for it. I find the system too vague.*

Some in borough used general practitioners because they were more accessible than the paediatricians in the main town, which could involve a journey of twelve miles or more. Others used them when they wished to underemphasise the significance of the events and the examination, as the following quotations illustrates:

> *We consider that to take the child to the general practitioner is a kind of assumption that you don't have to take it seriously because you know the kind of in-built signal is that you're toning the whole thing down.*

They would also be used, albeit rarely, if that was the only way to secure parental cooperation with an examination:

> *Our practice is if we think non-accidental injuries possibly will be diagnosed, we always encourage parents to go along with the children to the hospital. I think the only times we've perhaps veered from that is if the parents are particularly anxious about going to the hospital and it's a toss up between getting the child examined and so on, perhaps going to a place of safety or seeing about a bit of emergency protection. So I think we might consider using the general practitioner if it was a question of either getting the child examined or not getting the child examined but standard practice is to use a hospital.*

One of the consultant paediatricians in borough was seeking to increase the involvement of general practitioners in this sphere of work. This was partly to avoid concentrating the task in too few hands, which left a gap in expertise during absences on annual leave of sickness. He also thought it important to extend the use of general practitioners so that their own levels of interest and competence in this area of work increased. He gave some examples:

> *We get some referrals from social services that might well have been seen by the general practitioner. It might have been a bruise and the child had been subjected to previous bruises, it's a matter of documenting it maybe. The general practitioner may well know the family far better than we do. Sometimes we're asked to see them when, you know, it's a very minor thing that might be sorted out at another step, so I think it's important to involve GP's in child abuse.*

but

> *. . . it would depend on the age. If it's a small child with bruising, I'm more worried. If it's an older child, a school-age child with some bruising, it's query accidental, query dad did it or we know her mum admits dad is doing it. There's no great issue about that so I would ask the social worker to take her to the general practitioner.*

Summary

A high degree of coordination was revealed in the study in respect of arrangements for the medical examination of children suspected of abuse. An important objective has been to ensure that the minimum feasible number of examinations are carried out with sensitivity, in suitable locations and without undue delay as part of the sequential task performance at the investigative stage. These intermediate coordinated outputs were largely achieved in the case sample through a process undertaken in accordance with interagency procedures which instituted a relatively clear division of labour with the work concentrated largely in the hands of paediatricians and, in borough, a police surgeon. In a high proportion of cases in the sample there was only one medical examination. Although children's views were not sought in the study, the interviews generally revealed sensitivity to the potential trauma for the child. Unsurprisingly, in terms of the outcome of examinations, there were clearer findings in respect of physical than sexual abuse. There were higher levels of reported satisfaction with the examination of children suffering from suspected physical injury in city than in borough. General satisfaction was expressed about medical examination of children suspected of being sexually abused in both research sites, although the organisational arrangements differed.

Although the task of medical assessment of children suspected of abuse can be problematic (and was reported to pose particular difficulties for some in the study) the process appeared to be a routinised and accepted part of contemporary clinical practice and, in some ways, not too dissimilar from other circumstances in which a medical assessment and, if necessary, treatment is sought by a third party, such as a general practitioner. The task is essentially episodic and time-limited. However, the involvement of the examining doctors, and particularly of general practitioners, in subsequent interagency discussions and decision-making notably in child protection conferences, constituted a more radical departure from established working patterns as is discussed in Chapters Seven and Eight.

Chapter 7

Child protection conferences

The multidisciplinary case conference has been a key feature of the response to child maltreatment for many years and lies at the heart of interagency collaboration. In 1950 a government circular on children neglected or ill-treated in their own homes recommended regular meetings of officers of the local authority, other statutory services and voluntary organisations and advised that arrangements be made:

> *for significant cases of child neglect and all cases of ill-treatment coming to the notice of any statutory or voluntary service in the area to be reported to the designated officer, who would arrange for such cases to be brought before the meeting so that, after considering the needs of the family as a whole, agreement might be reached as to how the local services could best be applied to meet those needs. (Home Office, 1950).*

The advice was strengthened in the circular issued in 1974, following the inquiry into the death of Maria Colwell, which recommended a case conference 'for every case involving suspected non-accidental injury to a child' (DHSS, 1974(a)).

The government guidance in force at the time of the research, *Working Together* (1988), suggested that if case conferences were 'too large, wrongly timed, have no clear purpose, involve the wrong people or are poorly conducted they may not only fail to facilitate good practice but may also bring interagency working into disrepute and undermine good practice.' (DHSS and Welsh Office, 1988, p28). These issues, together with parental involvement and conference minutes, are considered in this chapter with reference to initial child protection conferences. The decisions made at conferences, child protection plans and perceptions of child protection conferences are discussed in Chapter Eight.

Timing

Although noting the potentially harmful consequences of wrongly timed conferences, *Working Together* (1988) did not give guidance as to appropriate timing. Nor did the local procedures in borough apart from noting the importance of arranging conferences so that those with inflexible commitments such as single handed general practitioners could attend. In city, the procedures noted that the timing of the initial case conference would vary but should certainly take place prior to the child's discharge from hospital or other place of safety.

In the sample of registered cases, 17 of initial child protection conferences were held within 1–10 days and a total of 32 within 14 days of referral, as is shown in Figure 7.1.

Figure 7.1 **Time elapsed between initial referral and initial child protection conference (N = 48)**

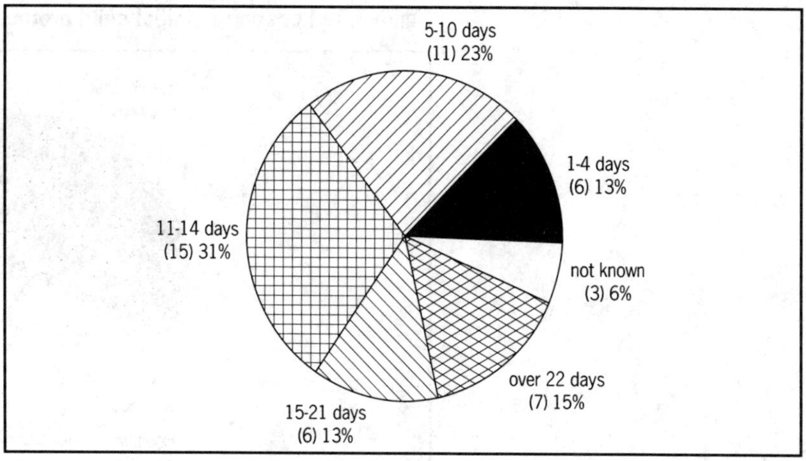

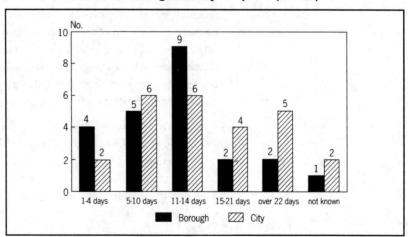

The patterns were similar in borough and city as is shown in Figure 7.2.

Figure 7.2 **Time elapsed between initial referral and initial child protection conference: borough and city compared (N = 48)**

Although at times, there were complaints that conferences had been called too quickly, leaving insufficient time for investigation and necessitating a reconvened conference at a later date, these were rare. In general, the timing of conferences was considered to be satisfactory.

Location

About half of the initial conferences were held in area social services offices, with almost a third held in hospital as is shown in Figure 7.3. Of the three held elsewhere, two were in the schools and one in the NSPCC office. The patterns were very similar in city and borough.

Figure 7.3 **Location of initial child protection conference (N = 48)**

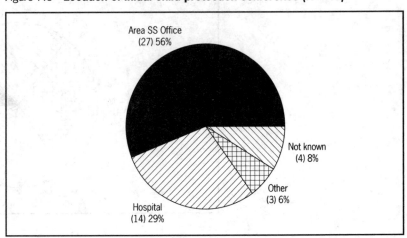

The suitability and quality of the venues for holding child protection conferences varied widely. Some social services offices had reasonable facilities either in purpose built modern offices or in the generously proportioned rooms of schools (now converted into social services offices) or former council offices built in the nineteenth century. However, some offices simply did not have the space or rooms of a size sufficient to accommodate conferences, and certainly not with any degree of comfort or welcoming surroundings. As one senior manager in social services said:

> *You've seen our offices, there's only one decent office and that's in [the main town]. I mean this is appalling. We haven't got a hot water system, for example.*

The lack of suitable venues was particularly problematic for minute-takers who described some as:

> *. . . abysmal. You very often go and have to balance your book on your knee and you sometimes can't see or you can't hear, people open the windows and there's traffic noise. There's no standard venue. I go all over the place and every place is different. Some are okay, others abysmal. We just make the best of it.*

One nurse manager who frequently attended cases conferences was exaggerating only slightly when she described the venues as:

> *sometimes completely hopeless, you're sort of sitting in a tiny room with a load of people falling out the window.*

There was a problem, too, if attempts were made to use venues which would encourage the attendance of other professionals. As one social services manager explained:

> *There's also a problem here about space to actually have conferences in. Our personal style is that we've tended to try and hold the conferences out on the area now and that meant fairly tacky surrounding to have a case conference in. But that actually meant that more people turned up for case conferences, for example if we have it here it seems to me we ony tend to get one person from the school, normally the head teacher. If we have it out on the area for example at the call-in office across the road from the school, we would have the head teacher and the class teacher you know, if we fixed it at the right time and similarly, well for all agencies we tend to get a better response if we held it out on the area.*

However, there was a tension between trying to meet the convenience of the different professionals involved, for example those paediatricians who would prefer to meet in hospital and teachers and others spread out across the localities concerned. Given the importance of the child protection conference for the future lives of children and their families, many of the venues fell short of reasonable standard, a deficiency further highlighted by the practice of family involvement in conferences.

Size and patterns of attendance

Seventy seven per cent (487) of those invited (629) attended initial child protection conferences. The average size of the 48 initial conferences was similar, at 10.6 persons per conference in borough and 9.7 in city. This is in line with other reports which show average conference size to be around ten for example, Hilgendorf (1987), Corby (1987) and Packman and Randall (1989). However the pattens were different, as illustrated in Figure 7.4, with only about a quarter of conferences in borough comprising eight people or less compared with 44% in city. The modal size in borough was 12. In interview, there was general satisfaction with the size of conferences.

Those most frequently attending the initial conferences in the sample of registered cases are listed in rank order in Table 7.1.

Figure 7.4 **Size of initial child protection conferences: borough and city compared (N = 48)**

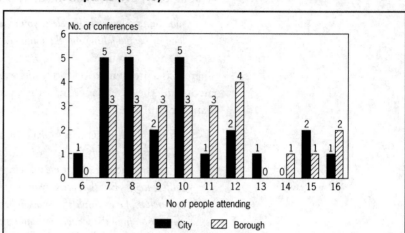

Table 7.1 **Most frequent initial child protection conference attenders by profession/rank, listed in order of frequency of attendance (N=401)**

	Borough	City	Total
Social worker	32	38	70
Police	21	27	48
Health visitor/school nurse	21	19	40
Principal social worker/Team Leader	12	21	33
Headteacher/Deputy	15	13	28
Minute taker	16	12	28
Nurse Manager	10	16	26
Education welfare officer	17	4	21
Local authority solicitor/court section	10	8	18
Child protection coordinator	4	12	16
NSPCC	14	2	16
Social services area manager/divisional officer	10	5	15
Consultant paediatrician	9	2	14
Class teacher	6	6	12
General practitioner	3	6	9
Paediatric junior doctor	1	6	7

This list of 401 'most frequent attenders' comprises 82% of the total attenders (487). The remainder of attenders, an average of about two per conference, included, interalia, psychiatrist, clinical medical officer, court welfare officers, family aide, social work assistant, hospital nurses, nursery nurses, probation officers, YTS workers and voluntary worker.

In many respects the patterns are not unexpected and they are broadly similar in both authorities, with social service department staff and the police as the most frequent followed by health visitors/school nurses and, since this was a sample of primary school aged children, head teachers.

These patterns were confirmed in interviews. The health visiting/school nursing service was reported to place high priority on conference attendance and to reschedule commitments in order to do so, reflecting the importance it attached to interagency collaboration. As one health visitor commented:

> *I'm glad that they're called and I'm glad to be there. I'm keen to attend and I would rearrange my workload in order to get there. In fact, I wish we could meet more often, perhaps more on an informal basis, have more case discussions before we get to the case conference.*

Schools, too, attached high priority to conferences. One head teacher said:

> *I think case conferences are the most important thing and I would always go to a case conference. It's just like the problems of a child on the at risk register they always come first no matter what else, you've got to drop everything and do it.*

There were problems in schools in releasing both the class teacher and the head or deputy, who was often the nominated child protection liaison teacher, to attend, since there was no spare capacity to cover classroom responsibilities in their absence. For that reason, often the head or deputy would represent the school, especially if more than one child in the school was to be considered at the conference which could involve several class teachers.

Police representation at initial conferences varied in the two authorities. In city, police officers from the Special Unit had been involved in conferences initially but as workloads had increased this had proved impossible and at the time of the research they attended few, selecting those where their involvement was seen as particularly important, for example if they had strong views about the action to be taken or if the child had given information to them but not to others involved. More usually, the police would be represented by an officer from the Crime Prevention and Community Division (formerly Community Liaison). These officers would brief themselves about the position from the Special Unit or other police divisions if they had been involved and would also organise the search of the criminal records of alleged abusers. In borough, the police were represented by the Special Unit although pressure of work sometimes made it difficult for them to attend.

While the patterns of attendance of social workers, the police, health visitors and teachers were broadly similar in both authorities, there were differences in respect of other groups, reflecting differences in the structure of service delivery and operational practices. One concerned education welfare officer who attended almost three quarters of the initial conferences in borough (17 out of 23) and only about a sixth in city (4 out of 25). Another was the presence of local authority lawyers, who attended almost half of the initial conferences in the case sample in borough, and none in city, although social workers from the court section attended about a third of the city cases in the sample to advise on care proceedings. A third concerned NSPCC workers who attended a high proportion of conferences as consultants in borough.

Nurse Managers

In general, the size of initial conferences was considered appropriate as were the patterns of attendance of those who came. However, one issue, the role of nurse managers caused comment and was explored in interview. In the case sample, nurse managers attended about two fifths of the conferences (10 out of 23) in borough and about two thirds in city (16 out of 25). This appeared to reflect a substantive difference in policy and practice, with a commitment in city to attending as many as possible ('we do try to make sure that all members of staff are actually accompanied') while in borough, patterns were more variable, with some nurse managers taking into account the experience and length of service of health visitors.

A police sergeant commented on the practice as follows, including the social services hierarchy in his observations:

> *The only people that go – shall I say, single-handed, are the police and the paediatrician. But what never ceases to amaze me is the fact that the social worker has always got his or her team leader, the nurse from the ward has got a nursing officer, health visitors have got a clinical nursing manager and, I think, they are probably being over-cautious and they are looking at protecting their member of staff's back, if you like. The health visitor always has a supervisor; they're always supervised. The health visitors are very experienced nurses, really gone through the mill in training and graduated to be well up in the nursing service and yet they still need somebody there to tell them what to say!*

The nurse managers, health visitors and school nurses did not share this perception of the nurse manager role. Many health visitors and school nurses welcomed the support, not only in the conference itself but also in preparation for it – an activity which appeared to be given higher priority in the health visiting/school nursing service than in many others. The nurse managers offered several reasons for their attendance. These included the support of staff in potentially difficult or threatening situations; ensuring that any health visiting or school nursing service contribution to the child protection plan was appropriate; overseeing, sharing and contributing to the interagency decision-making and briefing themselves in terms of their future supervision of the cases. The following quotations illustrate these themes and highlight both the anxiety, more evident in health visiting than in other professions, displayed by many about work in the field of child protection and the importance attached to staff support:

> *I am not prepared to have any health visitor or school nurse conned, drawn into, persuaded to, well to get involved in any recommendation to which they cannot agree . . . because health visitors and school nurses are concerned for the best for the child it's very easy to get dragged into offering to do more than you ought to be doing and therefore I see my role as pulling them back from the brink to some extent and ensuring that whatever they are offering to do and which is being accepted they are doing is possible both within the case load that they as an individual have and within the total case load that there is at that base; accepting that I have health visitors with case loads of three hundred plus and there's social workers out there with case loads of thirty, forty, you know. So I mean I think that's number one.*

> *This is a negative comment but I once heard somebody saying that if there's any aggro afterwards when it goes wrong, it's the health visitor and the social worker . . I think while the social services manager is there, a nurse manager should be. She's responsible for the service and for the output of that worker. She's there to give support, particularly in difficult cases but also to make sure plans are acceptable to the service . . . and to encourage the worker . . . to take something on if there's reluctance.*

Among the members of the interagency network, views about the practice of nurse manager attendance varied. A minority seemed to agree with the police view cited above. One social work manager for example said:

> *Health visitors have always got their manager with them. I don't think they need them but they always do. And their manager often just sits down and says nothing. Sometimes you get some good ones, which is fine. But most health visitors are so experienced at case conferences they are quite capable of saying what they need to say and also standing their ground and saying I'm not going to do that.*

Others did not view the practice as unhelpful, reporting that it was not a problem and some positively valued the nurse managers' perspective.

> *I value the joint contribution of health visitors and senior officers to case conferences, I now see it as normal and I bear it in mind that I wouldn't expect social workers to go to the CP case conferences without their team leader unless it was totally impossible, in which case I would expect them to have the support of another team leader.*

The resource consequences of staffing the rising numbers of initial conferences was however considerable and so the practice was under review:

> *I do at the moment because I still don't think everbody is good enough at case conferences and because the structure and the running of them hasn't quite got to the standard of excellence I dream about and I think there are exceptional cases. Perhaps in the future it may not always be necessary but if they don't go they certainly should be very well informed and have discussed it thoroughly before hand and certainly should need debriefing afterwards. I think the advantage of them not going is to cut down the numbers sitting round that table.*

Social work consultants

Different arrangements existed in each authority for the provision of social work consultants at initial child protection conferences. In borough this role was performed by members of the NSPCC child protection team. They attended about two-thirds of the initial conferences in the sample in this capacity. This is how one member of the team explained the role:

> *Advisory, consultant, picking up on things and clarifying, asking questions, making sure all the information is shared, I also actually try and encourage minority views, people who . . . We can't get away from the fact that there is a status hierarchy, that people are seen differently and even sometimes because a lot of people aren't used to conferences, they might not give as much information as they can and I see part of my role as saying 'I hope you don't mind but can I ask you some more', like the school teacher, 'you see this kiddie all the time, you're the next person to the parent who has the most contact with them, what are they like, friendships, relationships, meal times, dress, appearance, academically, everything not just their nine out of ten record whatever, everything, are they happy, are they pleasant, do they smile, what sort of person are they' and they give that information but you often need to tap it to get it, so that's something else that we try to do. Sometimes we also, we'll pick up on statements that are made inappropriately be they gender, race, whatever, and say that 'I do object to that statement being made', again*

you don't need to air it there but I would see that person afterwards, but we
tend now much more to say I needed to say I disagree with that.

The role of the consultant in highlighting the child's demeanour seems to be important in view of the forensic nature of the initial social work investigation, described in Chapter Four, where the focus was predominantly on the 'incident', its causes and the explanations offered rather than an overall initial assessment of the child. The issue could, of course, be raised by the conference chair. One explained her practice thus:

One of the questions I always ask is 'can you tell us about what the child's
feeling and the child's views are at this point' and people often look quite
gob-smacked really because it's not part of their thinking. But I think we'll
come to it. I don't think they're a million miles away. I just think they are
too harassed and with different styles developing some of these things will
change.

In city, a consultative role was provided by the child protection coordinators, who attended about half of the initial conferences in the sample. Since there were only two child protection coordinators in post for the whole city and their role involved various responsibilities including policy development, rewriting procedures, multi-agency training and working with the ACPC and its sub-committees, they were unable to attend all of the initial conferences, averaging from 30–60 per month. They were informed of all cases and selected using the following criteria:

I would only attend incident case conferences where there were difficult
issues. I would try and attend a case conference where a child obviously
had received serious physical injuries. Babies with fractures, I would try
and attend in respect of those to ensure basically that if we needed to
institute care proceedings then that was done. Also, maybe, cases of sexual
abuse that are particularly complex perhaps where youngsters who've been
abused have started threatening suicide and it's difficult to know quite
what course of action is going to help the child best. Case conferences where
the abuse is alleged against a member of staff in a children's home out of
city and where abuse is alleged against foster parents. So the sort of more
difficult types of situation.

The nature of the case as judged from the facts presented was used to prioritise the work but:

Occasionally I will be aware maybe that the worker or the team manager
isn't as experienced as they might be and I would maybe attend in those
circumstances if I had time but I would also maybe ensure that someone

else who was used to perhaps making judgements about care proceedings would attend, like a court social worker, if I couldn't myself go.

As with the role described by the NSPCC worker, the purpose was facilitative and clarificatory.

It's occasionally the case that I'm at a case conference and a child protection plan is very clear to me but the worker and the manager don't see it as clearly and I sort of would have to say 'well I think you should be doing this, this, this, and this, what does everybody else think?'

In both authorities the role was generally perceived as very important and welcomed, particularly by those in the chair, (although not all field staff in borough appeared to be so appreciative). Conference chairs did not appear to feel threatened by the external scrutiny but valued the support in a complex and sometimes stressful task. The following comments from conference chairs were typical:

I've certainly chaired a case conference where when it got to the recommendations I'd got some stuff scribbled down and I was working through these and the child protection coordinator kind of waded in and said 'I've got some proposals for the recommendation' and came up with things that I simply hadn't had time to work out. Excellent proposals, people regarded them as excellent. And I said to her afterwards 'you know I very much appreciated that input.'

Whenever they come their contribution is important, because they've got such a breadth of knowledge and see the whole span of these things and they can tell you when you're going off line and a sort of a quiet word here and I pick that up and I know I'm alright. So I value that but I don't get it. I say 'I'd like you to come' but they don't often come even if I say that. They have to make a judgement about where the priorities are.

I actually value their contribution. I do find it challenging because when chairing the conference some of the most difficult things are dealing with things like prejudiced statements, whether they're to do with gender or the role of women or ethnicity. Personally, I find there's a conflict if I'm chairing a meeting where I want to facilitate communication, if somebody is being blatantly racist I feel a professional dilemma because I actually want to challenge them and say 'I'm sorry I don't think you can express that view here' but I also know I've got to get what information they know out of them and it's actually extremely helpful to me to know that I can probably safely say in a meeting where I have a consultant, does anybody want to clarify what is being said in the knowledge that somebody else will say 'well actually I don't know where that's coming from but it's not appropriate here.' Because if they don't then I have to and I've got a confusion of roles then. So I actually value them, I think it's very challenging, well chairing is quite a difficult job. And it's nice to have somebody to throw things back and forth with who isn't embroiled in the other dynamics and has no other agenda than maintaining an overview of the information that's come across. I like to have them there.

The consultancy role provided by the child protection coordinators in city and by the child protection coordinator (who also chaired some conferences) and the NSPCC in borough was generally welcomed not only in case conferences but more broadly, in matters such as investigation and ongoing case management. They offered advice not only to social workers but to others in the interagency network. In both authorities, the key positions of the child protection coordinators in facilitating interagency work in advice about individual cases and in policy development was acknowledged and widely respected, although there were severe pressures on their time, given the number in post and the size of the task. They are in the position of reticulists and their competence and the respect in which they are held appears to be a critical factor in the interagency liaison, reported in both authorities to be generally good. This issue is further discussed in Chapter Eleven.

Non attenders

In Birchall's study, respondents indicated that better attendance would be the most significant improvement in the running of child protection conferences, ranked higher than items such as better chairing and shorter meetings (Birchall, 1992, p99). This did not prove to be the case in the present study in which attendance rates were not reported to be particularly problematic, with the predicted exception of general practitioners. In addition, child protection consultants would have been welcome at more conferences. Twenty three per cent of all professionals listed as having been invited to attend initial child protection conferences in the sample were recorded as unable to do so: 28% in borough and 16% in city. Different rates of attendance might be taken to indicate different degrees of collaboration as reflected in the willingness of professionals to invest time in case conferences. However, some invitations were sent as a matter of routine to staff in certain posts as a means of alerting them to concerns about a particular family without necessarily a clear expectation of their attendance. There is evidence of this practice in borough in respect of probation officers and nurse managers who accounted for 25 (27%) of the non-attenders, and in city in respect of child protection coordinators. The average number of persons invited in borough was 14.7 compared with 11.6 in city, and the average numbers attending were 10.6 and 9.7 respectively.

The missing general practitioners

As is shown in Figure 7.5 the largest group of non-attenders at conferences were the general practitioners, confirming other studies which noted their poor attendance record (Hallett and Stevenson, 1980, Parton and Thomas, 1983, DHSSI, 1988, 1989 and 1990(a) and (b), Birchall, 1992). It is difficult to know how much this matters. Government guidance has stressed the important role of general practitioners in child protection, most recently in *Working Together* where it is stated:

> *General practitioners have a vital role to play in the protection of children. As family doctors, working closely with health visitors, and other members of the primary health care team, they are well placed to identify at an early stage family stress which may point to a risk of child abuse, or to notice in the child indications of significant harm, or likelihood of significant harm. As more practitioners become involved in child health surveillance programmes their roles in preventing child abuse and in protecting children will increase. General practitioners' extensive knowledge of the family background enables them to make a particular contribution to child protection conferences and to the long term support of the child and family* (Home Office et al, 1991, p20).

Figure 7.5 Persons invited to initial child protection conferences who did not attend by agency/profession (N = 136)

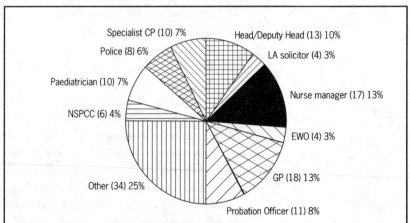

As was seen in Chapter Three, none of the 48 registered cases in the sample was identified by general practitioners in the course of their routine work. In the few in which they were the referral source, parents and, in one case, a child had presented to the general practitioner identifying child abuse as the reason for consultation. In only five of the cases did general practitioners undertake a medical examination of the child.

As is shown in Table 7.1, general practitioners attended under a fifth of the initial conferences in the sample, (9 out of 48). In general their record of attendance was described in interviews as poor but variable. In some of the smaller communities in borough, for example, the social services department claimed to have established reasonably close links with the local general practitioners and were 'not bad at getting them to turn up.' One health visitor said:

> *Some of them do, there are seven general practitioners here and they do seem to make an effort to come to case conferences, particularly the younger general practitioners who have been through the general practitioners trainee scheme.*

Elsewhere the position was more difficult:

> *I can't remember the last time I had a general practitioner at a case conference, initial or subsequent.*

> *Well, general practitioners never come. They should come but never come.*

Some spoke of having made considerable efforts to schedule conferences at times convenient to general practitioners and to facilitate their attendance in other ways. One social services manager explained:

> *The standard argument that was put out by the general practitioners was that we always held case conferences in a morning when they had surgery and they couldn't possibly attend, so I did an analysis of the case conferences that had taken place in the preceding twelve months and discovered in fact the majority of case conferences were held in the afternoon, in the early afternoon at a time when by and large GPs would not be holding surgery, I know that some of them have clinics etc., in an afternoon but I found that the general practitioners who are willing to attend can normally arrange a swap with a collegue to cover their clinic in order that they might attend. I mean we've got one or two GPs who are the model of case conference attendance. General practitioners who seem to work hardest are the ones who make the time to come to a case conference and there are certain practices her where that is the case where you would expect and would have the appropriate general practitioner. Sadly, all too often the general practitioners are not present. And we've tried to get over the other issue for example, some of them will argue from time to time on the length of a case conference, 'I can't sit there for two hours listening to people, I'm a busy man', we will take that on board, there's no reason why we shouldn't start the case conference and after brief introductory remarks regarding the nature of the abuse, ask the doctor for his or her opinion and then release them, that can be done and has been done.*

Another said:

> *But it is difficult, we've had gramophone records, well if you had the case*
> *conference at a different time they will come. We've had case conferences at*
> *a different time and they haven't come. They're very busy and I appreciate*
> *particularly in [the main town], it's exacerbated because of the number of*
> *single-handed practices.*

The logistics of accommodating the time preferences of a number of busy
people with fixed commitments was indeed problematic, described as an
'organisational nightmare'.

> *We come back to this timing of the case conference, you are never going to*
> *get an ideal time. If the paediatricians are involved we will normally try*
> *and arrange a case conference time to suit them, if they are going to give us*
> *evidence that is crucial, then they need to be there and we will normally go*
> *for the time that is convenient to them, then a school will phone up and say*
> *'well we can't come because we're teaching at the time, why can't you hold*
> *it after school or whatever?'*

A child protection coordinator explained the difficulties and the strategies
used, to date unsuccessfully, as follows:

> *Our relationship with general practitioners is, at an organisational level in*
> *terms of case conferences, very poor indeed. I can't find a system that*
> *actually is sensitive to their needs. Most of them are silent, so I don't know*
> *what most of them want but those who aren't silent say if you had these*
> *conferences at a time when I don't have my surgery I'd be able to come and*
> *I would want to come. There are people for whom we've organised*
> *conferences specifically at a time they said they could come and they still*
> *don't. Their response when they can't come is very varied. On the whole*
> *they are totally silent. There are a number of practices who are extremely*
> *good at contacting us to say we can't come to this conference but this is what*
> *we have by way of useful information, these are our views about this*
> *family, but they're a very small minority. The vast majority are just*
> *completely silent and we make the potentially dangerous assumption that*
> *if they'd known something they would have let us know. Which probably*
> *is the kind of thing that could be dangerous really, but that's the way it is at*
> *the minute. I've asked the family health services authority to try and*
> *debate with general practitioners how we might resolve this and I've asked*
> *that when they're looking at their contracts for independent practitioners*
> *they consider something about a commitment to the child protection*
> *procedures but they're sort of shrugging and saying 'these are independent*
> *people' you know so I don't know quite how that will result.*

A paediatrician described his strategy to involve general practitioners. He suggested that the way forward was not to issue guidance or directions since 'they have been doing that in the Area Review Committee since it was established in the seventies' and it had had little effect. He thought a more fruitful approach was to involve them on a case by case basis beginning from the starting point that they cared about their patients. When certain kinds of referrals were made to him he suggested that the child should be seen by the general practitioner and he was happy to discuss the case with the general practitioner over the phone and to suggest that it would be helpful if she/he could attend the conference. While not all general practitioners were experienced or interested in this kind of work, the paediatrician was optimistic about engaging some by this means.

Although time pressures were reported as the most common reason for the absence of general practitioners, it is not apparent that they face significantly greater pressures in this regard than some others in the network, particularly those with fixed commitments such as teachers with class teaching responsibilities or consultant paediatricians with scheduled clinics. Thus other reasons probably contribute to their placing attendance at conferences as a low priority in practice. Some of these, including a relative lack of familiarity and confidence in work with abused children and their families, the pace of their work which renders it rare for a general practitioner to devote a couple of hours at a time to only one patient, perceived problems about confidentiality and divided loyalties, were discussed in Hallett and Stevenson (1980). Over a decade later these issues still seemed problematic for many general practitioners, as indicated by the following responses:

> *Even when they do come they get all hot and bothered about confidentiality. When you have to go through it again and again that it's confidential and that sort of stuff. They've never taken that on and it's always strange to me why they do that when their colleagues at hospitals are so much more relaxed about the whole thing and are quite prepared to do that, I don't understand the difference in ethics there.*

> *They're caught up on the confidentiality thing, I think that's very often why they don't come. I think they hide behind that. I think there's a lot of GPs that are just frightened you know of crossing that barrier and perhaps, maybe because they are frightened of losing patients, I don't know.*

Since complaints about the non-attendance of general practitioners have been so frequent for so long, the question of whether their absence really mattered was probed in interview to ascertain whether the refrain was simply ritualistic. As expected, their contribution when they were present was perceived by some to be varied but, in general, valuable. This appeared to be more in respect of the information they could share at the conference than in terms of their own contribution to the child protection plan, although their future contact with the child and family might be expeced to include a concern with child protection if they had attended the conference. As one social work manager said:

> *I'm frequently pleasantly surprised by the knowledge that they have of the child, the parents and in a small relatively stable community like this, family history . . . They know the families and they're actually quite useful in terms of who the aunties are . . . if you need to look for some family support there's so and so in the next estate . . .*

Birchall's (1992) study confirmed that limited involvment of many general practitioners in child protection and their position on the periphery of the interagency network. Only 47% of the general practitioners in that study owned their own copy of the local interagency guidelines compared with an average of 66% for the sample as a whole. They ranked the usefulness of the procedures concerning their own role at 40%, second lowest compared with an average of 63%, and, with teachers, were least clear of their role in child protection of the six key groups sampled (Birchall, 1992, p59 and 197). As Birchall notes, upgrading their knowledge is a large task as would be any concerted strategy to overcome their apparent resistance to involvement. The issue is further discussed in Chapter Eleven.

Family involvement

In 1988 and 1989 at the time of the initial child protection conferences in the case sample in the study, neither authority operated policies of parental or child attendance for the whole of the conference. At the time of the field interviews in 1991, a pilot scheme was in operation in selected parts of borough but the issue was still under discussion in the Area Child Protection Committee and presenting considerable difficulty in city. In city, guidelines issued after *Working Together* (1988) included the phrase 'present ACPC policy does not permit attendance at initial incident case conferences'. Thus in neither area at the time of the study had there been full implementation of the advice contained in *Working Together* (1988) that parents 'should be invited where practicable to attend part of, if appropriate, the whole of case conferences unless in the view of the Chairman (sic) of the conference their presence will preclude full and proper consideration of the child's interest' (DHSS and Welsh Office, 1988, p 29).

Of the 48 initial child protection conferences in the sample, there was parental attendance in only three. The person who attended was the mother, in two cases in borough and one in city. In all three, attendance was for part and not the whole of the meeting. In borough, standard letters were sent to parents informing them of the conference, advising them of its powers and inviting them to make their views known, in writing or via the social worker, if they wished.

The persons informing parents of the outcome of initial child protection conferences are shown in Figure 7.6. The person informing the parents was not specifically recorded in 17 cases. The most frequent person was the key worker (the person nominated in the conference to take responsibility for case coordination) acting alone. The 'other' category comprises the NSPCC (one case), the key worker and a health visitor (one case), the key worker and a probation officer (one case) and a principal social worker (one case). As is shown in Figure 7.7 the conference chair or the chair and the key worker were also used in borough, but not in city.

Figure 7.6   **Persons informing parents of the outcome of initial child protection conferences (N = 48)**

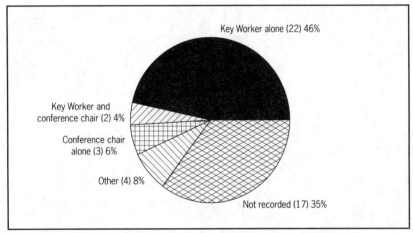

Figure 7.7   **Persons informing parents of the outcome of initial child protection conferences: borough and city compared (N = 48)**

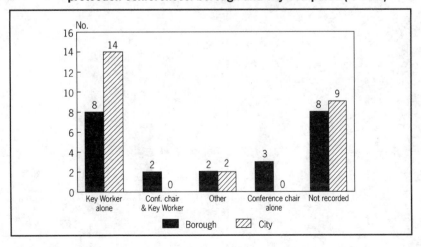

The means by which parents were informed was not specifically recorded in 23 of the 48 cases. As is shown in Figure 7.8, where it was recorded it was most often done by a home visit to the parents.

Figure 7.8 **The means of informing parents of the outcome of initial child protection conferences (N = 48)**

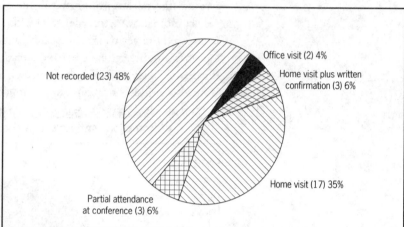

The slightly different patterns in city and borough are illustrated in Figure 7.9.

In few cases was there a record of written confirmation to the parents of the conference decisions on the social services department file. Central govern-

Figure 7.9 **The means of informing parents of the outcome of initial child protection conferences: borough and city compared (N = 48)**

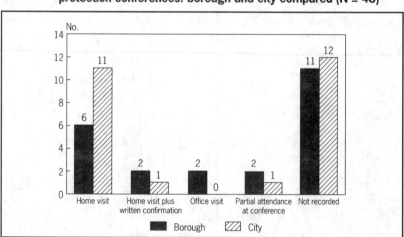

ment guidance in force at that time advised that 'written confirmation of the interagency action plan should, with the agreement of the agencies concerned, be provided for parents by the key worker' (DHSS and Welsh Office, 1988, p 30). Later guidance in *Working Together* (1991) recommended that those present should receive the minutes of initial child protection conferences and that 'others who were not present for the whole or part of the conference such as parents or other relevant family members and professionals should receive as a minimum written confirmation of the main findings of the conference, a note of who attended and who was absent and confirmations of the decisions and recommended plan of action' (Home Office et al, 1991, p 44).

At the time of the initial child protection conferences in the case sample, most of which took place in 1989 and 1990, parental and child involvement in the meetings was very limited. Nonetheless, since a pilot project was underway in borough and the issue was under active consideration in the ACPC in city and because of the significance of the topic, respondents were asked about it in interview. Many of those interviewed had experience of involving children and parents in review child protection conferences, in reviews of children in care or in other case discussions or planning meetings.

A number of respondents favoured parental involvement as a matter of principle and citizens' rights. For example, a nurse manager argued:

> *I've been to quite a few now where parents are there. Yes, they're not easy,*
> *I can see how important it is. I mean you only, in your mind, have to turn*
> *the situation around and think of somebody making a decision about your*
> *child and you can see that it sort of feels right that they should be there.*

One social worker said:

> *I think, looking at it from a parent's point of view, I think that there*
> *should be some way that they can have a say in that sort of forum,*

and another:

> *I think parents should have the right, whenever reasonable, to be in the*
> *case conference. It doesn't cause me any trouble at all.*

Finally, a police officer argued:

> *If you discuss the principle of it, I think they should be there because there*
> *are people saying things about them and their family and they don't get to*
> *challenge that and, based on what's been said about them and their family,*
> *very serious decisions may be taken and there's no-one there to challenge*
> *what's been said. And it's contrary to the root principle of law.*

Others, besides agreeing with the principle of parental involvement, argued that it led to more effective practice as noted by Thoburn (1992). For some, this was because the conference had access to better quality information, partly as a result of professionals taking greater care about the presentation and accuracy of their own contribution and partly because parents themselves could contribute additional information and correct errors. They were able to present themselves and their case to those conference attenders who did not know them personally, and had an opportunity to shape the recommendations made and to make a commitment to them.

The following quotations illustrate these views:

> *I think it's good for the parents to be involved because we are talking about them and their child or children and I think it's good to get them involved at a very early stage, you know, and I think by doing that maybe to build up trust with some of the parents and for the workers to work with them. At least it's in the open and they know exactly what's going on and the recommendations made. I think it is a good thing.*

> *I think we're new at it and I think people choose their words a lot more carefully, and maybe they should. I think they leave unsaid things but whether those things ought to be said in the first place if they can't be said in front of the parents is another argument. Yes, I think basically they do watch what they say, they leave things out but I'm not sure that's always a disadvantage. There are times when you can actually get hold of how to work jointly, genuine working relationship between the family and the group of professionals, the core group. People get more committed to it. You know they're in there making promises to each other, effectively, which is better than the professionals sitting round saying this is the plan we ought to present to the family, which is a kind of one sided arbitration. So when it works well, I think it works very well.*

Trends towards greater openness were reported in health visiting, social work and in other professions and some respondents argued that parental participation in conferences represented a welcome extension of their practice in being open and honest with parents outside the conference arena. As one social services manager explained:

> *All the staff we have in this office are able to be fairly open, honest and straight with parents but I can see that some other agencies who maybe haven't a chance to talk to the parents before the case conference, in terms of what their input was going to be, would maybe have difficulty*

and a social worker explained:

> *People know for the most part where they stand with me. I'm always*

straight up about the role that I have; you know, 'my role here is to assess whether you are a good enough parent or not and you have to show me what you can do and then I can go back to the court and say this is what this person has shown me they can do and, in the time that we've been working together, this is how it's changed and this is how it's improved but if you won't do that with me then it's your responsibility', and I dole it out like that and go for it.

A nurse manager said:

I think some staff will find it difficult, I think some people will feel uneasy with it. What we've tried to do, working towards it, is to talk to the staff about open recording and sharing. Several of the staff are actually recording at the time with parents and we're trying to push that more and more. We're now doing the Children Act training and it's given us another opportunity to reinforce it and we've used the staff to train staff rather than it coming from the seniors alone. So they've got their peers saying 'look we've got to be more open' as well as us saying.

As others have suggested (eg. Atherton, 1992, Monk, 1992) there was agreement in interviews that if parental involvement in conferences was to work successfully it needed to be founded not only upon a direct, open and honest approach in the rest of professional dealings with parents but also upon specific help and preparation for conference attendance itself. As one social worker said:

It's no good at all inviting a parent along to a case conference and them suddenly being overtaken by the case conference which so often happens. As social workers we are used to going to meetings, we're used to talking to a group of people, for a parent suddenly to be invited to a case conference with no preparation whatsoever they might as well not be there, they don't know what is happening. I think we're still of the opinion that we've invited them, what more do they want. I do think they do need preparing, they need to feel comfortable, if anybody can feel comfortable in case conferences. But I think we should do everything we could to make the parents be an active part of that meeting, otherwise there's just no point in them being there at all. I think it's about us getting our act together and seeing the needs of the parents or the carer.

However, not all of those interviewed were in favour of the changes which followed *Working Together* (1988). Some simply expressed themselves as uncertain, for example:

It's very difficult actually expressing an opinion when you haven't had an experience of parents attending a ghastly incident case conference all the way through. Because that's the tester isn't it, you know, because you think some people can't get it right when they're not there, what are they going to do when they are there?

Others were more antagonistic and, at the time of the study, the resistance of, for example, the police and the paediatricians in the ACPC in city had not been overcome. Some argued in principle for the rights of professionals to meet alone. For example:

We don't invite to initial case conferences because that's policy – it's a department view, which I actually agree with, that it should be a forum where professionals can meet and discuss views openly and decide a strategy on an initial incident.

More common were pragmatic concerns that the presence of parents would be detrimental to the conference for various reasons. One worry, frequently expressed, was that participants would be less than frank with each other. For example:

I'm not sure how I would feel where I have to say negative things. I just don't know.

I think it would inhibit a lot of the work that goes on in that forum because I think there's a lot of things that people couldn't say . . . it's going to be quite inhibiting and difficult.

and:

But I do feel, having been to case conferences with the parents present, that some of the people there are not saying what they would have said had the parents not been there and so you don't get the full information to share.

and from a paediatrician:

I do not support the idea of parents being at case conferences. They could, on occasion, but if one parent is the perpetrator or has significantly failed to protect the child, I think it would mean there was a prior conference where things were shared or some degree of inhibition which would not be to people's benefit.

A second concern was that the parents understandable anxiety and, at times, anger would disrupt the conference. Thirdly, some expressed the view that the parents' presence might distract the conference from its primary focus upon the child(ren) concerned:

I think it's possible to have parents attending incident case conferences and I think it's possible for it to be a positive experience for all concerned, however, I do think that there will be circumstances, many circumstances, where it will mean the children's interests aren't served and that's the problem that I've got. You tend to think that the Department of Health isn't looking at it too closely because if they did it would worry them really.

Fourthly, some, notably the police, expressed concern at the possibility of the parents incriminating themselves in conferences.

In common with experience elsewhere (eg. McGloin and Turnbull, 1986, Shemmings and Thoburn, 1990), some of those interviewed, however, reported that their concerns about these matters had been dispelled following experience of parental involvement in initial conferences in the pilot programme in borough, for example:

The advent of parental participation I think, in general terms, has benefited the system although I'd been personally opposed to it. My opposition to it has always been the fear that it becomes parent centred rather than child centred. At the moment I've only been involved in a couple of case conferences where you've had parental participation, it has not been an issue. It may just be the sample at the moment and it's not brought up the real problem cases. The conferences we've had so far, we've been able to keep it very clear that we are talking about the child, that the needs and wishes of the parent although they're understood and specific must not interfere with what is in the best interest of the child;

I'm actually at the stage where, those conferences where I haven't got parents, I'm feeling at quite a disadvantage which is interesting. I think it's not as difficult as I thought it might be, though it's not easy. The difficulties are about the balance of power and making sure that the parents are not patronised or all the conferences turned into a sort of therapeutic session and I try to deal with that by making it a very business meeting and I think some people think it's not fair on the parents who are probably not used to business meetings. I actually think that they are coping extremely well with these business type meetings but different people have different styles and I don't have the advantage of having been able to go and observe anybody else's because the very nature of them is that you can't have a whole host of observers, so I don't know what styles people are adopting. The actual presence of the parents has brought a different flavour to meetings which certainly makes them, in some way, more manageable from the chair's point of view because the professional network is still fairly intimidated by it so they review their information before they come to conference and if you ask the minute-takers, they'll say they're lovely.

In the pilot project the preliminary results were considered to be encouraging:

> *I think the pilot is going quite well. People have looked at 'what do I know, what is relevant' and they come prepared, instead of grabbing their case file on their way out of the office and thinking on the steps up to the conference room so, from that point of view, there's lots of advantages. I'm told they take a bit more time. I don't know what I feel about it actually facilitating ongoing work thereafter, that will be borne out by experience but it feels like you're making a start to a process and the preliminary feedback from parents is that they were glad they were there but they're not actually fooled into thinking they actually decided anything. They've got a fairly accurate assessment of what it's about, by and large, and I certainly don't pretend to them when I do my introduction bit that they are in a position to decide anything. I'm quite straight with them about 'you're here because it's useful for us to have you here basically. We need what you know to make a decent decision and not because we're doing you a favour or it's your right'. I don't see it in those terms, so I try to be fairly straight about the limitations of what we're doing but I haven't had big problems. By and large, in terms of participation, I think it's going along quite nicely. I'm pleased, I mean it encourages me. It's people like the police who frequently say 'well it's a pity Mrs so and so isn't here (in the ones that are non sample cases) because, you know, it would be really useful to have her here. You would understand it if you could hear her say it for herself.' Its fascinating.*

Such problems as there were in the pilot study were reported to be primarily logistical, such as adequate waiting rooms and child care facilities.

At the time of the research, there was an uncertainty about and little experience of involving children in initial child protection conferences. One social service manager argued that children's attendance should take priority because 'if we don't, then again we're seeing the children as chattel of parents'. But another suggested:

> *I've more reservations about child participation because our new procedures allow children who are sufficiently mature to attend the case conferences. I haven't had one where anybody's brought a child but I have a lot of anxieties about it because I think that the tension that there is about whether this is a damaging and difficult process for a parent is magnified a hundred times with the child. My feeling is that, in most families, there are lots of bits of family history that are not necessarily horrendous or earth-shattering but that have not been shared with adolescents. Very few parents, in my experience, will, for instance, have discussed their sexual relationship with their adolescent children or their previous relationships.*

They may or may not have been open about parentage of children within the family; they may or may not have shared with children medical histories, but I, as a chair, don't know what the child knows and I don't know what people have got up their sleeve and I'm really worried about the possible impact of a piece of casually tossed information to a child who doesn't know it and, as I say, I'm a lot more worried about that. I'm prepared to risk telling the parents something they didn't know but I'm worried about the child because I can't prepare them for what I don't know is coming. Child involvement in these conferences slipped through on the nod as uncontentious in our ACPC. They sort of thought, of course, children should be entitled. I think nobody had really thought that through and it was the notion of parents that was agitating people and I think, because of that, we haven't done the thinking through about the child policy.

This appears to confirm the findings in Birchall's study that respondents were less keen to see the involvement of children than parents in conferences. Only 7% of respondents thought children should be present for the whole of the conference, compared with 14% who thought parents should be. 53% thought children should be present for part of the conference compared with 66% who thought parents should be and 25% thought children should not be present at all, compared with 12% who thought so in respect of parents (Birchall, 1992, p 87).

Chairing child protection conferences

In appraising the value and effectiveness of initial child protection conferences, an issue discussed more fully below, there was agreement amongst those interviewed about the vital role of the chair. This is in accordance with government guidance in *Working Together* (1991) which states:

*The skills of the chair are crucial to the effectiveness of the interagency child protection conference. The chair should have a good understanding and professional knowledge of child protection. The selection and necessary training of those who chair child protection conferences is of great importance. (*Home Office at al, 1991, p 46*).*

It also reflects the findings of other studies, for example, Hallett and Stevenson (1980) and Birchall's study, in which the chairing was ranked fourth most important in a list of fourteen items for the improvement of conferences proposed by 204 recent conference attenders (Birchall, 1992, p 98).

The following quotations illustrate the perceived importance of the chair among those interviewed:

> *I think they are useful forums to gather all those people together if they're chaired well. When they're chaired well, they're chaired very well; when the chair doesn't know what they're supposed to do, they are abysmal;*

> *Some of the conferences that I've been to in (city) have been absolutely horrendous, they don't seem to be going anywhere;*

> *Some go on for too long. I've been to some that have lasted over two hours. That's an exception but I think we should be looking for sort of between an hour, an hour and a quarter and that's not to cut out any information, but it's to get people trained so that they give the information tht's required and very often I'm sort of wriggling in my seat because someone is saying something and we've heard that two or three times. That's where you need the strong chair and the strong chair also is important because if we just go in, sort of the eight of us and everybody is chipping in from the outset which occasionally happens, not quite as bad as that, but not far off. Then you don't get a clear picture and you're thinking 'wait a minute', you know, you get into a real muddle.*

The minute takers amongst others in both authorities identified the following characteristics as particularly important in good chairing: eliciting the information clearly at the beginning; having a clear agenda and sticking to it; managing the time; facilitating the participation of all who had something to contribute and clearly formulating the recommendations.

All but one of the initial conferences in the case sample was chaired by a member of the social services department, the exception being a conference chaired by the NSPCC, as shown in Figure 7.10.

Figure 7.10   **Role of person chairing the initial child protection conference (N = 48)**

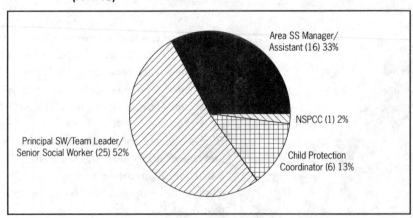

The patterns were different between the two authorities, as is shown in Figure 7.11 with more area social service managers/assistants chairing in borough than their equivalent, divisional officers, in city, and more principal social workers/team leaders chairing in city than in borough.

Figure 7.11 **Role of person chairing the initial child protection conference: borough and city compared (N = 48)**

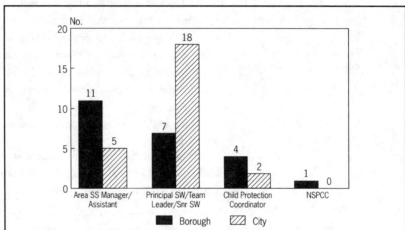

In both authorities at the time of the field research major changes were in train in respect of chairing conferences. In both the aims were to create a smaller pool of conference chairs, to boost their training, to ensure an independent chair and to try to effect greater uniformity across each authority in the style, format and content of conferences. The strategies for achieving this differed between the authorities. In borough, it was done through centralising the arrangements for conferences through the child protection coordinator and associated administrative staff. There, the problem in the past had partly been practical:

> *Before we had four office bases basically doing their own thing and because we're such a small area you could actually have all four, without knowing it, convening a case conference on the same day at the same time that required the paediatrician, the police surgeon, the legal adviser, a chair, a minute taker and a whole host of poeple and then all week there'll be nothing else happening. Which meant that a lot of conferences were happening without a legal adviser, without a whole host of very relevant people and all the other agencies were saying 'how are we supposed to choose which we go to'. And in reality they were saying 'we go to the area manager who'll shout loudest at us if we don't'. You know that was the*

> *basis on which these sort of crucial decisions were being made so that was the major motivating factor.*

but it was also a decision in principle:

> *Combined with my own and* Working Together*'s expressed concerns about line management chairs. I felt very strongly that there was a lot of role confusion for line managers who chaired case conferences and my observations were that that was reflected in the case conference minutes I was reading and that I felt that we needed to establish an independent chairing system and we needed to coordinate it. From an authority wide view we also got four different approaches to chairing and idiosyncratic agendas for case conferences and I felt it was important that we had this consistent approach and that we were all clear that we were working to the same kind of agendas and we were using the criteria in the same kind of way and applying some kind of consistency.*

At the time of the interviews, the system was newly implemented. Social workers generally expressed relief at having the time-consuming burden of arranging conferences removed from them:

> *The bulk of the ringing round and organising was falling on social workers, at a time when we had unallocated child protection cases and people were spending half the day doing basically an admin job, whilst goodness knows what kind of case was pending investigating in the unallocated basket so there were other reasons for bringing it in. But they're saying to me it's a great relief to them to be able just to hand it over to somebody and say please do it for me.*

There were some difficulties initially, including resistance by some of the pool of chairs to chair the conferences. There was said to be a temptation to plead other commitments in the hope that another might be called upon. The intention was to avert this by requiring chairs to offer blocks of time in advance (eg. each Tuesday morning). There was also some loss of flexibility as to timing, for example:

> *I want this on Tuesday afternoon and we say we're sorry we're already having one on Tuesday afternoon, you can have it on Thursday morning*

which was commented upon unfavourably by some in the interagency network, for example, social service managers, paediatricians and police surgeons. One area social services manager also observed that no longer chairing conferences in his own patch distanced him from the child protection cases in the area but others spoke favourably of the system and of the value of independence in the chair:

I think it's an improvement in that it offers and demonstrates impartiality, certainly referring to one of the cases that I recently chaired where there was parental involvement I found it extremely helpful to say to the parent that I was not tainted in any way by the case, I had no prior knowledge of it and I was not coming with a hidden agenda about you know, my social worker must be right or whatever, I was there to hear what had to be said from all sides, not to adjudicate, I don't see it as a form of legal proceedings, but in terms of the questioning that takes place in case conferences, normally that is initiated by the chair, I was able to reassure these parents that I would be neutral and objective.

In city, similar objectives were about to be implemented at the time of the research by designating a smaller pool of chairs within each of the divisions, reducing the number from 40 with different levels of experience and expertise to about 20 and also instituting a new training programme. It was expected that this would address the variation in chairing standard which existed across the city, upon which many commented in interview.

Preparation for conferences

Besides the quality of chairing, many of those interviewed stated that better preparation on the part of conference attenders would improve the running of conferences and possibly shorten them. One minute-taker commented as follows:

I just wish they'd be more prepared about what they're going to say. And even when they have it in front of them they don't seem to be able to pick out the relevant parts, they just say it all as if they've given no thought to it at all. Which is not helpful from our point of view, it's not helpful from everybody else's point of view, so preparation is something that everybody could be better at.

and a frequent conference attender said:

You often find people attend case conferences without preparation. That's very unhelpful because they haven't got dates, they are maybe expressing impressions and you want to know what these impressions are based on and they can't tell you because they haven't looked at the records recently.

As noted above, the health visitors and school nurses appeared to place most importance upon preparation for conferences. This may reflect their anxiety about them, which seem to be higher than that of others in the network, or maybe they were simply more willing to express it. One said for example:

I still feel intimidated. I usually prepare myself fairly well so that I have most of it in writing anyway what I want to say.

In addition, however, their management structures and recording practices reflected the importance attached to preparation. One nurse manager said when asked what contributed to successful conferences:

I think preparation really. It's enormously important to do that. I mean I was health visiting and I say it from humility, I was the first one to sort of grab a record card and go and so I don't say it from a sort of judgemental position. They really have to think what they're doing and how important it is and to make valid decisions. They have to be well run and I think the chairperson really is enormously important and the preparation from the people who are taking part.

In addition often to accompanying health visitors/school nurses to conferences as discussed earlier, nurse managers attached high priority to preparing for them with their staff. It was reported that in both city and borough all staff would be seen prior to the conference:

Yes, even if I can't go with them to conference then I spend fifteen minutes, half an hour, depending on the complexity of the case, going through what issues concern them, what is it that worries them as a health visitor, what are they concerned about, what do they want to make sure they put forward to corroborate their concerns, what evidence have they got to back it up and any other peripheral information that they feel is going to be pertinent.

In city, which had a structured recording system for child protection matters in health visiting/school nursing, there was a written proforma for completion, prior to the conference, by the health visitor or school nurse which incorporated details on the family composition, a brief family history and details of the involvement of the service with the child and family concerned. This formed the basis for discussion prior to the conference both about the information to be shared and the nature of any future health visiting/school nursing input to the child protection plan.

Clearly others in the interagency network prepared themselves for conferences, for example, the police in searching criminal records and updating themselves on the case and paediatricians and police surgeons in presenting the results of medical examinations. Social workers also often presented written reports of the initial investigation and had discussed the case prior to conference with the supervising senior team leader or principal who were closely involved in initial investigation and often attended the conference in support of the social worker. However, it seemed that the health visiting/

school nursing services in both authorities accorded more explicit priority to this task. This may be more feasible where, as in health visiting, child protection cases form a relatively smaller proportion of the total caseload than in services such as social services. It may, however, also reflect the importance placed on the role in government guidance issued to senior nurses on the management of child protection. (DHSS, 1988(a)). Nonetheless, it appears that better preparation could usefully be extended to others in the network.

Minutes

The minutes of initial child protection conferences are potentially key documents in interagency work in child protection, in recording agreements reached concerning the interagency protection plan, in serving as a baseline information source for workers and as a means of alerting those invited to conferences but unable to attend of the outcomes. Their importance is acknowledged in *Working Together* (1991) which reads as follows:

> *The written record of the child protection conference is a crucial working tool for all professionals. It should detail the essential facts, the decisions and the recommendations, the interagency child protection plan and an account of the discussion on which the decisions and recommendations are based. A copy of the minutes should be sent to all who attended the conference (*Home Office et al, 1991, p 47*).*

This is fuller than the advice in *Working Together* (1988), operative at the time of this study, which states as one of the main tasks of the conference chair to ensure that 'a written note of the case conference which records those participating, absentees and the recommendations, is made and its circulation list agreed' (DHSS and Welsh Office, 1988, p 29).

At the time of the research, the situation with regard to minute-taking was problematic in both authorities but was particularly severe in city. Of all the problems and resource difficulties in interagency work, this appeared to be the one most often raised spontaneously in interview and the one which attracted the most frequent highly critical comments, from within and outwith the social services department. The following comments are typical, but represent a small selection only:

from a school nurse:

> *What's been happening in [city] for a little while is that there are no minute-takers. Now that really worries me. I feel quite strongly we're dealing with people's lives and they are very powerful case conferences and the more you go sometimes to some of them, the more you realise just, well*

I do, I'm very conscious of what we're doing and I think if things had not been written down right then it's not very good.

from a social worker:

From a practitioner's point of view, from everybody's point of view, one of the banes of our life is case conference minutes. I mean [city] will not recognise that we need minute-takers and like it's just, it's horrendous. If these meetings are important enough to convene and get ten or twelve people to them, they're damn well important enough to be recorded and it's just shocking.

from a social services manager:

I think that this authority has been seriously remiss in failing to provide proper minuting of case conference.

and from senior management in social services:

. . . the minute-takers, which was obvious really, it was shouting as soon as I came. Minute-taking is absolutely fundamental and it hasn't been happening.

It was in this area, above many others, that workers expressed their vulnerability. One social services manager said:

The problem with not minuting is it is so dangerous. It's luck that there's not been a problem, I think. It leaves us personally wide open.

and a practitioner:

What people are now doing is refusing to take our own minutes but, again, I just think there but for the grace of God go we because it's only going to take one case conference where there's something serious is going to happen and we haven't got anything recorded.

The resentment this had caused was palpable. Practice in the past had been that where central minute-takers were not available, conference chairs had taken minutes (a practice explicitly criticised in the Beckford Report, (London Borough of Brent, 1985) and in *Working Together* (1988)) or the supervising principal social worker had done so. It was acknowledged that this was not good practice and in an attempt to pressurise for more resources, some social service managers were willing only to list the key recommendations from conferences and not attempt to provide full minutes:

I can't take the minutes and chair and contribute to the conference, it is absurd. I resent that.

The critical comments from many in the interagency network suggested that they did attach importance to conference minutes and used them as working tools. Although minute-takers and conference chairs reported that they did not generally receive many corrections, respondents acknowledged in interview that they did check the contents and correct them where necessary, although there was often a considerable delay between the initial conference and the receipt of the minutes. NSPCC staff acting as consultants to conferences in borough were reported to be particularly assiduous in checking the minutes. One of the team members gave the following example:

> . . . the other time I will also insist on it is if say a comment is made and that comment is minuted, an example was somebody saying 'but Mum likes the violence too; he hits her and she seems to enjoy it', and I said 'well if that's the case we need to know why this person puts up with that violence because nobody should be subject to violence' and when it came back, their comment was minuted and my reply wasn't and I did it from the point of view that somebody else was reading those minutes would think what on earth was the NSPCC doing there not to pick up on that, so that was sent back.

A nursing officer who read minutes as part of her advisory and monitoring role said:

> I've just had one set of minutes where it said the health visitor was going to maintain daily contact for six months. I've just dealt with that this morning and phoned up the health visitor and said 'have you read these minutes?' I think she said she was going to have weekly contact.

The lack of minute-takers was attributed to resource shortages, but also to a reluctance to acknowledge the importance of the administrative infrastructure in the department – a problem not confined to city but experienced in many social service departments (Stevenson and Parsloe, 1978) and in other services. This was confirmed in Birchall's (1992) study in which 40% of respondents were concerned about the need for a minutes secretary and the preparation of better minutes which, taken together, comprised the largest single area identified for improvement in the conduct of conferences. When asked about obstacles to interagency cooperation in child protection work, 47% of respondents in Birchall's study across the agencies identified inadequate secretarial support.

A shortage of secretarial support was acknowledged by some as a gender issue, a reflection of the gendered division of labour in social services departments and a reluctance of the part of key decision-makers to value the skill inherent in "women's work" (Hallett, 1989). As one social worker commented:

> There's a lack of acknowledgement of the role of women who do the minutes and organise the case conferences and stuff and without those women doing that work none of it would happen. In terms of working together they have a really important role which just isn't acknowledged, they do all the paperwork and all the letters and all the communication.

While many commented on the skill and training required to produce good minutes, this had not been reflected in the recruitment and pay of sufficient staff to do the work.

At the time of the field interviews, practice was changing in city. Additional administrative staff were being recruited to work with the child protection coordinator with minute-taking as one of their key functions. As with the introduction of specialist social workers, this was a development which was widely welcomed and seen as long overdue. The appointment of new senior management staff in the social services department was said to have helped effect the change.

The issue of minute-taking also posed problems in borough. There, too, the resource was newly centralised with the child protection coordinator making minute-takers available to initial conferences. The pressure of work in the section was such that:

> I've not been happy with the minuting situation, we've been under-resourced, at the moment our battle is huge. That's not just down to minute-takers, some of that's down to me. I mean I've got case conferences that I haven't had time to check the minutes of that are well overdue.

The format of minutes

While the key problem in both authorities at the time of the research was the supply of administrative staff to take the minutes, there were also continuing debates about their format. In both authorities where centrally supplied minute-takers were provided, the conference minutes were full, running often to twelve, fourteen or, at times, twenty pages. Some recipients thought them too long, arguing that key points were not highlighted and they were not easily assimilated by social workers on duty, or others wishing to read the file, for example.

> Case conference minutes must be seen as a tool and it's very easy for people to say the more complex the tool is, the more use it is and that is not the case and, if at all possible, reports should be on one piece of paper. Certainly once reports get to more than three pages, there starts to be a

disabling process of reading the whole report. What people tend to do is they look at the beginning first few paragraphs and move to the end. I think that in terms also of the efficient use of the minute-takers that they should be trained in the skilful, winnowing-out of the relevant information and not every piece in the case conference is worth minuting.

This is, however, a highly skilled task. The tendency to skim the beginning and the end rather than read the full minutes in city was, no doubt, accentuated by a filing system which filed papers through holes at the top rather than the side, combined with conference minutes printed on both sides of the paper. In order to read them the file had to be rotated through 180° on each page – a defeating task with bulky files.

Some staff were unsure what format and length of minutes they required, as one social services manager explained:

It depends what I want to do with them. If I want to read them to find out quickly what happened, I want them not in verbatim form. I want it both ways but I think, on balance, I would say it's more important to have full detail because there are things which don't seem significant at the time but some years later when you're looking back on the case conference minutes, small details, things that people say add up and, if you're going to put together a case to go to court, it can be important what people say but maybe there's scope for both, you know, some kind of abstract could be attached to it which sums up what they think the basic reasons are that caused it because there's a tendency, I think, if you're trying to find some information quickly, you're scanning through minutes up to twenty pages long.

Others argued that the style and length of conference minutes should vary from case to case. In particularly serious cases, where court proceedings or potentially a case review by the ACPC or other body might be required, there was a need for more detail. However, it was not always possible to predict which cases might end in case review.

Finally, some were clear that if conference minutes were to meet their varied purposes, they needed to be fairly detailed. This was particularly the view of child protection coordinators, who were increasingly called upon to review conference decisions.

When I ask myself 'what do we want the minutes for? what do we go back to them for?' there are only two things that we go back to them for – one is the recommendations and one argument says you could just do a recommendations sheet and send that out, and the other is when somebody says 'on what did you base that decision?' and 'did you really say that at the case conference?' and that tends to be in very contentious court proceedings where we are being asked to demonstrate from thread to needle the basis of our decision-making. I've actually been asked to go back to a decision that was made at a case conference and that was eighteen months after the event and had we not had very full minutes, I couldn't have dealt with that, what people's thinking was at the case conference about this. We couldn't have been able to recapture it.

One response to such a request would be to say that the detail was not available long after the event but

. . . the other side to that is that if we're in a highly contentious situation and being asked to review it, I'd actually like to be able to review it. I don't want to say, 'well I don't know why we decided it, we just decided it.' I'd like to actually be able to go back to it if I need to and say 'well, yes, did we actually think this through? was there a problem with the discussion? were there were other influences?' I mean the meeting before this meeting was with a guardian ad litem saying 'I think these decisions made at these case conferences were flawed, can I have your professional view?' Well, without the whole minutes, I'd be hard pressed to give him one because I wasn't present at it and he's coming to me and saying 'well, as a professional advisor to this authority, what's your view about this case conference?' Now one outlook can be very comfortable so I say 'I can't give you one because we don't record them' but at another, you know, wearing my professional hat, I'd actually like to know if he's right. I think we've got to be prepared to be accountable. They're important decisions aren't they? And if you can't back track and just find the basis on which they were made, then I think you've hit a problem.

The solution adopted was to standardise and structure the minutes so that a front sheet of about three pages recorded details of conference attenders, apologies, family structure, reason for convening the conference and then clearly identified recommendations at the end. However, between the two, the content of the discussion would remain fully recorded. It is, perhaps, surprising that although central government has issued guidance on matters such as the recommended format of ACPC annual reports, and the content and formal of local procedural handbooks, it does not appear to have done so in respect of conference minutes beyond the paragraph in *Working Together* (1991) quoted above.

Summary

This review of the arrangements for initial child protection conferences revealed that almost all were chaired by social service department staff and most (67%) were held within 14 days of initial referral. The majority were held in social service department offices but there was a shortage of suitable venues. With the notable exception of general practitioners, attendance rates were considered to be satisfactory, indicating a degree of commitment on the part of professionals in the interagency network to this piece of collaborative machinery. Despite the guidance issued in *Working Together* (1988), the involvement of parents and children in initial child protection conferences was not well developed at the time of the registration of cases in the sample (mainly in 1989 and 1990), although a pilot project was underway in borough in 1991. This is indicative of a time-lag in the local implementation of central guidance, discussed more fully in Chapter Twelve. Respondents' attitudes to parental involvement varied, with some in favour as a matter of principle and because of a perceived beneficial impact on practice, others uncertain and some opposed. There was more uncertainty about the wisdom and practicality of involving children.

Three issues were identified as important in improving the effectiveness of child protection conferences: chairing, better preparation on the part of participants and the production of minutes. Chairing styles and competence were said to vary widely and steps were being taken to limit the pool of chairs, to train them and to ensure that they did not hold line management responsibility for the cases under discussion, with a view to establishing greater consistency. The shortage of skilled minute-takers was a problem in both research sites, but particularly pressing in city and a source of anxiety and much resentment.

Chapter 8

Child protection plans and perceptions of child protection conferences

This chapter reviews the decisions made in initial child protection conferences in the case sample and explores the process of interagency decision-making and respondents' perceptions of conferences as a mechanism for interagency collaboration.

Decisions taken at initial child protection conferences

Working Together (1991) is unequivocal about the status of the initial child protection conference in relation to decision making. It states:

> *the only decision for an initial protection conference is whether or not to register the child. It discusses and records a proposed plan of action and it is for each agency representative to decide whether to accept the recommendations for action and their part in the plan. There should be a locally agreed procedure for confirming that these recommendations will be acted upon* (Home Office at al, 1991, p 42).

This built upon the advice of *Working Together* (1988) which noted that 'the results of the discussion are recommendations to individual agencies for action' (DHSS and Welsh Office, 1988, p 28). While this is the formal position, in practice de facto decisions were made in initial child protection conferences on matters other than registration, confirming Hilgendorf's (1981) observation that, whatever the constitutional niceties, case conference conclusions are frequently decisions. Part of the reason for the attendance of supervisory staff such as team leaders and principal social workers or nurse managers, discussed in the previous chapter, was to ensure that the decisions reached, or strictly the recommendations made, were acceptable to their agencies. Those, such as the police who attended alone, reported that in practice it was extremely rare for the recommendations to be challenged or overturned by their senior officers nor was it customary in the social services departments.

Since the case sample comprised only registered children, a decision was obviously taken to register the index child or children in each conference. The registration categories were 27 cases of physical abuse and 21 of sexual abuse, including five of grave concern (three of sexual abuse and two of physical abuse). Four of the five grave concern cases involved contact with Schedule 1 offenders, three of which involved sexual offences and the fourth physical assault. The remaining case of grave concern was one in which a mother had threatened to harm her children.

In line with central government guidance that 'if a decision to register is made, it will be necessary to appoint a named key worker' (Home Office at al, 1991, p 42), a key worker was appointed in all 48 initial child protection conferences with the task of coordinating the interagency work. In all but two cases this was an area team social worker from the social services departments. The exceptions were one NSPCC social worker appointed in borough and one hospital-based social worker in city. However, in a few cases because of pressure of work in the teams concerned the key worker was not named in the conference, with the decision as to who would act as key worker waiting until allocation of the case. In the interim, a principal social worker or team leader was named as the contact point for others in the interagency network. One school nurse summarised the position in these cases as follows:

> *There are even key workers that cannot be allocated, they cannot name a key worker because they haven't got the resources, now that is very worrying indeed. We insist, I say 'right, could we have a name then please' and usually the principal social worker will give you his name, so you do have a name but you don't have an allocated key worker. There is pressure, there's a lot of pressure.*

The child protection plan

Central government guidance in force at the time of the initial child protection conferences in the case sample specified that one of the main tasks of the conference chair is to ensure that 'a plan, based on assessment and clearly understood by all concerned, is developed and agreed, for recommendation to the agencies concerned, and any reservations or dissenting views recorded' (DHSS and Welsh Office, 1988, p 29). This is one of the clearest indicators of a coordinated output.

In almost all of the initial child protection conferences in the sample, some kind of child protection plan was agreed at the conference. In three cases, no plan was outlined. In two this was because the conference decision was that further investigation and a reconvened conference was required before a plan could be formulated and in the other, because the key worker was appointed following the conference and had the task of formulating the plan, the conference having decided to register the child concerned.

The conference minutes scrutinised in the course of the research revealed that much of the focus of initial child protection conferences was upon the 'incident' or cause for concern which had precipitated the conference, on establishing whether abuse had occurred, and if so, the need for and category of registration. In this process, much attention was focused on the initial investigation of the alleged abusive incidents – for example the outcome of medical examinations, police inquiries or social work interviews – and then on the presentation by conference participants of their knowledge of and previous contacts with the children and families concerned. When this was clear, the discussion often turned to whether children met the criteria for registration and, only subsequently, to the formulation of a child protection plan. As one social service manager explained:

> *I've had the sense at several case conferences that you've spent two hours working out, well discussing whether or not registration should take place, discussing the police investigation where it might go from here or whatever, and people are exhausted by the time you get to that stage and often I think if there isn't a proper child protection plan worked out, a detailed one it's simply because people have got to the stage when they're just exhausted and they really think having to do that is too much. And the chair sort of responds to that somehow and allows them to get away with it.*

In interview, some acknowledged that this was not in accordance with central government guidance which stresses that children's names should be placed on the register only when they meet the criteria for registration *and* an interagency child protection plan is required. For example:

> *I think they take decisions about registration and then formulate the child protection plan, where in reality it ought to be the other way round.*

This study, therefore, confirms Farmer and Owen's (1993) finding that, in a sample of 120 child protection conferences, the average time spent discussing the child protection plan was only nine minutes. The emphasis in conferences upon investigation and the labelling and classification of 'the abusive incident' has also been noted by others, for example Hilgendorf, 1981, and the SSI Report on Rochdale (DH 1990(b)). It is a feature and possibly a requirement of a system with clear categories of registration, the potential involvement of the criminal justice system in respect of abusers and the need for evidence in respect of compulsory measures of care. It is reported to be a much less marked feature in systems, such as those in Holland, parts of Germany and parts of Belgium where the approach is more voluntaristic and therapeutic and where there is de-facto a large degree of decriminalisation of child abuse. Christopherson, for example, reports that in the Dutch case notes he studied details of the abuse were sketchy because the abusive incident was of secondary importance to the family's overall functioning and needs (Christopherson, 1989, p 86). Marneffe, too, describes how, by comparison with the British system, little attention is paid in a treatment centre in Brussels to the abuse itself, with a focus instead on the child's needs and the family's functioning (Marneffe, 1992). Some writers, however, Purvis (1988), for example, emphasise the need to explore the situational nature of the abusive act in great detail covering both its history and circumstances and the motivation and opportunities of the alleged offender in order to assess future risk. In the British child protection system as it currently operates, attention to both aspects – the abusive incident and the child and family's functioning and needs – is required, perhaps with varying emphasis from case to case. The problem seems to be how to encompass a consideration of both aspects within the constraints and desired length of the child protection conference.

The content of child protection plans

As is shown in Figure 8.1, in 45 cases (94%) the children were to be protected following the initial child protection conference by voluntary support. In 42, this was by support in their own homes or much more rarely those of extended family members and in a further three cases by voluntary admission to care, as it was then called. In only three cases were care proceedings or place of safety orders (as they were then called) sought following the initial conference. The patterns differed between the two authorities as is shown in Figure 8.2, with city opting for a greater degree of voluntary support in the cases in this case sample.

Figure 8.1   **Action following initial child protection conferences (N = 48)**

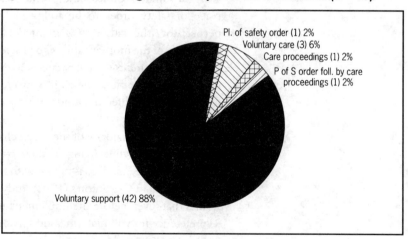

Pl. of safety order (1) 2%
Voluntary care (3) 6%
Care proceedings (1) 2%
P of S order foll. by care proceedings (1) 2%

Voluntary support (42) 88%

In the only case in the sample recommended for care proceedings during the initial conference, a place of safety order had been taken prior to the conference. This was a case of a five year old child living with his natural father and stepmother, referred by the father who acknowledged that the child had been bruised and asked for the child to be removed from home. The

Figure 8.2 **Action following initial child protection conferences: borough and city compared (N = 48)**

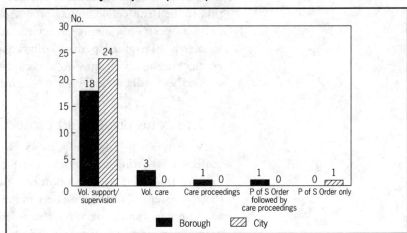

social worker reported the child to be 'tense, rigid and frightened' and asking to go to residential care. The two place of safety orders were taken in cases of sexual abuse. One was a case in which the family had temporarily disappeared with the children on learning of the allegation and it was decided to seek a place of safety order to be followed by care proceedings if the alleged perpetrator (the father) was granted bail, since the conference was not convinced of the mother's ability to protect the children. The other was a case in which the parents were separated and each made accusations about the care provided by the other. The children were removed on a place of safety order following the conference and care proceedings followed, after a spell in voluntary care.

Thus the vast majority of the index children (81%) were subject to a child protection plan while living in their own homes (or with relatives), as is shown in Figure 8.3. This is in line with but slightly higher than the figure of 74% reported in Creighton's (1992) study and confirms the findings of other stuides that, even before the implementation of the Children Act 1989 with its preference for voluntary measures, compulsory measures of care were used only infrequently (Hilgendorf, 1981, Dingwall at al, 1983, Corby, 1987, Packman et al, 1986). Although the numbers are small, there was in this sample a greater tendency towards the use of substitute care in borough as is shown in Figure 8.4. In eight of the 48 cases there were no other siblings in the household. In the 40 cases involving siblings they, too, were likely to live at home following the conference as is shown in Figure 8.5.

The elements of the child protection plan (in addition to registration and the appointment of a key worker) were classified from the minutes of the

Figure 8.3 **Place of residence of index children following the initial child protection conference (N = 48)**

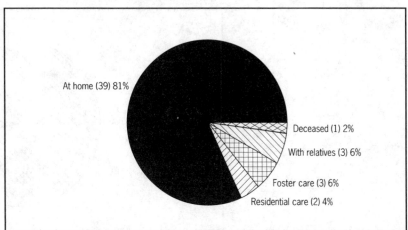

Figure 8.4 **Place of residence of index children following the initial child protection conference: borough and city compared (N = 48)**

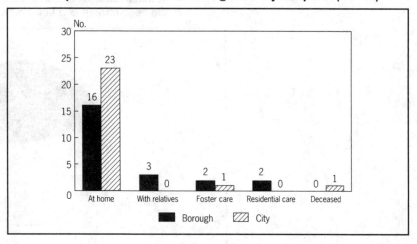

initial child protection conference using the following non-exclusive broad categories: police investigation, prosecution, assessment, social services department involvement, other agencies' involvement. It may be argued that any involvement with a child or family inevitably requires assessment and reassessment in the course of intervention and certainly key workers appointed at or following initial conferences would be likely to undertake assessment as part of the child protection plan. However, in some conferences the word 'assessment' carried implications of a fuller, more structured assessment along the lines of the 'orange book', the Department of Health guide to assessment entitled '*Protecting Children*' (DH, 1988). In Figure 8.6,

Figure 8.5 **Place of residence of siblings following the initial child protection conference (N = 40)**

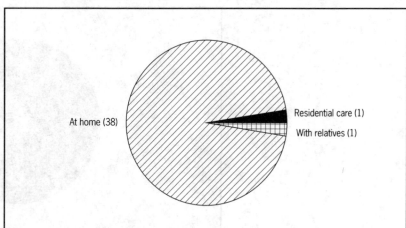

Figure 8.6 **Principal components of child protection plans as recommended at initial child protection conferences (excluding registration and the appointment of a key worker) (N = 102)**

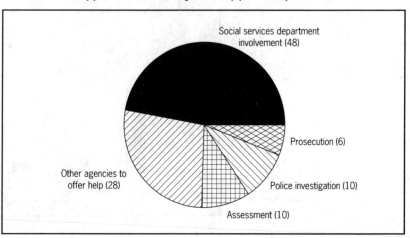

which presents the frequency of the principal components of child protection plans, assessment is reserved to those cases where a fuller assessment of this kind appeared to be intended.

The decisions concerning police activities in Figure 8.6 do *not* represent the sum total of police action in the case sample, since in some cases, investigations were completed or proceedings recommended before the initial conference was held. In total, police were involved in investigation in 32 of the cases and prosecutions resulted in 12 of the cases and police cautions in a further two, as discussed in Chapter Five.

Since the need for an interagency child protection plan is specified as a prerequisite for registration in government guidance, it is perhaps surprising that the role of other agencies in the network besides the social services department is mentioned in only 28 (58%) of the 48 cases (although this is in line with Farmer and Owen's (1993) finding that, in 30% of registered cases studies, the only intervention recommended was social work contact). The frequencies with which particular agencies were identified in the child protection plan is shown in Figure 8.7.

Figure 8.7 **Number of times in which specific agencies were mentioned in child protection plans (N = 101)**

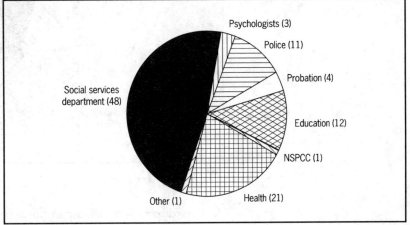

The patterns were broadly similar in borough and city, as is shown in Figure 8.8.

Figure 8.8 **Number of times in which specific agencies were mentioned in child protection plans: borough and city compared (N = 101)**

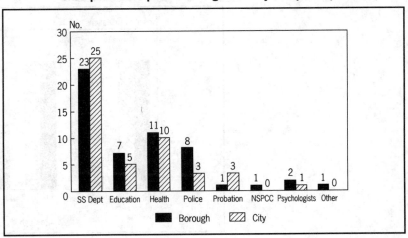

After social services, health was the service most often identified, in 21 of the 48 cases, followed by education in 12 of the 48. The separate components of health service activity identified in the 21 cases and the frequency with which they occurred are shown in Figure 8.9 for the sample as a whole.

Figure 8.9 **Number of times different health service professionals were identified in initial child protection plans (N = 28)**

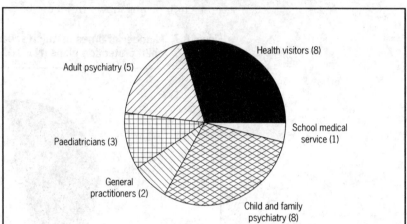

The patterns were almost identical in borough and city as is shown in Figure 8.10.

Figure 8.10 **Number of times different health service professionals were identified in initial child protection plans: borough and city compared (N = 28)**

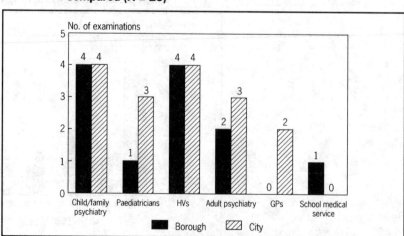

One of the two most frequently identified health resources was child and family psychiatry, although this only applied in eight of the 48 cases. This was more frequent than their reported involvement in response to the long case vignette presented in Birchall's (1992) study, which may reflect the fact that, in borough and in city, child and family psychiatric services had developed valued assessment and treatment resources in the field of child abuse but that there is local variation in service provision in this field across the country. The low levels of paediatric involvement following initial conferences confirmed their key investigative/diagnostic role in the field of child protection rather than sustained involvement in the treatment or follow up of the majority of the children concerned.

In the context of *interagency* child protection plans, it is surprising that the roles and expectations of those with routine contact with children and families are not spelled out more clearly. It appeared from interviews that health visitors and school nurses, who attended many of the conferences, gave much thought about the nature and scope of their future involvement with the cases, but this seems rarely to be reflected in detail in the child protection plans. General practitioners were less frequent conference attenders but conference minutes would be forwarded both to those who had attended and those who were absent. However, the expectations of them, if any, in relation to future handling of the case were not spelled out. A third example are the teachers. Although the case sample comprised primary school aged children, in only a quarter (12 cases) was the education service specifically mentioned in the child protection plan, as is shown in Figure 8.7. Of these, six referred to the need for the school to monitor the child, two to work on identifying alternative educational placements, two to the role of the educational welfare service in liaising with the schools concerned and reporting absence to the social services department, one to the work of a preschool liaison teacher and another to the need to contact the school for further information about a child. Despite the fact that schools have a role in monitoring children on the child protection register, in reporting any future concerns and prolonged absences of the child, this was noted in only a small number of the cases. It might be argued that this is common knowledge amongst teachers and does not need stating explicitly. However, data from this and other studies, for example Maher, 1987 and Birchall, 1992, suggests that familiarity with child protection matters should not necessarily be assumed on the part of all teachers.

In general, the child protection plans, as recorded for the social services departments files, did not always outline explicitly the roles of agencies in the interagency network in connection with future management of the case. This may be a missed opportunity since it should not be assumed that all will be conversant, through training, experience or knowledge of the local guide-lines, with what may be required of them for the future protection of the child concerned – a point discussed further in Chapter Eleven.

The services or resources to be offered to children and families as identified in initial child protection plans are listed in more detail in Table 8.1. These should not be taken as indicative of the entire range of services in fact supplied to and used by the various agencies to the children and families concerned. First, it was evident that some services offered were not, in fact, taken up, or not for long, by the families concerned. Secondly, it was clear from the social services department files that additional services, not specified in the original plan, were in fact provided by social workers. Thirdly, interviews suggested that it was likely that, in some cases, services additional to those specified in the child protection plan were provided by other agencies, for example, paediatric follow-up.

Table 8.1. **Number in cases in which service/resource specified in child protection plan (N = 104)**

	Borough	City	Total
Social work support	17	21	38
Child and family assessment	6	3	9
Child and family psychiatry	4	4	8
Health visiting	4	4	8
Social work advice/advocacy	6	1	7
School monitoring and support	4	7	11
Adult psychiatry	3	2	5
Respite/voluntary care	4	1	5
Paediatric follow-up	0	4	4
Day nursery/playgroup	1	2	3
Family aide	2	1	3
Financial/material aid	1	2	3
TOTAL	52	52	104

Nonetheless, the data in Table 8.1 do indicate the nature of the response and the envisaged scope of multiagency activity at the stage of the formulation of child protection plans. Three points emerge clearly. First, social services departments are at the forefront of the plans. When all the services/resources provided by them in the above table (support, advice and advocacy, respite care, family aide, financial/material aid) are totalled they comprise over half (56) of the total (104) resources and services specified in the initial plans. So following the peak of interagency involvement at the initial child protection conference, it diminishes thereafter, leaving the prime responsibility not just for case coordination but also for service provision with the social services department as the lead agency. Secondly, apart from the social services department, on-going involvement is concentrated in relatively few other services, notably schools, health visitors and child and family psychiatric services. Thirdly, there is very little joint, hands-on interagency collaboration in intervention. The various services may work in parallel and keep each other more or less closely in touch with their activities and developments in the case, but little joint, multidisciplinary intervention was envisaged or, in fact, took place.

These findings confirm many other studies including the Beckford Report, (London Borough of Brent, 1985), Corby and Mills, 1986, Gough et al, 1987, Weightman, 1988, Creighton and Noyes, 1989, the Social Services Inspectorate, (DH 1989), and Birchall, 1992. Gough et al, for example, studied 147 families (202 children) on the child protection register in Strathclyde and noted the low level of interagency work with registered children, particularly the absence of psychological and psychiatric advice and a paucity of health data, especially the limited contributions from general practitioners and community medical officers. They concluded that 'it is surprising to find such low levels of formal involvement of other agencies in what is meant to be an interdisciplinary monitoring system' and that 'at present the interdisciplinary case conference system does not really justify the name' (Gough et al, 1987, p 125 and 126).

The content and focus of the initial child protection plans varied widely in their breadth, depth and specificity from case to case. Some were extremely brief. One, for example, noted only that a decision had been taken to register a child in a particular category, that a key worker had been appointed and a core group would be established to monitor the child's progress and another that care proceedings and the prosecution of the alleged offender would follow. Others, by contrast, were more detailed. In one case, in which a mother had referred herself to her general practitioner having physically injured her child, the child protection plan included the following: a decision to register the index child in the category physical abuse but not to register the siblings; voluntary support since care proceedings were not warranted; the health visitor to visit regularly to offer advice about child management, to help with one child's enuresis and to try to arrange for a playgroup place; the education welfare officer to monitor school attendance; the police to consider the need for a police caution on receipt of the conference minutes; the social services department to offer support and advice about marital and financial problems and to monitor the care and well-being of the children; and finally, the establishment of a core group comprising the teacher, the educational welfare officer, the health visitor and the social worker.

For analytical purposes, the child protection plans may be sub-divided into five broad groups, the 'family supported', the 'abuser removed' the 'assessed', the 'cared for' and the 'monitored'. The categorisations are crude and there is a degree of overlap – for example, there is, or should be, a concern with monitoring the well-being of all registered children. Similarly many would say that whatever the focus of the plan their aim was to support the children and families concerned. However, the categorisations are intended to point to the primary orientation of the child protection plan as discerned from the case conference minutes and the social services department files. The frequencies of the categorisations are as shown in Figure 8.11 for the sample as a whole and with borough and city compared in 8.12.

Figure 8.11 Primary Orientation of Child Protection Plans (N = 46)

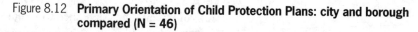

`family supported' (17)

`assessed' (4)

`monitored' (4)

`abuser removed' (13)

`child cared for' (8)

Figure 8.12 Primary Orientation of Child Protection Plans: city and borough compared (N = 46)

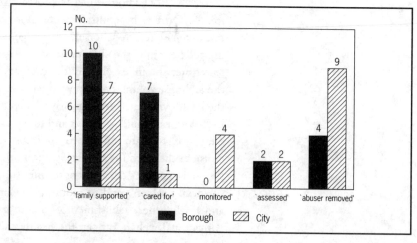

No.
12
10   10
8   7   7
6
4   4   4   4
2   2   2
0   0
   'family supported' 'cared for' 'monitored' 'assessed' 'abuser removed'

■ Borough   ▨ City

Two cases in city are uncategorised, one was a case conference held following the death of an infant following which the mother was charged. It was considered that a child protection plan would only be required if she became pregnant in the future. The second was a case in which a key worker was to be allocated following the conference and the case notes contain no entry for the six months following registration so it was difficult to discern the nature of the involvement.

The 'family supported'

These were mostly cases of physical abuse (13) and tended to be self-referred (10). As in Packman's (1986) study, abuse often proved to be only one concerning factor in an over-stressed family. In these cases, a voluntaristic approach was sought to improve the children's standards of care and well-being while they remained at home.

An example of such a case was one in which the mother called the police to the home, alleging that her cohabitee had injured her son. Physical abuse was confirmed, but there was also concern about neglect, particularly the general standards of cleanliness in the home, and there was a history of voluntary social work involvement over the preceding six years. The abuser was prosecuted and placed on probation. A child protection plan was developed, involving work with the cohabitee on his drinking problems and help for the family with material standards and child care, and a core group was established. The social worker's account is quoted in some detail since it illustrates well the nature of interagency involvement which can occur in such cases and also, incidentally, the complex situational judgements involved:

> *Setting core groups up initially is a bit of an effort but it is worthwhile and, in this case, it's been quite helpful to get regular updates about how children are performing in school because sometimes schools – unless you phone them up they are a bit reluctant to phone if they feel they're making a complaint about the care of the children and, in this case, its the physical appearance of the children . . ., they feel a little bit awkward really. So I think if you have regular meetings it's much easier for them to feel comfortable and give us some more information and for us to agree how we deal with it. It has actually been useful in this case because we've had a lot of good information and I've done a bit of work with the school nurse in trying to improve standards at home with mother, with mother's cooperation, it has been helpful. We're inviting the mother now to case conferences. It was a bit tricky at first because there was a lot of the school workers saying difficult things so I had to do a bit of work first, to ease the way until things are on the up, but things are on the up now to some*

extent. So she's going to be coming along to core group meetings in future. As a matter of practice, I think it's good if parents can come along.

Part of the plan was to work with the cohabitee on his alcohol problems. The expectations were set out in writing, including the following:

My team leader and I feel that the help which this organisation is willing to offer you will give you the professional support and counselling you need to help you look seriously at your drink problem and get it under control . . . We would expect you to take up the offer of help, attend the sessions, take it seriously' . . . etc.

The social worker explained:

I don't like operating with people on a basis of saying one thing to their face and saying other things behind their back in case conferences. I tend to be upfront and try to be as sympathetic and caring about it as possible. You know, I don't put people up against doors and say 'you will do this, this and that'. The approach is slightly different but I try to get the point across clearly, in fact, in writing too usually, I try and do that so that people know exactly what's expected.

The other part of the plan was to work with the mother about standards in the home. The case notes record the social worker sitting down in the bedroom with the older child to speak to him in private about conditions in the home and his reactions to them. In interview the social worker said:

He was upset about it. This is why I've been taking . . . I don't try and be judgemental with parents about conditions because conditions vary and, with this family, there's always been a lot of love between mother and the children's behaviour has shown that they are generally happy children so I think that's the bench-mark, the emphasis. But it became increasingly apparent with the children, especially this child, as he was getting older he was becoming more aware of the conditions at home and was upset about it.

The social worker provided material help (new bedding, a hoover and carpet shampoo) and explained his approach as follows:

The approach I've taken is to try to help her set the standard that she'd ideally like for herself rather than impose some standard from outside, either mine or somebody else's and she's sort of responded to that. There's a certain amount of laziness as well. I mean she will actually make an effort with the areas that are visible to the outside, ie the front room and the kitchen and ignore the upstairs. So it's been trying to get across to her really that the children as they get older are going to be affected by that, that it's going to be less acceptable as the children get older that if the children are unhappy about that, protest about it, and the children are getting some victimisation at school because they were smelling and she actually responded to that. She actually responded to that very well, she understood that and she's turned the children out okay after that, you know, cleaner. She's had to run round chasing one of them for washing, etc and she's actually done that and the school is saying that the children's appearance is a lot better. So it's trying to . . . it's difficult because just going there and saying 'Look, this isn't good enough. Let's have a tidy up', that's not helping her really to internalise that for herself. She has to set reasonable standards for herself. That's just as likely to alienate her, cause her not to want to cooperate. So it's trying to go at her pace really, trying to get a reasonable standard that seems livable, and we've put some practical help in. The bedrooms look a bit brighter, or the bedding looks a bit brighter and it's easier to wash. I feel, it's still not good enough but it's not so bad that I feel we need to make an emergency out of it. We're still trying to help her over a period of time to get her standards better but it's not so bad that we need to put a public health warning on the front door.

The work on the cohabitee's drinking problem was ultimately unsuccessful and the mother finally sought an injunction to keep him from the home. In interview the school nurse and the teacher acknowledged the improvement in the children's appearance.

It should not be inferred that all the parents in the 'family supported' category would necessarily view the involvement of social workers and others as supportive. On the contrary, there is evidence in the case files of understandable parental anger and resentment about registration, particularly in cases where parents had initially sought help, and this had been followed by medical examinations, investigation, possibly involving the police, and a case conference in which, at the time of the sample, they were not present. However, it was suggested in interview that the anger usually subsided. As one social services manager explained:

It's rare though that you don't get access to people, very rare. Usually they get grumpy for the first few days after a case conference, most people understand . . . it's rare that people actually just put up the barriers completely. I don't know whether that's actually out of fear of the consequences but people don't seem to be able to sustain anger for very long really.

Another said:

The social structure of our caseloads is very, very, very heavily weighed towards the unskilled working class or the no-skilled working class and,

> *quite frankly, the apathy in the wake of centuries of whatever, people accept*
> *these things so passively.*

There was an example in the case sample where a school had referred a child with bruising, the mother admitted that the father had punished the child for his misbehaviour and the family was initially uncooperative with attempts to arrange a medical examination. The police were not asked to investigate the assault, although they considered they should have been informed. The case record notes the family as initially very hostile to the social worker. However, over time the social worker helped the family for example with visits to the child psychiatrist and she also happened to be present when the child needed emergency surgery and had offered support and practical help in taking them to hospital. The case notes record the following:

> *She (the mother) said she did not think social workers could be so helpful.*
> *She thought they were just for taking kids away and she didn't know what*
> *they would have done without me during the last week or so.*

In a few cases, however, the hostility persisted and these cases, categorised as 'monitored', are discussed below.

The 'abuser removed'

The 'abuser removed' group were the second largest category, comprising just over a quarter of cases (13 of 48). They were cases predominantly of sexual abuse (10 of the 13) in which an alleged abuser (in this sample, all men) had been clearly identified and the protection of the child was effected through prosecution of the alleged offender and/or the departure or the removal of the alleged abuser from the home or its environs.

The focus of work in such cases was explicitly child protection rather than general child welfare. It sometimes involved work with the children by social workers or specialist resources such as child psychiatry to help them work through their experiences and/or to develop their protective skills and capacities, and work with the mothers to help them protect their children and to support them in their decisions to separate from violent or abusive men. In one case, for example, two children in separate families disclosed child sexual abuse, involving the same abuser. The social worker worked with both mothers and the children in a number of sessions helping the children to develop their capacity to protect themselves using books about good and bad touching, and their mothers to support the children. When the alleged abuser was not prosecuted for lack of evidence, a police officer attended one of the sessions to explain why it had not been possible to prosecute and to reaffirm that this did not mean that the children had not been believed.

The 'cared for'

The next largest group was the 'cared for' comprising a sixth of the cases (8 of the 48), in which the children were protected by removal from home, through care proceedings or voluntary reception into care (as it was then known). Five were cases of physical abuse and three of sexual abuse. Although the numbers are small, this was more common in borough than in city. These were cases in which either the degree of risk was assessed to be such that the children could not be protected within the home or in which parents themselves asked for the children to be removed for fear of future harm.

The 'monitored'

A small group of four cases has been categorised as 'monitored'. These were cases in which abuse had been identified, where there was a degree of parental hostility and resistance to engaging in work to protect their children, but where the risk was not considered to be great enough to justify removal of children from home. The aim was to put in place a network of surveillance of the children, through schools and health visitors/school nurses and others in the interagency network so that the child's well-being could be monitored. An example is of a family where older daughters were alleging that their father was beating the children, including their younger brothers. Injuries were found but the father denied the alleged assault when interviewed by the police. The family was resistant to social work involvement, a problem exacerbated by the shortage of interpreters since English was not the family's first language. Those in the interagency network believed the children's account and were worried by the level of reported violence in the home, both to the children and the mother, but felt unable to effect any change or to do anything beyond monitoring the situation in view of the family's resistance to help, including that of the mother.

A social services manager spoke of these kind of cases in interview as follows:

> *There are some cases where it is not perhaps about effecting any change, more about just monitoring. I think there are some cases where it's up front really that you are saying to the family, 'look, the reason I'm here is because your child is on the register. I know you're not happy about me coming or I know you can't understand why I'm coming but I have a job to do and that is to come and to check that everything is ok' and you do it on a kind of formal footing almost, you go once every three weeks and you make a point of having a look at the child. You know the sort of policeman role rather than the family friend sort of helper. There are times when you do that because that's more acceptable to them. They don't want you there every day but they know that they've got to put up with that and they*

> *push you as to whether the child comes off the register and that sort of thing*
> *so they can do away with you. But it's a more formal footing that you are*
> *on with people, it's possible to do something and what you're doing is*
> *monitoring and that you're seeing that the child is okay, and things aren't*
> *deteriorating, who's in the household, but it's limited you have to accept*
> *that it's not, you're not guaranteeing anything, you're maybe picking up*
> *on early signs of any major problems.*

The 'assessed'

Finally, there was a small group of only four cases categorised as 'assessed'. These were cases in which abuse had been identified but full assesment was required to identify and clarify the nature of risk and the components of a child protection plan. These were not the only cases in which assessment was undertaken but those where at the stage of formulating the plan this was the primary focus of the work. In the sample of cases in this study, this form of assessment was infrequent. The research did not reveal whether this was because full assessment of the kind recommended by the Department of Health guide *Protecting Children* (DH, 1988) is perceived as irrelevant to case needs or unrealistic in terms of the time and resources required or whether it is not widely known among practitioners in the research sites.

The child protection conference and the formulation of child protection plans

Views and practice varied about the appropriate role of the conference in specifying the content of the child protection plan. Some suggested that the case conference should set a broad outline of a child protection plan noting the involvement of various agencies but that more detailed work should be carried out by the core group or within the social services department.

While some initial child protection plans were rather vague, others argued that developing a detailed plan in the initial conference was important both in protecting the child and in sustaining interagency involvement thereafter. For example:

> *I think if a good plan is made at case conference and a plan for reviewing in*
> *whatever form is made then people are very clear about the roles that*
> *they're doing and about the resources that are going to be used and I think*
> *it is the job of the case conference to say this is how people are going to*
> *work, this is what they're going to do and then we'll meet in a certain time*
> *and review what they're doing. Then everybody's very clear about what*
> *the plan is. I think if at that point the conference is wishy washy then*
> *maybe what happens afterwards is wishy washy too.*

I think sometimes child protection plans are maybe too broad and need to be pinned down because if you say adequate monitoring when in fact what you mean is health visitor will go round every fortnight, paediatrician will see the child once a month until, and list those things, unless you do that you haven't got a clear idea who your core group is really. So I think people could sometimes do with a bit more detailed thought on that.

Consensus and dissent in child protection conferences

A striking finding in relation to the case sample was the high degree of interagency consensus in relation to conference decisions concerning both registration and the child protection plan, as evidenced in conference minutes and other indications on the social services department file. For the purposes of this research, dissent was noted either when it was recorded as such in the minutes, with particular individuals or agencies having asked for this to be done, or when the conference minutes indicated that there had been interprofessional disagreement over certain topics in the course of the discussion. Dissent was recorded in the initial conference minutes in only three of the 48 cases, two in borough and one in city. Slightly higher levels of disagreement (in seven of the 48 cases) were identified from the discussion as reported in conference minutes, but these cases had not all led to a formal noting of dissent from the recommendations. Three were in borough and four in city.

The first of the three cases in which dissent from the recommendation was formally recorded was one in which a mother had overheard her children talking of sexual matters and witnessed sexual activity between them. When questioned, one said that his uncle had abused him. No clinical findings of abuse were found on medical examination and the children concerned did not reveal or say anything when interviewed by the police Special Unit. The conference decided to register the case as grave concern of sexual abuse but the head teacher and legal officer disagreed, the latter arguing that grounds for registration were not met.

The second case was one of the few cases in the sample where the mother had contacted the general practitioner, having attacked her son and inflicted bruises. The general view was that the mother was concerned and caring but was severely stressed with a large family and marital problems over debts. The mother admitted that she had difficulties controlling her son and the conference decision was to register only this child and not the siblings, in the physical abuse category. The disagreement at the conference was with the police who thought the mother should be interviewed by them since there had been a serious assault but this was opposed by the general practitioner, health visitor and social worker, who all expressed the view that it would be unhelpful. It was agreed in the conference that the mother would attend the divisional police station (not the Special Unit) for interview and that the social worker would accompany her. The following information was extracted from the social services department file. Since this case was not in the sub-sample which generated the respondents for the interviews it was not discussed with the professionals concerned. It is possible that the police might give a different account. The case record notes that while the family was not pleased that their child's name was on the register, they accepted it without an 'overly negative response' and were prepared to cooperate with social work visiting. On the next visit the social worker informed the mother that the police wished to interview her and the record reports that the mother was 'not at all happy'. She did not see herself as a criminal and would not 'be spoken down to by the police'. At the Police Station after an initial interview, it is reported that the Police Inspector informed the mother that she was being cautioned, and referred to her criminal assault on the child.

The social worker notes that the police comments were not factually incorrect but they provoked a negative response. The mother is recorded as having yelled that she did not consider herself a criminal and would not accept the caution and it was discontinued, the mother being subsequently photographed and fingerprinted for police records. On the two social work visits in the succeeding days the family was reported to be very hostile to the social worker who explained that someone from social services needed to visit but that she would seek to transfer the case to a new worker. This was done. In the succeeding month, the mother sought legal advice and was not prepared to be cautioned, which was reported to the police. It was reported that there would be consultation with superior officers but it was likely that no further action would be taken.

This was the clearest example in the case sample of someone who, in Packman and Randall's terms, 'asked for help and got control instead' (1987, p 107). It should, however, be noted that it was rare for disagreement to exist between the police and others in network on these matters as was discussed in Chapter Five.

The third case in which dissent was recorded in the minutes was one in which the paediatric consultant, police, health visitor and class teacher were critical of the social services department. In this case, the school had referred a burn on a child to the social services department, noting that it was not the first time they had noticed marks on the child and that the child said the burn was inflicted by a relative. The family did not cooperate with a medical examination at the hospital and the police were subsequently contacted. They argued that they should have been contacted at the outset since it involved a serious assault. The child was subsequently examined following a visit by three police officers and a social worker to the home. At the case conference there were revelations of earlier injuries and the social services department's response in the past was perceived to be inadequate. The minutes record that 'the case conference ended on a general note of discord between the various agencies concerned that positive action had not been offered by the social services department in the past'.

In the remaining four cases in which disagreement was evident from the minutes but no formal dissent was recorded, one concerned a disagreement between a teacher and a health visitor about whether sexualized behaviour was or was not a problem in a particular school; another in which a teacher disagreed with a conference recommendation not to inform a father (separated and living elsewhere) of the registration of his child; the third a case in which the police expressed a wish to investigate but this was not accepted by the conference and the police accepted the advice; and a fourth, an unusual case concerning a dead child where medical advice was that registration should be delayed until the cause of death was established.

In the majority of the cases, however, the conference recommendations and indeed the discussion as recorded in the minutes were characterised by consensus rather than dissent. This was confirmed in interviews. Comments such as the following were typical, from a police officer:

> *I've never come up against a vast void between the two sides – we're usually thinking the same way.*

from a social services manager:

> *In very, very few cases I feel, is there much controversy.*

from a teacher:

> *I've never been deeply unhappy with the decisions.*

Questions were asked in interview about two particular matters, whether there was usually agreement over the decision about registration and also about the child protection plan. Reaching decisions about registration were said to be relatively unproblematic and consensual, and undertaken within the framework of the interagency procedures. Comments such as the following were typical.

> *Registrations are fairly easy, they either fill the criteria or they don't and if they do then they're registered.*

> *I don't think there's too many fights about registration actually.*

There were exceptions. The cases cited with those in which social workers were arguing that registration was unlikely to be helpful. One police officer gave an example:

One of the areas that we often, well not often but there is disagreement from time to time is where a social worker would say that she does, he or she would say that she doesn't see what good registration would do, how it would help the young person and that she feels that it might badly influence her relationship with the family, that is said occasionally. My view on that is that there's a procedure there for registration and that we follow that even though it might make life a little bit difficult between her and the parents. I can hold the red book that lays out the procedures. But having said that I don't think it's just a case of saying the procedures say this. It's a case of saying 'look they're there to safeguard the child'. It sort of indicates our concern. It means for instance if the youngster should turn up at hospital and these are words I used exactly this morning, where the social worker was not saying they shouldn't be registered these particular children but he was just sort of tossing in his own mind the benefit of it and I said 'look it's a case that if they do turn up for treatment, perhaps not referred through the doctor, it would just ensure that the medical staff at the hospital took that extra little bit of care and had the past history', which is what it's all about. So yes I would get my own way simply because I can fall back on that but I think it's important not just to say the book says but really just go over, not that one should have to perhaps, you know, the reasons why the procedures are there.

The child protection plan was said to provoke a little more disagreement, but again consensus was more marked than dissent, as the following quotations illustrate:

There's a fair degree of agreement. We usually agree on what needs to be done.

and:

there's generally a consensus view about what should happen.

One not unexpected point of difficulty was that sometimes others in the interagency network perceived social workers to be too keen to pursue voluntary approaches with families and to leave children at home or to rehabilitate them with families rather than to take them into care, which confirms a similar finding in Birchall's (1992) study. In the course of interviews with teachers, health visitors and paediatricians, for example, cases were cited which obviously had distressed them greatly when they had had to 'watch and wait' and press for more decisive intervention. However, although such cases clearly made a very significant impact, they were acknowledged to be relatively rare. As a nurse manager explained:

I think that the point at which debate actually does take place and to be very honest there has only been once when I actually did end up hammering the desk, well not quite hammering the desk there wasn't a desk but actually saying I wasn't prepared to go with it is when it comes to what I've always crudely called disposal of child, ie where should that child be going? are they safe to go home? have we got to look at a place of safety, care proceedings? etc., and that has been the point at which contention has come. At the end of the day the reality of life is that if social workers wish to take certain decisions on placement there is nothing I can do to stop them but what I can do is to have it made very clear that I am unhappy and therefore they are doing it against our wishes.

A paediatrician said:

Case conferences are sometimes marked by dissent . . . It tends to be more with cases where you can predict that children are going to be anti-social, violent teenagers if nothing is done to intervene and yet they are repeatedly returned home. That is what is worrying, when parents are unable to give them what they need, apart from any physical aspects. More often than not one can persuade the case conferences or social workers to go along with one's professional view.

A social worker commented on this from his perspective:

I think case conferences are useful but perhaps up to a point. Obviously people who are invited to case conferences are normally involved with the case but sometimes they are not, they're more brought in aren't they and I feel don't perhaps always see the full view of things . . . I think it should be more viewed as a whole rather than specific things like injuries and I think sometimes they're not, and if you haven't got the whole view it can sometimes colour your judgement. Because I have actually worked with people, who yes I appreciate have over chastised their children and I'm not saying there's ever an excuse for it but I think had they looked at things perhaps from a different angle. Sometimes the consequences of case conferences are quite severe, aren't they? I've never been in one where I've disagreed that the child should be registered. But sometimes about receptions into care.

This was one of a few social workers who expressed criticism of a preoccupation of conferences with specific incidents and establishing whether or not abuse had occurred as distinct from a broader concern with child and family welfare. It is a matter for debate whether the high degree of consensus is a matter for concern. As one social worker put it:

Yes, we agree but that's what we're supposed to do, isn't it?

Some, for example (Dingwall et al, 1983), would argue, however, that the involvement of varied professions in decision-making can act as a brake on the coercive use of the power of the state in relation to family life and that this will only be effective if there is real discussion and disagreement around the table. If processes are operating to stifle debate this would be a cause for concern. Otherwise there is a danger of collusiveness amongst powerful agencies which may be inimical to the well-being of children and families, as Blagg and Stubbs (1988) suggest. One social services manager explained it thus:

> *There is a very high degree of consensus, worryingly high. The thing is when you've been doing it a while and in the same area you come up with the same faces at each case conference generally, and I suppose it must be more so in smaller areas. You do get the same people and I don't know whether the level of consensus is about the fact that there's mutual trust and understanding and respect, when you've said your bit you really know what the decision is going to be because you've come across these situations before and that's that. Or whether that's more about, well I don't want to upset them because I know them and I've got to see them next week and I don't want to put them on the spot because I think they're talking rubbish because none of us, nobody likes conflict in that sort of situation. I wonder whether it would be different if we were all total strangers or having to make a decision when we'd not have to meet each other again, whether we'd come to different conclusions about it, whether people might be likely to tell us much more, I sometimes feel that. I feel like it myself sometimes that I don't press somebody particularly hard on a point because I quite like them really and I don't want to upset them, embarrass them in front of everybody else. I hope I don't let that influence my judgment of that but I'm conscious that I do it, or the fact there's a feeling I have about that. Whereas I might think what they're actually saying is dangerous or worrying or whatever I think perhaps I wouldn't be as hostile to them as somebody that I didn't know at all, so yes on the whole there is a pretty high level of consensus.*

Power and participation

Another possibility in explaining high levels of consensus is that some participants might feel diffident about or excluded from expressing a dissenting viewpoint. In general, those interviewed said that they were given the opportunity to participate at conferences and that they considered their contributions were listened to and taken seriously. As one school nurse said:

> *On the whole I think it's very democratic, I think they listen to what you have to say.*

and an education welfare officer:

> *the only people I worry about are school staff who are not normally at case conferences. I worry then that they are not quite as sure as the people on the circuit that are always there, you are aware, you know you've come to say what you have to say.*

Some added that they were confident enough to make sure this happened. One head teacher explained:

> *I think they'd gone in with the intention of writing him off and lightening their case load. I got the impression, but the school nurse and I were there fighting our corner. So you've just got to make sure you say what you say haven't you. I think that's another reason for sending a head teacher*

and a police officer said, laughingly, of himself:

> *I'm a dogmatic Yorkshireman and if I've got something to say well then they'll have to listen to it before I go, they'll have to hear it.*

A further reason for the degree of interagency consensus might be a perception that the social services department as the lead agency would enter the conference with a predetermined plan which it would be futile or difficult for other agencies to challenge. However, this was not reported to be the general experience of those interviewed. The social workers varied in the extent to which they had a preconceived plan. Some argued that, as the lead agency, they should:

> *We rarely go to a conference with no idea of what we want to do, with no conception of what the protection plan is going to be. I hate that. There's been the odd occasion when it's been inevitable because the conference has been arranged so quickly. There's a lot to be said for not having a conference quickly if we haven't had time to get that, I find it a very unhelpful experience.*

However, it was suggested that they would listen to other points of view and modify the plan as necessary. The above quotation continued:

> *So, for the majority of conferences, we formulated a view, not a fixed view, an interim view and as a consequence we've got an interim, a proposed protection plan. There's a danger that you could become emotionally committed to your view and your protection plan and, therefore, you could pack it to push it through. I hope we don't do that too much.*

and another said:

I tend to find that, especially if you know the family well and you can argue at the case conference, it carries a lot of weight but I think that you have to accept that other professions quite often know the children sometimes as well as, if not even better than you, and they might bring information to bear that you aren't even aware of, so you have to be flexible and not too dogmatic. You have to accept that other people have just as much interest in the care of the children as you have . . . So I think you have got to be open-minded, you've got to be willing to have your view changed, not be too dogmatic and too blinkered really.

One chair explained his conscious practice to try to be impartial and not to push the social services viewpoint:

Often there is a consensus view and so, you're not as it were taking the social services view point, you're sharing the view that has been generated by the meeting, by multi agencies. I've found where there is actual controversy it is possible to stand back and . . ., for example, I would try not to influence the decision or in fact defer and say 'well if you want to register for example these are the pluses, if you don't want to register these are the reasons why you shouldn't register' or care proceedings or whatever, you've got to have the pros and cons of the situation, not over influence the voting and not vote myself.

and another commented:

We try, wherever possible, to pair up with the other team leaders so that they chair case conferences of our cases and I do theirs and so on. That's what we try and do, not always possible but wherever we can do that. We're doing it more and more I think now I think we've found the benefit of that. I've certainly felt it's very useful. Because I mean clearly, particularly if you're involved in a very difficult case you're in an impossible position, trying to appear as an independent chair who allows everybody choice but you've got an angle there you want pushed and you're not being fair to people because I know that I've manipulated case conferences to get the outcome I wanted and that's because it's a tough arena and you know given the power I would use it, and abuse it and I know I do so. I'm happier if I can say, from the position of not being the chair, say what I want and feel okay about that.

Occasionally, however, participants reported that they thought the social services department had tried to impose a particular line, as the following quotation illustrates:

I think sometimes the principal social workers who are chairing the meeting influence a little bit too much what was being said. For example,

> *I remember a few years ago we were having a case discussion about a family that various people had got concerns about and the principal who was actually sitting in and chairing this case discussion did actually say 'well if you wish to push this any further I must warn you now this may go to court'. I felt like saying 'excuse me but you know if we have concerns then we have concerns' and if it leads on to having to go to court, which it did actually I ended up going to court with this family. That's how it's been very sadly but you don't stop something just because, he may have just been making up aware of but the way he said it sort of almost . . .*

Those interviewed in social services departments were conscious of their powerful positions vis a vis some conference participants and the readiness of some others in the interagency network to leave decisions to them, accentuating consensus in conferences. One social worker said:

> *I always wonder how much other professionals that are involved in that decision really understand the meaning of that, you know I really do. I have been in case conferences where people will continually abstain and I've often wondered if that's because they don't really know. No one ever asks do we know the meaning of the register. I think, that we've got a long way to go in educating and letting other professionals know and perhaps we ought to incorporate in a case conference a bit of blurb about saying what it means, you know, what they're voting on if you like. But I think there are people who will go along with the flow, you know, they'll just think well they'll err on the side of safety.*

A social work manager commented:

> *In terms of shared decision-making, I'm probably a little jaundiced. I think we're the lead organisation and I think people are quite happy to have us as the lead organisation. What tends to happen, in my view, is that we say what we'd like to do and people either agree or disagree and it's not often they disagree.*

It was expected that there may have been a struggle for dominance in the case conference arena between doctors and the social services department. This would have accorded with much previous work on the difficulties experienced when doctors, with high status, occupational prestige, ascribed and assumed authority and traditionally male gender are required to work collaboratively with others in health and welfare generally (Dingwall and McIntosh, 1978, Ducanis and Golin, 1979, Webb and Hobdell, 1980, Dingwall, 1980, Clifford, 1985) or child protection in particular (Oppé, 1975, Mazura, 1977, Davoren, 1983, Dingwall et al, 1983, Bross et al, 1988). However, this did not appear to be a marked feature of the cases in the case sample although consultant paediatricians only attended 11 of the 48 initial conferences. Nor was it a dominant theme of the interviews, although a few social workers referred to it. One paediatrician acknowledged the possibility in the following quotation, although stressing the severe logistical problems of fitting conference attendance into a timetable pre-booked with fixed commitments such as out-patient clinics in the context of a heavy clinical workload:

> *Case conferences present great difficulty. I usually try to go because an experienced medical opinion will often guide the way things go and the decisions made. Often it is not so much the precise findings but the total picture which will indicate the degree of risk. I try to go myself but it is extraordinarily difficult.*

This may partly be explained by the patterns of attendance at conferences by consultant paediatricians in the two research sites and differences between the personnel. In city, in only two of the 25 initial conferences was a consultant paediatrician present, with junior hospital doctors representing paediatric services in a further six. In borough, consultant paediatricians attended nine of the initial conferences and a junior doctor only one. It was in city that concerns were raised in interview about the difficulties of working with one consultant. These were attributed to a particular personality and were not generalised to other consultants in the locality. In borough, as was reported in Chapter Six, some of the consultants were experienced as diffident and lacking in confidence in child protection matters and showing some reluctance to express a clear clinical view. It is unlikely, therefore, that they would assume a directive or authoritarian role in discussion of the case. Whatever the reasons, interprofessional struggles for dominance and disagreements as to action in child protection cases were not, in general, marked features of the role relations between hospital medicine and social services in this study.

The perceived value of initial child protection conferences

Previous studies, for example, Castle (1977), Corby (1987) and Brunel (1988), had found child protection conferences to be effective, useful and supportive. In Birchall's study, 80% of respondents considered that child protection conferences were generally helpful to the child concerned (Birchall, 1992, p 84). These findings were confirmed by this study in which respondents in interview stressed the value and importance of the child protection conferences as mechanisms for interagency coordination, echoing the key role ascribed to them in government guidance and local procedures.

As noted in Chapter Seven, there were criticisms of their functioning, particularly when they were badly chaired, poorly structured and too long. Some noted with concern the variations in standard across both authorities. But, in principle and in practice, respondents accorded them high priority and valued them. The following are typical responses to questions on the topic. From a social services manager:

I think they're an absolutely vital part of the process;

from a head teacher:

I always feel they are worthwhile and I'm glad I've been;

from a nursing officer;

They are generally valuable and they usually achieve their purposes;

from a police officer;

Yes I feel that you do achieve something with case conferences personally speaking, yes I'm quite happy with them and the recommendations. And you see the other angle as it were, from the family, from the social worker side, yes I'm quite happy with case conferences;

and, perhaps unusually, from a general practitioner:

every case conference I've been to, I think I've felt it's been worthwhile. Certainly, the one with this family, the last one I went to, I think it went on for a couple of hours but it was appropriate. No, I think they're very important and I think they're not a waste of time. It is difficult sometimes to fit the timing around us but they do. The social workers try very hard to accommodate us and we're not the only people who have problems and commitments. No, I think it's good.

A child protection coordinator summed up the views of the majority of the respondents:

They are absolutely essential, because they are the only structured formal multidisciplinary forum. And being that, it's the only place where you can fit different bits of information together about a child and get a proper impression really. You would be putting the most terrible dreadful onus on the social worker and that would be very inappropriate because you would be then formally taking responsibility for other agencies decisions which would be nonsense really. But case conferences are like courts they focus the mind wonderfully and it's really 'come up with the goods time' and I think the discipline of a case conference assists people in making decisions. Case conferences often involve people taking action which frightens them, taking risks which frighten them equally and it's only when the child's circumstances are all laid out in front of you that people have a proper response to what's going on. It's really easy to make decisions at the end of a telephone somehow. It's not easy when everybody else is there and you really have got to say what you think and act on what you think and case conferences are good because of that.

Not many would dissent from the following:

Oh yes, despite the fact that I make criticisms, I actually think that we don't do a bad job at the end of the day.

Summary

In examining the decisions made in initial child protection conferences concerning the registered cases in the sample, the study found that the vast majority of the children were living at home at the time of the initial conference and that most continued to do so following registration. In only three of the 48 cases were care proceedings or place of safety orders (as they were then called) sought. Study of the child protection plans revealed that social services departments played a key role in subsequent intervention, not only as the lead agency but as the principal provider of support and services. The interagency protection plans revealed clearly that interagency involvement diminished markedly following registration and that continuing intervention was concentrated in relatively few hands besides the social services department, notably schools, health visitors and child and family psychiatric services. There was little joint multidisciplinary work in intervention. The child protection plans were found to vary considerably in their breadth and specificity. For analytical purposes, the primary orientation of the plan was categorised as 'the family supported', 'the abuser removed', 'the cared for', 'the assessed' and 'the monitored'. The first, voluntary support, was associated with physical abuse and self referral and was the most common. The removal of the abuser was associated with the protection of children from men who had sexually abused them. Together these categories comprised 65% of the registered cases.

In reviewing respondents' perceptions and experiences of child protection conferences, the high levels of consensus about registration and the child protection plan were noted. Despite some criticisms of aspects of the organisation and functioning of conferences discussed in the previous chapter, this study confirmed the findings of previous research in revealing positive evaluations of the multidisciplinary conference as a mechanism of interagency collaboration.

Chapter 9

Intervention, monitoring and review

This chapter explores interagency collaboration in child protection in intervention, case monitoring and review. The study found considerable variation in the extent to which the interagency child protection plans were implemented. As one social services manager said:

> *We're not bad at the investigation, we're not bad at coming up with a plan to protect the child, what we are bad at is following it up.*

In this chapter, aspects of organisation and practice relevant to this topic are discussed. They include: social work records, parental involvement (or the lack of it), change and complexity in the cases, resources for intervention (or the lack of them) and sustaining interagency involvement throughout intervention. The chapter ends with a discussion of core groups and the arrangements for case monitoring and review.

Interagency work in intervention in the case sample

In the pilot work on the data collection instrument, attempts were made to map the interagency contacts in the intervention phase. The intention was to extract information about the patterns and nature of intervention, including who contacted whom, by what means, with what frequency and for what purposes eg passing on information, seeking action by the other party, seeking joint activity etc. The uneven nature of social work recording and the apparent frequency with which interagency contacts went unrecorded rendered this impracticable. In the study, therefore, data extracted from social service case records concerning patterns of interagency contact were confined to meetings, which appeared to be recorded more fully, because formal minutes or at least a brief note of the meeting was kept.

As is shown in Figure 9.1, subsequent child protection conferences were held in 26 of the 48 cases in the sample between the initial child protection conference and the time of data collection (an average of 15.8 months). The pattern of subsequent conferences varied between borough and city as is shown in Figure 9.2. They were held in borough in nine of the 23 cases and in 17 of the 25 in city. The principal reason for the difference was that, at the time of the study, child protection cases in borough were routinely reviewed by a multiagency meeting known as district review, discussed at the end of this chapter.

As is shown in Figures 9.3 and 9.4, neither the chairs nor locations of the 38 subsequent child protection conferences varied markedly from those of

Figure 9.1 **No of cases in which subsequent child protection conferences were held and their frequency (N = 48)**

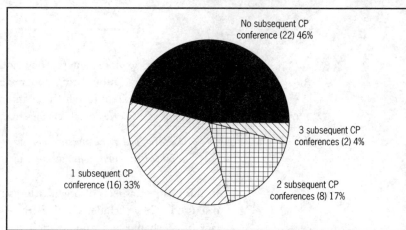

Figure 9.2 **No of cases in which subsequent child protection conferences were held and their frequency: borough and city compared (N = 48)**

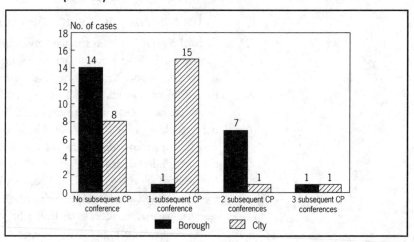

the initial conferences. The average size of the conferences was 9.5 in borough and 10.2 in city, not dissimilar from the initial conferences discussed in Chapter Seven. There were, however, slight differences in attendance rates. Data about patterns of attendance were available in respect of 34 of the subsequent conferences. In total, 469 people were invited and 338 attended, a rate of 73%. As is shown in Figure 9.5 the rate of attendance was higher in city (82%) than in borough (64%). The figures confirm a slight fall in interagency involvement when compared with an overall 77% attendance rate at initial conferences (84% in city and 72% in borough). Nonetheless, as with initial

Figure 9.3 **Location of subsequent case conferences (N = 38)**

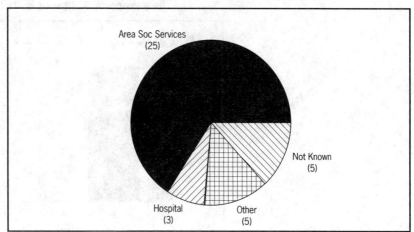

Figure 9.4 **Chair of subsequent case conferences (N = 38)**

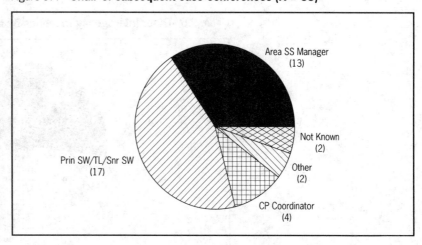

conferences, the attendance rate indicates a significant degree of interagency commitment to the formal machinery of collaboration.

The frequency of other interagency meetings following initial registration is shown in Figure 9.6

The patterns are very different in borough and city, partly because of district review meetings in the former but when these are excluded there remains a tendency for more interagency meetings other than subsequent child protection conferences to take place in borough than in city. Excluding district reviews, the size of the other interagency meetings was small, most commonly three or four people, as is shown in Figure 9.7, confirming a tendency for interagency activity in respect of on-going cases to be concentrated in relatively few hands.

Figure 9.5 **Numbers attending subsequent child protection conferences as a proportion of those invited: borough and city compared**

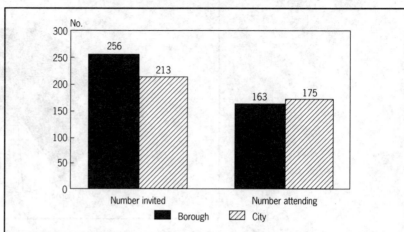

Figure 9.6 **Other interagency meetings by frequency and type (N = 84)**

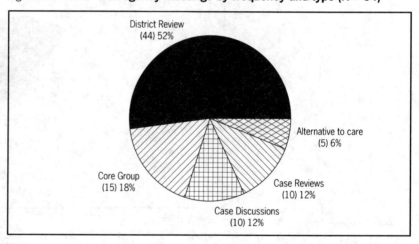

Social work records

The recording practices of social workers, which were highly variable, posed a problem in the study in tracing interagency work in ongoing intervention. Some files contained what appeared to be full recording of contacts with children, families and others in the interagency network. Others were much less complete. This appears to confirm the findings on this matter in Birchall's study, which reported, for example, that social workers were less likely than health visitors and teachers to record internal exchanges

Figure 9.7   **Other interagency meetings by frequency and type: borough and city compared (N = 84)**

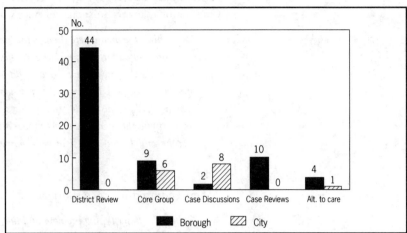

Figure 9.8   **Size of other interagency meetings (excluding district review) (N = 40)**

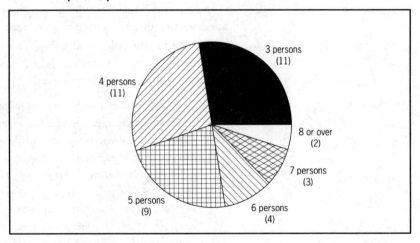

of information concerning child protection cases, with less than two thirds of social workers reporting that they did so 'always' or 'often'. Lower proportions reported confirming exchanges of information with other agencies in writing (Birchall, 1992, pp54–56).

The uneven and sometimes poor practices in social work recording have been noted in child abuse inquiry reports and in SSI Reports and appear surprising in view of the social workers' potential vulnerability and openness to scrutiny in child protection cases. For many social workers in the study recording did not appear to rank as high priority and the problem was compounded by serious deficiencies in the amount of administrative support. One senior manager in social services summarised the position:

> *So I think the area where there is the greatest poverty is in administrative support, particularly typing support. If you've read some case files here, I should think you'll have cried a bit over the quality of some of the presentation, and I'm very worried about that. I think there's a strong feeling that you just can't get a typing service here. You almost have to be halfway up the hierarchy to get proper attention, to get a proper secretarial service and I think that is a very worrying state of affairs professionally . . .*

Others endorsed resource shortages:

> *There's a major typing problem and they're not typing case records and in fact until recently there was a two week delay on letters, there's a major typing crisis which I think doesn't help the condition of those files;*

This confirms Birchall's findings that almost half of the respondents across the agencies identified inadequate secretarial services as impeding interagency collaboration (Birchall, 1992, p74). The filing systems in operation in city and borough were not user friendly.

A social work manager remarked:

> *Our files are an extremely poor tool for professional social workers. They are under resourced, people have to deal with very old bulging files that are falling apart, or new cheap tatty inappropriate files that if you want to take one sheet of paper out of, it takes you about ten minutes to struggle it out and another ten minutes to struggle it back in again. You might not be able to read the words in the corners of the page, all sorts of bizarre things like this. Quite frankly this department would benefit from spending about twenty or thirty thousand pounds on completely replacing the filing system on a phased basis because people feel demotivated because of the physical states of the files.*

Some social workers clearly gave recording a high priority, but others did not. In consequence:

> *what you're left with is workers not being able to give a proper good account of the work that they've done. And it's sheer pressure of work that's led to them being in that situation.*

This variation in recording practice was confirmed by study of the files. A few were excellent, but by comparison with the recording of child protection investigations and the initial child protection conferences, the quality of recording often deteriorated in the intervention phase. It proved to be difficult in the study (although this was not unexpected) to trace events and, in particular, to identify the reasons for taking particular courses of action or deciding not to do so. While for a researcher this may be simply tiresome or disappointing, it has consequences in practice for the ease with which, or indeed whether at all, the file can be used as an effective work tool either by the social worker in reviewing her or his intervention and evaluating its outcome or by those with responsibility for supervising or monitoring the work – a point discussed more fully later in the chapter.

Parental commitment to the child protection plans

A related problem in implementing child protection plans in some cases concerned the degree of parental commitment to them. As noted in Chapter Seven, parental participation was rare in initial child protection conferences in city and borough at the time of the study. While in some cases parents met some conference members following the meeting to hear the decisions, and in others a written note of the child protection plan was supplied in addition to an oral explanation, it could not, in general, be said that agreements had been worked out in partnership and with full parental participation. Perhaps unsurprisingly therefore, there was, in some cases, difficulty in securing parental compliance with the plans. Child and family psychiatric services were an example, having been identified as part of the child protection plan in several cases. However, it sometimes transpired that parents and children attended once and failed to keep further appointments or proved otherwise difficult to engage and so the case would be closed in the clinic. One child psychiatrist interviewed acknowledged the difficulty:

> *If the professionals' main concern is the protective attitude of the parents, I think that, as a group, we've done very badly with them and I worry a lot about them. I wonder whether more work through the divisional social worker may help and try to do more work at home if possible or whether there are other ways of somehow getting it going. So far it's not one that we've been able to address. I've had several cases where I've felt I am frustrated . . . we've not been in a position to offer a home based service and it isn't probably a shared agenda and they don't see the point in coming.*

Cases such as these raise the issue of whether any particular part of the intervention was a requisite as opposed to merely a desirable part of the child protection plan and, if the former, then what subsequent action would be taken if there was non-compliance. In the cases categorised above as 'abuser removed', contingency plans were sometimes formulated at the planning stage, particularly in respect, for example, of what should happen if the alleged abuser were released on bail, or otherwise returned to the home. However, this occurred less in other cases where the objectives of intervention and the minimum levels of required change were less clearly articulated in the child protection plan. This made the monitoring of implementation of the plan difficult and the assessment of the consequences of non-compliance for the continued protection of the child problematic.

Change and complexity in the cases

A third factor militating against the neat implementation of the child protection plans was the pace of change and the complexity of life faced by many of the children and families in the sample, a factor also noted by Packman and Randall (1989) and Farmer and Owen (1993). For some but not all of the families, child protection concerns were just one of the many difficulties they faced to different degrees and in differing combinations. There were problems of domestic violence, relationship breakdowns, severe debt and financial hardship, unemployment, unsuitable housing, psychiatric disorder, racial harassment, marital stress, and rapidly changing household composition, to name but a few. The resilience and coping strategies of some families in the face of severe and multiple problems and the inadequacies of a range of social policies appeared to be remarkable. It was, however, manifestly difficult for social workers and others in the interagency network to keep abreast of the changes and their eye firmly on the ball of child protection in the midst of such turmoil and need. Given the pace of change:

> *Sometimes decisions which appear from case conference minutes to be absolutely vital, when you look at it in supervision with a worker maybe some weeks later, you think well what were we worrying about, or well we know it's changed because the abuser's left now or whatever.*

Resources for intervention

A fourth factor affecting the implementation of child protection plans concerned the manifest shortage of resources for intervention with children and families. These included access to basic services such as housing, income and employment plus the basic resource of social work time and specialist resources of advice and help to work with abused children, their families and abusers.

The following quotation illustrates this point:

> *We're very good at the investigation side, we get our referrals, we know how to do something about it, we don't just think 'well I don't know what*

to do here. I'll put it in the bin', we actually know that there is a problem that needs teasing out, we do what we can in terms of getting the thing teased out and brought to case conference, we pick up the concerns of other agencies roundabout, we end up then with the case allocated to social services and we don't have the social workers to work with it. It is that fundamental resource issue which is the biggest problem to child protection in this area and I presume in a lot of other areas as well, we need to have sufficient staff to actually work with these cases.

It may be expected that in facing the gap between unmet need and desired responses, all social workers, as indeed other professionals, would complain of lack of resources – it is a leit motif of work in health and welfare services. In fact, a few social workers and their managers did contrast their own resource position in settled local communities with those elsewhere and suggested that they were sufficiently well resourced to cope with the volume of work, for example:

We're not in a position where we feel that we're having to grapple with an overwhelming flood coming in and swamping us . . . I think were in a reasonable position. If everybody else was in our position things would be a lot better for a lot of children and an awful lot more social workers.

In a similar vein, one senior health visitor contrasted the resource position in her patch with those of her colleagues elsewhere:

The health visitors in our sector are lucky in that the number of cases are manageable for them as individuals, comparable to others. I think that's the key. We're reasonably lucky with staffing levels, so the HVA recommendation of 250 families per health visitor full time means we've in fact been able to apply so that's the first thing that makes it easier. Whether that stays that way anybody can tell, but that is how it has been so far, we've been fortunate. The child protection issues, if you actually look at the community we serve, we've got quite a lot of very tight knit self supporting communities where the support networks to families are quite good. We have a low unemployment rate, we've got only certain pockets of the higher than average incidence of single parent families and because we've got limited mobility of families it means that they know where the resources are so we've got quite a lot of positives going. We do have pockets where there are concerns, where there are families who have got all sorts of social deprivation, high rise flats, low income, single parents, some drug abuse, some alcohol abuse the same as everywhere else but not throughout the sector . . . its in pockets, it's not throughout the whole sixty two thousand population of the sector.

It must be emphasised that these staff were in specific locations and they formed a very small minority of those interviewed. Nonetheless, it does suggest that staff are able to appraise the issue of resources realistically and that complaints about resource levels are not inevitable. Few others considered themselves to be in this favourable position. An indication of this was the existence of unallocated child protection cases in both social services departments. The numbers varied but it was considered unacceptable by the departments themselves and by others in the interagency network.

In terms of social work time for intervention with children and families there were serious pressures, as social service managers explained:

> *I think that the situation here is extremely dangerous in that we have too few social workers doing too many cases and because of that you end up with a situation where decisions are made on the hoof. There are not very many decisions that are carefully thought out because you haven't got the time to do it. It's alright saying to social workers you know 'well good practice now says you should have taken on board all that's come out of Cleveland, all that's come out of Rochdale'. When can they get time to read these? They don't, so how can they take it on board? We are not protecting our staff, we are not saying to them to do this piece of work you need time, not just the time to actually get out there with the client and be doing whatever it is you've got to do, you need thinking time, time to go to a book to read it, to find out what current thinking is, what good practice is etc etc. We just assume that they'll know it and if they didn't know it it's their fault because they've been trained, and that is the bit that frightens me. The numbers game is so gross now; presumably we've only got a fraction of what one of the London boroughs has got but in terms of the staff and number we've got it's gross. Ten years ago I think there were something life fifty cases on the child protection register and there's now three hundred, so that's six fold. Right. Have we had a six fold increase of staff? We haven't. Okay, I can see that you don't just add a number of six fold to your staff of whatever but I do think that you need to at least double your staff if you're going to cope.*

In these circumstances:

> *The reality is that people are doing their best and trying to do their best but under lots of limitations and that's one of the big problems with the media and media presentation which can't help how children and parents perceive us because they home in on the sensational cases. And there's nothing to redress the balance about the number of workers that are working with children. I know it's really awful but I actually am surprised that more things don't go wrong, given the number of people working the hours they're having to work and what they're having to deal with, I think that's*

> *quite a credit to the people who actually stick at it and put in as much as I think they can.*

Another manager explained the position, and the management strategy employed to cope with it:

> *There is a major problem here of overload, an enormous pressure of work. Because we've got such a large amount of work coming in, there's a constant need to prioritise so there's a constant need to close cases in order to keep open ones coming in, so we frequently close cases knowing that they're going to come up again. My general preference would often be to keep on some cases quite a bit longer in a general supportive role. But that's impossible on this division it has to be a fairly ruthless closing of cases in line with the same ruthlessness about prioritising and what work we do, what we pass out and how we monitor it. The team leaders have become really good at that at that stage and it's one of my skills which I have acquired which I'm not very happy about, acquiring a skill of being ruthless with cases. And it's an unpleasant skill I find that I've got but the division couldn't survive.*

Many others in the interagency network shared these views about the limited capacity of the social services departments to meet the need in registered child protection cases, and in preventive work in child care. In interview a teacher gave the following example:

> *I can remember at this particular case conference where there were loads of us round and I gave a little formal report on the children, how they were getting on at school and the background and history of the family was laid bare, all the problems, the financial problems, emotional and psychiatric problems, the relationship problems with stepfather, all this kind of thing and things were set up that there was going to be this homemaker going in and then it sort of transpired sometime later that the whole thing broke down because the homeworker left her job and had never been replaced; etc, etc, and you thought gosh all that time and effort, they were discussed fully, that was going to happen, it hasn't and the family's kind of gone back to square one again. I think oh, was it worth it. The homeworker hasn't gone into the family, have we actually done that child any favours and you lose heart a bit, not in the social workers particularly but in what they are actually able to do with the resources they've got available.*

Another teacher, with experience in a London borough commented of the position in city:

> *the social services here do seem to be even more hard pressed than they were in my last authority. They are very, very hard pressed.*

A clinical nurse manager expressed similar views:

> *I sometimes feel that, particularly where we've got lots and lots of concerns, there'll be a social worker involved but I sometimes think that we don't actually get what we want. In other words I'd like more action as it were. I think we need more day care. Certainly I need more health visitors but I think social services need more social workers and we have home makers but we need more of those. There almost isn't a service because they're so thinly spread. The social workers are stretched to the limit and so are the health visitors. They can't allocate and until they do we have got families sitting on the shelf. I know they can't allocate.*

Besides social work time, four other resource shortages within social services were identified: family support services such as day care and family aides or homemakers; residential and foster care, particularly specialist care to meet the needs of abused children; specialist treatment resources for abused children, their families and abusers and the specialist advice and support provided by the child protection coordinators, two in city and one in borough. The following were typical comments:

> *We do have some quite serious gaps really. Nursery placements are like hen's teeth really. You can never get an emergency nursery placement, it's not an option you consider in child protection case conferences because it's not there, the whole issue of resources is poor and that's not to knock the authority. They probably do their best but family centres, nurseries, we're scratching the surface all the time.*

> *I see that the whole of child protection is vastly under resourced. And it also strikes me that the coordinators work to such a high standard that in many ways they keep an under resourced service limping along because of the standard of work they put in. Maybe it would have ground to a halt if it wasn't for their commitment and their standard of work.*

One senior social services manager explained the position as follows:

> *It has profound significance when two day nurseries you have are in 1937 buildings and we have to close one on health and safety grounds and the third one you have is in a large Victorian house and it's about to be condemned because of the poverty of its wiring for goodness sake. Now what has been happening in previous years? There comes a point where you've got to call a moratorium on blame and you've got to say in order to provide a service of child protection in this area, this area needs that amount of resources. Blow your rate support grant, whether it's a labour controlled council or liberal or conservative, it doesn't matter. If you've got children who are hurt then this is what needs to be provided. As a*

department, the range of resources available to support families and treat
abuse in families is pitiful.

Efforts had been made in both authorities to develop treatment resources for
abused children, their families and abusers and some advances had been made
for example in child and family psychiatry, in probation and in developing
social work skills.

As one social services manager said:

> *In terms of resources, to be honest I think we're developing more resources*
> *for children and families just now. We've got a specialist unit who are*
> *looking at children who've been sexually abused, who if they don't work*
> *with them, will offer support and advice to the social worker who is. So at*
> *least it's beginning to feel that we can call on some specialist resources for*
> *advice or to actually take on a piece of work. Where in the past we haven't*
> *had that we've just had to pull together what we could.*

Nonetheless, severe shortages persisted. As was the case in respect of referrals
and preventive work discussed in Chapter Three, there was a resigned and
weary and, as some of the above quotations indicate, demoralised acceptance
of the resource position by those in the interagency network. One social
service manager commented:

> *I think we've come to the point now where we recognise that yes we don't*
> *have the resources and I guess we don't fight about those anymore. I think*
> *there's a general understanding that everybody's in the same boat and we*
> *wish to be able to undertake therapy in a totally different way if only we*
> *had the resources. And that phrase is said many times, 'if only we had the*
> *resources we could do this, that and get it right' but we don't so we don't*
> *fight about those now.*

The constraints on intervention placed by the resource position were real and
pressing. Alongside them, however, there appeared, from reading the child
protection plans and from interviews, to be some uncertainty about how best
to intervene in child protection cases. This, no doubt, reflects the predominant focus in the development of British child protection services upon
identification and investigation rather than upon the development of treatment skills and resources. It is also probably linked with the difficulties of
measurement, the very limited data on the outcomes of intervention and
treatment programmes and, perhaps, a reluctance to address these issues
(Monck, 1992).

One social worker voiced these concerns as follows:

> *Dare I say it? I don't think really we've worked out the right forms of*
> *treatment for these people. I think that we go in, don't we, we investigate,*

> *we make decisions about people's lives, we may split up families but at the end of the day is that really helping? I would say that more often than not it doesn't. So I think we've got to be looking, yes you can't ignore that investigations have to take place, I'm not saying you wipe all that away. We've got to have more resources and more therapeutic treatment coming, from whatever source. There is no point in going in . . ., it's like the old thing isn't it you go in, you make an assessment of what the problem is but then what do you do about it, how can you really solve that problem or whatever? So effective treatment is a very important issue to look at, what we're actually doing in the department.*

Certainly the aims and content of intervention and the indicators of successful outcome were not often spelled out in the plans. One respondent commented:

> *There are certainly big gaps in resources but I think our problem is with planning, not with the actual resource. I can't substantiate that too easily but my view is, my observation is that in those cases where we've actually positively identified a sort of service delivery plan, the resources can usually be found. But sometimes we don't actually get down to planning.*

However, this was not the dominant perception and experience of the dire resource position in the social services departments. The above discussion about resources should not be taken to imply that it was only the social services departments who were struggling to cope with high workloads and high levels of need with straitened resources. The interviews revealed, inter alia, difficulties in schools, in the health visiting/school nursing service, in the police Special Units and in paediatrics. The position in respect of social services has, however, been highlighted here because of the key responsibility placed upon them, as the lead agency, in implementing child protection plans. They did not, however, do so alone as the following discussion illustrates.

'Left holding the baby'

A final issue in implementing the interagency child protection plan was the difficulty reported in many, but not all of the cases, in sustaining interagency interest and involvement following the investigation and initial child protection conference. This confirms the finding of Gough et al's (1987) longitudinal study of 202 children on the child protection register in one region in Scotland, which noted the low level of interdisciplinary work achieved with cases while they were on the register. Creighton and Noyes (1989) and Farmer and Owen (1993) also note the central role of the social services department and possibly the overreliance of the interdisciplinary system upon it.

For some professions, for example the police and paediatricians, withdrawal at an early stage was in many cases appropriate. One social service manager commented:

> *You wonder where they've all gone, but in some ways it's a relief. Because I mean there are so many people sometimes who are actually involved in the investigation, sometimes just keeping them all in touch is very very difficult. It's a relief sometimes just to whittle it down to just the health visitor and the social worker and maybe a school teacher, me keeping contact with them to make sure they all keep in touch. That's as it should be really you can't have forty people really but providing the key agencies who've made a commitment at the case conference to be involved do follow that through, and by and large they do, then generally it's not a major problem.*

However, others in social services departments perceived it differently as the following quotation illustrates:

> *I would say interagency working is extremely good in the initial period after case conference, what tends to happen in terms of interagency working is that it fades away, assuming the situation gets better it fades away and then we end up holding the baby, well, we feel like we're on our own. With maybe a health visitor if it's a younger child, maybe a school knowing the child if it's older because they've got a lot of other things to get on with they're not concerned about the child any more because things seem to have improved, therefore, the commitment isn't there; it's perhaps unfair but from my perception and I think the perception of social services workers generally there is a feeling that other agencies, although they want to be involved in the decision-making process, they want to shift the responsibility to social services and to a named person like the key worker on the case. I think there's a sense in which they think the responsibility is with social services and they should get on and do it. I think sometimes it is difficult to include people in responsible decision making because they talk about co-working and I think sometimes people get the wrong idea, it's you visiting and me visiting, it's not sharing responsibility and decision making and that sort of thing and sometimes there's still a tendency to see social services as carrying that responsibility. So I think there's a tendency to push it back towards social services and just volunteer information that they have.*

However, this was not a one-way process and it was suggested that in working with children and families on the child protection register some social workers were less diligent about interagency liaison than in earlier phases of the case. One social services manager explained:

> *I know school staff feel very isolated sometimes when they are dealing with a child who is on the register and we have had you know child protection liaison teachers ringing us up and saying 'is this child on the register or not?' and the fact that they haven't known is a cause for concern really. I think it may be the old story, that when people's anxiety level is raised at the investigation time they do do the liaison but afterwards when everything's settled down and there is a protection plan in place, I think they probably do the bare minimum really.*

and another said:

> *The school sees the kids a lot, they are a very important source of information, not just about counting arms and legs but whether the child looks happy, whether the child can concentrate or not. I'm not sure we get the best out of that. That's partly us. Not getting to the school enough, not spending the time that we need to do with the teacher who's experiencing the child all the time. We tend to just assume that because this is mainstream activity for us, it's mainstream activity for other people . . .*

A social worker endorsed these views:

> *Sometimes we are open to criticism that we forget that actually there are a lot of people, a lot of other professional agencies who may actually be with this child a lot more than we are, who can give us valuable information about that child and I don't think we do it enough and acknowledge that these people do have something important to say about these children because they are seeing these children. And that's a very funny quirk and one of the contradictions of field social work, you're supposed to be the key worker, the most important person da de da, quite often we're the ones who have the least contact with the child and even the opportunities that they do have with the child what they're really doing is working with the family, with the parents or the adults or the carers in that family not doing individual work with those children.*

Many commented that core groups could be a valuable mechanism in overcoming these obstacles, a finding confirmed in Birchall's (1992) study.

Core groups

At the time of the initial child protection conferences in the case sample, core groups were established in only six of the 48 cases. The membership, shown in Figure 9.9, reveals clearly the concentration of on-going work in

Figure 9.9 **Membership of six core groups**

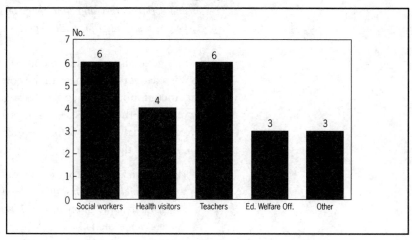

child protection in the hands of social workers, health visitors and, in this primary school-aged sample, teachers and school nurses. The 'other' category comprises one community psychiatric nurse, one psychiatric social worker and one psychologist. By the time of the interviews, core groups were reported to be much more extensively used. They were generally welcomed, both as a mechanism for sustaining interagency involvement and ensuring that plans were implemented and also as a means of working in partnership with parents, (although this was not a feature of the case sample), as the following quotations illustrate:

> *Core groups are brilliant. They really are. We meet four-weekly, myself, the nursery and health visitor and I don't know what we'd have done without that because the three of us are very closely involved with this family, and in terms of being able to keep in touch and to know what we're doing and what's happened from month to month, it's been invaluable. We're continually in touch on a regular basis. And you can't have that sort of dialogue over the telephone; if there is going to be an input to a family by a number of agencies then a core group will be set up and mandated to meet regularly so that there can be an exchange of information, continuously updating people who know where everybody's at with the family. If there are any significant problems arising during the treatment process then that core group can address those problems and resolve them.*

> *When you get people together that's valuable, that's when information gets exchanged and you get updated a little bit more, they're useful and they keep a sense of the case being alive for everybody, you know if you're committed to that routine. Things don't drop and you also build up some trust between the workers then. You talk about working together I mean*

> *that's the embodiment of it when you get that group of people, the teacher and social worker and that group of staff, meeting on a regular basis keeping each other in touch. That's useful.*

Although generally warmly welcomed, a few concerns were expressed that there was a danger of 'cosiness' in the core groups, which usually met without management input, and of concentrating too much power in the hands of the key worker and the social services department. The following examples, the first from a social worker from the NSPCC and the second from a health visitor, illustrate these worries but they were not commonly expressed views:

> *What worries me about core groups is that sometimes core groups are given power to make decisions that I think should be done within a case conference scenario. In my first week here, my first two weeks here I went to a core group, and I had never been to one before. I didn't know what was going on and a decision being made that these two little boys should go home and I'd never met the family but my guts were going, that is wrong, and I came back and said 'I've said yes in the meeting but I think I mean no' and I was right you know, because the social worker was bulldozing people.*

and:

> *I think this then comes down to perhaps personalities with, occasionally you get social workers who I think they perhaps feel that, (I don't know how to say this) that their view is right, okay, now everybody else yes, they may contribute but really their view is right, not all social workers are like that. And that is hard. You know if they are very strong personalities if you're not careful you can be swept under the table.*

The expansion of the core group periodically to form the basis of review child protection conferences was one means to avoid insularity and dominance by one profession or a powerful individual.

Monitoring and review

Effective systems of internal monitoring and of external interagency review of child protection cases are designed, inter alia, to oversee the implementation of child protection plans and reassess them as required. At the time of the interviews, the mechanisms of interagency review were in the process of change in both authorities.

In borough, cases in the case sample had been reviewed by an interagency meeting known as district review. The district review, chaired by the NSPCC team leader, involved representatives of middle management of the various agencies (social services, health visiting, education welfare, probation, the police, community medicine). The meeting reviewed cases usually on a four-monthly cycle, considering 18–20 cases in a day, scheduled at twenty minute intervals. The review operated on the basis of written reports from members of the interagency network, supplemented by the presence of the key worker. At the time of the interviews, the system was on the point of change to one in which an expanded core group with an independent chair would review cases three months after the initial child protection conference and at six-monthly intervals thereafter.

In city, at the time of the interviews, the review of child protection was undertaken by the provision of written reports to the custodian of the register, a principal clinical medical officer, and an administrative clerk. The forms were issued every six months to the key worker and others involved with the case. As in borough, the system was about to change with the transfer of the register to the social services department, in 1992, implementing the recommendation in *Working Together* (1988, para 5.33). Although it was acknowledged that the arrival of the forms might act as a spur to interagency or other activity in cases which had been allowed to drift, prompting a visit to the family or a phone call to colleagues in the interagency network for example, it was generally agreed that the system was not well suited for the rigorous reassessment of cases or review of the implementation of the interagency plan. As in borough, a new system based on expanded core groups was about to be implemented to allow for more comprehensive review, interdisciplinary discussion and to offer scope for parental participation in case review. It was clear from the interviews that there was widespread acceptance of the need for interagency review of the child protection plans. The following view was typical:

> *I think it's important because again it's involving other agencies in the decision. Don't forget the decision was made by a case conference so if we're talking about working together, it's got to be a must, hasn't it? Otherwise social services are left again. We're asking the question should just social services be involved in child protection, or should other agencies continue to be involved? Because at the moment the feeling is social services are the child protection agency or NSPCC, so it's over to them. If we're talking about working together, if we're talking about the sort of guidelines we're getting from the government about a multidisciplinary approach, we've got to have a multidisciplinary review system but also to involve the parents and to involve the workers on the case on the ground level not just the senior officers. There's a process started off in this interagency way and it should be finished off in this interagency way.*

However, concerns were expressed about the resource implications of the new systems, which in both authorities would considerably increase the number and/or the length of review conferences.

Deregistration

At the time of the study, the process of deregistration varied between the two authorities. In borough, deregistration required the approval of the multiagency district review. In city, practice varied. In some cases deregistration took place following a letter to the other agencies involved seeking their approval of a proposal to deregister, in others, particularly where other agencies raised an objection there was a review case conference. The position in city was explained as follows:

> The reviews can take place in a variety of different ways really and the reason for that is again lack of resources, lack of social work time. We are aware obviously that the best sort of review is a meeting with parents present but that would involve social workers in an awful lot of work, that would be new work because a lot of workers haven't done that sort of thing before. So under the procedures they're still able to do a paper exercise review where the least that is required of them is that they get information in writing from the various agencies involved, collect all the reports together and discuss with their team leader what should happen and go on from there. And they then have to fill in the form from the register to say that this review process has happened.

There had been an expectation in the past in city that clear cases of abuse (registered as 'overt' rather than 'suspected' in terms of the local registration criteria) would remain registered for a minimum of three years, although there was a possibility of earlier removal. However this, too, was about to change to more focused, briefer child protection intervention associated with a more rigorous management approach and interagency review system.

In neither area were decisions about deregistration said to be particularly contentious. For example, from a teacher:

> I would say usually we are in agreement, I mean I can think of a couple of instances when I have said well you know, 'just look at this a little bit longer that is what we're saying to you', and you asked me are we normally taken notice of – I've got to say yes we are, they do value what the staff at the school say, I'm not saying they always do what we say . . .;

from a paediatrician:

> *I think it's probably reasonable in [city]. If one has strong objections to a child coming off, they will leave the child on but usually one can agree.*

from a local authority solicitor:

> *Well, we get consulted. We get consulted but I think it's just really as a formality you get the document through to say that this is proposed and you're being consulted because you were a member of the case conference. I don't think it's a point of interprofessional conflict as far as I'm concerned;*

from a clinical nurse manager:

> *I don't think they're kept on in this area anyway longer than is necessary, generally speaking. I do think sometimes they are taken off perhaps earlier than we would wish. Having said that, up to now they haven't come unstuck with it.*

The social workers, too, considered that they were usually able to secure interagency agreement to deregistration when they thought it desirable, for example:

> *I haven't had a lot of experience of disagreement. If it did get any disagreement then we'd have to set up a case discussion and look at it. I think usually you've carried most of the professions along with you as you've been working with the case so you've got a core of agreement anyway.*

Thus, in deregistration as in initial registration of the cases, the interagency network generally operated on the basis of consensus rather than sharp and frequent interprofessional disagreement.

Internal monitoring

An important component of the mechanisms for interagency review are the internal supervision and monitoring systems within the constituent agencies. Since the focus of this study was interagency coordination, the internal monitoring and management systems within each of the separate agencies involved were not examined in detail. Nonetheless, in the course of interviews significant differences emerged which appeared to have a bearing on the working of the interagency network in child protection and in the implementation of child protection plans.

One of the most important was the differing degrees of supervision and support offered to field staff. At one end of the continuum was the health visiting/school nursing service. While there was some variation across borough in the level of support provided, in city there was a clear system of accountability, based on written records specifically designed for the purpose. In general across both authorities, the levels of monitoring and staff support in respect of child protection cases held by school nurses and health visitors was high. It was reflected in the support offered to staff before and after child protection conferences, in preparing their contribution and identifying their role in the child protection plan. At the other extreme were consultant paediatricians, and, when they were involved, general practitioners who operated with high levels of professional discretion. Also in this category were police officers who reported that, while they operated within formal systems of hierarchical accountability, their recommendations were very rarely overturned by their superior officers.

In between were the social workers where the arrangements for the supervision, monitoring and staff support varied considerably within the authorities. In some teams, supervision of child protection cases was reported to be close and was welcomed as supportive by the social workers. In others, it was more patchy and in some it appeared almost non-existent, at least in the intervention phase when child protection plans were implemented. The systems often required social workers to seek help reactively as difficulties arose. In both authorities supervision was closer in the initial investigation phase and in both authorities supervisory staff were involved, in different ways, in the systems of interagency review, at a minimum by countersigning written reports from the key workers. In neither authority was there extensive evidence of supervisory input in on-going intervention, recorded in the case files, either in written accounts by social workers of decisions reached in supervision or of the supervisors having themselves read the files. There were, however, some exceptions to this general observation.

A lack of supervisory input was acknowledged as particularly problematic in the social services department in city and part of the departmental reorganisation, imminent at the time of the research study, was to strengthen the supervisory capacity in child care at team level. It seems likely that the variability in the supervision offered to key workers had an impact on the difficulties in implementation of the child protection plans discussed earlier.

In city and borough, responsibility for the quality of work in child protection rested principally with the line managers in the areas and divisions. There was, however, no formal monitoring or 'product sampling' carried out by them, by the ACPC or by the child protection coordinators although, informally, their advice and intervention had an impact on the standard of work. The management information available from the child protection registers, neither of which was computerised at the time of the study and both of which were relocating to the social services departments, was regarded as inadequate. As one said:

> When we get that information into the computer it will be superb, but
> simple things like how many unallocated case have they? No idea. How

many families have we got where English isn't their first language? No idea. How many cases is this particular key worker carrying? No idea. What proportion of case conferences do GPs come to? I can't tell you and it's incredibly frustrating because there is no way I can access what we've got.

The interviews and records confirm Birchall's finding that interagency coordination in child protection was perceived to work less well in the intervention phase than in referral and investigation. In that study, 22% of respondents considered interagency coordination worked very well in the initial phases and 61% rated it 'rather well'. In on-going work only 9% ranked it 'very well' and 63% 'rather well'. The proportion who considered it worked 'rather badly' rose from 14% in the initial phases to 24% in subsequent intervention (Birchall, 1992, p66).

In city and borough the interagency case monitoring and case review systems were in the process of change but there was a lack of accessible management information which was important not only for the social services departments but for the interagency system as a whole. In its absence, the quality control mechanisms were more likely in many, but not all, of the agencies involved to be activated only when things went wrong and required case review by the ACPC, an issue discussed in the next chapter.

Summary

Following the peak of interagency involvement evidenced in the initial child protection conference, subsequent intervention was concentrated in very few hands, and predominantly within the social services department. Problems in the implementation of the child protection plans were identified, including a severe lack of resources to help abused children and their families, difficulties in securing parental compliance with intervention plans and complexity and the pace of change in turbulent families. There were also reported to be difficulties in sustaining interagency involvement once the anxiety and peak of activity associated with initial investigation and registration had passed. Core groups were identified as a significant mechanism for promoting active interagency involvement among those most closely concerned with the children and families.

Internal mechanisms for monitoring child protection work varied within and between servies. The interagency monitoring systems were in the process of change to establish case review procedures which involved the interagency network in both authorities and facilitated family involvement in the process. As with other aspects of interagency decision-making reviewed in the study, the process of case deregistration was revealed to be generally characterised by consensus rather than dissent.

Chapter 10

The machinery of interagency collaboration in child protection

A distinctive feature of the British system of child protection is the elaborate machinery established for interagency collaboration from the 1970s onwards. Two key components of this – the child protection register and the child protection conference have been discussed earlier. Here the local procedural guidelines and the bodies which produced them, Area Child Protection Committees, are reviewed. The data are drawn from interviews and from the questionnaire completed by 81 respondents, described in Chapter Two.

The local procedures

As required by central government guidance, the Area Child Protection Committees in city and borough issued local interagency procedures. In city, the version in operation at the time of the study was published in 1989, implementing many but not all of the recommendations in *Working Together* (1988). In borough, the publication of the revised procedures did not take place until 1991. Their initial production was slow while an interagency working group prepared a draft prior to the appointment of the child protection coordinator. They were then delayed while an internal case review was conducted by the ACPC since it was thought that procedural changes might flow from this. However, as the timescale for the review extended, a decision was taken to publish the procedures as they stood. They were therefore issued in 1991 in the knowledge that they would imminently need revision to take account of the implementation of the Children Act 1989 and the revised *Working Together* (1991).

Availability of the procedures

Questions were asked in interview and in the questionnaire about the availability of the procedures to members of the interagency network. As Figure 10.1 shows, most respondents (83%) possessed their own copy of the procedures. This compares with a level of ownership of 66% reported in Birchall's study (1992, p 57) reflecting the greater involvement of the sample in city and borough in child protection work.

Of the nine reporting that they did not have their own copy, eight were teachers (three in borough and five in city) and one was a social worker, in borough. Six of the teachers reported that a copy was available in the building in which they worked, usually in the staff room but two teachers, one in each authority and including a child protection liaison teacher reported that they had never seen them. It was stated in interview that it was policy in authority to make a copy available in each school.

Figure 10.1 **Number of respondents with a personal copy of the local procedures (N = 63)**
(This question was excluded from the questionnaire for ACPC members, hence the smaller number of replies).

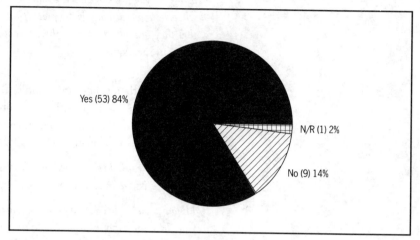

In borough it was said of schools:

> *I sometimes wonder how often they're read, you know we can only encourage people. Every school has copies, it's part of the local authority's instruction that they should be on clear display in every staff room. Part of the training of what you do as a designated teacher you must let every member of staff know that this exists, and all the rest of it, but you can lead horses to water but you can't make them drink can you. There's a great pressure on schools and in some schools it will take a high priority and in other schools it won't because of the make up of the catchment area of the children who are there. I appreciate and others appreciate that child abuse is not restricted to certain parts of the town. I don't think that some teachers would accept that . . . the children that they teach were as open to the chances of abuse as others. I think it is fair to say that in certain parts of the town there's more awareness of child protection than in others.*

Education welfare officers in borough reported that they had personally delivered the revised procedures to head teachers and child protection liaison teachers, explaining the key changes and offering to address all teachers on the topic.

In city, the procedures had been distributed through the constituent agencies of the ACPC and it was said:

> *We still get, even now, some two years after the production of the procedure manual, schools ringing us direct and saying we haven't got one, we never received one. So I think there's a big question mark about how thorough the Education Department were and how important they regard it as being. So you just have a sense that some of the schools or a number of the schools are not actually being provided with the information and support that they actually need from the centre as it were, being let down by the centre in some respects.*

In interviews with teachers in schools, their awareness of the procedures varied. Some were familiar with the contents and knew where the school copy was to be found, others were more vague, as the following quotations from child protection liaison teachers illustrate:

> *I haven't a copy. I've been led to believe since I asked [the school nurse] that there is one in school somewhere. I presume [the head] has it.*

> *I know about it. I've read it once. I know where it is! I'll go and fetch it for you. It's funny that because I didn't know of it's existence until about a year ago when I was on a course and they gave us it, but I didn't know it existed until then. So, I don't know if other people use it or not. I was interested to read it to find out what the procedure was supposed to be . . . It probably exists in school but nobody's ever given it to me. Probably in the office somewhere.*

The variation in the teacher's knowledge of the interagency child protection guidelines confirms the findings about varied levels of awareness of child protection in schools, discussed in Chapter Three, in connection with interagency referral. It highlights the difficulty of ensuring that a large workforce on dispersed sites is informed about a topic which, although vital for an individual child, represents only a small fraction of their daily concerns. It also confirms findings in Birchall's (1992) study that teachers were the profession least likely to own their own copy of the guidelines, followed by the general practitioners. In general, however, efforts to distribute the guidelines across the interagency network had been successful and this was confirmed in interviews with observations such as:

> *You see them all over the place, people do refer to them*

and

> *When you go to case conferences you see four or five copies.*

Some concerns were expressed, however, about how familiar people were with the contents in practice. In city, the social services department had organised training sessions to familiarise field social workers with the revised procedures but this had not taken place in borough. One social worker who had been in post for nine years at the time of the study when asked whether she had ever used the procedures replied:

> No. I mean I've used people around me I think. I've never sort of gone to a book to see what I should do.

This was, however an exception, although a few other social workers reported relying on their seniors rather than the procedures. Figure 10.2 reveals that in response to a question in the questionnaire about their most recent use of the procedures, 45 people (71%) reported using them within the preceding four weeks, of whom 15 had used them within the previous week and nine in the last twenty-four hours. Only two respondents reported never having used the procedures. This was a higher rate of usage than in Birchall's study, where 37% of respondents reported that they had used the procedures in the preceding four weeks, of whom 11% had done so in the preceding week. This reflects the different sampling strategy used in the two studies.

Figure 10.2 **Respondents reported most recent use of procedures (N = 63)** (This question was excluded from the questionnaire for ACPC members, hence the smaller number of replies).

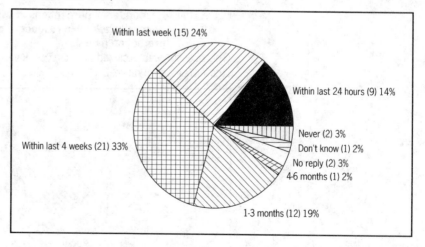

Most respondents found the procedures helpful, as is shown in Figures 10.3 and 10.4. Again, the figures differ from those found in Birchall's study where a smaller proportion of respondents (63%) reported that they found the procedures helpful in respect of their own role and a larger proportion (29%) that they did not know. In Birchall's study 60% of the respondents found the procedures helpful concerning the role of other professionals and 35% did not know, compared with 86% and 6% in this study.

Figure 10.3 **Respondents' perceptions of whether the procedures are generally helpful in respect of their *own* role in child protection (N = 63)**
(This question was excluded from the questionnaire for ACPC members, hence the smaller number of replies).

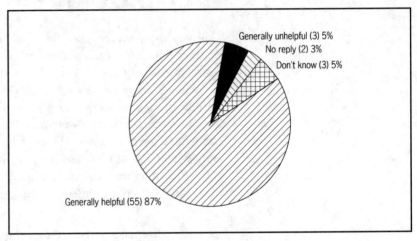

Figure 10.4 **Respondents' perceptions of whether the procedures are generally helpful in respect of other professions' roles in child protection (N = 63)**
(This question was excluded from the questionnaire for ACPC members, hence the smaller number of replies).

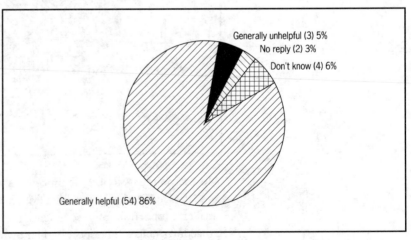

These responses to structured questions in the que[...]
borne out in interviews with most respondents confi[...]
procedures and found them helpful. The following w[...]
interview to questions about their use and value:

from a probation officer:

> *I think my feeling is that they are there, they are necessary. We have to give a high priority to child protection, it's right that we do so.*

from a paediatrician:

> *They are helpful and necessary. It is important that staff know what to do.*

and from a police officer:

> *I think they are useful. I think they're essential, to have guidelines. I've never been involved in drawing them up. I just sort of follow them but they seem to be very reasonable as far as I'm concerned.*

It is possible that if the interview sample had contained a larger proportion of doctors the picture might have been less positive. Parton and Thomas observe

> *In our experience social services departments tend to implement the procedures quite vigorously (but) the medical profession tends to be more laissez-faire (1983, p 60).*

One police officer in the present study, who observed that copies of the procedures were regularly in evidence at child protection conferences added 'but you never see the paediatricians with them'. The data in Birchall's (1992) study indicate that the procedures were not widely available among general practitioners nor perceived as particularly helpful by them.

In responding to questions in interview about the usefulness of the procedures, respondents identified several different strands. Some stressed their help as a check list in ensuring that the necessary tasks were completed at a time of stress as the following quotations illustrate. A clinical nurse manager said:

> *I think one of the dangers otherwise is that at a time of stress it is very easy for everybody to omit doing something that is very obvious . . . because it was the stress of the moment and that is the way that mistakes happen and children fall through the net. And we end up with both of us in front of an enquiry and a dead or badly injured child on our hands. At least with procedures it gives the flexibility for people to follow those procedures in whatever order is appropriate at the time but it does provide that sort of check list of have I done blomb blomb blomb blomb and if I haven't done,*

> *then why haven't I done it and generally if you haven't done it there's a definite reason why you haven't done it and that's fine because you can justify it but you're justifying it with a reason rather than just because you forgot it;*

an NSPCC social worker:

> *I do need them. Its useful for me to actually just check that I'm, yes, following a line, is it security? Yes I suppose it is to some extent. Investigations, even though I've done loads, they are very anxious times. I like them but they are anxious times and I find myself going to the procedures, it's like a life line I suppose. Just a quick flick, right you're all right off you go. Right, just a mental check;*

and finally, two social workers:

> *I use procedures as I would a legal reference, that if necessary before going out I will look at them. In fact, yes, I can say I do that every time, even with something I think is straight forward because it's quite easy to miss the tick list as it were, forget to contact somebody, forget to do this or do something in the wrong order and I think we all do that;*

> *I've never done such a bulk of work of this kind, you know some social workers will be perhaps doing many a month or many in six months, and I suppose some of the aspects of it will become second nature and I wouldn't need to sort of check out but I think nowadays they're on the whole sufficiently complicated for one to feel it's best really just to recheck as you go along.*

A few respondents pointed to the value of the procedures in resolving interagency disputes. For example, a social worker said:

> *Yes. They're useful in terms of just checking whether some disagreements about whether police should be involved or not, etc. and what the process is. I mean if you are doing a joint piece of work with somebody and somebody disagrees with you, you can refer them to this and get it sorted out.*

and a police officer explained how he would use them to press for decisions about registration at initial conferences, as discussed in Chapter Seven.

It was surprising that respondents only rarely reported that the existence of the procedures helped them in their direct work with families, when they could invoke them as the reason for taking difficult decisions or courses of action. A health visitor gave one of the few examples:

> *I think you need the machinery . . . and in the cases where it's a family I knew and I've picked up for instance a slap mark on the face which I've*

done twice with two separate families. One time when I was on holiday, one of the mums shoved a note under the door for my attention, but that was on the Friday and I came back on the Monday to find this letter to say she was really sorry, apologising to me she was really sorry but she had gone really mad with this child and she had hit him a lot of times and could I come to see her, and that the child was covered in bruises he really had a lot of bruises, she'd gone absolutely bananas. I just said to her 'I'm sorry, this isn't between you and me, there is machinery we've got to put in operation and we'll just try and do it together' and I'm glad that there is the machinery . . . I think it's very important that families know that there is no possibility whatever of keeping this thing between you and them . . . It helps to say, 'listen this is how it is, this is the contract of my employment, you know that, now you and me and this little boy we are going to casualty, now come on we'll go', and that makes it much easier.

Some workers welcomed the procedures for their role in ensuring some standardisation in response and ensuring minimum standards of good practice in an important area of work.

I think inevitably they must constrain practice but they do result in hopefully everyone acting in the same professional way across the board irrespective of the case . . . Otherwise you get a variety of practice which is in some cases might be very good, very appropriate and others it might be very shoddy. I think this is the only way you can try and ensure that professional response is appropriate and equal across the board.

I think they're realistic, there are always some things where the procedures could be tighter but I think what underlines procedures is good practice and if people are tuned in to what is good practice anyway, then the procedures are there to make sure that takes place.

Finally, some respondents pointed to the role of the procedures in protecting and safeguarding them, as noted also by Corby (1987). The following views are from social workers and a clinical nurse manager:

It's pressure at the time but at the end of the day I feel comfortable with it, because I've followed the procedures and if anything else occurs then at least I've done that:

I find it helpful that things are laid down, the guidelines are there and you must follow them. I think basically it's to protect ourselves which is right, but it's also got to be in the interest of the client to make sure that you are following the word. I do really.

In a situation like this where people can feel very anxious about child protection work generally and don't want to be in a situation where they will be held publicly accountable if something's gone wrong, then you hold to whatever structures you can.

I think people are frightened enough about dealing with child abuse to be very grateful for them on the whole. They're very clear and very easy to follow and I think most health visitors welcomed them with open arms when they were first composed and circulated and I think that by and large people use them.

Such views were particularly prevalent among health visitors and some social workers, confirming the finding in Birchall's (1992) study that anxiety about work in child protection was more evident among these two professions than others. Their exposed role as front line workers and the criticisms of their role performance in many child abuse inquiry reports no doubt contribute to this. The role of the procedures in offering such protection to police officers or to the small number of doctors interviewed was much less prominent.

The extent of general approval and appreciation of the procedures was somewhat surprising in view of the criticisms made of them in the past, particularly by social workers as a fetter on their professional discretion, see for example, Popplestone, 1977, HC 329-II, 1977, p 250, HC 329-III, 1977, p 515, Hallett and Stevenson, 1980. Although, as is discussed below, some were critical on this score, they were a small minority. Several factors appeared to have contributed to this. One was clearly a generation of workers who had never known another way of working, for example:

As a newly qualified worker I suddenly came in and there was a pile of cases on my desk and a procedures manual, so I've got to say that the procedures have helped me. When I become more comfortable with the procedures and perhaps a little bit more confident with myself, perhaps they'll burden me but at this moment in time they're not a burden nor have they restricted me in any way. Apart from the paperwork and having to read them, I found them very helpful. I wouldn't have been able to survive without them.

Others accepted them as part of the customary way of proceeding, confirming other findings in the study of a relatively, although not entirely, unquestioning acceptance of the status quo, as the following quotation illustrates:

Maybe I've been ground down over the years, I don't know. I'm the last spark of radicalism left, really, but I don't feel . . . there's nothing in it that matters that we have to do that we wouldn't do anyway.

But, perhaps most important, many workers welcomed the structure and safety which they considered was afforded by the procedures in a stressful field of work.

Anxiety and fear in child protection

Discussion of the child protection procedures in interview illustrated well the heavy burden of responsibility and accountability carried by many in the interagency network, and a degree of fear that acted as a spur to coordination and to procedural compliance. Although many said that they found the procedures helpful, discussion of them provoked some anxiety and defensiveness among those interviewed, who clearly feared a test of their knowledge of them when the subject was introduced. The following replies were typical of many in borough where revised procedures had been issued just prior to the research interviews:

from a health visitor

> *I've not read it yet, it's a failure I should have done.*

from a social worker

> *Yes I do have a copy, are you going to ask me if I've read them now? . . .
> no really, I haven't touched them.*

from another

> *You're going to ask me what I think of them and I've not looked at them
> yet.*

In city, where the revised procedures had been available for much longer, similar observations were made; for example by a teacher:

> *Yes, I can't say it's as well thumbed as it should be*

and by a social worker:

> *I mean I haven't read it from cover to cover.*

Although the procedures were generally viewed as helpful and supportive, they were also the standard against which performance would be judged and thus carried the potential to catch people out. As one senior manager in social services said:

> *Their primary purpose, in my view, is they are meant to be a tool for staff
> and certainly we wrote them with that intent in mind. But I'm also*

> *conscious that if we have a child protection tragedy and a need for a case review then the procedures are the things that are looked at. If we get a Rochdale it's somewhere the SSI are going to head for.*

A social work manager expressed it thus:

> *Yes, it sits there on my desk and when I pick it up and look at it I don't feel 'gosh this is reassuring and refreshing, thank goodness this is here'. I feel this is something which I'm going to be measured by, not something which is here to guide and instruct me, this is here to trip me up if I get it wrong. And it may be, that's just my experience but that's what's happened you know, people have used it in that way to beat me over the head rather than to say 'have you thought about using this? You have a problem, let's look at the child protection manual and see how we can resolve this problem'. That's what it feels like.*

While the fear and anxiety of work in child protection was most acutely perceived, or perhaps more openly expressed, in this study by health visitors and their managers, they were not alone. The police, for example, acknowledged child protection as a high profile and demanding activity:

> *I think we are confident to an extent about what we are doing but I think it is a dangerous position to become too confident about this sort of work . . . There are some very controversial cases that we deal with, abuse in children's homes and abuse in schools and abuse in foster homes, abuse by professional people and all the sort of stuff that's going to make banner headlines; and of the ordinary cases that have been dealt with in the force every day (and there are 3,000 officers) the ones that are coming to us are really controversial, difficult investigations; and you've got to deal with it properly and with due regard to the implications of what you're doing to everybody.*

Unsurprisingly, some social workers and their managers too, expressed similar concerns:

> *There is the fear in this job which if I didn't mention it would be dishonest really; for all that you try to work in an imaginative and constructive way with clients the fear of getting it wrong is important. It affects judgements. I know it does and you get defensive decisions made in situations because if you take a risk in this game you're pilloried if it goes wrong. That troubles me really;*

> *My big problem really is the amount of knowledge, time and sheer resources of all descriptions that are required now to come anywhere near meeting the good practice standards and the requirements of the Children*

> *Act . . . We haven't got the resources to deal with this . . . It't quite worrying actually because when we get a call there'll be the social workers that stand there, not the director, not the councillors, not the government. We're on a hiding to nothing;*

> *As a senior officer, I wouldn't want a career in child protection. The emotional demands of it are a kind of public kick in the teeth and watching your back. If I had to go back to fieldwork I'd be heading for the elderly, pronto.*

It was, however, suggested by some members of the social services department in city that the relative lack of local political interest in child protection and of senior management engagement with it in the past, coupled with the absence of a major and critical public inquiry, contributed to a position where, for some, there was a degree if not of complacency then a lack of awareness of the responsibilities carried. This was said to be reflected in matters such as the absence of specialist practitioners and of minute takers in some conferences. Social workers and senior staff spoke of this, as in the following examples:

> *I think [city] has sat down on its laurels; because we haven't had major tragedies we haven't had anything to jump up and down about and I've often said 'look, there but for the grace of god, go we'. I just think sometimes it's a matter of time.*

and

> *[city] has not learned to get scared about child protection. The culture is not quite right. The focus is not sharp enough.*

A social worker expressed surprise at the relatively laid back approach of some colleagues:

> *. . . What surprised me, because quite often I'll go out on NAI investigations with other teams, what is surprising working with other social workers is sometimes, not only that they're not familiar with the procedures in very clear ways, for the child, but they're not very clear about it in terms of themselves.*

This social worker gave the following example of a report by a school nurse of anal bruising on a registered child, following which a home visit was paid to investigate:

> *When we got there the mother was in the house but the father was with this particular child at a daughter's house. There had been a history of agression in this family in the past and mum was basically saying that she*

didn't know how this bruising has occurred. He could have fallen down, he could have been pushed by his older brothers. Mother was very antagonistic; we knew father from the past was antagonistic and eventually mother was saying 'well, as it happens, we have an appointment at the Children's hospital the following morning anyway as a routine appointment, can I not take him to be examined then?' The social worker involved said 'yes, that might be a good idea', because I think there was concern about the aggression if we had insisted on taking the child that evening. And when we left the house I was saying 'I think nevertheless we still need to go and see this child. It may be perhaps appropriate that we leave it until the following morning but if we're doing that (a) we need to consult with management and (b) we need to see the child' and the response back was 'but we know the school nurse has seen the child today'. I said 'yes but we haven't seen the child . . . It really doesn't matter if five other people have seen the child, we haven't seen the child, and if we are anticipating leaving this child to be examined until the following morning, which, may be appropriate because the bruising was old bruising, and it may be appropriate for those reasons to try and work with the family rather than against the family by trying to drag this child to a hospital at about 6/7 o'clock in the evening, nevertheless we need to consult with managers because we are leaving ourselves totally vulnerable to not having seen this child and to be making this sort of a decision' . . . But I was certainly bothered enough to have rung a manager myself to make sure that at least they know that information. And it's in scenarios like that that I'm quite staggered that sometimes social workers are not protecting themselves, leave alone the child.

Critics of the procedures

While the great majority of respondents found the procedures helpful, there were some critics as the following examples from social services departments illustrate:

There's a kind of nil win, where some staff will take the view that what's in there is kind of patronising, over the top and doesn't allow them professional judgement. Other staff argue it is not clear what they are expected to do. Most try and strike a balance in that, I think we've got a reasonable balance. I'm quite clear that not everybody would support that view. If everybody was just disagreeing on one end of the spectrum it would be less of a problem.

There are various factions really in the department. People who are very pro-parent and see their role as supporting the parent to protect the children don't like the procedures. They see them as a sort of punitive process that

> *parents have to be put through if they've abused their child somehow.*
> *Although I wouldn't say by any means that that was a prevalent view, it's*
> *sort of little pockets and certainly I think some of the volutary agencies in*
> *[city] feel that as well. There's at least one pocket of workers who perceive*
> *the procedures as not being stringent enough and they're really with the*
> *right of the child to be protected from abuse at all costs and feel that the*
> *procedures don't achieve that. So there's that other end of the scale. I think*
> *there are still those workers who are frightened of the hostility that*
> *implementing the procedures might involve them in with parents but most*
> *people I think are using the procedures very closely and find them helpful.*
> *One or two people are a little bit sceptical and probably won't give them*
> *the attention they deserve.*

A few social workers argued that the procedures constrained them and fettered their discretion:

> *I think the idea behind them is partly to protect the system in a sense as*
> *well as protect the children that we are supposed to be protecting. So there*
> *is no room for individual judgement . . . It's like step one, you do this*
> *then you do step two then three. There's no room in there, is there, for any*
> *individual assessment or judgement of what the situation is?*

> *I wish that the procedures allowed for some sort of thing between the*
> *response at the moment, you know we either invoke the procedures or we*
> *don't, there's no half way house . . . I wish we had a less intrusive and*
> *less serious looking response which would do the job without the*
> *procedures. Where there is actually an injury which has been caused non-*
> *accidentally, I would say our procedures don't allow us to not case*
> *conference that.*

Other social workers, while not deeply critical of the procedures themselves, emphasised the importance of good practice underpinning the procedures, for example:

> *procedures can never operate successfully unless you have the other part*
> *which is to do with the social work, from my point of view as a social*
> *worker the social work task sorted out. And I think there are major*
> *problems with that. And I think if that is not addressed as well then no*
> *amount of procedures will actually help children.*

Compliance

Respondents considered that there was, in general, a reasonable degree of compliance with the procedures, although it was acknowledged that there was slippage from time to time, for example in matters such as checking the child protection register and cross-referrals between the police and the social services departments, as the case sample had also revealed. Departures from the procedures were not, however, in general perceived to be patterned. One exception concerned the accident and emergency department in borough with which difficulties were reported over the exchange of information concerning injured children. The other involved one part of borough where the rate of child protection conferences was lower than expected given its population size. Interagency links there were reported to be close and workloads in the social services department and health visiting service were perceived to be more manageable than in some other areas. There the procedures were reported to be scrutinised for the maximum discretion to avoid formal child protection conferences in circumstances where inter-agency work was already taking place and children's welfare being promoted. It was explained as follows:

> *our conferencing rate has been significantly low compared to the rest of the authority, and there's been a tradition of using some discretion. That might have been dangerous for individual professionals. I hope its been more dangerous to the professional than to the kids. I think it has . . . There has been a culture of planned meetings, discussions between agencies outside of the child protection procedures . . . Most of the time there is contact early enough that we don't have to wait for somebody to come and panic. The child will have been observed before . . .*

and:

> *We don't case conference everything that moves here and it seems to work out alright for us, touch wood.*

It was, however, usual for the procedures to be followed fairly closely and it was apparent that they had made a significant contribution to the insti-tutionalisation and routinisation of interagency collaboration in child protection.

Area Child Protection Committees

The remaining piece of the machinery of interagency work in child protection for consideration in this study is the Area Child Protection Committee (ACPC). Local authorities were advised in the DHSS Circular issued in 1974 to establish area review committees (as they were then called) in localities where they did not exist. Their main functions were to devise and advise on procedures for dealing with cases, to review the work of case conferences and to provide education and training for staff. Their membership was to be at 'senior level' from the local authority, health authority, the police, the probation service and the NSPCC. *Working Together* 1988 redesignated them Area Child Protection Committees as a joint forum for developing, monitoring and reviewing child protection policies and outlined their main areas of activity as follows:

a   to establish, maintain and review local interagency guidelines on pro-
     cedure to be followed in individual cases;

b   to review significant issues arising from the handling of cases and reports
     from enquiries;

c   to review arrangements to provide expert advice and interagency liaison;

d   to review progress on work to prevent child abuse;

e   to review work related to interagency training (DHSS and Welsh Office,
     1988, p 39).

In the revised *Working Together*, 1991 the list was expanded to include additional functions (b, g and h below), and a more pro-active stance was indicated by replacing the words 'to review' with 'to scrutinise' and requiring recommendations to be made subsequently to the responsible agencies.

a   to establish, maintain and review local interagency guidelines on pro-
     cedures to be followed in individual cases;

b   to monitor the implementation of local procedures;

c   to identify significant issues arising from the handling of cases and reports
     from inquiries;

d   to scrutinise arrangements to provide treatment, expert advice and
     interagency liaison and make recommendations to the responsible
     agencies;

e   to scrutinise progress on work to prevent child abuse and make recom-
     mendations to the responsible agencies;

f   to scrutinise work related to interagency training and make recommen-
     dations to the responsible agencies;

g   to conduct reviews required under Part 8 of this Guide;

h   to publish an annual report about child protection matters (Home Office
     at al, 1991, p 5).

This revised guidance was issued towards the end of the fieldwork for this study, although a draft was in circulation. At the time of completion of questionnaires and of the interviews the effective guidance governing the operation of the ACPCs was *Working Together* 1988.

As is explained more fully in Chapter Two, twelve people interviewed in city and borough were members of the ACPC and they received an adapted version of the questionnaire which included a brief series of questions on its functioning. In addition, in borough only, the questionnaire was sent to the remaining members of the committee. In total 18 questionnaires were completed by ACPC members, In interview, members of the ACPC were asked about their experiences of its functioning and other field staff and their managers who were not members were asked about their knowledge of the ACPC and its impact, if any, on their work. Several significant structural problems were identified including issues of representation and budgets.

Interagency coordinating committees

Interagency committees are a common device for promoting coordination in health and welfare generally, as well as in child protection, in the UK and USA (Skaff, 1988). Typologies of such committees usually employ the idea of a continuum locating the mechanisms between informal arrangements at one end through more formalised structures to centralised federations or mergers at the other end. One such typology is proposed by Whetten (1981) and Mulford and Rogers (1982) who follow Clark's (1965) schema and propose three strategies of coordination: mutual adjustment, alliance and corporate. Mutual adjustment strategies are informal and low key with a focus on specific cases while the corporate strategies have a formal authority structure to promote coordination, often with a strong centralised administrative unit. In between are alliance strategies which are efforts to coordinate autonomous organisations without the authority of a formal hierarchy. Whetten (1981) identified two further interorganisational forms within the alliance category, the first, often associated with federation, usually involves the formation of some kind of centralised administrative unit and possibly the direct employment of staff. The second form of alliance is a coalition or council where the authority system is more informal and power remains vested in each anticipating member agency. Whetten suggests the coordination is more difficult to orchestrate in such circumstances, given the absence of a third-party mediator, a point of relevance to Area Child Protection Committees which approximate closely to this form of alliance. However, the establishment of budgets and moves to appoint staff to work directly to Area Child Protection Committees suggest that they may be moving towards a more formalised and centralised form of alliance.

Davidson (1976) also characterises interorganisational relations along a continuum with dimensions such as the degree of formalisation in arrangements and structure, specificity about objectives and willingness to cede some organisational autonomy characterising the five stages from the least formal mechanism, communication, through cooperation and confederation to federation and, finally, merger, as shown in Figure 10.5.

Figure 10.5 **A typology of interorganisational relationships from Davidson, 1976, p118**

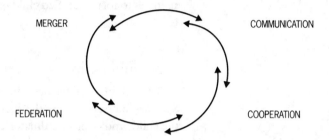

Davidson suggests that it is possible to proceed through the steps in a cyclical way. He proposes that:

> *If two or more agencies are communicating, they are doing no more than talking together, sharing information, ideas and feelings about the shape of their shared world. When mere communication leads to the suggestion that organisations 'work together' on some small project, they may be said to be cooperating. This stage is characterised by informality of the arrangements and a degree of the vagueness of the tasks to be accomplished or even of the broader goals to be achieved. When the arrangements become more formalised and tasks more clearly limited and well-defined, the nature of the relations may be thought of as a confederation, still loose and without formal sanctions for non-participation. When the organisations are willing to define the goals and tasks and when they are willing to cede a degree of their autonomy to that joint structure, a federation exits. When the structure is formalised to the point that the original organisations are willing to give up their identities as organisations, at least regarding the specific domain(s) in which the cooperation has occurred, they may decide to merge to form a new organisation (Davidson, 1976, p 120).*

Area Child Protection Committees seem, at present, to fall between the third and fourth stages – confederation and federation. There are no formal sanctions for non-participation although no doubt strong informal pressure would be exerted if agencies at local levels refused to participate at all. There is a formal structure and, to the extent that agencies agree to follow the procedural guidelines, they have ceded some of their autonomy for entirely independent action. The suggestion was made in the Kimberly Carlile Report (London Borough of Greenwich, 1987) that, because the inter-agency arrangements had failed again, consideration should be given to establishing a new merged organisation combining health and social services functions at local levels in a new child protection agency. The muted response in professional and policy circles to this proposal suggests that it is unlikely that the fifth stage outlined by Davidson – a merger of the participating agencies to form a unified child protection service – will be established in the UK.

Membership

The ACPC was chaired in each authority by the Director of Social Services and serviced by the social services department principally through the child protection coordinator. Although those responding to the question-naire reported that they 'very regularly' or 'regularly' attended as is shown in Figure 10.6, it was clear that there were problems of attendance from others less closely involved, for example in borough, representatives of accident and emergency, orthopaedic and obstetric services. This was predicted as likely to continue to be problematic as the local hospital moved towards trust status since as a paediatrician (who was a regular attender) remarked in interview:

> *an afternoon spent at the ACPC is a session spent not generating income*
> *for the hospital.*

In both borough and city there were reported to be problems about the nature and level of representation. *Working Together* 1991 states:

> *all agencies should recognise the importance of securing effective*
> *cooperation by appointing senior officers to the ACPC. Their appointees*
> *should have sufficient authority to allow them to speak on their agencies'*
> *behalf and to make decisions to an agreed level without referral to the*
> *appointees' agencies* (Home Office et al 1991, p 6).

It was clear that this was far from easy to achieve. The biggest problem was perceived to be with health authority representation. Partly this was a result of the complexity of the structures which resulted in multiple representation. When ACPC members were asked in the questionnaire whether there were any professions or agencies currently represented on the ACPC who did not need to be, four of the 18 respondents replied yes. When asked to specify them the answers included 'too many medical representatives who do not attend' and 'over representation from different aspects of the health auth-ority'. But there were also difficulties, notably in respect of general prac-

Figure 10.6   **Regularity of attendance at ACPC meetings as reported by respondents (N = 18)**

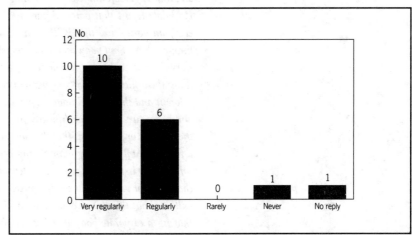

titioners because they represented no agency and were unable to commit autonomous, independently contracted practitioners. This led one respondent in the questionnaire to suggest that general practitioners should not be represented on the ACPC since 'each acts independently anyway'. Problems were reported too, in respect of the representation of the Family Health Service Authority, which was reported to have effectively withdrawn in borough:

> they are members but they don't turn up, they didn't think there was any point in turning up, they couldn't control general practitioners which is what we're after. They haven't got any money to invest which is what we're after and they kind of said, 'send us the minutes and if there's anything that particularly affects us we'll come to that particular meeting'.

More broadly, difficulties were reported in respect of the health service members and of education in terms of securing a level of representation which carried with it budgetary control, the capacity to implement policy, to ensure effective feedback of ACPC business to the agencies concerned and to demonstrate ownership of the committee's business. This contributed to a position in which there was a tendency for ACPCs to be characterised not as pro-active, dynamic committees but as slow and ponderous 'talking shops', as the following quotation illustrates:

> I only would seek to comment on how the Department of Health seems to assume that they work which is, seemingly, fairly incisive and dynamic bodies that are capable of actually grasping issues and taking them through to some satisfactory resolution but the experience in [city] would lead me to be somewhat sceptical about that. I think it's fundamentally wrong to

hold that sort of concept if that, indeed, is what the Department of Health do think. I guess I am referring to things like glib recommendations in the Rochdale report that parental participation will be brought on stream in every authority and the ACPCs and social services have taken the lead through that. That body should overcome any resistance. Full stop. End of story. Very succinct and simple sort of concept. If only it were like that! I think the difficulty is that we consistently in the Area Review Committee before it and the ACPC now, despite a change of membership and status and so on, we have great difficulty in actually getting people to represent the agencies or professions that they are supposedly there to do . . . there is a fundamental difficulty with getting people to do that . . . They don't sort of bring issues spontaneously or few of them do, they always have to be chased up or asked to do specific pieces of work and then sometimes they will do it but there's no spontaneity in that sense. You don't get the sense that it's a corporate body that has a common aim, as it were.

Another respondent in borough characterised the position a few years ago and contrasted it with a subsequent improvement as follows:

There were about twenty seven people there and it was heavy with silence and there was this dead agenda . . . it had to change and there was the task of making people speak. It's a very important and serious business child protection, it really is. Either you have a view or you shouldn't be there. Now I've not actually said that to people but I think they've got the flavour and its working better now.

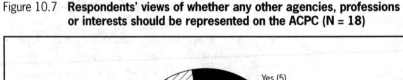

Figure 10.7   **Respondents' views of whether any other agencies, professions or interests should be represented on the ACPC (N = 18)**

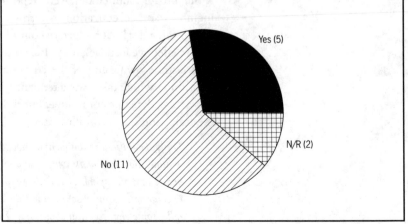

In response to a question about whether other agencies, professions or interests should be represented on the ACPC, most thought not as shown in Figure 10.7. Those wishing to see additional members identified members of the judiciary, court administration, consumers of child protection services and senior officers from the district health authority as potentially making a valuable contribution.

Budgets

At the time of the field research, neither ACPC had succeeded in establishing an identified budget for its activities. In both authorities, funds had in the past been secured from joint finance and were used, for example, to finance the transfer of the child protection register, the production of procedure manuals, the annual report, training posts and minute-takers for child protection conferences. As one member observed:

> *I think we've enjoyed a great deal of support from joint funding and the JCC. Had that not been the case, I don't know, I can't imagine what sort of difficulties we'd have been in really.*

Some members, for example those representing health visiting, reported that they had no funds available within their budgets to contribute in cash rather than kind to the operation of the ACPC, and other members for example, a general practitioner/police surgeon had no budget as such at all.

In borough, it was reported:

> *We haven't got a decision on the budget issue, but it's coming. I'll go and see the health authority about section 27 and I shall tell them that in child protection work of course this is particularly important. I want at least thirty thousand and I'd like £73,000, to run the ACPC child protection service at the moment, so they've got to make a contribution and next year they'll put it in their budget!*

In city, a budget proposal was, at the time of the study, being pushed through the Joint Consultative Committee (JCC).

There was recognition both of the importance of a budget, actual and symbolic, and some resentment that the advice in *Working Together* (1988) which reads:

> *It will be the duty of the agencies represented on the ACPC to reach agreement for funding the ACPC. Agencies should allocate funds to the ACPC in accordance with agreed arrangements at the beginning of each financial year so that the ACPC has an annual budget* (DHSS and Welsh Office (1988), para 7.11)

was not more specific about the apportionment of costs. This view was particularly well highlighted by a police representative on one of the ACPC's, whose responsibilities in the police authority required him to be a member of five ACPC's and 23 sub-committees. Not surprisingly, he argued strongly for a greater degree of central direction so that individual budget negotiations described as a 'nightmare' with each ACPC, 'all structured differently' could be avoided:

> *I would like to see some guidelines or instructions saying this is what we have to put in and we have to put it in on all ACPC's because then everybody knows how they stand and everybody would be getting the same service.*

This point was generalised to other ACPC functions, for example the preparation of local procedures and identifying significant issues arising from inquiries:

> *It would be nice from our point of view to have a full set of procedures for the whole area. I certainly feel that I'd like to see a full set of procedures for Great Britain, you know and then we wouldn't be having, I don't know how many ACPC's there are, but we wouldn't be having say sixty separate sub-committees looking at each recommendation from each report. Think of the waste of time that there is. I find that because I'm on separate sub-committees looking into the same part of a report everybody's looking into it, all coming up with different conclusions. I mean surely something should be right, no that's wrong, they may well all be right but some things are going to be more right than others, and that frustrates me, to be quite honest, in my role.*

While the local variations across the country may make the production of standardised local procedures difficult and may lead to less local ownership than when the ACPC produces its own (itself no mean task, it appeared from this study), there does seem to be scope for rationalisation and more shared activity, for example, in publicising the lessons of major inquiries.

The functioning of the ACPC

As is discussed more fully in the next chapter, the personal relationships at senior officer levels in both city and borough were generally characterised by goodwill and courtesy. This was reflected in the answers in the questionnaires on topics such as the degree of consensus in the ACPCs, as shown in Figure 10.8.

This may also reflect the fact that the committees were relatively settled in their membership, as shown in Figure 10.9.

Figure 10.8   **Respondents' perceptions of the frequency of agreement about matters under discussion in the ACPC (N = 18)**

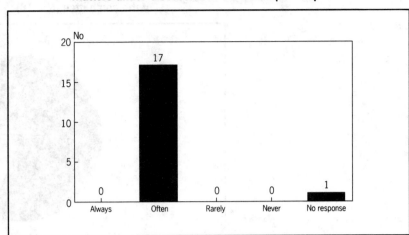

Figure 10.9   **Respondents' length of service on the ACPC (N = 18)**

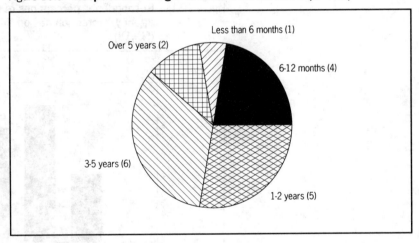

Several respondents mentioned in interview that the ACPC provided a valuable opportunity to meet counterparts in the other professions and to transact business informally. As is shown in Figure 10.10, most respondents thought that the representation of their agency or profession on the committee was important.

The two who responded 'not very important' to the question were a probation service representative and on of the police representatives. Similarly, as is shown in Figure 10.11, most respondents thought their agency or profession wielded 'a modest amount' or greater degree of influence on the decisions reached in the ACPC.

Figure 10.10 **Respondents' perceptions of the importance of their own agency/profession's representation on the ACPC for the work of the committee (N = 18)**

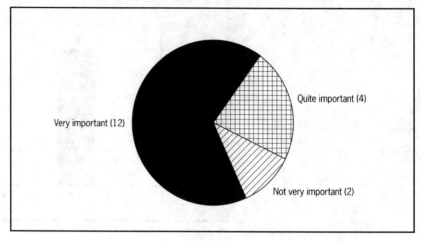

Figure 10.11 **Respondents' perceptions of the degree of influence his/her agency/profession has on the decisions reached in the ACPC (N =18)**

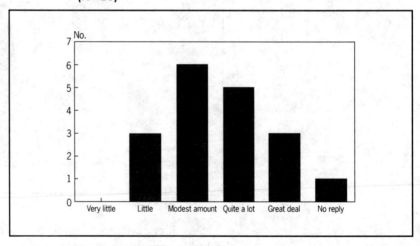

Those responding a 'little' to this question were a child psychiatrist and two representatives of schools (one from the primary and one from the secondary sector). Those replying 'a great deal' were two of the social services department representatives and one of the police representatives. In betwen claiming a 'modest amount' were six representatives from community nursing, the police, probation, an education officer and clinical medical officers (2) and five claiming 'quite a lot', community nursing (2) the police, the social services department and a police surgeon.

Respondents were asked in the questionnaire and in interview how well they thought the ACPCs of which they were members functioned. Some respondents could contrast the position in borough and city with experiences elsewhere, as the following quotations indicate:

> *All the ACPCs have got different strengths and weaknesses, I suppose. I don't see [borough] functioning as the worst one, I don't see it functioning as the best, I think it just functions okay;*

and, of city:

> *Comparing it with others I think it's at least as good as any ACPC arrangements that I've come across. They're not amazingly impressive set ups when you're dealing with them. They tend to sort of shape up under pressure and under exceptional case review investigation pressures when people really get closely working together but that's not really the point. So I think a fairly kind of mixed picture, at least average if not above average of the ones I've come across.*

As is shown in Figure 10.12, the members expressed a relatively high level of satisfaction with the overall functioning of the ACPC. This may be indicative of a rather bland, accepting view, evident at other points in the data. One respondent replied, when asked about the utility of the ACPC:

> *Well, the framework for the ACPC is so well established now through Mark I and Mark II Working Together, I think the time when I debated its utility is rather past. I have done, going back to the Area Review Committees and some of the other rather elaborate bureaucratic arrangements which they sprouted, I was questioning about them. The requirements are now so scrutinised by SSI, the procedural requirements, the exceptional case review requirements that I rather accept them as given.*

However, answers to scaled questions concerning performance in respect of the five main areas of ACPC activity (as outlined in *Working Together* (1988)) suggest that an uncritical acceptance was not the case. As is shown in Table 10.1, the tasks perceived as being best performed were those concerned with the production of local interagency procedures and the review of significant issues arising from cases and inquiry reports, while the least well performed task concerned prevention.

In interview, ACPC members shared the view that they had performed reasonably well in conducting internal case reviews:

> *I think when there's a public profile, like with the death of a child, it doesn't do too badly. I think we've learnt a lot. It was virgin territory. I think if we had to do another one tomorrow, God forbid, we'd do it better.*

I don't think they do too badly at that and I think that all the agencies were very open in provision of information, (except for casualty) you know, by and large, I think it didn't do badly but that's the public profile side.

Figure 10.12 **Respondents' perceptions of the overall functioning of the ACPC (N = 18)**

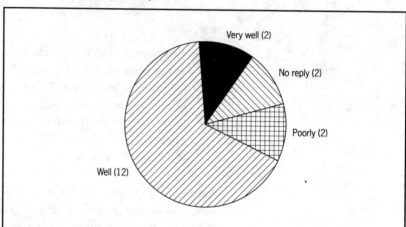

Table 10.1. **Respondents' perceptions of the performance of the ACPC with respect to five key tasks (N = 18)**

	Very well	Well	Poorly	Very poorly	Don't know	No reply
to establish, maintain and review local interagency guidelines on procedures to be followed in individual cases	4	13	0	0	0	1
to review significant issues arising from the handling of cases and reports from inquiries	4	12	1	0	0	1
to review arrangements for interagency liaison	2	10	3	0	2	1
to review progress on work to prevent child abuse	1	6	9	0	1	1
to review work related to interagency training	2	9	6	0	0	1

However, in neither ACPC was there regular monitoring by the committee of the quality of ongoing work in child protection, as opposed to the ad hoc and in-depth investigation of appeals or specific cases which aroused particular concern. In city and in borough, regular monitoring was expected to be easier following the computerisation of the register and its transfer to the social services department:

> *It's going to mean that we're much better at monitoring the sorts of cases that we're actually faced with, how they're being responded to, what the outcomes are and so on.*

At the time of the study, however, it was clear that, although there was wide variation across the areas concerned, there was an absence of routine monitoring and quality assurance:

> *I think in terms of reviewing processes when things haven't gone wrong and looking at good practice, we're not very good. We don't do any random sampling. We review on error.*

The high ranking by members of the ACPC's performance in relation to reviewing individual cases is interesting, since this was the issue of which field staff were most critical. When asked in interview about their knowledge of and contact with the local ACPC, many teachers, health visitors, police officers and social workers said that both were minimal. Many could not name their agency's representative on the committee or state the frequency of its meetings, and many asserted that its impact on their work was minimal. This is surprising since many claimed to follow the local procedures issued by the ACPC, but it appeared that the provenance and auspices of the procedures were not particularly significant for field staff. Some of those interviewed, particularly social work managers were more knowledgeable about the existence of the ACPC but critical of its remoteness from daily practice and the concerns of front-line staff, as the following comments illustrate:

> *It's marginalised to the point of non existence. I mean we receive copies of minutes of ACPC meetings but my view is that the service delivery people are not keyed into that in any kind of way . . . I don't deny they produce useful strategic pieces of work [such as the procedures] but I don't have any feel about ACPC as a corporate body wanting to be keyed into the interface between practitioners and families in the community.*

> *No, not really, is the honest answer no. We know that our child care coordinator is the link person in there and our director has a role in there but from where I sit, no they're a long way away. Generally we listen with interest to the debates that are going on up there and wait for them to be translated into action . . . I think there's a far more positive feeling on the*

ground about involving parents in case conferences than we're getting from the ACPC at the moment. I think it could be worked out on the ground. But they're not at that stage yet with this.

I often wonder if they're taking any notice or listening to what field workers, front line workers are doing, do they know what we're doing?

However, when staff had been involved in case reviews they had more direct knowledge and were critical on two principal grounds, namely lack of information and feedback and lack of staff support. At the time of the field research, this issue was being addressed and in borough a protocol had been issued for the support of staff in the event of a serious episode, including the designation of someone to keep the social workers involved informed about progress, to offer them time off and external counselling support if required, and to help in respect of media attention. The issue was, however, addressed in the context of serious episodes, where there was sufficient cause for concern to instigate a case review. Ongoing staff support for social workers in the routine management of child protection cases was less well developed in both authorities by contrast with the health visiting/school nursing service and with the police who, in the Special Unit in borough at least, had access to external counselling support.

Suggestions for change

Although ACPC members were, in general, relatively satisfied with the task performance of the committees, there were suggestions for improvement. As is shown in Figure 10.13, while the majority saw no need for change in the ACPC remit, three respondents did.

Figure 10.13 **Respondents' perceptions of the need for change in the remit of the ACPC (N = 18)**

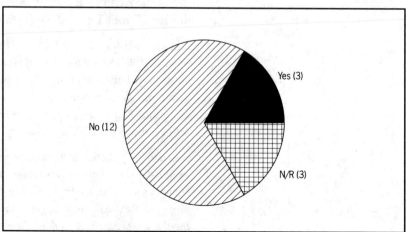

Eleven answered that there were changes which in their opinion would improve the effectiveness of the ACPC as is shown in Figure 10.14.

Figure 10.14 **Respondents' view as to whether there were any changes which would improve the effectiveness of the ACPC (N = 18)**

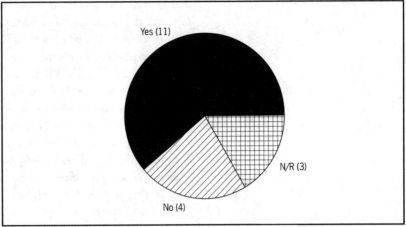

Among the changes suggested were: shorter agendas; earlier circulation of the papers; more contribution from members, particularly medical representatives; representation at a level which carried the power to commit agencies to the decisions reached; clearer delegation of responsibility to members from agencies; direct management of the register and conference system to protect its independence; empowerment of the ACPC to be directive, eg when agencies were not following the guidelines or to enforce joint training with the police; formal arrangements for feedback from representatives to their own agencies; evaluation of the ACPC; and permanent accommodation with tea and coffee facilities! In addition several respondents emphasised the importance of securing a budget for the ACPC and, in borough, the need for a small executive committee to expedite business, which was being established at the time of the study.

   Those most closely involved with the ACPC's, particularly the child protection coordinators, upon whose enthusiasm and commitment so much turned, were the most critical of the structural constraints. One remarked upon the importance of:

> *ACPC's being properly established and funded. I think there's been a lot of double speak from central government about the role of ACPC you know this high status group of definitive professionals who will make decisions and are totally powerless. It doesn't tie up. In the form that it was I could have lived without it. Not because I don't think we need one but because it wasn't achieving anything.*

This respondent put the case for more radical change:

> *I actually think they are necessary. I think it's vital if you really believe that there is a need for interagency influence in child protection to have something that is not within the control of any one agency as an overriding control. The temptation for any one agency to manipulate procedures in line with the constraints that are upon them organisationally would be enormous without it, and I think it is vital. I would actually like to see it totally independent. I'd like to see an independently financed top sliced organisation that has some clout and a proper budget because at the moment they're tokenist. I'd be quite happy to see somebody appointed as an administrator from business or whatever or certainly a chair who was properly financed and had an independent voice, that you could second your staff time into. I actually think they should have an enhanced role. I don't think they're sufficiently independent of the organisations. And I mean we can all ignore them can't we, we do what we want and I don't think that's appropriate because I think it's in an area that there's so many potential conflicts that we ought to actually have to come up with the goods. I don't see how we can protect services internally, well I know we can't. One of the values of centralising the administrative support for child protection services is that we can identify how much it costs and if we can get a commitment and a recognition that that is a child protection service and get it protected by the ACPC we stand a chance of keeping it. Otherwise we might well find ourselves in a totally unmanageable situation, because local government finance is just so dire.*

Markets and prices: 'paying each other for what's done'

One of the characteristics of the British system of child protection is that a degree of coordination has been achieved at local levels, through the establishment of mechanisms for working together. These include cross-referral systems between agencies, the child protection registers, initial and review child protection conferences, procedural guidelines and the ACPCs. The relatively uniform pattern of publicly provided services in health, education, social services and the police across the country had made a degree of rational planning for collaboration possible. This was strongly buttressed and reinforced by central government guidance. It was founded on professional acknowledgement of the need to work together and also what Glennerster terms an element of the old social administration paradigm namely 'the belief in rational planned allocations, in collaboration not competition, in professional responsibility and public service as organisational motives, not financial incentives and competition' (1992, p 18).

In the course of interviews several respondents raised concerns about the challenge to that collaborative tradition posed by the changes in the political economy of social welfare in the late 1980s, and particularly the introduction of internal markets, purchaser/provider splits and locally managed units. In this study, it was particularly apparent in health care and in education but was extending to other arenas, notably policing and to social services departments, although at the time of the study neither city nor borough operated a purchaser/provider split in their child care operations within social services.

Working Together (1991) took account of the changes brought about by the NHS and Community Care Act by stipulating that, in health care, 'the commissioning authority should ensure that child protection is included in the contracts that they agree with providers and that monitoring arrangements are set up.' (Home Office et al, 1991, p 18). At the time of the field research almost all of which preceded publication of the revised *Working Together*, the impact of the health service reforms was beginning to be felt in child protection. It raised important issues of the appropriate representation of purchasers and providers of child health services on the ACPC and of the extnt to which in practice, the requirements of child protection would be recognised by purchasers. In city, as explained in Chapter Six, there was a valued tradition of arranging for the admission to hospital of abused children, pending further investigation and the holding of a child protection conference, but it was reported:

> *The whole attitude has changed because the medical staff have changed and the economic atmosphere in which the National Health Service is now operating has changed, the Children's Hospital are seeking trust status from April of next year. There has been mention at the ACPC on several occasions of social services being required to buy beds, contract for beds at the Children's Hospital and everything is moving in a very different direction. It's been mentioned by the paediatrician certainly. I feel very ambivalent about it. I don't feel at all happy with the basic principles, about the direction in which it's going but I'm anxious to save this kind of approach really because it has worked very well in the interests of children, families, professionals alike.*

In borough, at the time of the study, the hospital had not applied for trust status, although it was expected to do so in the third wave of applications. There, a senior manager in social services said that:

> *Planning children's health, the more general contextual issue, is I think it's quite problematical. We went along to talk to all the consultants about the Children Act. I'm going to meet with the health authority in about four weeks time, five weeks time and I'm tempted to say sort them out but that's pejorative; share with them some of the critical issues. The first*

> *statement that was made in this meeting of consultants was by our community physician and he said 'the first thing you've got to realise is that if you're going to be coming to the new health service and asking for a service you are going to have to pay for it'. And the first thing I said was 'we do not have a budget to pay the national health service for services that we need to have that are free'. I've already mooted the idea of charging people for access to the child protection register and of course it wouldn't work. But I felt so cheesed off with some of the policies that were coming out, everybody else can charge us. I had had three bills for £137 for attendance at a case conference, £120 for a small report, one paragraph for a report to court on a child protection case, this is just not on. So I sent them straight back and said 'the NHS is paying you, not me'. So I mean that has caused some ruffles but I've had no more, so that's fine.*

Concern was also expressed in both city and borough about the impact of GP fundholders on child protection if this meant they would be reluctant to refer children to hospital for diagnosis and any subsequent paediatric or psychiatric follow-up required. In city, the child psychiatry service received referrals in respect of treatment for sexually abused children direct from a variety of sources, including paediatricians, school doctors, social workers, teachers and general practitioners:

> *At the moment it's an informal referral system, the managers are saying that our job is to ensure that the population gets a chance to have this service and as long as they are appropriate referrals, we don't mind and that's what I would like . . . I've had a lot of concern about whether GP fundholders would be paying for the child psychiatric services that their patient's receive. Would that mean that they wouldn't have to pay for it if they ask a social worker to make a referral? It just gets very silly.*

In respect of schools, the concerns were focused upon the impact on child protection of local management of schools and of local financial management. This was particularly serious in respect of in-service training for child protection as the following examples illustrate:

> *I think as schools become more independent and seem to be getting more and more problems with their budgets we're encountering more difficulties because they can't release staff for training so easily. Because if you release a staff member for training with the new arrangements of funding you have to pay for a supply teacher to cover the class out of your budget. For instance one head teacher is saying 'well do I send my staff on the refresher course or do I replace my windows, you know do I board up this window giving them training, or do I let the children have daylight?' So, I mean, they're difficult situations for them to judge. So that at that level there are*

problems and basically the legislation didn't help them with that because there is no top slicing that protects those kind of priorities;

and:

When we went to court for two days there were three members of staff there, myself and two teachers. At that time we didn't manage our own budget and if I remember rightly the head teacher rang up the authority and they said we could have supply cover. Now, at the moment, we're under local financial management. I can't think we'd have paid for that out of our money, who would we have gone to? . . . I don't think we've had to pay for child protection training in the past and there's been cover provided, I'm almost sure of that, but there won't be now.

I've been on one course. Well again, you see this is to do with funding. When it was set up, we had an initial course where all school teachers for child protection went for training but that must have been just at the end of central funding and now, of course, it's all gone.

Another concern was that schools would be less responsive to the needs of children with multiple difficulties, including child protection concerns. As a school nurse said:

We often have children who are on the child protection register and they're excluded from school, so you may not, there may not be any health workers attached, other than GPs. There will be issues about medication, and problem pupils and they have to be placed somewhere else but in the real world that we live in schools have got a budget now and you know they cannot accommodate too many people who are causing problems.

The third concern was that the difficulties of securing a high profile for child protection and ensuring awareness and implementation of the local procedural guidelines, already perceived to be problematic when schools were in local authority control, would be exacerbated. As one respondent said:

Schools generally have treated child protection seriously, the take up of training courses has been high. But organisationally the more schools are removed from the LEA then on issues like child protection it becomes an influencing role rather than an accountability or directing role and I am somwhat unhappy about that.

The practice of trading across market or quasi-market boundaries was also affecting other areas of collaborative activity. As one police officer observed:

Some of the ACPCs are saying 'well we're going to charge you for our secretary coming and then we're going to charge you if you make a referral

> *and we check our records' and we're going to say 'well we're going to charge you if we check a conviction'. Who is going to suffer, it's the kids who are going to suffer isn't it you know we're playing sillies . . . In child protection we've all got our various roles to play and I don't see how we can charge for 'oh we've done the investigation it's three police officers and a detective inspector' and the CPS will say 'well we studied the file and took it to court that's going to cost so much'. I see it that we shouldn't be billing because it's a primary function that we've got, a primary role that we should do is investigate, well it's the protection of life and property, prevention and the investigation of crime, well it fits right into what we should be doing. It's what we're here to do you know, it's right at the core so we shouldn't be charging for our services. As I say I just think it'll come to a sorry state if we do, my views are old fashioned there.*

A clinical nurse specialist raised the issue of charging for contributions on child protection in in-service, basic qualifying and multi-agency training, first giving an account of the nature of the in-service training sessions which had been provided for health visitors and school nurses:

> *The first round of study days raised awareness. I realised there was a fair amount of ignorance about child care law and about what is in the procedure book. In a way that didn't dismay me too much because I feel health visiting and school nursing is positive health and we shouldn't be obsessed, this is just one bit and a very little bit for some. But we started off the first round of study days with a set of about twenty qustions for them to sit and work their way through, a quiz I called it which silenced everybody. It was wonderful, we joked about the power of that and by the end of the day I said we need to have got an answer for all of those, so the rest of the day was geared to answering that with a discussion at the end. The second set that we did last year took on the aftermath of Cleveland because I felt they hadn't time to read the thing that's the size of a telephone directory. That's what I'm in post for and I gave them an outline of the outcome of Cleveland and what had gone wrong based on the official report. We looked at local movement in coping with child sexual abuse . . . And also on that day we asked the court principal social worker (he very kindly came free of charge. I fear this may not happen again). He came to talk to them about appearing in court and what the law was last year and so of course we've just embarked on a series of workshops over the Children Act.*

However, the basis of charging was about to change:

> *We've given quite an input and I've been very happy to do this because the boundaries have allowed me to do it, money-wise it's this market economy*

that's bothering me . . . . It's just that if we've been asked to speak in the School of Nursing and the Polytechnic and I've talked to nursery teachers, other agencies training or made a contribution and I've been very happy to do this and I feel that will be sad if that gets ruled out. I think there may be a change in what we're asked to do. In the future people have to pay each other for what's done, that's putting it very simply but it comes down to that and I think one of the improvements in breaking down misunderstandings is to share that sort of input. I think it will be sad if we lose those opportunities.

A clinical nurse manager also said:

The ACPC has provided significant amounts of training for health visitors for which we must owe them thousands of pounds but the training would not have happened if we had had to pay the real cost in cash resources.

These policy developments were relatively new at the time of the field research. The objectives of the creation of internal markets in health, of local management in schools and of the extension of the principles of pricing in other public services are far removed from a concern with interagency coordination in child protection and their success needs to be appraised against this broader canvas. Nonetheless, their actual and potential impact upon interagency collaboration in child protection which, until then, had been effected without direct cash transactions was perceived as harmful or unhelpful among those interviewed. Glennerster has suggested that:

We are in the midst of a process that is systematically stripping local government of its power to run or even regulate local services. Local housing estates, schools, trust hospitals are floating off into a world of semi-obscure accountability (1992, p 17).

If this is the case, its impact and that of changes in the health service upon child protection services is serious and requires urgent study.

Summary

This chapter reviewed two aspects of the mechanisms for securing interagency coordination in child protection – the local procedural guidelines and ACPC's. The procedural guidelines were found to be available to the majority of the interagency network, although some teachers were unfamiliar with them. In general, respondents reported that they found the procedures helpful (concerning their own roles and those of others) and they did not appear to regard them as unduly constraining. Reasonably high levels of compliance with the procedures were reported, although some lapses were reported in interview and were also apparent from the case files. Introduction of the topic of procedures in interview raised anxiety in some respondents, who were conscious that they constituted a standard against which their performance might be judged and illustrated the heavy burden of responsibility, accountability, anxiety and sometimes fear carried by many of those working in the field of child protection. The procedures proved to have been important in securing an institutionalised and routinised interagency response in child protection.

In respect of ACPCs, there appeared to be a disjunction between a perception of them as pro-active high-powered dynamic bodies and the practical difficulties of making them work effectively at local level. Among the difficulties were issues of the level and status of representatives on the committee and ensuring commitment to the committee's work. As in other aspects of interagency work studied in this research, discussions at the ACPC were reported to be generally characterised by consensus rather than interprofessional disagreement. The members of the ACPC in borough considered that the committee performed better in respect of the development of procedural guidelines and reviewing significant issues from case reviews and inquiry reports than in matters such as reviewing work in the prevention of child abuse. In both research sites, there was a lack of awareness among many front-line staff of the role and function of the ACPC.

The chapter concluded with a brief review of the impact of broader changes in the political economy of welfare, notably reforms in the NHS and the education service introducing internal markets and local management. These were perceived to be damaging to the practice of interagency collaboration in the protection of children. The structural and constitutional problems facing ACPCs suggest that they are not well placed to respond to these developments.

Chapter 11   Interagency work experienced

This chapter brings together and reviews respondents' experiences of and views about interagency work in child protection. It draws on two data sources. The first is the final section of the interview in which respondents were asked questions about working together, exploring, inter alia, the extent to which they accepted or welcomed the mandate to work collaboratively. Among the questions asked was whether or not they agreed with Blyth and Milner's observation that 'given the opportunity, professionals would probably work better alone' (1990, p 195).

The questionnaire issued to those interviewed and to some other members of the Area Child Protection Committee in borough (see Chapter Two for details) provided the second data source. The scaled questions sought views about the ease of cooperation with particular professions, preferences as to collaborative partners, role clarity and role overlap, the extent of agreement about child abuse, the degree of urgency with which various professions approached the task, the importance of the professions involved and perceptions of competence in respect of child protection in the various professions.

The need for and value of cooperation

Almost unanimously, those interviewed accepted the importance of working together and appeared to value it. That was also the finding of Birchall's (1992) study. It should, however, be acknowledged that the respondents in both studies are likely to be those with at least some commitment to interagency work in child protection. In Birchall's study in particular, those who chose to return the postal questionnaire were more likely than not to under-represent those who were actively hostile or deeply uninterested in the topic. In the present study, the names of those approached for interview were drawn from social service case files which indicated that they had some involvement with a case of child abuse, again probably excluding those who were deeply resistant or successfully engaged in avoidance strategies in respect of interagency work in child protection. However, the individuals whose names were drawn from the case files could not reasonably be taken to represent only the very enthusiastic. The great majority nonetheless endorsed the need for and utility of an interagency approach to child protection. This may in part be attributed to a rather uncritical acceptance of the status quo, implied by a response such as 'that's the way we've always done it and you accept that as the way it's being done'. Given the rhetorical appeal of coordination, and the combined weight of public inquiries, central government guidance and local procedures it would be a brave person who argued for a single agency approach and ploughing a lone furrow in child protection. However, the responses from many in varied professions appeared to be more positive than this. For example:

from a police officer:

> *I'm very much for the agencies having to work together, I really am;*

from a school teacher:

> *I think we've got to work together, oh I think that you've got to. Certainly we have because we haven't got the powers to do obviously what we think might need to be done or even the resources;*

and from a social worker;

> *It has to involve health professions, education departments, youth service; it has to involve so many people so how could you possibly do that alone. I fundamentally believe in making sure that what I do is done properly and it's more than paying lip service. I mean it isn't about just covering my neck, though there's an element of that, but it's because I do believe that we're all coming at it from different angles with all our own beliefs and there is no way that we can assess that child's needs just from a social work point of view;*

and from the health visiting/school nursing service:

> *Oh it's got to be. The days when you could live in your own little corner and not talk to anybody else went out an awful long time back. I think one of the lessons that comes from every child death enquiry that there has been is that the bottom line is that communication was awful. I think, therefore, for anybody to sit there and say we can live in our little ivory tower and we are not going to talk to this agency or that agency or the other agency, they're living in cloud cuckoo land because professionally it's indefensible.*

These views appeared to be shared by staff at many levels in the heirarchies in the various agencies although, in arguing for a multidisciplinary approach, respondents emphasised different factors. Some stressed the need for the varied skills to be brought together; for example, health visitors said:

> *I think we've all got different skills and different jobs; I think we can all bring something to it;*

and:

> *I don't think one agency can fill the needs of a family in distress, with young children. You need the medical point of view to make the diagnosis of what's happened, you need the social workers' skill that we don't have, you need the health visitor for the basic knowledge of young babies and children from feeding onwards and I think it's crucial that we all work together.*

Social workers, too, argued in a similar vein:

> *Sometimes interagency work, working with other agencies is difficult but I would prefer to work with other agencies. They've got expertise I haven't got. They know, you know, and there's no getting away from that. If you come from a standpoint, which I do, that child protection is a multiagency responsibility and it's a jigsaw and the social workers can't do it on their own, they need the other agencies to assist them, we haven't got all the skills right. We need other skill areas.*

Some also invoked the concept of an obligation or duty to collaborate viewed as a professional responsibility, as expressed by a head teacher:

> *I've got no doubt in my mind that if I've got something that I'm concerned about then it's my duty to be concerned with other professionals and if I don't do that, I shouldn't have my job.*

Others stressed the dangers of working alone, some pointing out the positives of support in a difficult task, others pointing to the dangers of censure for failing to collaborate, echoing the views of D'Agostino, 1975, and Bourne and Newberger, 1980. As health visitors said:

> *No I don't believe that people prefer to work alone. It's an awful responsibility to take a caseload on and look to every aspect of the needs of it; it's nice to be responsible for day-to-day chores but responsibility, I think, we'd like to share with people;*

> *It's just important to get together and share information and concerns . . . I would like somebody else to be involved really. I suppose it's like a back-up because you're frightened that if anything happens you are on your own. If you feel somebody else is involved the burden's sort of halved a little bit;*

> *It's comforting to know if it's something that you are initially involved with that it isn't just you, you're not carrying this, there's now a whole load of other people sharing this;*

> *I do feel the multiagency approach is crucial and I think it's very dangerous for people to work and think they can deal with it all.*

and two social workers:

> *People have an opportunity to say what they think, whether they take that opportunity or not is entirely up to them, but if they don't they can't crib about it later. And we can't, as the key workers, be criticised for not listening to information, if it's not given to us, can we? So it makes me feel safer because at the end of the day when decisions are made, I can say to myself 'it wasn't just my decision, it was a case conference decision';*

> *I mean there's so much in child protection you're covering your back and all this, whether we like it or not and you can't do that alone, you can't'.*

Thus, among those interviewed, interagency coordination was widely accepted and valued for increasing the skills and knowledge brought to bear on a particular case, and as a support in sharing responsibility in difficult situations. Finally, respondents acknowledged the likelihood of censure if they failed to observe guidance and guidelines advocating a multidisciplinary approach.

The importance and contribution of the varied professions

The professional practice literature from work of Helfer and Kempe (1968) onwards has emphasised the aggregation of the skills and resources from different professions as vital to effective child protection practice, although this has been more often asserted than demonstrated. Mouzakitis and Goldstein suggest typically

> *no one discipline could understand and handle such a complex problem. The wide range of social, psychiatric and psychological problems involved in abuse requires that social workers, physicians, nurses, lawyers, judges, psychiatrists and many other professionals work together if the cycle of abuse and neglect is to be broken. These various disciplines make distinct contributions to a comprehensive diagnosis of the abusive family and the abused and neglected child as well as the planning and treatment of such cases (1985, p 218).*

Pettiford makes a similar point:

> *The multidisciplinary . . . approach to the identification and treatment of child abuse and neglect emerged out of the recognition by practitioners of various professions that child abuse and neglect problems do not lend*

*themselves to simple treatment approaches rendered unilaterally by a
single discipline. The multiple problems exhibited by both the abused/
neglected child and the abusive/neglectful parent(s) require intervention
and treatment that is generally beyond the scope and expertise of any
single discipline (1981, p 1).*

Many others write in a similar vein, for example Steele, 1976, Besharov,
1977, Wallen et al, 1977, Mills et al, 1984, Jones and Pickett, 1987, Bross et al,
1988. It was, therefore, not surprising that a significant strand of the responses
to questions reported above about the value and necessity of a multidisciplinary approach was an acknowledgement of the importance of the aggregation
of different skills and resources. A question on this was posed in the
questionnaire as follows: 'How important do you think the role of each [of
the following professions] is in child abuse cases?' While it may be expected,
and the data confirm this, that there would be a reluctance to designate any
profession as 'not at all important', nonetheless the responses do distinguish
between the various professions as is shown in Table 11.1.

In this, as in all similar questions reported in this chapter, the tables exclude
the responses of the particular profession in question so that, for example, all
social service department staff are excluded from the answers concerning
social work, all community nurses and their managers from answers concerning health visiting and school nursing and so on. This accounts for the
different number of responses recorded for the various professions.

Unsurprisingly the lead profession, social work, was ranked as essential by
92% followed by the investigative agencies, paediatricians 65% and the police
58%, with accident and emergency departments ranked next at 54% (despite
their relatively low profile as a referral source in the case sample in this study)
and health visitors at 53%. Thus the findings in this study reflect the
dominance of investigation in child abuse cases. The comparable rankings in
Birchall's study were, in order, social work, health visiting, paediatricians, the
police and teachers, (Birchall, 1992, p 199).

When the scores for 'essential' are combined with 'important', six
professions emerge with a rating of over 90% – social workers (98%), the
police (96%), teachers (95%), health visitors (95%), paediatricians (94%) and
general practitioners (90%). (In this, as in other tables, the lower figure of 66%
for school nurses is affected by the lack of experience of respondents in
borough where separate school nurses were not employed at the time of the
study). The comparable data from Birchall's study are very similar, with the
following ratings: social workers (94%), teachers (90%), the police (83%),
health visitors (90%), paediatricians (85%) and general practitioners (90%).
These figures suggest that the view publicised following the rediscovery of
child abuse in the 1960s, and reinforced by government guidance and local

Table 11.1. **Respondents' perceptions of the importance of other professions' role in cases of child abuse**

Importance

	Essential %	Important %	Not Very Important %	Not At All Important %	No Opinion %	Varies %	No Response %	No Experience %
Social workers (N = 48)	92	6	0	0	0	0	0	2
Teachers (N = 62)	34	61	2	0	2	2	0	0
EWO (N = 62)	21	61	11	2	0	2	0	3
Health Visitors (N = 66)	53	42	3	0	0	0	0	2
School Nurses (N = 66)	27	39	14	2	2	0	0	17
Police (N = 71)	58	38	1	0	0	0	1	1
GP (N = 76)	33	57	9	0	0	0	0	1
Paediatricians (N = 76)	65	29	1	0	0	0	1	5
Psychologists (N = 76)	12	47	16	3	7	1	0	13
Psychiatrists (N = 76)	12	47	16	5	5	1	0	13
A & E (N = 76)	54	30	5	0	1	0	1	9
Lawyers (N = 77)	22	47	14	2	5	3	1	5

procedures about the necessity of a multidisciplinary approach is widely accepted in the 1990s; a finding confirmed by the interview data.

Role clarity

An important objective of interagency coordination in child protection reflected in the interagency procedures is the institutionalisation of a relatively clear division of labour amongst the key professions. This was explored through the question 'How clear/unclear do you think the role of each is in child abuse cases?' which revealed that there were differences in the perceived clarity of the contribution of the various professions. As Table 11.2 shows, the

Table 11.2. **Respondents' perceptions of the clarity of role of other professions in cases of child abuse**

Role Clarity

	Very Clear %	Fairly Clear %	Rather Unclear %	Very Unclear %	No Opinion %	No Experience %	Varies %	No Response %
Social workers (N = 48)	69	25	4	0	0	2	0	0
Teachers (N = 62)	19	44	32	3	0	2	0	0
EWO (N = 62)	37	34	21	2	0	3	0	3
Health Visitors (N = 66)	33	44	14	2	2	3	2	2
School Nurses (N = 66)	24	29	15	3	5	23	2	0
Police (N = 71)	38	50	9	0	1	1	0	1
GP (N = 76)	16	32	34	11	1	4	1	1
Paediatricians (N = 76)	43	40	7	1	3	5	0	1
Psychologists (N = 76)	13	43	20	2	4	17	0	1
Psychiatrists (N = 76)	12	33	25	4	5	20	0	1
A & E (N = 76)	36	32	8	9	3	13	0	0
Lawyers (N = 77)	30	35	12	4	5	10	4	0

least clear roles were seen to be those, first of general practitioners with 34% of respondents regarding their role as 'rather unclear', followed by teachers with 32% of their role as 'rather unclear'. These patterns broadly confirm findings in Birchall's study where general practitioners and teachers jointly headed the list of those with 'rather unclear' roles, at 32% (Birchall, 1992, p 196). When the 'rather unclear' and 'very unclear' rankings are combined, the relative position of general practitioners and teachers remains the same, but the proportions rise to 45% and 35% of respondents respectively. By contrast, the social workers' role is perceived as very clear by over two thirds of respondents, followed by the paediatricians at 43%, while only about a third of education welfare officers, accident and emergency doctors and health visitors have very clear roles. However, when the 'very clear' and 'fairly clear' rankings are combined, social work is the highest at 94%, with the police and paediatricians nearly as high and the health visitors perceived as having clear roles by about threequarters of respondents.

Role overlap

The literature on interdisciplinary working reflects two views on the issue of role overlap or role blurring. Some argue for role clarity, for example Bourne and Newberger, 1980, Hilgendorf, 1981, Payne, 1982, Watt, 1985, and Corney, 1988. Others, particularly when writing of multidisciplinary teams as opposed to the coordination of looser service networks, favour a degree of role blurring and role overlap (Faller and Zeifert, 1981, Sgroi, 1982, Mousazkitis and Varghese, 1985). The nature of coordination practised in child protection as revealed by this study which principally, although not exclusively, involved information exchange, the synchronisation of separately performed tasks and some degree of shared decision-making rather than joint collaborative activity suggests that a high degree of role overlap is likely to be unhelpful. The data in Table 11.3, which derives from responses to the following question in the questionnaire: 'How often, if at all, do you find each of the following professions overlapping with you in child abuse cases?' suggests that several of the professional roles were clearly delineated.

Several professions, general practitioners (69%), psychologists (68%), psychiatrists (65%), lawyers and teachers (64%) and accident and emergency doctors (59%) were perceived to overlap with the roles of others either 'very rarely' or 'not often'. By contrast, those whose roles were perceived to overlap 'frequently' or 'very often' with others in the network were social workers (55%) and health visitors (45%).

It is likely that this reflects, in part a degree of overlap specifically between social work and health visiting which has been noted elsewhere in the literature (for example, Fox and Dingwall, 1985). Nonetheless, in this study, health visitors and their managers articulated clearly the general health promotion role of health visiting and expressed a keen wish not to be involved inappropriately in offering support to families which could, and they argued should, more appropriately be provided by social workers. This stress on their preventive and advisory functions and their role in identifying and referring problems is also reflected in the professional literature, for example, Mowat (1982), Musanandara (1984) and the Health Visitors Association (undated). However, as the interview data revealed, the thresholds of intervention and the resource position in social services departments were such that, in practice, health visitors were required to work supportively with families, undertaking tasks similar to those of social workers.

However, in general, as the data in response to questions about role clarity and role overlap indicate, a relatively clear division of labour has been established in the field of child protection, at least from the perspective of the professionals involved. Whether this perception would be shared by parents and children involved with a multiplicity of professionals was not explored in this study.

Table 11.3.   **Respondents' perceptions of the degree of overlap between their own role and that of other professions in child abuse cases**

Role Overlap[1]

	Very Rarely %	Not Often %	Frequently %	Very Often %	No Opinion %	No Experience %	No Response %
Social workers (N = 36)	6	19	33	22	6	8	3
Teachers (N = 47)	26	38	23	6	4	0	4
EWO (N = 47)	21	32	26	4	4	6	6
Health Visitors (N = 51)	18	24	31	14	4	8	2
School Nurses (N = 51)	18	24	22	6	8	22	2
Police (N = 56)	20	32	21	7	5	9	5
GP (N = 60)	32	37	12	2	3	10	5
Paediatricians (N = 60)	20	32	17	8	5	13	5
Psychologists (N = 60)	30	38	5	0	3	20	3
Psychiatrists (N = 60)	40	25	3	0	5	23	3
A & E (N = 59)	34	25	10	0	7	20	4
Lawyers (N = 60)	42	22	10	0	5	18	3

[1] This question was excluded from the questionnaire for ACPC members, hence the smaller number of replies.

Improvements over time

A significant feature of the general responses in interview about people's experience of working together was that interagency relationships had improved in recent years. This was a recurrent theme, particularly of relationships between the police and social workers and health visitors and social workers. The following comments from the police are typical:

> *I have been their [social workers] most voluble critic for a long time in my early experience with them, but I'm not nearly as critical now because I've learnt to understand their limitations and I've also learnt to understand their attitudes which are basically different. We address the same problem but from different directions. So long as we understand the direction that they have got to come in and they understand the direction that we've got to come in, we're going to get a better result;*

> *I think what we've got the benefit of, certainly at grass roots level now, is that we've got two and a half years' experience of these units being set up, you know, and a lot of bridges have been built and I see that as a very positive thing that has come out of it. They are, the people on the ground, certainly working together, you know and they know the first names of people. The way they've been training together, I think there is a joint ownership. It's important to understand that we also know more about each other's role and in that police officers now don't believe that social workers have all got open toed sandals and Citroen 2CV's you know, we understand why things happen within their organisation and what their part is. We've all got separate parts to play in the procedure but it is important that we're all going down the same path playing our parts and I think there's that understanding that has come about now. Like the close liaison that there is is good, I'm not saying that we've got it 100% right but certainly the feedback I get from social services and police is very, very positive;*

and from social workers:

> *It feels a little bit better. I think people are actually taking on board some responsibility for child protection. Certainly the police, I feel a lot more comfortable with the police than I have done in the past, yes. Formerly I thought, yes they were interested in the criminal stuff. Yes they still are but they are, I suppose, shifting to some extent that they've got a responsibility in the child protection plan.*

Similar improvements in role relations were reported to have taken place between health visitors and social workers and between senior staff in both professions, for example:

There is a sharing, there's been a lot of work gone on not only at my level but obviously at higher levels, ACPC level and at field level, to actually get this teamwork approach and I think we're winning. I wouldn't say we're there because inevitably it takes a long long time but we are winning. In terms of the working together, obviously there are good days and there are bad days, but overall I'm aware that it works a lot better now than once upon a time it did;

Going back to when I started health visiting in 1973, oh, I mean everybody was very possessive then. I think we've worked very hard over the years, not just us but social services, whose principal social workers have worked very hard at developing the interagency links, and now we've reached a point where it pays off, by and large.

Improvements were not confined to these three professions, however, and respondents reported a general improvement as they had learned to work together over time, which contrasts with the pessimism and problematisation of interagency work identified in the literature, to which reference was made in Chapter One.

Ease of cooperation

The largely positive views expressed in interview concerning improved interagency relations in recent years were confirmed in the responses to the following question in the questionnaire: 'How easy/hard do you generally find it to collaborate with members of each profession?' As is shown in Table 11.4, health visitors were ranked top of the list of those with whom it was 'very easy' to cooperate by 32% of respondents, followed by education welfare officers (31%), social workers (27%) and school nurses (26%).

Over threequarters of respondents ranked collaboration with four professions as 'very easy' or 'fairly easy' with education welfare officers top, followed by health visitors, teachers and social workers. (The rankings in Birchall's study were first health visitors, followed by school nurses, teachers, the police and then social workers, (Birchall, 1992, p 192)). By contrast, only a few respondents found general practitioners and accident and emergency doctors very easy, followed by local authority lawyers, paediatricians and psychologists. Paediatricians headed the rather difficult ranking (25%), followed by accident and emergency doctors (24%), general practitioners and psychiatrists at 22%. The prominence of doctors in the list of those perceived as difficult to collaborate with suggests that the status and power differentials identified as problematic in many previous studies of interprofessional collaboration (and discussed in Chapter Eight) continue to pose problems in the field of child protection.

Table 11.4. **Respondents' perceptions of the ease of collaboration with other professions**

Collaboration

	Very Easy %	Fairly Easy %	Rather Difficult %	Very Difficult %	No Opinion %	Varies %	N/R %	No Experience %
Social workers (N = 48)	27	50	13	2	0	2	2	4
Teachers (N = 62)	13	66	11	0	0	2	3	5
EWO (N = 62)	31	56	5	0	0	3	0	5
Health Visitors (N = 66)	32	50	6	0	2	0	3	8
School Nurses (N = 66)	26	47	0	3	0	0	0	24
Police (N = 71)	13	47	18	0	3	4	3	13
GP (N = 76)	8	40	22	15	1	1	1	12
Paediatricians (N = 76)	11	42	25	0	3	3	0	17
Psychologists (N = 76)	15	46	12	1	3	1	1	21
Psychiatrists (N = 76)	13	26	22	1	5	0	3	29
A & E (N = 76)	8	28	24	8	4	1	3	25
Lawyers (N = 77)	9	44	14	1	4	1	1	25

People and places

The interrelated aspects of locality, including the size, complexity and stability of the interagency network, and the impact of particular personalities were explored in the study.

Professional stability and mobility in the interagency network

An important dimension of working together is the degree of mobility in the professional population. This topic was explored in the questionnaire with reference to three issues – respondents' length of experience of working in the locality, in their profession and in their current rank. The results, presented in Table 11.5 for the sample as a whole, shows that 30 (38%) of the sample had worked in the locality for over 10 years and a further 33 (41%) for between three and nine.

Table 11.5. **Length of experience in locality, profession and rank: total questionnaire sample**

	Education	Social Work	Nursing	Doctors	Police	Other	Total
Years in locality							
10 years and over	13	12	1	3	1	0	30
3–9 years	4	11	10	3	4	1	33
up to 3 years	1	7	3	0	4	2	17
	18	30	14	6	9	3	80
Years in profession							
10 years and over	16	19	8	5	9	2	59
3–9 years	1	9	4	1	0	1	16
up to 3 years	0	2	2	0	0	0	4
No response	1	0	0	0	0	0	1
	18	30	14	6	9	3	80
Years in rank							
10 years and over	7	6	1	2	4	1	21
3–9 years	7	14	9	3	1	2	36
up to 3 years	4	10	4	1	4	0	23
	18	30	14	6	9	3	80

Only 17 (21%) had worked in the locality for less than three years. This, together with Birchall's (1992) study, is an important corrective to the picture of very high staff mobility experienced, for example, in some London boroughs. The figures for city and borough are presented separately in Tables 11.6 and 11.7. Somewhat surprisingly, these show that the length of work experience in the locality was higher in city than in borough.

The length of service in the profession also shows only four people (two social workers and two health visitors in borough) with less than three years in post. These findings confound popular images of very inexperienced workers, particularly social workers, at the front line. By contrast, it appeared that staff engaged in child protection were in post and remaining in the locality long enough to build the interprofessional relationships required for collaborative work, as is discussed below.

Table 11.6. **Length of experience in locality, profession and rank: city**

	Education	Social Work	Nursing	Doctors	Police	Other	Total
Years in locality							
10 years and over	5	7	0	1	1	0	14
3–9 years	2	3	5	2	3	0	15
up to 3 years	0	1	2	0	1	1	5
	7	11	7	3	5	1	34
Years in profession							
10 years and over	6	7	3	2	5	0	23
3–9 years	1	4	4	1	0	1	11
up to 3 years	0	0	0	0	0	0	0
	7	11	7	3	5	1	34
Years in rank							
10 years and over	4	2	0	0	3	0	9
3–9 years	0	3	6	2	1	1	13
up to 3 years	3	6	1	1	1	0	12
	7	11	7	3	5	1	34

Table 11.7. **Length of experience in locality, profession and rank: borough**

	Education	Social Work	Nursing	Doctors	Police	Other	Total
Years in locality							
10 years and over	8	5	1	2	0	0	15
3–9 years	2	8	5	1	1	1	18
up to 3 years	1	6	1	0	3	1	12
	11	19	7	3	4	2	46
Years in profession							
10 years and over	10	12	5	3	4	2	36
3–9 years	0	5	0	0	0	0	5
up to 3 years	0	2	2	0	0	0	4
No response	1	0	0	0	0	0	1
	11	19	7	3	4	2	46
Years in rank							
10 years and over	3	4	1	2	1	1	12
3–9 years	7	11	3	1	0	1	23
up to 3 years	1	4	3	0	3	0	11
	11	19	7	3	4	2	46

Locality

Geographical proximity and coterminous boundaries have frequently been highlighted as important in the literature concerning interagency collaboration (Norton and Rogers, 1981, Skinner et al, 1983, Armitage, 1983, Williams, 1986, Westrin, 1987, Challis et al, 1988, Broussine et al, 1988). They proved important factors in this study. Both the research sites were selected so their social services and education boundaries were co-terminous with the health authorities and it was clear that, at senior officer levels, relationships were generally close. This was particularly marked in the borough, where the scale was smaller than in city. The following comments illustrate the point. The first from a senior manager in social services:

> *We have a tremendous capacity for collaboration here which is a great strength:*

the second from a senior officer in the education department:

> *It's a small authority; we have coterminous boundaries and it works reasonably well. Being coterminous has great advantages in that many difficulties that would arise in a larger area are minimised, people know one another . . . people have an identity, being a small authority, and that in itself, aids understanding because you can slot people in when you know what their roles are. It's probably because of that that things work reasonably well;*

and the third from a police surgeon:

> *We all know each other; we're on first name terms.*

The position was well summarised in the following quotation:

> *In terms of small is beautiful – I mean it doesn't actually feel like it sometimes – but the potential for getting well coordinated services in an area where your health authority, police division, probation division, etc. are coterminous, it has to give you a head start. Because we're not just small organisationally, it's also in terms of getting to know each other sufficiently well to develop good working relationships. We've had a fair turnover of staff in social services, I suppose the police have suffered that as well, but other agencies tend to have a fairly stable staff group, and parts of our areas have very stable staff groups.*

At field level too, especially in parts of borough away from the main town, there were small, relatively stable, professional communities which appeared to have a beneficial impact on the interagency network. For example,

> *This is an area where everybody knows everybody. I know most of the professionals, this is a small town – it's easier to build up relationships. When you've got a population of, what, 12,000 here, your agencies are just across the road so you do build up this working relationship, so working together is much easier in that way.*

Some respondents were, however, aware of the potential drawbacks of a close, settled and small interagency network. The following quotations illustrate the concerns:

> *One of the things about [borough] is that people are very comfortable with each other. I think we work well together. I've sometimes questioned whether we work well from the child's point of view; I think sometimes we're quite good at getting on but we're not so good at teasing out areas that might cause conflict because of the implications of that;*

> *That's the danger as well, because you can actually get quite cosy and the danger of it being so small is that you're not taking it on people's professional skills but on their personality and stuff like that, and that's the danger. Such and such a body's all right as a mate or a friend but they're useless at their job, but because they're nice and friendly then you don't actually tackle the work issues; that's the danger;*

> *I'd want to stress that there is room for improvement and I think the danger in [borough] is because people know each other very well that we actually sit back and say we've got it right and we haven't: there is room for improvement. What I don't want to give is the impression that [borough] has got it right, and that is around, 'We're alright, we've got it sussed! Right. We work together really well' and we don't, there are differences, but what I keep hold of is there is the dialogue and people are prepared to listen, not everybody but yes, there are people around who will listen.*

It appeared to be the case that structural arrangements, goodwill and, especially in borough, the size of the network facilitated interagency collaboration.

Nonetheless, this study confirmed the conclusion reached by others that while structural conditions may afford a more (or a less) conducive environment, they could not, in themselves, guarantee close interagency relationships (Wistow and Fuller, 1986, Pugh-Thomas, 1987, Challis et al, 1988). Physical proximity was not sufficient. Nor, of itself, was a small locality with a stable professional community. This was well illustrated in one of the small towns in borough. Although superficially similar to others where interagency relations were widely reported to be close in terms of the configuration of the interagency network, there were perceived to be important differences. As one health visitor said:

I found it much more productive there [in another town in borough], the work with the social workers. They had a very positive view of health visitors and the health authority and what that health authority could provide and they were very pally basically and they would drop in and we would drop in on them and, in my naivety, I thought that this is how it was everywhere. I now realise that was largely down to the attitude of the senior social worker who regularly dropped in just to say 'Hi', to sit down and have a butty and a cup of tea and then go on his way, who was very keen to see the student health visitors. He was very keen to bring the student social workers to see us. None of that happens here and I find that very hard to come to terms with. I mean I came running over here with a big smile on my face expecting it all to be the same and it isn't. It comes down to personalities. If the person at the top and if the person leading the team is supportive and positive and, you know, enthusiastic about other agencies, I think then the other social workers pick it up. There certainly is a difference here, other than cases that we're working on, we have very little contact, no contact with them.

The emphasis in the above quotation on personalities is critical for understanding interagency work. There were several examples in this study of the significance and impact of particular individuals playing key roles as instigators or sustainers of coordination (described in the literature as reticulists), reinforcing the finding of other studies (Norton and Rogers, 1981, Shane, 1982, McKeganey and Hunter, 1986, Riordan et al, 1988, Gamache et al, 1988, Wistow, 1989). Notable among the reticulists were the child protection coordinators. In city, too, changes in the senior management team within the social services department were reported at the time of the study to be having a beneficial impact upon the priority accorded to child protection. In borough, many commented on the importance and impact of the person in charge of the special police unit which had seen a succession of changes prior to the study. The interest and expertise of individual consultant paediatricians was also reported to be critical. In city, a clinical nurse manager commented on the importance of staff in key positions, contrasting two social services offices:

I think it's personalities; I would say it stems from the principal social worker, as to the way they lead the team. It's the same with health visiting and school nursing, it comes down to us as clinical nurse managers and the emphasis that we put in and the sharing that that leads to. If I sit here and am negative about it, I mean if I sit here and say 'oh these social workers, don't tell me they want yet another report out of us' and I start saying that to my staff, my staff are going to turn round and think 'oh well if she feels like that, you know, why should we bother?'

In borough a pre-school liaison teacher gave an example of the effect of a change in personnel in the social services department:

> *Prior to the new senior coming, it was abysmal and you just felt you were getting nowhere, nothing was being taken up and you were getting no liaison whatsoever and, in fact, downright resistance on occasions. So you see we're now into a different ball game because we're now into a whole era of cooperation of working together and actually being invited to meetings and involvement being recognised and none of that happened before. [X] has brought a whole breath of fresh air to social services, with her coming the whole thing has changed completely and it's very open and very much everybody wanting to work together, to be seen as working together rather than little power struggles going on and it sounds silly when we were all working with the same families to the same end when all's said and done.*

The senior in question remarked:

> *If somebody was discussing a case with me I would think it was a matter of good professional practice to involve the other agencies, . . . because you're obviously missing out on vast quantities of information if you're not getting that feedback. So if there was any effect because of my being here it would be because when I came I sat down and talked about what was good professional practice and encouraged people to go out and do it.*

It was in this team that one of the few deliberate attempts to foster interagency links was reported to have occurred, at the suggestion of a team member. She explained it as follows:

> *I organised – just a little thing, isn't it – but we were talking about six or seven months ago about how we work with all these different people and we don't know them so we actually had a dinner upstairs, we actually sent out invitations to all these diffent agencies and said come along and have lunch please and they came. It was marvellous, we ran out of food and everything else. We asked people from schools, we asked health visitors, we asked occupational therapy officers and some home care officers . . .*

A similar strategy had been tried in city.

> *My team particularly were very keen on establishing a base on the patch and we did establish a base where the team meetings are held, where we try to hold case conferences and we made a lot of effort in the area to actually get to know our contemporaries on that level of the agency because that's something that worries me. It's all very well having the procedures on multiagency work but it's really with the contemporaries that it matters and so we've done a lot of work with that and it seems to be easier to keep*

*that link up. We did it by inviting people on coffee mornings which we
kind of had, a kind of social really, come and meet us; we do it in a variety
of ways.*

This respondent went on to outline the importance of attention to interpersonal relations in the process of interagency collaboration. She suggested:

*It's important to me as well who you actually invite to meetings, who you
make a point of asking to come and how you actually handle those people
when they come to any kind of meeting, about what you ask them and
how you value what they've said to you because it isn't just about bringing
people to the meetings, is it? It's about how you actually enable them to
talk and how you value what they say and that's quite worrying because it
seems to me, like a lot of people at case conferences and meetings we have,
many people aren't empowered to speak so getting to know other agencies
has been about that too.*

Two NSPCC workers in borough also emphasised this aspect. One said:

*We see that every single person is equally important and they have
something to offer and it's harnessing that and sharing that and pooling
ideas and let's look at this together, the 'we' bit rather than the 'you' bit
and the more I think that we get that across in the work that we do and
also on an informal level, the better. So I think yes we spend just a lot of
time as well when we're in the conferences saying positives, 'that was really
good, that was really helpful' or if it's somebody we don't know saying
'where are you based, you know, what do you do' because then, if I get a
referral at that school, I can phone and say I haven't met your head teacher
but I have met such and such at a case conference and it just increases – it
puts faces to names – and just increases and improves working
relationships.*

It is perhaps significant that the respondents who spontaneously raised in interview these issues of the *process* of working together were all women. This appears to offer some confirmation for the observations about the greater importance attached to these interpersonal processes by women managers in social services departments when compared with their male counterparts (Eley, 1989).

Nonetheless, these conscious attempts to foster interagency collaboration were relatively rare, which appears to confirm Wise's observation that:

*It is ironic indeed to realise that a football team spends 40 hours a week
practising teamwork for the two hours on Sunday afternoons when their
teamwork really counts. Teams in organisations seldom spend two hours*

> *per year practising when their ability to function as a team counts 40 hours*
> *per week* (Wise, 1974, quoted in Brill, 1976, p 45).

While the analogy of the team is not ideal, when considering the more disparate interagency network which characterises much child protection work, nonetheless the general point is of relevance. The development of interagency collaboration appears to require informal time to establish links and get to know people (see, for example, Gustaffson et al, 1979, Topper and Aldridge, 1981, Sgroi, 1984, Krugman, 1984) but this requires resources of time and space for its achievement.

The study revealed, unsurprisingly, that knowing the other professionals concerned clearly had an impact upon the ease and quality of collaboration. Many respondents answered questions about working with others principally in terms of personal relationships rather than role, for example:

> *It depends on who the other professionals are;*

and:

> *I think it's an interpersonal issue. There's particular people that I would be*
> *very pleased to go and do some work with, like the police surgeon that I*
> *would feel quite comfortable to take kids to time and again. There's some*
> *social workers and one or two police officers that I would feel uncomfortable*
> *with but the other thing is unless you actually take time to get to know*
> *people it's dead easy to dismiss them.*

Most thought that it was not necessary to know people but it helped greatly, as the following quotations illustrate:

> *You don't need to know people in order to work with them but sometimes*
> *it helps. If they know their job and you know your job I think you should*
> *be able to just get together and get on with the job in hand. It shouldn't*
> *matter whether you know them. I've been here so long now I've got used to*
> *working with different people and knowledge like that is useful, it speeds*
> *up your work knowing who to pick up the phone to, who to speak to,*
> *knowing who you're speaking to but I'm not sure you need to know*
> *them;*
> *I enjoy working with other agencies. I found it a lot easier once I've got to*
> *know the person I'm working with, it's awful talking to somebody on the*
> *phone you don't know, in a building you don't know and not appreciating*
> *the job but I think once you get more experience and get to know people it's*
> *easier and they know how you work and you know how they work.*

This confirms Webb's (1991) observation that practitioners consistently highlight interpersonal relations when discussing coordination and collaboration.

Preferred collaborators

The above quotations from the interviews highlight the importance of personalities and of interpersonal relationships in interagency work. Data from the questionnaire also confirm the importance of personal knowledge of collaborative partners. Table 11.8 shows answers to the question: 'In general, to what extent do you prefer to work with each of the following agencies/professions in child abuse?'

The answers again display a positive view of others in the network, with very few respondents scoring the 'prefer not to' and fewer still the 'much prefer not to' columns in respect of other professions. The professions heading the list of preferred collaborative partners are social workers and health visitors, 81% and 80% respectively when the 'much prefer to' and 'prefer to' columns are combined, followed by teachers and education welfare officers. The high ranking of social workers and health visitors may reflect the fact that they are at the heart of child protection activities and that familiarity and frequent contact reinforces a preference for working with them amongst network members.

The relatively high rankings of teachers and education welfare officers reflect their high ranking also in the list of those with whom it was perceived as easy to collaborate (Table 11.4), which suggests that despite some lack of clarity in the roles of teachers (Table 11.2), interpersonal relations were not perceived as difficult. Those who rank lowest in the list of preferred collaborators (psychologists at 49% and psychiatrists and lawyers at 40%) are those less frequently involved, as the numbers in the 'no experience' column demonstrate. The low ranking for lawyers as preferred partners and their place at the top of the list (24%) when the 'much prefer not to' and 'prefer not to' columns are combined, probably reflects the fact that for many in the network extensive contact with them arises only rarely when court proceedings are in train. This was reported in the interviews, especially by health visitors, school nurses and teachers, to be particularly anxiety-provoking. The police also figure prominently, (at 21%) along with general practitioners (at 22%) in the list of those with whom respondents preferred not to collaborate. Since the police are a key profession at the investigation stage, this suggests that role tensions still remain for some respondents.

Trust and respect

Having personal knowledge of potential collaborators in the network not only usually eased interpersonal exchanges. It also afforded the opportunity

Table 11.8. **Respondents' preferences for working with other professions in child protection**

| | Preference[1] | | | | | | | |
	Much Prefer To %	Prefer To %	Prefer Not To %	Much Prefer Not To %	No Opinion %	Varies %	No Experience %	No Response %
Social workers (N = 36)	31	50	6	0	6	3	6	0
Teachers (N = 46)	4	74	13	0	4	2	0	2
EWO (N = 46)	20	57	11	0	7	2	4	0
Health Visitors (N = 50)	18	62	6	0	2	0	10	2
School Nurses (N = 50)	14	50	8	0	8	0	20	0
Police (N = 54)	9	50	17	4	7	4	9	0
GP (N = 59)	7	49	19	3	7	2	12	2
Paediatricians (N = 59)	20	46	10	0	10	2	12	0
Psychologists (N = 59)	3	46	14	2	12	2	22	0
Psychiatrists (N = 59)	3	37	10	3	12	3	29	2
A & E (N = 59)	12	44	15	0	8	2	19	0
Lawyers (N = 59)	3	37	22	2	8	3	24	0

[1] This question was excluded from the questionnaire for ACPC members, hence the smaller number of replies.

for the build up of trust and respect for the competence of others, identified in the literature as an important prerequisite for cooperative activity, see, for example, Ducanis and Golin, 1979, Mayhall and Norgard, 1983, McGloin and Turnbull, 1986 and Webb, 1991. Of course, personal knowledge and contact also had the potential to do the opposite. Many respondents commented on the judgements, based on their previous experience, they made about individuals when working together, as illustrated in the following quotations:

from one social service manager:

> *There are some agencies and some professionals that we work with where we know them and can trust them and there are other people whose predicted response is likely to be of less good quality;*

from another:

> *It depends on who you're dealing with. You get to know from the ground the people who you can take their word that if they're worried then there really is something to be worried about;*

from a paediatrician:

> *You get to respect social workers when you work alongside them and see they don't all want to remove children;*

and, finally, from a police officer, discussing the deregistration of cases:

> *I think you base your judgements, well I do certainly, on the social worker who's sent me the letter. You know, if they are saying they should be off [the register] and she knows her business – that's good enough for me. I'd agree with it but when you see it with the less experienced eye you go into it a bit more thoroughly. Because we know the social workers, sort of intimately (not quite the right word!) and you say she really knows what she's doing, if she's saying that, she knows the family better than me, that's good enough for me and so that is the way that we do business. That is trust and that is personal relationships and understanding.*

Such relationships were disrupted when individual people changed jobs. Some respondents referred to the need to build up their personal credibility and trust on moving jobs, a point also noted by Dingwall et al (1983). One police officer spoke of his experience in a liaison role as follows:

> *'When I came into the department, I had a fortnight with my predecessor and, in that fortnight, I went to two or three case conferences where my face became known and probably for six months after that I was getting phonecalls asking for my predecessor and I'd say 'sorry he has left, I'm [X] and I'll be coming to the case conference' and I was treated with, I'd like to think it was respect, but probably I was treated as an outsider until they knew me and the way that I worked. And over the four years after that initial six months I've built up a close relationship with all the agencies. Now if I should come to leave this post . . . In my opinion to make unnecessary moves is not in the best interests of this part of the business because it is an essential part of our job to have these relationships and,*

> *without them, you've got a real problem. Now it is possible that within the next six months I'll be moved and someone then is going to have a long job to make the contacts, to establish the relationships, to be trusted and, for that period of time, there's got to be . . . but there's nothing you can do to legislate against that. The only thing we can do is introduce our successors, if you like, into the system and get their face known and with the best will in the world my predecessor took me round the various divisions of social services and introduced me to, if not all the social workers, certainly to the team leaders and said 'look this is [X], he's taking over from me,' but then you've still got to get into the system and be accepted by other people.*

A clinical nurse manager who reported considerable success in establishing good working relationships with her counterparts in social services in the adjacent building commented:

> *I think you can safely say we've got those relationshps well-established. However with decentralisation in [borough] they're all going to move so we're back to square one of setting relationships, that's problematic.*

Clearly some job mobility is necessary, desirable and inevitable. Nonetheless this study suggested that the impact on interprofessional relations of both repeated structural reorganisations in health, welfare and other services and of staffing policies which require frequent moves (for example into and out of Special Units in the police service) may have been underestimated.

Role performance

The responses in interview concerning issues of trust and respect in interprofessional work reported above indicate that judgements about the competence of others in the network were frequently made on the basis of personal contact with individuals rather than ascribed to the role of others. This experience was generalised by respondents in answer to the following question in the questionnaire: 'How well do you think each agency/ profession carries out its role in child abuse cases?'

As is shown in Table 11.9, while there was a marked tendency to avoid the answer 'very poorly' nonetheless the answers do appear to reflect discriminating choices. Among those ranked 'very well' are, in order, paediatricians, social workers, health visitors, then school nurses and the police. Comparable findings in Brichall's study identified the same five professions, but they were ranked in the order health visitors, paediatricians, social workers, the police and school nurses, (Birchall, 1992, p 203). As Table 11.9 shows psychologists and psychiatrists ranked lowest at 4% (albeit with a quarter of respondents

Table 11.9. **Respondents' perceptions of how well other professions carry out their role in child abuse cases**

	Very Well %	**Fairly Well** %	**Rather Poorly** %	**Very Poorly** %	**No Opinion** %	**No Experience** %	**Varies** %	**No Response** %
					Agreement			
Social workers (N = 48)	23	67	2	0	2	4	2	0
Teachers (N = 61)	7	48	32	2	5	2	2	2
EWO (N = 61)	15	55	16	0	3	7	2	2
Health Visitors (N = 65)	21	55	6	0	2	11	5	0
School Nurses (N = 65)	17	41	9	0	9	21	0	2
Police (N = 70)	17	56	11	0	3	9	3	0
GP (N = 75)	8	22	37	11	1	15	4	1
Paediatricians (N = 75)	24	45	13	0	1	12	3	1
Psychologists (N = 75)	4	43	11	3	11	24	1	3
Psychiatrists (N = 75)	4	29	16	5	13	26	1	4
A & E (N = 75)	13	32	18	8	5	17	4	1
Lawyers (N = 76)	9	39	12	1	10	21	4	3

reporting 'no experience') and then teachers at 7% and general practitioners at 8% but with smaller numbers in the 'no experience' category. When the 'very well' and 'fairly well' categories are combined, social workers are ranked top with 90% of respondents placing them in this category, followed by the health visitors, the police and paediatricians so ranked by about threequarters of the respondents.

This finding of generally favourable perceptions of the role performance of the key professions of social work, health visiting, the police and paediatricians confirms much of the interview data. The positive views of social work expressed by other professionals in the network may be surprising in view of the bad press they have repeatedly received from child abuse inquiries. However, as indicated in earlier chapters, the interview data reveals their interprofessional partners in child protection as generally understanding of the difficulties of the role and of the resource position faced by social services departments and, by and large, supportive in their views.

By contrast to the favourable views of the core professions, general practitioners and teachers headed the rankings of those who were considered to perform 'rather poorly' at 37% and 32% respectively. The same rankings are reported in Birchall's study (1992, p 203). When the 'rather poorly' and 'very poorly' columns are combined, general practitioners head the list at 48% followed by teachers at 34% and accident and emergency doctors at 26%. It is possible that this may reflect unrealistic expectations by other professionals of practitioners whose individual experience of child abuse may be limited, whose primary professional focus and preoccupation lie elsewhere and only a small minority of whose pupils or patients are expected to comprise abused children. This would, however, also be the case for health visitors and school nurses with their concerns for universal populations and for accident and emergency department doctors and others on the list, all of whom receive higher ranking by their fellow professionals, which suggests that dissatisfactions with the role performance of general practitioners and of teachers in child protection reflects real dissatisfaction, based on experience.

Consensus in the interprofessional network

A degree of consensus is acknowledged in the literature as important to cooperative activity (Levine and White, 1961, Reid, 1964, Warren, 1967, Van de Ven, 1976, Norton and Rogers, 1981, Armitage, 1983, Williams, 1986, McKeganey and Hunter, 1986, Zeifert and Faller, 1981 and Skaff, 1988). As was indicated in Chapters Three and Eight, there was relatively little dissent about the appropriateness of referrals, about decisions about registration or about the broad shape of child protection plans. The responses in the questionnaire shown in Table 11.10 broadly confirm that the professionals involved consider that their concerns are similar to others in the network.

The data split broadly into three groups: first, those closely involved in child protection (social workers, health visitors, paediatricians) where the combined ranking of views as 'very' or 'fairly similar' totalled 90%, 82% and 74% respectively; secondly, a group of professionals (psychologists, psychiatrist, accident and emergency doctors and lawyers), who were less often involved and whose views were considered less similar at 49%, 38%, 50% and 35% respectively but where about a fifth of respondents reported no experience of having worked with each profession. Thirdly, less than half (49%) of the respondents reported that they shared very or fairly similar concerns with the police (49%) and with general practitioners (44%), yet most respondents reported experience of working with these groups. The police received the highest ranking in the 'not very similar' category at 31%. This suggests that despite the emphasis on the importance of the welfare of the child in recent circulars of guidance on the police role in child protection (discussed in Chapter Five), a significant proportion of members of the interagency network nonetheless, and unsurprisingly, considered the police focus to be distinctively different from their own. Among the core professions, with the exception of the police however, there appears to be a considerable degree of consensus, sufficient to sustain a degree of collaborative activity in child protection.

Table 11.10. **Respondents' perceptions of the extent to which other professions share similar concerns in handling cases of child abuse**

	Agreement							
	Very Similar %	Fairly Similar %	Not Very Similar %	Very Dissimilar %	No Opinion %	No Experience %	Varies %	No Response %
Social workers (N = 48)	38	52	4	0	2	4	0	0
Teachers (N = 61)	11	56	26	2	2	0	2	0
EWO (N = 61)	27	50	11	2	2	3	2	2
Health Visitors (N = 65)	35	47	2	2	0	11	2	2
School Nurses (N = 65)	21	39	12	2	6	18	0	2
Police (N = 70)	14	35	31	7	4	4	3	3
GP (N = 75)	16	28	28	8	4	11	1	4
Paediatricians (N = 75)	32	42	12	0	2	11	1	0
Psychologists (N = 75)	8	41	15	4	9	21	0	1
Psychiatrists (N = 75)	9	29	24	5	7	24	0	1
A & E (N = 75)	16	34	17	8	5	18	1	0
Lawyers (N = 76)	5	30	30	7	5	22	0	0

Urgency

Besides the extent of agreement about the nature of the problem and of appropriate responses, another reported difficulty in interagency work is the different degree of urgency accorded to the problem by different professions. The problems resulting from discrepant timescales have been noted by Urzi, 1977, Hallett and Stevenson, 1980, Ruber, 1988, and Blagg and Stubbs, 1988. Given the recommended timescales in matters such as medical examinations and holding initial child protection conferences and the speed with which they occurred in this study, significant interprofessional differ-

Table 11.11. **Respondents' perceptions of the degree of urgency with which other professions approach their work in child abuse**

	Urgency							
	Much more urgency %	Some more urgency %	Less urgency %	Much less urgency %	No Opinion %	No Experience %	Varies %	No Response %
Social workers (N = 48)	17	36	27	4	2	4	4	6
Teachers (N = 61)	5	11	52	11	5	2	5	8
EWO (N = 61)	3	21	42	7	11	3	5	7
Health Visitors (N = 65)	5	27	24	5	8	11	3	17
School Nurses (N = 65)	0	20	27	6	12	23	3	8
Police (N = 70)	7	27	30	4	9	7	3	13
GP (N = 75)	1	8	37	22	8	9	4	9
Paediatricians (N = 75)	3	30	28	0	12	8	4	15
Psychologists (N = 75)	0	5	30	16	24	16	1	7
Psychiatrists (N = 75)	0	5	25	16	22	22	1	7
A & E (N = 75)	5	25	20	11	12	9	3	15
Lawyers (N = 76)	1	7	33	14	17	17	3	8

ences in these or in referral would be likely to lead to difficulty. The questionnaire, therefore, included the following question:

In general, do you think each of the followng agencies/professions' approaches its work in child abuse with more or less urgency than your own agency/profession?

The data shown in Table 11.11 show that there are few outliers in the 'much more urgency' or 'much less urgency' responses, which suggests that the timescales among the network are reasonably well synchronised. When the 'much more urgency' and 'some more urgency' rankings are combined and compared with the combined rankings of 'less urgency' and 'much less urgency', social workers remain ahead of the 'more urgency' rankings (53%), followed by the police (34%) and paediatricians (33%). Thus the core investigative professions are perceived to approach the task with urgency, a finding generally confirmed by the cases in the case sample. Teachers at 63% lead the 'less urgent' ranking followed by general practitioners at 59%. If the urgency with which different professions are perceived to approach their involvement in child protection is also a reflection of the importance they attach to it, this may reflect some distancing of general practitioners and teachers from a central concern with the task, a finding indicated elsewhere in the data.

Summary

This review of the aspects of working together revealed that there was widespread acceptance of the need for and value of interprofessional collaboration in child protection. Its importance in the aggregation of different skills and resources, and in offering support in a difficult task was stressed. Many respondents were also aware of the likelihood of censure if they challenged the orthodoxy. Interagency coordination in child protection was reported to have improved significantly in recent years. The data concerning role clarity and role overlap confirm that a relatively clear division of labour has been established in child protection, at least as perceived by the professionals. There was a high degree of reported consensus (as revealed also in the case sample and discussed in previous chapters) and reasonably congruent time-scales.

The research sites were characterised by relatively stable staffing patterns. These, together with coterminous boundaries, provided a conducive base for the establishment of interagency coordination. Nonetheless, the significance of interpersonal relationships in collaborate activity was illustrated together with the importance of reticulists in sustaining coordination.

Throughout the chapter the data revealed concerns about the role of general practitioners and, to a lesser extent, of teachers in child protection – an issue which is explored in the final chapter.

Chapter 12

Conclusions

In this chapter, the conclusions of the study are presented. The study explored interagency coordination in child protection using a case study approach. The main data sources were the social services case records of a sample of 48 registered child abuse cases; in-depth interviews with varied professionals involved with a sub-sample of those cases; questionnaires issued to those interviewed and a small number of key others; and policy and procedural documents available in the research sites and at central government level. The study sought to relate the findings to Birchall's exploration of the topic which used a different research design, namely a postal questionnaire survey to which 339 professionals from six key groups responded (Birchall, 1992). It also sought to relate the findings to the literature on interagency coordination and child protection, reviewed in Hallett and Birchall (1992).

The cases in the case sample

The nature of the cases in the sample was outlined in Chapter Two. They were 48 cases of primary school aged children registered mainly in 1989 and 1990 for physical or sexual abuse or, in a few cases, grave concern thereof. In over half of the cases the initial referral was from a family member (usually the mother) or the child him/herself. The children came disproportionately from families in which the birth mother lived with a father substitute, and in which there were four or more children. 27 of the 48 were girls, and 21 were boys. Six were from minority ethnic groups.

In the 21 cases of sexual abuse, penetrative sexual contact had occurred in eight, non-penetrative sexual contact in five. In the 27 physical abuse cases, 23 had injuries classified as moderate in Creighton's (1992) terms, that is soft tissue injuries of a superficial nature. The physical injuries were not of a life threatening nature and in many cases they represented only one of several problems identified in the families concerned. While it may be argued that no child should be subject to physical violence, it is possible that the physical abuse suffered was not the most pressing problem in the lives of the primary school aged children concerned, many of whom faced lives of deprivation, hardship, turmoil and disruption in an unequal society and in the face of the inadequacies of a wide range of social policies.

In 41 of the 48 cases, there was one alleged abuser per case. In 34 of the 48 cases the alleged abuser(s) were men and in 11 women, with male and female abusers involved in a further two cases. All alleged abusers in the cases of sexual abuse were men, the majority being related to the children concerned. The majority of the families had had prior contact with the social services department, twenty-six of them having been the subject of prior child protection referrals.

The widespread practice of routinised coordination

The study revealed that widespread routinised interagency coordination was central to child protection practice. While there were occasional reported lapses and certainly some frictions and difficulties in the process, the automatic mode of operation at referral, and if cases progressed further into the system, at the investigation and initial child protection conference stage was a multidisciplinary one. This was reflected in a routinised and relatively clear division of labour among the key agencies, operating largely sequentially, particularly in the early phases of the construction of a case of child abuse.

The rise and fall of interagency collaboration through a 'case career'

Government guidance in *Working Together* (1991) suggests that an individual case career through the child protection system may be envisaged in the following six sequential stages:

i   referral and recognition

ii   immediate protection and planning the investigation

iii   investigation and initial assessment

iv   child protection conference and decision-making about the need for registration

v   comprehensive assessment and planning

vi   implementation, review and, where appropriate, deregistration (Home Office et al, 1991, p 26–27).

These phases were explored in the study but, as the guidance notes, there is likely to be some overlap as the stages do not necessarily stand alone nor are they clearly divided in time. A clear finding of this study is that the level, intensity and spread of interagency involvement is not uniform across all stages of a case career. Interagency collaboration is much more highly developed in the initial phases, up to and including the initial child protection conference, than it is thereafter. This is reflected in the content of the interagency child protection plans, discussed in Chapter Eight. The majority of children in the case sample were to be protected by voluntary support.

Although a prerequisite for registration in government guidance is that an *interagency* protection plan is required, in almost 40% of the cases in the case sample there was no mention in the child protection plan of other agencies besides the social services department. The roles and expectations of other agencies in routine contact with the children concerned were not always identified clearly in the plan and social services departments, as the lead agency, were at the forefront of the plans. Besides them, ongoing involvement was concentrated in relatively few hands; specifically (in this sample of primary school aged children) in schools, health visiting and child and family psychiatric services. Thus, in ongoing intervention the social services department played a dominant and sometimes, it appeared, almost exclusive role. As in the initial stages, there was very little joint hands-on collaborative work in intervention. Interagency activity was largely confined to information-exchange and some limited shared decision-making, for example in the core groups, which were emerging durng the fieldwork for this research as a valued device for sustaining interagency involvement following registration.

Although the mechanisms for review and deregistration were in the process of change in both research sites at the time of the study, in both at this stage of a case career there was the episodic resurgence of interagency involvement as professionals came together (or were consulted) about the progress of individual cases and deregistration.

The fifth stage in the six-stage model outlined by *Working Together* (1991), namely comprehensive assessment and planning, did not figure prominently in the cases in the case sample. In only four of the 48 cases was there full assessment of the kind recommended by the Department of Health guide *Protecting Children* (Department of Health, 1988). The much more common practice in the research sites at the time of the study was to proceed from the child protection plan based upon initial assessment to on-going intervention with the family.

The intermediate outputs of coordination

The principal facets of interagency coordination revealed by this study were frequent information exchange, a degree of joint planning to clarify the division of labour and to ensure largely sequential task performance and some shared decision-making. With the possible exception of some joint police/social work investigation, there was little evidence of more radical forms of coordination.

Information exchange

Information exchange was the most prominent form of coordination. It was particularly evident at the referral stage and in initial child protection conferences and, although to a lesser extent, in case intervention, in case reviews and in core groups.

At the referral stage, as is discussed in Chapter Three, there were ready and easy contacts between social services departments and most of the key agencies of which, in this study, schools and health visitors were identified as particularly important. The nature of referrals received from the interagency network was broadly perceived by the social services department staff to be appropriate both in terms of the thresholds at which cases were identified and passed on and in terms of the timing of the referrals. It appeared that the system, which is founded on the voluntary reporting of professional (and lay) concern in accordance with local interagency procedural guidelines, rather than a specific statutory duty to report, worked reasonably well.

At the initial stage of referral, it was clear that the extensive routine checks were made by social workers of others in the interagency network who may have had knowledge of the child and family concerned. It appeared from the case records, however, that not all such checks were fully recorded. As is discussed in Chapter Three, the nature and quality of information received varied. Some professions, notably general practitioners, were perceived as less forthcoming than others. Nonetheless, there was a routinised and frequent resort to the interagency network in appraising referral information from professional and lay sources concerning possible cases of child abuse.

The social services departments' response to serious allegations, defined in practice principally as those concerning sexual abuse and some cases of physical injury, was reported by other professional groups to be timely and generally adequate. There was less contentment with the capacity to respond to less clear-cut or lower threshold referrals as is discussed further below.

Clarification of the division of labour in child protection

The findings of this study indicate that interagency coordination policies and practices have institutionalised a relatively clear division of labour for most of the professions engaged in child protection. This is confirmed by data from the questionnaires concerning respondent's perceptions of the clarity of role of the various professions involved. For example, 94% of respondents considered social workers' roles to be very clear or fairly clear, followed by the police at 88%, paediatricians at 83%, and health visitors at 77%.

Concerning the perceived degree of role overlap, a number of professions, for example, general practitioners (69%), psychologists (68%), psychiatrists (65%), lawyers and teachers (64%) were perceived to overlap with the role of others in the interagency network either 'very rarely' or 'not often'. An exception to this general observation concerns the roles of social workers and health visitors, 55% and 45% of whom respectively were perceived to overlap frequently or very often with the roles of others in the network. Much of this may be with each other and is longstanding (cf. for example Fox and Dingwall, 1985). It arises from their shared role in the support of vulnerable families in the community using broadly similar techniques of intervention, notably counselling, support and advice-giving, often in the family home. Nonetheless, in this study, health visitors and nurse managers articulated clearly the health promotion role of health visiting and expressed a keen wish not to be involved inappropriately in offering support to families whose primary needs were for material assistance and social work support. Nonetheless, the dominance of child protection and the high thresholds for acceptance of cases into the social services departments meant that, in practice, health visitors continued to work with families in need in the community often without social work support. When both agencies were involved with the same family, the potential for role overlap between these two professions appeared to remain considerable, although this may not necessarily be undesirable.

The division of labour in child protection was evident throughout referral, initial investigation and subsequent intervention. At the investigative stge it principally concerned the allocation of responsibilities among the core professions of police, paediatricians and social workers. With the exception of some joint investigative work undertaken by the police and social workers (discussed below), coordination principally involved the sequential ordering of tasks undertaken by separate professions to ascertain the status of the case and to avoid muddle, duplication and unnecessary trauma in the form of multiple or inappropriate interviews or medical examinations for the children concerned. As was discussed in Chapter Six, the arrangements for medical examination of children suspected of physical or sexual abuse differed between the two research sites. In both, in the sample of registered cases, medical examinations were conducted in the majority of cases (88%), and predominantly by paediatricians (in 62% of the cases). In about threequarters of the registered cases in the sample in which a medical examination was carried out, only one was undertaken, two were undertaken in about a fifth of cases and in one case only, three were carried out. Most medical examinations were carried out speedily, with most taking place on the day of referral and 69% taking place within two days. The outcome of the referrals in terms of clear physical findings of abuse varied, as was expected, between cases of physical and sexual abuse. In both research sites, the arrangements for getting medical examinations done appeared to work reasonably well although, as is discussed below, the skills, experience and interest of individual clinicians were crucial to the the outcome of the examinations.

As is discussed in Chapters Four and Five, the division of labour between social workers and the police in initial investigation was rather less clear cut. Some cases (19%) were initially investigated by the police alone, some by social workers alone (33%) and 48% were, at least nominally, joint investigations. However, even when the police and social worker jointly investigated cases, in only 11 of the total sample did they engage in a potentially more radical form of coordination, namely undertaking joint interviews with the children concerned. This confirms a clear finding of this study that interagency coordination was more focused upon the exchange of information, some joint planning and the sequential ordering of tasks than on hands-on collaboration involving two or more professions working together. This was true both of the investigative stage and in subsequent intervention.

There was little evidence in the case records of repeated, intrusive interviewing of children. In the cases investigated by social workers alone, only one interview was carried out with the child in half the cases, two in a further six and in two cases, four. In cases investigated jointly, only one interview was carried out in just under half the cases, and the majority had two interviews. Indeed, there is some evidence that the direct contact with children at the early stage of a case may have been relatively superficial, resulting in a lack of information at case conferences about the child, his/her well-being and reactions to the abuse, as is discussed in Chapter Four.

Shared decision-making

The third component of coordinated activity revealed by the study was some shared interagency decision-making. Part of this occurred in initial investigation, in discussions for example between police and social workers in strategy meetings or elsewhere about the timing and nature of interviews with children, families and/or alleged abusers. It was most clearly seen in initial child protection conferences, and in subsequent child protection conferences or reviews of specific cases.

Issues of power and participation and consensus in these interprofessional encounters were explored in the study. A dominant finding was that despite the varied professional backgrounds and agency functions of those concerned, decisions were characterised by consensus rather than dissent. There is evidence for this at several points in the data. For example, dissent from child protection conference recommendations was recorded in the conference minutes in only three of the 48 cases in the sample, and disagreement identified in the discussion at conferences as revealed by the minutes in a further four. It may be that a high degree of consensus would be expected in the data derived from the case files, since these were cases in respect of which, by definition, there must have been sufficient interprofessional agreement in the initial child protection conference to warrant registration. They were also cases of physical or sexual abuse. As was indicated in Birchall's (1992) study, these types of case produced both more uniform and more serious ratings when the professionals in the sample were asked to rank brief vignettes.

Vignettes concerning emotional abuse and neglect were ranked as less serious and revealed more interprofessional and intraprofessional dissensus.

However, in interview, consensus was said to characterise interagency work generally, with disagreement about registration reported to be very rare and about intervention plans only slightly less so. Similarly high levels of interagency agreement were reported in respect of discussions at the ACPCs (discussed in Chapter Eleven) and in answer to the questions in the questionnaire about the extent to which other professions shared similar concerns in handling cases of child abuse. The latter revealed high levels of shared similar concerns amongst three of the four key professions – social workers, health visitors and paediatricians. The exception among the core professions was the police, with less than half of the respondents (49%) reporting that they shared very or fairly similar concerns in handling of cases of child abuse with them. This appeared to reflect a different orientation and task focus but not to create overwhelming problems in interagency collaboration between the police and the rest of the network.

The degree of consensus is surprising in view of the literature on interprofessional work which stresses the difference between professions in matters such as training, occupational socialisation, frames of reference, techniques and timescales of intervention, all of which carry the potential for disagreement about the nature of the problem under discussion and about what should be done. The question, therefore, arises as to why dissensus was not a more marked feature of interagency collaboration in this study. Several possibilities suggest themselves. One is that the procedural system devised for processing cases acts to limit disagreement. One essential task is to aggregate information to ascertain the status of the case including the degree of risk to the child concerned. The components to be integrated are relatively clearly identified and the parameters of the decision-making and possibilities for action limited both by the shortage of the resources and by custom and practice. Thus, the process appears to be circumscribed, bureaucratic and technical rather than one in which sharp ideological differences surface between the professions. There is some evidence for this in the data, especially concerning feminist perspectives on child sexual abuse. Several of those interviewed, mainly social workers in social services departments and the NSPCC, articulated clearly in interview perspectives on the nature and experience of child sexual abuse which were informed by feminist perspectives concerning the abuse by men of their power. While several respondents were angry about the apparent inability of the criminal justice system to respond appropriately to abusers, they nonetheless managed to work within the system to further the interest of women and children as they perceived them. They did so without being in a permanent state of conflict with others whose views about the nature of sexual abuse might be very different from their own.

A second possibility, discussed in Chapters Eight and Eleven, is that the relative stability of the local professional networks and the likelihood of the need to collaborate with individuals in future also serves to minimise disagreement or to limit its open expression. A third is that in the context of considerable anxiety about decision-making and fear of the consequences of getting it wrong, tendencies towards consensus and deferring towards those deemed to 'know' are accentuated.

A fourth possibility is that working within any system or organisation limits fundamental questioning of its dominant paradigms. There is some evidence for this at several points in the data in the general acceptance of the status quo and lack of critical evaluation of the direction and nature of the child protection system (although there were some exceptions reported in the text). It is certainly hard both to work within and stand outside the system; there is a tendency to accommodate over time.

It is for debate whether the degree of consensus matters. Many commentators point to the importance of consensus in sustaining interagency coordination (eg. Levine and White, 1961, Armitage, 1973, Williams, 1986, McKeganey and Hunter, 1986) and a permanent state of conflict and disagreement among the professionals concerned is unlikely to be helpful to decision-making or to the children and families concerned. Nonetheless, there is a powerful argument (eg. Dingwall, 1983, Blagg and Stubbs, 1988) for vesting decisions to intervene in family life in many hands and requiring interprofessional agreement for action as a brake on the coercive power of the state. If the culture among those professions is so uniform that disagreement as to proposed action is very rare, this may pose a threat to the civil liberties of some children and families.

Issues in the division of labour

The role of the police

One of the most significant changes in the division of labour in child protection confirmed by this study concerns the role of the police. Parton has characterised the change in the last twenty years as one from a socio-medical to a socio-legal discourse (Parton, 1991). This study revealed the police to be inscribed at the heart of the response to what comes to be labelled as child abuse. They had some involvement in the investigation of 32 of the 48 cases in the case sample and were invited to attend all the initial child protection conferences. As was discussed in Chapters Five, Eight and Eleven, relationships between the police and other agencies were not revealed to be particularly fraught whether in the case sample, in interview or in answer to questions in the questionnaire. However, there were difficulties in joint investigation. Some were logistical. Others, notably the problems experienced in interviewing young women in the context of allegations of sexual abuse, appeared more intractable, representing fundamental differences in style and approach.. It is not clear that they would be easily resolved following the implementation of the Memorandum of Good Practice on video recorded interviews (Home Office and Department of Health, 1992).

Some important questions are raised by the study concerning the outcomes of police involvement. Government guidance and the police respondents interviewed stressed that successful prosecution is not the sole nor necessarily the most important criterion for judging the outcome of police involvement. The welfare of the child was also identified as important. There was, however, some tension and conflict between the objectives of the welfare of the individual child, and of justice, including the protection of future victims, as was discussed in Chapter Five. In the case sample, alleged abusers were prosecuted in twelve cases, seven cases of sexual and five of physical abuse. In seven of these a custodial sentence was imposed, at an average length of two years two months. It was found that police and others with whom they worked often wished to see more offenders prosecuted. They were frustrated with the difficulties of securing good enough evidence, especially in cases of sexual abuse, and of convincing the Crown Prosecution Service to proceed with the cases. Certainly, the position was revealed in this study to be one in which, despite extensive police involvement, the contribution of the criminal justice system to the protection of children from abuse was very limited.

The role of general practitioners

This study confirmed the findings of much previous research about the difficulty of securing the attendance of general practitioners at child protection conferences. They proved to be the largest single professional group of non-attenders at initial child protection conferences in the case sample comprising 18% of those who did not attend. The study further revealed them to be minimally involved in the initial identification and referral of cases of child abuse. Four of the cases in the sample were initially referred to the social services department by a general practitioner but in each case the family or child had contacted the general practitioner identifying child abuse as the reason for having done so. No cases of child abuse in the sample were identified by general practitioners themselves in the course of their routine contact with children and families. Their pattern of use of the child protection register in city, where general practitioners accounted for 1% of the calls in 1990, suggests that they are not prominent as front-line identifiers of abuse. In intervention with families following registration their role was also minimal; a specific function for general practitioners was identified in the child protection plan in only two of the 48 cases in the sample.

The questionnaire data reveal general practitioners (together with teachers) to head the list of those with roles which were considered to be 'very' or 'rather' unclear. Birchall's (1992) study indicates that general practitioners themselves share this perception, with only teachers considering their own roles to be less clear. In the present study, general practitioners headed the list of those perceived to perform 'rather' or 'very' poorly in child protection, this being the view of 48% of respondents.

These findings raise important issues. It seems clear the mandate to work together is not widely accepted by general practitioners, who may have the status and independence to ignore it. It may be that despite the emphasis placed in official guidance on the importance of this role, that they have, in fact, little to contribute and the system can and does function in the main without their active participation. However, this was not the view of the respondents in this study, 90% of whom considered that the general practitioner's role was 'essential' or 'important' in child protection. The difficulties of ensuring their attendance at child protection conferences was expressed as a source of sadness and, at times, frustration in interview.

It should be noted that there are individual exceptions to these general statements. One occurred in the case sample where the general practitioner had played a key role in ensuring the well-being of a young woman who had initially disclosed physical abuse in the household to her. It may be that further research is required to illuminate the nature of the contribution which can potentially be made by general practitioners and to document the circumstances and means by which their participation in interagency work in child protection can be facilitated and maximised, for example, through changes to their contract of employment. However if general practitioners are to be generally more closely involved in child protection, the findings from this study indicate the size of the task to be faced in increasing their knowledge and generating interest and commitment in this small part of their work.

Teachers

Some similar issues arise for teachers. They share with general practitioners contact with a universal or near universal child population; they have a primary task orientation which is far removed from child protection and, individually, each may expect to encounter a case of child abuse rather rarely. However, teachers differed from general practitioners in this study in referring 19% of the cases in the sample and they were confirmed in interview (and by Gibbons et al's 1993 study) as a key referral source. They also, with the health visitors, were the agency most likely to be involved along with the social services department in ongoing intervention with the child following registration.

The study revealed the teachers' key role in identifying abuse and their close knowledge and observation of children in school which were valued both in initial conferences and in monitoring the well-being of children. However, as was discussed in Chapter Three, the interviews revealed considerable variation in the extent to which teachers were familiar with the interagency referral procedures and the local procedural guidelines. Some were clear; others much less so. They were also perceived by the questionnaire respondents to have unclear roles in child abuse, only exceeded by the general practitioners. As with the general practitioners, Birchall's (1992) study revealed that they, too, were unclear about their role, scoring highest of all professions with 29% of all teachers considering they were rather or very unclear about their own role in child protection cases.

The difficulty of ensuring that awareness of the problem of child abuse and knowledge of the procedures to be followed were evenly distributed across a large workforce in dispersed locations was acknowledged in both research sites. The position was considered to be becoming more difficult in the context of changes in the education system distancing or removing schools from local education authority control, as is discussed more fully below.

The policy implications of these findings are that it may be necessary to spell out the teacher's role more clearly in child protection plans, rather than assume that they will be aware of what is required. In this study, although all cases in the sample were primary school aged children, a future role for the education service was specified in only twelve of the plans. Secondly, given their key role, efforts need to continue to be directed to raising the levels of awareness and of knowledge about how to respond so that all may reach the standard of confidence and commitment displayed by some in this study.

The mechanisms of interagency coordination

Four key devices to promote interagency coordination were studied in the course of the research: the child protection register, the multidisciplinary child protection conference, the local procedural guidelines and the ACPC. In addition core groups were studied although they were not widely used in the sample of cases initially registered between 1988 and 1990.

Initial child protection conferences

Two mechanisms, the multidisciplinary child protection conference and the local procedural guidelines were particularly valued in facilitating interagency work. As is discussed in Chapters Seven and Eight, the generally very positive evaluation of initial child protection conferences confirms previous research and echoes the key role ascribed to them in government guidance and local procedures. There were some criticisms of aspects of their functioning, for example that some were poorly chaired, and thus too long and poorly structured, that participants could be better prepared, that there was shortage of minute-takers and suitable venues. Nonetheless, in principle and generally in practice, the majority of respondents valued them and accorded them high priority and considered them a vital forum for interagency collaboration.

Procedural guidelines

Rather more unexpectedly, similarly positive evaluations were reported of the local procedural guidelines issued in each research site by the ACPC, following central government guidance. Criticisms of procedures as constraining professional discretion, of being unrealistic and of protecting agency staff at the expense of the well-being and interests of children and families were not prominent in the study as they had proved to be earlier (Hallett and Stevenson, 1980). On the contrary, most reported that they found the procedures helpful as a list in structuring and organising the work, in clarifying different professional roles and in resolving interagency difficulties. More respondents reported them to be helpful in containing the anxiety engendered by the work than found them to be a hindrance or constraint, although some were conscious of their status as the yardstick against which performance would be judged if there were failures of compliance and tragedy occurred.

The child protection register

The social services departments' files revealed that a record of a register check having been completed existed in only 21% of the cases in the sample. Interviews with respondents suggested that consulting the register may have occurred rather more frequently although it went unrecorded, but it appeared that this varied within and between work sites and professions. Some argued that they would already know the register status of families within their areas and acknowledged that the procedures (which required a register check) were not always followed. The research showed that, at the time of the study, the register was used more as a management tool rather than as a central point of inquiry for professional staff.

The ACPC

This research revealed the ACPCs in both research sites to be bodies considered to be performing useful functions but hampered by their status, resources and membership. There was a gap between an ideal of ACPCs as dynamic, corporate, pro-active bodies and a perceived reality of them as somewhat slow, cumbersome, with unresolved difficulties about membership, particularly the capacity of all members to represent their professions and agencies and to ensure effective implementation of ACPC policies.

When ACPC members in one research site were asked to review the performance of the committee, they reported that it performed best in establishing, maintaining and reviewing local interagency procedures and in reviewing significant issues arising from particular cases or from inquiry reports and least well in reviewing progress on work to prevent child abuse.

The study revealed a gap between field staff and the ACPC, the former often having little knowledge of the ACPC and generally regarding it as remote and out of touch.

The interagency network

The interagency network in child protection was revealed in this study to be characterised by heterogeneity. The respondents in the present study varied greatly between the professions in matters such as the amount of time they spent working with child abuse. There was also variation in the amount of coverage of the topic in their basic or post-qualifying training. In respect of the latter, social workers reported the most and teachers the least. This heterogeneity was not unexpected and confirms the findings of Birchall's (1992) study. It does, however, illustrate how diverse is the network in terms of role, task, the salience of child protection in the overall workload, the amount of experience and training and thus, presumably, confidence and competence with which the various professions approach the task.

Rather more surprising, although this was also confirmed in Birchall's (1992) study, the research found the interagency network to be relatively stable. These matters are likely to vary across the country but in the two research sites in this study, 38% of the questionnaire respondents had worked in the locality for over 10 years and a further 41% for between three and nine years. 74% of respondents had worked in their profession for over ten years. Only four staff, two social workers and two health visitors, had worked in their profession for less than three years. These figures are an important corrective to popular ideas both of great staff mobility and of very inexperienced staff working at the front line in child protection. The stability is importnt in offering a base upon which interagency work could develop since, as is discussed below, the importance of establishing personal links between professionals proved important in developing and sustaining interagency coordination.

The interpersonal base to interorganisational relations

Despite the dominance of mechanisms and structures in much of the literature on interorganisational relations, this study pointed to the importance of interpersonal relationships in initiating and sustaining interagency work. It confirmed Webb's observation that 'practitioners consistently highlight the level of interpersonal relations when discussing coordination and collaboration' (1991, p 237). This was illustrated in responses to the question about the ease of collaboration with other professions (presented in Chapter Eleven), in which there was an association between little experience of contact with particular professions and perceived difficulties in collaboration. The critical role of the child protection coordinators as reticulists was illustrated, inter alia, with reference to the working of ACPCs where their energy and drive was perceived to be vital. Elsewhere in the data, respondents in interview referred to the importance of personal knowledge of collaborative partners, of a degree of trust and familiarity and the problems which could result if this was broken by frequent staff moves or had not yet been established, as was often the case at the time of the study in the joint police/social work investigations.

The importance of personalities was also illustrated, for example the impact of the lead officer on the style and functioning of police special units, or of changes in senior and middle management within social services departments. The effect of the competence and interest of consultant paediatricians in child abuse work was also revealed as particularly important, given their relative scarcity and, therefore, prominent role in the interagency network in a particular locality.

The policy implications of this are both positive and negative. Positive in that it appears that people do matter and that, despite a structured and bureaucratised system, the interest and commitment of individuals can and do impact upon interagency coordination and thereby, it is hoped, on service delivery. The negative implication is that key individuals who lack the requisite skill or interest and who may be reluctant to address the deficit through post-qualifying training can seriously impede the quality of service provided. The element of chance poses problems for a system which relies upon and assumes a willingness and capacity to work together in the interests of children.

The changing political economy of welfare

The study was undertaken at a time of transition in the political economy of welfare which proved to be affecting coordination in child protection. Interagency coordination in respect of child abuse was developed in the UK in a social welfare system with relatively uniform patterns of state provision in health care, education and the personal social services. These had facilitated a degree of coordination which was high by comparison with more fragmented welfare systems elsewhere. It was reinforced by a tradition of rational planning in public policy in which the coordination of services was a prominent policy goal from the late 1960s onwards (Challis et al, 1988). This tradition was challenged in some services during the 1980s as increasing emphasis was placed, rhetorically at least, on the importance of service users seeking and coordinating their own service packages in the mixed economy of welfare. However, in child protection, the dominant coordinating paradigm survived largely unchallenged throughout this period. Services were largely uncosted at the point of service delivery and there was little trading across *market* as opposed to service boundaries. The social control element of child protective services no doubt contributed to this since it placed a responsibility on the state to ensure that coordinated services were available to vulnerable children, whose carers could not necessarily be expected to seek out services on their behalf.

As is discussed in Chapter Ten, this research study revealed clear evidence of a threat to the dominance of the old paradigm which rested on a

> 'belief in rational planned allocations, in collaboration not competition, in professional responsibility and public service as organisational motives not financial incentives and competition' (Glennerster, 1992, p 18).

The impact of the health service reforms with the creation of NHS trusts, of fund-holding general pratitioners and of a purchaser-provider split in health care were said by some respondents to be undermining the former collaborative traditions and practices. Similar difficulties were reported to be occurring in respect of schools, as they implemented local financial management and lost the support for child protection provided by 'top-sliced' local education authority funding. Objectives such as decentralisation, a market driven approach and the independence of service units (hospitals or schools) from health or local authority control render the planned coordination of public services increasingly problematic as was reported in this study. The structurally insecure ACPCs were not well placed to resolve the resulting difficulties.

Resources for child protection

The study revealed a child protection system severely constrained by resource shortages. This was evident at all stages and in many parts of the interagency network. In investigation, despite the high priority accorded to the task by social services department staff, there were reported difficulties in conducting the required number of initial investigations to the standard deemed desirable. In initial child protection conferences, resource shortages included unsuitable venues and, most worrying for the respondents interviewed, inadequate secretarial services to provide minutes. The lack of investment in secretarial services also had a deleterious impact on case recording. Perhaps most serious of all, however, were shortages of resources to help children, familes and alleged abusers following registration. As discussed in Chapter Nine, there was a lack of day care, of homemakers or family aides, of substitute care in foster or residential care, and of specialist treatment resources for abused children, their familes and for abusers whether provided within or outwith the social services departments. There was also a shortage of social work time, leading to an incapacity at times to nominate key workers at initial child protection conferences, with the consequence that cases were temporarily carried by first-line managers (a practice condemned in the Kimberley Carlile Report (London Borough of Greenwich, 1987)) and in the Second Report from the Health Committee on Public Expenditure on Personal Social Services (HC 570–1), and there were some unallocated child protection cases in the research sites.

The issue of financing local government in general and social services departments in particular is arcane and complex and beyond the scope of this study. There are heated debates about whether the standard spending assessment accurately reflects real needs; about the precise effects on the personal social services of attempts to limit local spending levels in the absence of hypothecated funding and about the extent to which resource difficulties in child protection reflect poor management practices or genuine resource shortages. The Department of Health reported an increase in spending on the personal social services of 27.2 per cent for England as a whole between 1984/5 and 1990/91 (when the fieldwork for this research took place). When deflated by a personal social services specific deflator to take account of the relative price effect of pay and prices in that sector, the increase was 21% for England (HC 570–1, 1991). A survey published by the Association of Directors of Social Services in 1991, however, reported that of the 83 authorities who responded, over half anticipated a reduced or standstill budget in the social services department in 1991/92 (ADSS, 1991).

Whatever the truth of the claims and counter-claims about resource levels, the position in this study was that child protection, which was claimed by the social services departments and acknowledged by others in the interagency network to receive high priority, was severely hampered by a level of resources which was insufficient for the task. As was discussed in Chapter Nine, the social services departments were not alone in facing resource shortages. Difficulties also emerged in the study in respect of staffing in the police Special Units, health visitors' workloads, the paediatric services, schools and elsewhere.

Implementation of the mandate to coordinate

The findings of this study reveal that the implementation of interagency coordination policies in child protection may be viewed as largely successful. There was widespread acceptance of the need for and value of working together in child proteection among practitioners at field and senior management levels in the key agencies. (The principal exception was the general practitioners whose status as independent contractors appeared to enable many of them to stand aloof from the problem of child abuse and from the procedural guidelines). There was also evidence of varied outputs of coordination in matters such as interagency referral systems, child protection plans and arrangements for case review. Coordinated outputs were evident at all three levels of child protection services identified by Carter (1976), namely ad hoc case coordination, systematic case coordination (in child protection conferences) and programme coordination (in ACPCs).

In accordance with much current implementation research, this study explored a policy issue (interagency coordination) in the context of a policy network rather than the implementation of a single specific decision. It thus paid considerable attention to the motivations and experiences of local actors in the policy process. However, viewed from a top-down perspective, two caveats may be entered to the picture of a relatively successful policy implementation revealed in the study. The first concerns a time-lag in implementation. While at one level, the scale of the changes in interagency working established over a relatively short time-scale, notably since the mid-1970s, is remarkable, nonetheless the time-lag in implementing specific pieces of guidance may, from a 'top down' perspective, be less welcome. For example, in neither research site in 1991 had the guidance contained in *Working Together* (1988) (DHSS and Welsh Office) been fully implemented, for example, in the routine involvement of parents in initial child protection conferences. In borough, it was not until 1991 that revised procedural guidelines were issued to implement the recommendations of the 1988 guidance.

The second, more problematic, concerns the degree of variation evident in policy implementation. Variations in operational practices were noted at several points in the data. In respect of social services departments they were reported to occur, for example, in the quality of initial social work investigations, in recording practices, in compliance with the requirement to check the child protection register, in differential responses to child protection referrals between various area teams and in the quality of chairing initial child protection conferences. The variations were not confined to the social services departments however. Although the numbers were small, there were differences in the prosecution rates of alleged abusers between the two research sites. There were also differences in the services reported to be provided by the consultant paediatricians and in the responses made by teachers at the referral stage.

These variations may reflect different levels of skills, knowledge, competence and possibly interest in the topic of child protection on the part of staff concerned which may be difficult or expensive to rectify. From a 'top down' perspective, they highlight a perennial problem in human service delivery, namely the inherent limits to control of those at the front-line who, in child protection as in other fields, exercise professional power and/or delegated discretion in the course of their work (Blau, 1955, Smith, 1965, and Lipsky, 1980).

A standard response to such variations (used in the defence of local as opposed to central government as a service provider) is that they reflect an appraisal of and considered response to differing local circumstances. However, it was not clear that this was the case within the study, since the variations seemed less patterned and more idiosyncratic – the product of 'accident' not 'design' – rather than a reflection of conscious policy choices. They thus raise issues of 'territorial justice' – to what extent should citizens of one authority or local area be entitled to levels and standards of service provision comparable to those provided elsewhere?

The variation in operational practice and standards also raises issues about quality assurance in child protection. While some initiatives were in progress at the time of the research to standardise practice (for example, the selection and training of a smaller pool of conference chairs), in general, there were not well developed mechanisms of quality assurance in place. As was discussed in Chapter Ten, the pattern had been for ACPCs to review cases sporadically in response to error rather than to engage in the routine monitoring of practice. Nonetheless, it should be noted that a lack of attention to outcomes also reflects the content of the policy guidance issued by central government, as is discussed below.

In general, however, the study revealed a high degree of coordination based on the institutionalisation of routines, a relatively clear division of labour, a dependable set of assumptions about role performance and some degree of convergence (or, at least, toleration of difference) of professional values and paradigms among core workers. This had been established, with some difficulty since the early 1970s. It is the more remarkable since it was achieved in a complex interorganisational context which, the literature suggests, poses particular challenges to policy implementation (Scharpf, 1978, Hanf, 1978, Mountjoy and O'Toole, 1979). Furthermore it was achieved without the deployment by central government of the more potent means of controlling the periphery, namely primary or secondary legislation or significant specific financial incentives. Instead, circulars of guidance were used.

The status of government circulars in this sphere is somewhat uncertain. The Local Authority Social Services Act, 1970 (Section 7(1)), requires local authorities to act under the general guidance of the Secretary of State for Social Services in their social services functions, thus vesting circulars with some kind of statutory authority. Nonetheless, the Department of Health explains the difference between primary legislation, secondary legislation (regulations), codes of practice and guidance as follows:

> *One might sum up the differences between the requirements of these*
> *various official documents like this: Regulations say 'You must/shall';*
> *codes say 'You ought/should'. When guidance explains regulations it*
> *reaffirms the 'You must' messages. However, when it goes beyond*
> *regulations in setting out good practice, it conveys the message that 'It is*
> *highly desirable to . . .' or 'Unless there is good reason not to, you should'*
> *rather than 'You must'* (DH, 1989).

In the same document the Department of Health places guidance documents
such as *Working Together* (1988) (which was effective during the fieldwork for
this research) in the category of 'stand alone' guidance (that is not issued
alongside regulations) and thus in the weakest category of policy instrument.
Further reference was made to the status of the guidance in the preface to
Working Together (1991) which noted that it was issued under Section 7 of the
Local Authority Social Services Act, and that:

> *As such, this document does not have the full force of statute, but should*
> *be complied with unless local circumstances indicate exceptional reasons*
> *which justify a variation* (Home Office et al, 1991, piii).

While this clarifies the status of the guidance for local authorities in the
exercise of their social services functions, it does not do so for services such as
the police, health or the voluntary sector.

In 1977, the Association of Directors of Social Services commented to the
Select Committee on Violence in the Family on the circular on non-
accidental injury to children (DHSS, 1974(a)) and suggested that:

> *a letter of guidance from central government has had more effect in*
> *moulding the development of services and shifting resources than a major*
> *piece of legislation such as the Chronically Sick and Disabled Persons Act*
> *or even the Children and Young Persons Act* (HC 329–III, 1977,
> p 132).

The development of interagency collaboration in child protection since then
has continued to rely on circulars of guidance rather than legislation. Despite
this, implementation has been relatively successful.

In trying to account for the implementation success, it should be noted
that routinised coordination is not, of course, confined to child protection. It
is clearly seen, for example, in the division of labour within western medicine
where there are clear processes of referral and arrangements for the sequential
performance of tasks between general practitioners and a wide range of
specialist practitioners. In bio-medicine, this reflected an organic development. In child protection, by contrast, coordination occurred in an interprofessional arena, with considerable angst and difficulty as is reflected in the

problematisation of the topic in the literature. It is possible to speculate that developments in interagency collaboration might have occurred organically as part of a process of professional maturation, for example in social work, and professional change in response to a newly re-emerged social problem. It might, therefore, be suggested that mandated coordination in child protection served simply to accelerate a process which was likely to have happened anyway. This may be so, but scrutiny of the policy content and of the process of implementation suggest that other more powerful factors were at work in the sphere of child protection.

Mandated coordination can depend for successful implementation, either on sufficient authority for it to be imposed from the top down or sufficient shared agreement amongst the professional actors in the network on rational corporate aims, or both. Despite the interest in coordination expressed in British public policy since the 1950s, neither the model relying on central imposed authority nor the rational model of shared goals among the implementation network have been strikingly successful in community care for example. What, then, accounts for the relatively successful implementation of mandated coordination which was revealed in this study?

One factor is that, although coordination was mandated by central government, it was founded on the accepted tenets of good practice which have characterised the professional literature on the topic of child protection from the late 1960s onwards. It worked with rather than against the grain of received wisdom among the professional leaders of the time. The DHSS was not, therefore, issuing novel and unexpected policy at 'the top' in 1974 for implementation at local level. Rather it was engaged in an interactive process where policy reflected practice and emerged out of a process of dialogue and negotiation with the structured interests (such as local government associations and professional bodies) who bore responsibility for implementation. To a very considerable extent, as Whitmore (1984) demonstrates, the professional perspectives and organisational interests shaping the dominant paradigms of child abuse and appropriate policy responses in the DHSS also exercised considerable influence among health and welfare agencies at the periphery.

Secondly, despite modifications and incremental changes to respond to new situations and forms of abuse, notably the rise in identified cases of sexual abuse, the basic policy requirement of interagency coordination has remained remarkably constant over a period of over twenty years. As Sabatier (1986(b)) has noted, much implementation research takes place over too short a time scale, often less than five years, which accentuates the tendency to identify implementation deficits and policy failures. Many respondents in this study identified significant improvements in interagency collaboration in recent years suggestting that the changes to working practices required even by routinised coordination take some time to develop.

However, both these factors – a professional acceptance of the desirability of coordination and a continued policy emphasis on the need for it – also characterised other fields where less progress in implementation was achieved. In the sphere of child protection, however, there was, in addition, close specification of the mechanisms of collaboration. While this too occurred in fields such as joint planning between health and social services with the establishment of joint Consultative Committees, the coordinating mechanisms and intermediate outputs required by central government in child protection were detailed, specific and extended to the case level. They included the establishment of ACPCs, child protection registers and child protection case conferences, and later, interagency child protection plans. Perhaps most important of all, however, and distinct from many other fields was the requirement for ACPCs to produce local interagency guidelines. As this study showed, these routinised and reinforced the requirements for coordination in handling specific cases and they guided and constrained the activities of field staff in child protection.

This raises the question of why the machinery was specified more closely in the field of child protection. It appears that there was a greater urgency and degree of purpose about the task than in some related fields, where the advice remained exhortatory and coordination was achieved more in form than in substance. The key seems to lie in the external environment in which the policy response to child abuse developed, notably the impact of the public inquiries into child abuse. These shaped not only the content of the policy itself for example, a greater specificity about the mechanisms for collaboration, but also had a profound impact upon the implementation context.

Parton (1988) has documented the sense of crisis surrounding child abuse in 1973 and 1974 at the time of the Maria Colwell inquiry and a number of authors have pointed to the relationship between a perception of a 'crisis' and a propensity for interagency collaboration (Warren, 1967, Form and Nosow, 1958, Reid, 1975). Klonglan at al (1975), reporting on a demonstration project, suggests that support for a coordination programme is most likely to be obtained if the organisation involved can first agree that there is a genuine, pressing problem. They suggest exploiting a crisis, presenting figures documenting the seriousness of the problem, and making comparisons with practice elsewhere as strategies which can be used to build commitment to the problem. These were evident in the policy response in 1974. In the absence of coercion or the use of legislation or of financial incentives to encourage agencies to comply, the government faced the position where, as Scharpf suggests, it either had 'to persuade participants that it is in their own interest to join a proposed policy network . . . or that it is their duty to do so' (Scharpf, 1978, p 366). In the case of child abuse in 1974, both applied.

While perception of a crisis may act as an initial spur to interagency coordination, its influence and impact could be expected to diminish over time. However, in the field of child protection in Britain, the sense of crisis was episodically but powerfully reinforced by the succession of inquiries which followed the Maria Colwell case. An important theme of each was the need for improved interagency coordination. As the empirical research reported here demonstrates this generated a climate of professional anxiety and fear for many, which acted as a spur to compliance.

The child abuse tragedies, with the associated publicity, constituted a level of scandal which served as a critical catalyst in promoting interagency coordination. It changed the context of exchange between professions and transformed the costs and benefits for those involved, especially the costs of non-compliance. Exchange and rationality had not, in themselves, proved sufficient. The achievement of a high degree of routinised coordination in child protection, in contrast to other policy spheres, can be attributed in great part to the desire to avoid tragedy and scandal. This fostered a degree of interprofessional convergence about the importance of protecting the child from harm. It was also a somewhat defensive stategy, focused on the avoidance of disaster rather than the long-term welfare of children.

This potentially has two consequences. The first is that there is a danger that the degree of interprofessional convergence and consensus and the existence of routines may mean that there is only a limited capacity to respond when an exceptionally difficult or unusual case occurs, which may fundamentally challenge the value consensus and require a more radical form of coordinated response. Secondly, a defensive, routinised form of coordination may serve to accentuate the tendency towards conservatism noted by some writers.

Interagency coordination, child protection, child welfare and conservatism

In Chapter One, the potential for interagency coordination to act as a force for conservatism was noted. Reference was made, inter alia, to Weiss' observation that coordination simplified the problems in human services by implying that the worst problems are merely administrative and Benson's (1982) view that interagency coordination suggests that advanced societies face no structural problems or contradictions and that problems can be resolved through an interorganisational technology.

The policy response to child protection in Britain did not place new statutory duties on the health and welfare agencies, did not require the development of new services and did not provide significant earmarked resources for the resolution of the newly emerged problem. It worked within a definition of abuse as primarily caused by aberrant individuals and to be resolved more by identification and registration (the determination of case status) than by effective intervention. The focus was administrative and case-managerial with an emphasis on process and outputs rather than outcomes. Walton (1993) is critical of this, noting that government policy is deficient in its failure both to set goals and objectives for child protection services and to specify a radical agenda for change to remedy child abuse. She asserts that 'in child protection we have a large problem which is thought capable of a disproportionately small solution' (1993, p 155). It should be noted, however, that, had the government sought to set clear objectives or develop a more radical approach to the problem, it would be likely to have faced greater difficulties both in securing agreement in principle to the policy and in the course of implementation. As it was, a significant shift in the allocation of resources was effected without primary legislation and without providing significant additional specific funds.

The study offers considerable support for the view of interagency coordination strategies in child protection as tending towards conservatism. By definition, the cases in the sample had met the criterion of interprofessional agreement at an initial child protection conference that they should be registered. In interview, respondents suggested that thresholds for intervention in general were too high rather than too low, with none suggesting that the child protection services were intervening unwarrantedly or engaged in the intrusive surveillance of families. This study did not explore the extent to which the children and families concerned shared this professional view. The focus of interagency activity was on the early stages of the construction of a case rather than on therapeutic intervention and was case-managerial rather than service oriented. As suggested above, it was largely defensive, motivated by a desire to secure the protection of children and to avoid tragedy and scandal.

The study revealed clearly, however, that there were concerns about the incapacity of the social services departments to intervene preventively at earlier stages with families in difficulties in the absence of clear signs of physical or sexual abuse. This was reported to be a consequence of resource shortages regretted both by those trying to refer cases into the system, notably teachers and health visitors, but also by the social workers themselves.

The Children Act 1989, implemented in 1991 as the fieldwork for this study came to an end, envisages support services provided for children in need which are 'acceptable non-stigmatised responses to the normal problems of family life' (Department of Health, 1993(b), p 33). This study points to the size of the task faced by social services department and other health and welfare agencies in moving from the existing practices found in the research sites to the position envisaged by the Children Act. The Children Act Report 1992 suggests that the research sites may not be unusual, noting that some local authorities were being rather slow to develop adequate children-in-need initiatives and finding it difficult to move from a social policing to a more proactive partnership role (Department of Health, 1993(b), p 33). It is probably correct that entry to the child protection system is reserved for serious cases, given the consequences for children and families of engagement with the child protection procedures, usually an unwelcome and stigmatising process. However, if this is the case, the child welfare needs of children and families need to be met through accessible, supportive, non-stigmatising and *available* services, which requires a commitment to providing the resources to make this possible and those within the child protection system require pro-active interventive resources to promote welfare as well as to undertake routinised, defensive case management.

References

AIKEN, M., DEWAR, R., DI TOMASO, N., HAGE, J. and ZEITZ, G. (1975) *Coordinating Human Services*, San Fransisco: Josey-Bass.

ALDRICH, H. E. (1972) An organisational environment perspective on cooperation and conflict between organisations in the manpower and training system in(ed) NEGHANDI, A. *Interorganisation Theory*, Kent, Ohio: Kent State University Press.

ALDRICH, H. E. (1976) Resource dependence and interorganisational relations *Administration and Society*, 7, 419–54.

ALDRICH, H. E. (1979) *Organisations and Environments*, Englewood Cliffs, New Jersey: Prentice Hall.

ALFORD, R. (1975) *Health care politics: ideological and interest barriers to reform*. Chicago: University of Chicago Press.

ARMITAGE, P. (1983) Joint working in primary health care *Nursing Times*, 79, 28, 75–8.

ASSOCIATION OF DIRECTORS OF SOCIAL SERVICES (1991) *Press Statement –* issued 14 March 1991 cited in HC 570–1, pxvi.

ATHERTON, C. (1992) Ten practical points to consider when calling a child protection conference in (ed) THOBURN, J. *Participation in Practice – involving families in child protction*. Norwich: University of East Anglia.

BALBO, L. (1987) Crazy quilts: rethinking the welfare state debate from a woman's point of view in Showstak SASSOON, A. (ed) *Women and the State*, London: Hutchinson.

BARRETT, S. and FUDGE, C. (eds) (1981) *Policy and Action*. London: Methuen.

BARRETT, S. and HILL, M. (1984) Policy bargaining and structure in implementation theory *Policy and Politics*, 12, 219–40.

BECKER, S. and McPHERSON, S. (1986) *Poor clients: the extent and nature of financial poverty amongst consumers of social work services*. Nottingham University: Benefits Research Unit.

BENJAMIN, M. (1981) Child abuse and the interdisciplinary team: panacea or problem in (ed) Irving, H. *Family law: an interdisciplinary perspective*, Toronto, Canada: Carswell.

BENSON, J. K. (1975) The interorganisational network as a political economy *Administrative Science Quarterly*, 20, 229–49.

BENSON, J. K. (1982) A framework for policy analysis in (ed) ROGERS, D. L. and WHETTEN, D. A. and associates *Interorganisational coordination: theory, research and implementation*. Iowa: Iowa State University Press.

BESHAROV, D. J. (1977) US National Centre on child abuse and neglect: Conference highlights *Children Today*, 10, 6, 12–16, 36.

BESHAROV, D. J. (1987) Contending with overblown expectations *Public welfare*, Winter, 7–11.

BIRCHALL, E. (1992) *Report to the Department of Health: Working Together in Child Protection: Report of Phase Two: A Survey of the Experience and Perceptions of Six Key Professions*. Stirling: University of Stirling.

BLAGG, H. and STUBBS, P. (1988) A child centred practice? Multiagency approaches to child sexual abuse *Practice*, 2, 1, 12–19.

BLAU, P. (1955) *The Dynamics of Bureaucracy*. Chicago: Chicago University Press.

BLYTH, E. and MILNER, J. (1990) The process of interagency work in Violence Against Children Study Group *Taking Child Abuse Seriously*. London: Unwin Hyman.

BOND, J., CARTLIDGE, A., GREGSON, B., PHILIPS, P., BOLAM, F. and GILL, K. (1985) *A study of interprofessional collaboration in primary health care organisations*. Newcastle: University of Newcastle upon Tyne Health Care Research Unit.

BOOTH, T. A. (1981) Collaboration between the health and social services: Part 1, A Case Study of joint care planning *Policy and Politics*, 9, 1, 23–49.

BOURNE, J. D. and NEWBERGER, E. H. (1980) Interdisciplinary group process in the hospital management of child abuse and neglect *Child Abuse and Neglect* 4, 2, 137–44.

BRILL, N. (1976) *Teamwork: working together in the human services*. Philadelphia: Wippincott.

BRITISH PAEDIATRIC ASSOCIATION and BRITISH ASSOCIATION OF PAEDIATRIC SURGEONS (1973) NAI to children: a guide on management *British Medical Journal*, 4, 656–60.

BROSKOWSKI, A., O'BRIEN, G. and PREVOST, J. (1982) Interorganisational strategies for survival: looking ahead to 1990 *Administration in Mental Health*, 9, 3, 198–210.

BROSS, D., KRUGMAN, R. D., LENHERR, M., ROSENBERG, D. and SCHMITT, B. D. (eds) (1988) *Child Protection Team Handbook II*. New York: Garland Press.

BROUSSINE, M., COX., P. and DAVIES, F. (1988) The significance of interprofessional stereotyping in the health and social services *Local Government Studies*, 14, 3, 57–67.

BRUNEL SOCIAL SERVICES CONSORTIUM (1988) *The professional management of child abuse* (unpublished draft report). Uxbridge: Brunel University.

BRYMAN, A. (1988) *Quantity and Quality in Social Research*. London: Unwin Hyman.

CAMPBELL, B. (1988) *Unofficial secrets: child sexual abuse – the Cleveland case*. London: Virago.

CARTER, J. (ed) (1976) *The Maltreated Child*. London: Priory Press.

CASTLE, R. (1977) Case conferences – cause for concern in (ed) FRANKLIN, A. W. *Child Abuse – prediction, prevention and follow-up*. Edinburgh: Churchill Livingstone.

CHALLIS, L., FULLER, S., HENWOOD, M., KLEIN, R., PLOWDEN, W., WEBB, A., WHITTINGHAM, P. and WISTOW, G. (1988) *Joint Approaches to Social Policy: Rationality and Practice*. Cambridge: Cambridge University Press.

CHILDREN'S RESEARCH FUND INTERNATIONAL COLLABORATIVE COMMITTEE FOR CHILD HEALTH (c1987) *The medical aspects of child abuse*. Liverpool: Children's Research Fund.

CLARK, B. R. (1965) Interorganisational Patterns in Education *Administrative Science Quarterly*, 10, 224–37.

CLARK TURNER, J. and TEN HOOR, W. (1978) The nimh community support program: pilot approach to a needed social reform *Schizophrenia Bulletin*, 4, 3, 319–44.

CLIFFORD, C. (1985) Nurse-doctor relationships: is there cause for concern? *Nursing Practice*, 2, 102–8.

CLYDE, J. (1992) *The report of the inquiry into the removal of children from Orkney in February 1991*. Edinburgh: HMSO.

CM. 412 (1988) *Report of the inquiry into child abuse in Cleveland, 1987*. London: HMSO.

CMND. 3703 (1968) *Report of the Committee on local authority and allied services*. London: HMSO.

CMND. 5055 (1972) *National Health Service Reorganisation: England*. London: HMSO.

COOK, K. S. (1977) Exchange and power in networks of interorganisational relations. *The Sociological Quarterly*, 18, 62–82.

CORBY, B. (1987) *Working with child abuse*. Milton Keynes: Open University Press.

CORBY, B. and MILLS, C. (1986) Child abuse: risks and resources *British Journal of Social Work*, 16, 5, 531–42.

CORNEY, R. (1988) Social work and primary care – the need for increased collaboration: discussion paper *Journal of Royal Society of Medicine*, 81, 29–30

CREIGHTON, S. (1992) *Child Abuse Trends in England and Wales, 1988–90.* London: NSPCC.

CREIGHTON, S. and NOYES P. (1989) *Child Abuse Trends in England and Wales 1983–87.* London: NSPCC.

D'AGOSTINO, O. (1975) Strains and stresses in protective services in (ed) EBELING, N. and HILL, D. *Child Abuse: Intervention and Treatment.* Acton, Mass: Publishing Sciences Group Inc.

DARTINGTON, T. (1986) *The limits of altruism: Elderly mentally-infirm people as a test case for collaboration.* London: King Edward's Hospital Fund for London.

DAVIDSON, S. M. (1976) Planning and coordination of social services in multiorganiational contexts *Social Service Review,* 50, 1, 117–37.

DAVOREN, E. (1983) Powers struggles in the child abuse field *Children Today,* 12, 6, 14–16.

DEPARTMENT OF HEALTH (1988) *Protecting children: a guide for social workers undertaking a comprehensive assessment.* London: HMSO.

DEPARTMENT OF HEALTH (1989) *The Care of Children Principles and Practices in Regulations and Guidance.* London: HMSO.

DEPARTMENT OF HEALTH (1991) *Children and Young Persons on Child Protection Registers Year Ending 31 March 1990 England.* London: DH.

DEPARTMENT OF HEALTH (1993(a)) *Children and Young People on Child Protection Registers Year ending 31 March 1992, England.* London: DH.

DEPARTMENT OF HEALTH (1993(b)) *Children Act Report 1992.* London: HMSO.

DEPARTMENT OF HEALTH AND SOCIAL SECURITY (1970) *National health Service: the future structure of the National health Service.* London: HMSO.

DEPARTMENT OF HEALTH AND SOCIAL SECURITY (1972) *Battered Babies.* Letter LASSL(76)2.

DEPARTMENT OF HEALTH AND SOCIAL SECURITY (1973) *A report from the Working Party on Collaboration between the NHS and Local Government on its activities to the end of 1972.* London: HMSO.

DEPARTMENT OF HEALTH AND SOCIAL SECURITY (1974(a)) *Non-accidental injury to children* LASSL(73)14.

DEPARTMENT OF HEALTH AND SOCIAL SECURITY (1974(b)) *Report of the Committee of inquiry into the care and supervision provided in relation to Maria Colwell.* London: HMSO.

DEPARTMENT OF HEALTH AND SOCIAL SECURITY (1976) *Non-accidental injury to children. Area Review Committees* LASSL(76)2.

DEPARTMENT OF HEALTH AND SOCIAL SECURITY (1980) *Child Abuse: Central Register Systems* LASSL(80)4.

DEPARTMENT OF HEALTH AND SOCIAL SECURITY (1982) *Child Abuse: a study of Inquiry Reports*. London: HMSO.

DEPARTMENT OF HEALTH AND SOCIAL SECURITY (1988) *Diagnosis of Child Sexual Abuse: Guidance for Doctors*. London: HMSO.

DEPARTMENT OF HEALTH AND SOCIAL SECURITY SNMAC (1988(a)) *Child protection: guidance for senior nurses, health visitors and midwives*. London: HMSO.

DEPARTMENT OF HEALTH AND SOCIAL SECURITY AND HOME OFFICE (1970) *Battered Babies*. Letter CMO 2/70.

DEPARTMENT OF HEALTH AND SOCIAL SECURITY AND WELSH OFFICE (1988) *Working Together: a guide to arrangements for interagency cooperation for the protection of children from abuse*. London: HMSO.

DEPARTMENT OF HEALTH SOCIAL SERVICE INSPECTORATE (1988) *Inspection of Cleveland social services department's arrangements for handling child sexual abuse*. London: DH.

DEPARTMENT OF HEALTH SOCIAL SERVICE INSPECTORATE (1989) *Report of inspection of child abuse services in Cumbria SSD*. Gateshead: DH.

DEPARTMENT OF HEALTH SOCIAL SERVICE INSPECTORATE (1990(a)) *Report of an inspection of collaborative working arrangements between child protection agencies in Cleveland*. Gateshead: DH.

DEPARTMENT OF HEALTH SOCIAL SERVICE INSPECTORATE (1990(b)) *Inspection of child protection services in Rochdale*. Manchester: DHSSI, NW Region.

DERTHICK, M. (1972) *New Towns In Town*. Washington: Urban Institute.

DICKINSON, J. (1993) The Strengths of 'Working Together', Unpublished paper, Central Region Area Child Protection Committee Chairs Conference, Leicester.

DINGWALL, R. (1980) Problems of teamwork in primary care in (ed) LONSDALE, S., WEBB, A. and BRIGGS, T. *Teamwork in the personal social services and health care*. New York: Syracuse University Press.

DINGWALL, R. (1986) The Jasmine Beckford Affair, *Modern Law Review*, 49, 4, 489–507.

DINGWALL, R., EEKELAAR, J. and MURRAY, T. (1983) *The Protection of Children: state intervention and family life*. Oxford: Blackwell.

DINGWALL, R. and McINTOSH, J. (eds) (1978) *Readings in the Sociology of Nursing*. Edinburgh: Churchill Livingstone.

DIXON, B., BOUMA, G. and ATKINSON, G. (1987) *A Handbook of Social Science Research* Oxford: University Press.

DUCANIS, A. and GOLIN, A. (1979) *The interdisciplinary health care team.* Germantown: Aspen Systems Corp.

DUCKETT, J. (1977) The coordination of welfare and health services in Australia *Australian Journal of Social Issues*, 12, 3, 188–99.

ELEY, R. (1989) Women in Management in Social Services Departments in (ed) HALLETT, C. *Women and Social Services Departments*, Hemel Hempstead: Harvester Wheatsheaf.

FALLER, K. and ZEIFERT, H. (1981) The role of social workers in multi-disciplinary collaboration in (ed) FALLER, K. *Social work with abused and neglected children.* New York: Free Press.

FAMILY RIGHTS GROUP (1986) *FRG's response to the DHSS Consultation Paper Child Abuse Working Together.* London: FRG.

FANDETTI, D. (1985) Issues in the organisation of services for child abuse and neglect in (ed) MOUZAKITIS, C. and VARGHESE, R. *Social work treatent with abused and neglected children.* Springfield, Illinois: Charles C. Thomas.

FARMER, E. and OWEN, M. (1993) *Decision-making, intervention and outcome in child protection work.* Draft report to the Department of Health. Bristol: Department of Social Policy, University of Bristol.

FIELDING, N. and LEE, R. (1992) *Using computers in qualitative research.* London: Sage.

FINKELHOR, D. (1984) (ed) *Child sexual abuse: new theory and research.* New York: Free Press.

FINKELHOR, D. (1992) 'Master class: Child Sexual Abuse' unpublished paper, International Congress on Child Abuse and Neglect, Chicago, USA.

FLIN, R. (1988) Child witnesses: the psychological evidence *New Law Journal* 26.8.88, 608–10.

FLIN, R. and TARRANT, M. (1989) Children in the witness box *Social Work Today*, 2.2.89, 18–19.

FORM, W. H. and NOSOW, S. (1958) *Community in disaster.* New York: Harper and Row.

FOX, S. and DINGWALL, R. (1985) An exploratory study of variations in social workers and health visitors definitions of child mistreatment *British Journal of Social Work*, 15, 5, 467–78.

FROST, N. and STEIN, M. (1989) *The politics of child welfare.* Hemel Hempstead: Harvester Wheatsheaf.

GAMACHE, D. J., EDLESON, J. L. and SCHOCK, M. D. (1988) Coordinated police, judicial and social service response to woman-battering: a multiple-baseline evaluation across three communities in (ed) HOTALING, G., FINKELHOR, D., KIRKPATRICK, J. and STRAUSS, M.. *Coping with Family Violence: Research and Policy Perspective*. California: Sage Publications.

GEACH, H. (1983) Child Abuse Registers – time for a change? in GEACH, H. and SZWED, E. (1983) *Providing civil justice for children*. London: Edward Arnold.

GELLES, R. J. (1975) The social construction of child abuse *The American Journal of Orthopsychiatry*, 45, 363–71.

GIBBONS, J., CONROY, S. and BELL, C. (1993) *Operation of child protection registers*. Report to the Department of Health, Social Work, Development Unit, University of East Anglia.

GIL, D. (1981) The United States versus child abuse in (ed) PELTON, L. *The Social Context of Child Abuse and Neglect*. New York Free Press.

GIOVANNONI, J. and BECERRA, R. (1979) *Defining Child Abuse*. New York: Free Press.

GLASER, D. and FROSH, S. (1988) *Child sexual abuse*. London: Macmillan.

GLENNERSTER, H. (1992) Paying for Welfare: Issues for the Nineties, Unpublished paper, Social Policy Association Conference, University of Nottingham.

GOLDBERG, E. and WARBURTON, W. (1979) *Ends and Means in Social Work*. London: Allen and Unwin.

GOUGH, D., BODDY, F, DUNNING, N. and STONE, F. (1987) *A longitudinal study of Child Abuse in Glasgow, Volume 1: the Children who were registered*. University of Glasgow: Social Paediatric and Obstetric Research Unit.

GUSTAFFSON, L., LAGERBERG, D., LARRSON, D. and SUNDELIN, C. (1979) Collaboration in practice: experiences from a multidisciplinary research project on child abuse and neglect *Acta Paediatrica Scandinavia Supplement*, 275, 126–31.

HAKIM, C. (1987) *Research Design*. London: Unwin Hyman.

HALL, P., LAND, H., PARKER, R. and WEBB, A. (1975) *Change, choice and conflict in social policy*, London: Heinemann.

HALL, R. (1977) *Organisations – structure and process*. New Jersey: Prentice Hall.

HALL, R. and CLARK, J. P. (1974) Problems in the study of interorganisational relationships *Organisation and Administrative Sciences*, 5, 45–66.

HALL, R., CLARK, J., GIORDANO, P., JOHNSON, P. and VAN ROEKEL, M. (1977) Pattens of interorganisational relationships *Administrative Science Quarterly*, 22, 457–74.

HALLETT, C. (1989) Child abuse inquiries and public policy in (ed) Stevenson, O. *Child Abuse: Public Policy and Professional Practice.*

HALLETT, C. (1989) *Women and social services departments.* Harvester Wheatsheaf.

HALLETT, C. and BIRCHALL, E. (1992) *Coordination and Child Protection: A review of the literature,* Edinburgh: HMSO.

HALLETT, C. and STEVENSON, O. (1980) *Child Abuse: aspects of interprofessional cooperation.* London: Allen and Unwin.

HAMMERSLEY, M. (1990) *Reading ethnographic research.* London: Longman.

HANF, K. (1978) Introduction in (eds) HANF, K. and SCHARPF, F. *Interorganisational Policymaking: limits to coordination and central control.* London: Sage Publications.

HANF, K. and SCHARPF, F. (eds) (1978) *Interorganisational Policy Making: Limits to coordination and central control.* London: Sage Publications.

HC 329–II (1977) *First Report from the Select Committee on Violence in the Family Session 1976–77: Violence to Children Vol II Evidence.* London: HMSO.

HC 329–III (1977) *First Report from the Select Committee on Violence in the Family Session 1976–77: Violence to Children Vol III Appendices.* London: HMSO.

HC 570–1 (1991) *Health Committee – Second Report Public Expenditure on Personal Social Services: Child Protection Services* Volume 1. London: HMSO.

HEALTH VISITORS' ASSOCIATION (undated) *Health visiting in the 80s.* London: HVA.

HELFER, R. E. and KEMPE, C. H. (eds) (1968) *The Battered Child.* Chicago: Chciago University Press.

HERZBERGER, S. D. and TENNEN, H. (1988) Applying the label of physical abuse in HOTALING, G., FINKELHOR, D., KIRKPATRICK, J. and STRAUSS, M. (ed) *Coping with Family Violence: Research and Policy Perspectives.* California: Sage Publications.

HILGENDORF, L. (1981) *Social workers and solicitors in child care cases.* London: HMSO.

HILL, M. (190) The manifest and latent lessons of child abuse inquiries *British Journal of Social Work,* 20, 3, 197–214.

HJERN, D. (1982) Implementation research: the link gone missing *Journal Public Policy,* 2, 3, 301–8.

HOME OFFICE (1950) Joint Circular with Ministry of Health and Education *Children neglected or ill-treated in their own homes*

HOME OFFICE (1988) *The Investigation of Child Sexual Abuse Circular 52/1988.*

HOME OFFICE (1990) *Criminal Statistics for England and Wales.* London: HMSO.

HOME OFFICE, DEPARTMENT OF HEALTH DEPARTMENT OF EDUCATION AND SCIENCE, WELSH OFFICE (1991) *Working Together under the Children Act: A guide to arrangements for interagency cooperation for the protection of children from abuse.* London: HMSO.

HOME OFFICE and DEPARTMENT OF HEALTH (1992) *Memorandum of Good Practice on video recorded interviews with child witnesses for cirminal proceedings.* London: HMSO.

HORLEY, S. (1988(a)) Homing in on violence *Police Review*, 96, 4946, 226–7.

HORLEY, S. (1988(b)) Police and the abuse of women *Social Work Today*, 20, 1, 18.

IRVINE, R. (1988) Child abuse and poverty in (ed) BECKER, S. and MACPHERSON, S. *Public Issues, Private Pain.* London: Insight.

JONES, D. and MCQUISTON, M. (1988) *Interviewing the Sexually Abused Child* 2nd edition. London, Gaskell: Royal College of Psychiatrists.

JONES, D. N. and PICKETT, J. (1987) Case management and interprofessional liaison in (ed) MAHER, P. *Child abuse the Educational Perspective*, Oxford: Basic Blackwell.

JONES, D., PICKETT, J., OATES, M. and BARBOR, P. (1987) *Understanding child abuse.* Basingstoke: Macmillan.

KAHN, J. and THOMPSON, S. (1971) Teamwork: theoretical and practical issues *Medical Officer*, Jan 8th 25–6.

KEMPE, C. H., SILVERMAN, F. N., STEELE, B. F., DROEGMUELLER, W. and SILVER, H. K. (1962) The Battered Child Syndrome *Journal of the American Medical Association*, 181, 17–24.

KING, M. and TROWELL, J. (1992) *Children's Welfare and the Law: the limits of legal intervention.* London: Sage.

KLONGLAN, G., MULFORD, C., WARREN, R. and WINKELPLECK, J. (1975) *Creating interorganisational coordination: Project Report.* Iowa: Sociology Report No 122A, Dept of Sociology, Iowa State University cited in WHETTEN, D. (1981).

KNAPP, M. (1984) *The Economics of Social Care.* Basingstoke: Macmillan.

KRUGMAN, R. (1984) The Multidisciplinary treatment of abusive and neglectful families *Paediatric Annals*, 13, 10, 761–4.

:VINE, S. and WHITE, P. (1961) Exchange as a conceptual framework for he study of interorganisational relationships *Administrative Science Quarrly*, 5, 583–601.

LINDBLOM, C. E. (1959) The science of muddling through *Public Adminis-tration Review*, 19, 2, 79–88.

LIPSKY, M. (1980) *Street-level bureaucracy*. New York: Russell Sage.

LONDON BOROUGH OF BEXLEY (1982) *Report of the panel of inquiry into the death of Lucie Gates*. London: Borough of Bexley and Bexley Health Authority.

LONDON BOROUGH OF BRENT (1985) *A Child in Trust: the Report of the panel of inquiry into the circumstances surrounding the death of Jasmine Beckford*. London: Borough of Brent.

LONDON BOROUGH OF GREENWICH (1987) *A Child in Mind: the protection of children in a responsible society*, London: Borough of Greenwich.

MAHER, P. (ed) 1987 *Child abuse: the educational perspective*, Oxford: Blackwell.

MARSH, D. and RHODES, R. A. W. (eds) (1992) *Implementing Thatcherite Policies*. Milton Keynes: Open University Press.

MAYHALL, P. and NORGARD, K. (1983) *Child abuse and neglect: sharing responsibility*. New York: Wiley.

MAZURA, A. C. (1977) Negligence – Malpractice – Physicians' liability for failure to diagnose and report child abuse *Wayne Law Review*, 23, 3, 1187–1208.

McKEGANEY, N. and BLOOR N. (1981) On the retrieval of sociological descriptions: respondent validation and the critical case of ethnomethodol-ogy *International Journal of Sociology and Social Policy*, 1, 3, 58–69.

McKEGANEY, N. and HUNTER, D. (1986) Only connect: tightrope walking and joint working in the care of the elderly *Policy and Politics*, 14, 3, 335–360.

McGLOIN, P. and TURNBULL, A. (1986) *Parental participation in child abuse review conferences*. London: London Borough of Greenwich.

MILES, M. and HUBERMAN, A. M. (1984) *Qualitative data analysis*. London: Sage.

MILLS, L., GRAVENER, B. and McRAE, K. (1984) Child abuse in Winnipeg: hospital and community together *Canada's Mental Health*, 32, 2, 10–15, 23.

MOLIN, R. and HERSKOWITZ, S. (1986) Clinicians and caseworkers: issues in consultation and collaboration regarding protective service clients *Child abuse and Neglect*, 10, 201–210.

MONCK, E., (1992) Unpublished paper on 'Treatment Outcomes' Depart-ment of Health Seminar on Child Abuse Research, Dartington, Devon.

MONK, D. (1992) The experience of a social services manager of involving parents in child protection conferences in (ed) THOBURN, J. *Participation in*

Practice – involving families in child protection. Norwich: University of East Anglia.

MORAN-ELLIS, J., CONROY, S., FIELDING, N. and TUNSTILL, J. (1991) *Investigation of Child Sexual Abuse: an Executive Summary*. Surrey: University of Surrey.

MOUNTJOY, R. and O'TOOLE, L. (1979) Towards a theory of policy implementation: an organisational review, *Public Administration Review*, 39, 5, 465–476.

MOUZAKITIS, C. M. and GOLDSTEIN, S. C. (1985) A multidisciplinary approach to treating child neglect *Social Casework*, 66, 4, 218–24.

MOUZAKITIS, C. M. and VARGHESE, R. (ed) (1985) *Social Work Treatment with abused and neglected children*. Springfield, Illinois: Charles C. Thomas.

MOWAT, S. (1982) Cutting out the abuse *Nursing Mirror*, 155, 10, 28–31.

MRAZEK, P., LYNCH, M. and BENTORIM, A. (1981) Recognition of child sexual abuse in the United Kingdom in MRAZEK, P. and KEMPE, C. (eds) *Sexually abused children and their families*. Oxford: Pergammon.

MULDOON, L. (1981) *Incest: confronting the silent crime*. St Paul, Minnesota: Department of Corrections.

MULFORD and ROGERS (1982) Definitions and models in (ed) ROGERS, D. and WHETTEN, D. *Interorganisational coordination: theory, research and implementation*. Iowa: Iowa State University Press.

MUSANANDARA, T. (1984) Communication between workers: the key in cases of child abuse? *Health Visitor*, 57, 233.

NATIONAL CHILDREN'S HOME (1992) *The Report of the Committee of Enquiry into Children and Young People who sexually abuse other children*. London: National Children's Home.

NEGHANDI, A. (ed) (1975) *Interorganisation theory*. Kent, Ohio: Comparative Administration Research Institute, Kent State University Press.

NELSON, B. (1984) *Making an issue of child abuse: political agenda setting for social problems*. Chicago: University of Chicago Press.

NEWSON, J. and E. (1978) *Seven Years Old in the Home Environment*. Middlesex: Pelican.

NORTON, A. and ROGERS, S. (1981) The health services and local government services in (ed) McLACHLAN, G. *Matters of Moment*. Oxford: Oxford University Press.

O'TOOLE, R., TURBETT, P. and NALEPKA, C. (1983) Theories, professional knowledge and diagnosis in (ed) FINKELHOR, D., GELLES, R., HOTLAING, G. and STRAUS, M. *The Dark Side of Families*. Beverly Hills: Sage.

OPEN UNIVERSITY (1993) *Investigative interviewing with children – trainers pack*. Milton Keynes: Open University.

Oppé, T. (1975) Problems of communication and coordination in (ed) White-Franklin, A. *Concerning Child Abuse*, Edinburgh: Churchill Livingstone.

Packman, J., Randall, J. and Jacques, N. (1986) *Who needs care? Social Work decisions about children*. Oxford: Blackwell.

Packman, J. and Randall, J. (1987) Decision-making at the gateway to care in (ed) Stevenson, O. *Child Abuse: Public Policy and Professional Practice*. Hemel Hempstead: Harvester Wheatsheaf.

Parton, N. and Thomas, T. (1983) Child abuse and citizenship in (eds) Jordan, B. and Parton, N. *The political dimension of social work*. Oxford: Blackwell.

Parton, N. (1985) *The Politics of Child Abuse*. London: Macmillan.

Parton, N. (1991) *Governing the Family: Child Care, Child Protection and the State*. Basingstoke: Macmillan.

Payne, M. (1982) *Working in teams*. London: Macmillan.

Pelton, L. H. (1981) *The Social Context of Child Abuse and Neglect*. New York: Human Sciences Press.

Perrow, C. (1979) *Complex Organisations*, 2nd Edition Glenview. Illinois: Scott Foresman.

Pettiford, E. (1981) *Improving Child Protection Services through the use of Multidisciplinary Teams*. Washington: American Public Welfare Association.

Pföhl, S. J. (1977) The discovey of child abuse *Social Problems*, 24, 3, 310–23.

Platt, J. (1988) What can case studies do? in (ed) Burgess, R. G. *Studies in Qualitative Methodology*, Greenwich, Connecticut: JAI Press Inc.

Popplestone, R. (1977) Moving the balance from administration to practice *Social Work Today*, 8, 13.

Pressman, J. and Wildavksy, A. (1973) *Implementation*, Berkeley: University of California Press.

Pugh-Thomas R. (1987) *Joint planning and collaboration at the interface of NHS/SSD*. Social Services Inspectorate: DHSS Southern Region.

Purvis, H. (1988) Dangerous clients: further observations on the limitation of mayhem *British Journal of Social Work*, 18, 6, 592–609.

Reid, W. (1964) Interagency coordination in delinquency prevention and control in Zald, M. (ed) *Social Welfare Institutions: a reader*. New York: John Wiley.

Reid, W. (1975) Interorganisational coordination in social welfare: a theoretical approach to analysis and interaction in (ed) Kramer, R. and Specht, H. *Readings in Community Organisation and Practice*. Englewood Cliffs, New Jersey: Prentice Hall.

RHODES, R. A. W. (1981) *Control and power in central-local government relations* Aldershot: Gower.

RHODES, R. A. W. (1986) *The national world of local government*. London: Allen and Unwin.

RHODES, R. A. W. (1988) *Beyond Westminster and Whitehall*. London: Unwin Hyman.

RHODES, R. A. W. (1990) Policy networks: a British perspective *Journal of Theoretical Politics*, 2, 3, 293–317.

RIORDAN, J., BRAMHALL, B. and BLACKHOUSE, T. (1988) Teamwork to serve the elderly *The Health Service Journal*, 19 May, 564–6.

ROGERS, D. L. and WHETTEN, D. A. and ASSOCIATES (1982) *Interorganisational coordination: theory, research and implementation*. Iowa: Iowa State University Press.

RUBER, M. (1988) *Child Sexual Abuse: a report on interagency cooperation from the perspective of Social Services Departments in England and Wales*. Heywood, Lancs: DHSS SSI.

SABATIER, P. (1986(a)) Top-down and bottom-up approaches to implementation research: a critical analysis and suggested synthesis *Journal of Public Policy*, 6, 1, 21–48.

SABATIER, P. (1986(b)) What can we learn from implementation research? in (ed) KAUFANN, F., MAJORIE, G., OSTROM, V. and WIRTH, W. *Guidance, Control and Evaluation in the Public Sector*. Berlin: Walter de Gruyter.

SABATIER, P. and MAZMANIAN, D. (1980) A framework of analysis *Policy Studies Journal*, 8, 538–60.

SCHARPF, F. (1978) Interorganisational Policy Studies: issues, concepts and perspectives in (ed) HANF, K. and SCHARPF, W. *Interorganisational policymaking: limits to coordination and central control*. London: Sage Publications.

SCHMIDT, S. M. and KOCHAN, T. A. (1977) Interorganisational relationships: patterns and motivations *Administrative Science Quarterly*, 22, 220–34.

SGROI S. (1982) *Handbook of clinical intervention in child sexual abuse*. Lexington: Lexington Books.

SHANE, P. (1982) *Special Analysis: Interagency coordination*, San Fransisco: G H White and Co.

SILVERMAN, D. (1993) *Interpreting Qualitative Data*. London: Sage.

SKAFF, L. (1988) Child maltreatment coordinating committees for effective service delivery *Child Welfare*, LXVII, 3, 217–31.

SKINNER, A., PLATTS, H. and JILL, B. (1983) *Disaffection from school: issues and interagency responses*. Leicester: National Youth Bureau.

SMITH, D. (1965) Front-line organisation of a state mental hospital *Administrative Quarterly*, 10, 381–99.

SMITH, M. (1993) Parental control within the family: a normative study of the nature, extent and background factors of physical violence to children in the home, Unpublished paper presented at Department of Health seminar Research into Child Abuse, Dartington Hall, Devon.

SOCIAL TRENDS 1992 (1993). London: HMSO.

STALTMEIR, A. and MACKENZIE, D. (1987) *A study of child abuse initial case conference reports: the management and reporting of case conferences.* London: London Borough of Tower Hamlets.

STEELE, B. (1976) Experience with an interdisciplinary concept in (ed) HELFER, R. and KEMPE, C. H. *Child Abuse and Neglect: the family and the community.* Cambridge, Mass. Ballinger.

STEVENSON, O. and PARSLOE, P. (1978) *Social Service teams: the practitioners' view.* London: HMSO.

STEVENSON, O. (1988) Multidisciplinary work – where next?, *Child Abuse Review*, 2, 1, 5–9.

SUDMAN, S. (1976) *Applied Sampling.* New York and London: Academic Books.

TERR, L. (1986) The child psychiatrist and the child witness: travelling companions by necessity, if not by design *Journal of the American Academy of Child Psychiatry*, 114, 10, 1432–9.

THE RESEARCH TEAM (1990) *Child Sexual Abuse in Northern Ireland.* Belfast.

THOBURN, J. (1992) (ed) *Participation in Practice – involving families in child protection.* Norwich: University of east Anglia.

THOMAS, T. (1988) Working with the police *Social Work Today*, 20 October.

TIBBITT, J. (1983) Health and personal social services in the UK: inter-organisational behaviour and service development in (ed) WILLIAMSON, A. and ROOM, G. *Welfare States in Britain.* London: Heinemann.

TOPPER, A. and ALDRIDGE, D. (1981) Incest: intake and investigation in (ed) MRAZEK, P. and KEMPE, C. *Sexually abused children and their families.* Oxford: Pergamon.

URZI, M. (1977) *Cooperative approaches to child protection: a community guide.* St Paul, Minnesota State Department of Public Welfare.

VAN DE VEN, A. (1976) On the nature, formation and maintenance of relations among organisations *Academy of Management Review*, 4, 24–36.

VAN METER, D. and VAN HORN, C. (1975) The policy implementation process: a conceptual framework *Administration and Society*, 6, (Feb), 445–88.

WALLEN, G. PIERCE, S., KOCH, M. and VENTERS, H. (1977) The inter-disciplinary team approach to child abuse services: strengths and limitations *Child Abuse and Neglect*, 1, 359–64.

WALTON, M. (1993) Regulation in child protection – policy failure? *British Journal of Social Work*, 23, 139–156.

WARREN, R. (1973) Comprehensive planning and coordination – some functional aspects *Social Problems*, 20, 355–64.

WARREN, R. L. (1967) The interorganisational field as a focus of investigation *Administrative Science Quarterly*, 12, 396–419.

WARREN, R., ROSE, S. and BERGUNDER, A. (1974) *The structure of urban reform*. Lexington, Mass.: Lexington Books.

WATT, J. W. (1985) Protective service teams *Health Social Work*, 10, 3, 191–8.

WEBB, A. (1991) Coordination: a problem in public sector management *Policy and Politics*, 19, 4, 229–241.

WEBB, A. and HOBDELL, M. (1980) Coordination and teamwork in the health and personal social services in (ed) LONSDALE, S., WEBB, A. and BRIGGS, T. *Teamwork in the personal social services and health care*. New York: Syracuse University Press.

WEDLAKE, M. (1978) A police view of the present position in (ed) WHITE-FRANKLIN, A. *Child Abuse: prediction, prevention and follow-up*. Edinburgh: Churchill Livingstone.

WEIGHTMAN, K. (1988) Managing from below *Social Work Today*, 29.9.88, 16–17.

WEISS, J. (1981) Substance vs symbol in administrative reform: the case of human services coordination *Policy Analysis*, 7, 1, 21–45.

WESTRIN, C.-G. (1987) Primary health care: cooperation between health and welfare personnel *Scandinavian Journal of Social Medicine* Supplement 38.

WHETTEN, D. A. and LEUNG, T. K. (1979) The instrumental value of interorganisational relations: antecedents and consequences of linkage formation *Academy of Management Journal*, 22, 325–47.

WHETTEN, D. (1981) Interorganisational relations: a review of the field *Journal of Higher Education*, 52, 1, 1–28.

WHITMORE, R. (1984) Modelling the policy/implementation distinction: the case of child abuse *Policy and Politics*, 12, 3, 241–67.

WIDNER, R. (1973) Evaluating the administration of the Appalachian Regional Development Program *Growth and Change: a journal of Regional Development*, 4, 25–9.

WILLIAMS, S. (1986) Case studies in collaboration *Family Practitioner Services*, 13, 3, 39–43.

WILSON, R. and AKANA, P. (1987) Coordination with intergovernmental and private agencies in (ed) ANDERSON, W., FRIEDSON, B. and MURPHY,